The Blackwell Encyclopedic
Dictionary of
Operations Management

THE BLACKWELL ENCYCLOPEDIA OF MANAGEMENT

EDITED BY CARY L. COOPER AND CHRIS ARGYRIS

The Blackwell Encyclopedic Dictionary of Accounting
Edited by A. Rashad Abdel-khalik

The Blackwell Encyclopedic Dictionary of Strategic Management
Edited by Derek F. Channon

The Blackwell Encyclopedic Dictionary of Management Information Systems
Edited by Gordon B. Davis

The Blackwell Encyclopedic Dictionary of Marketing
Edited by Barbara R. Lewis and Dale Littler

The Blackwell Encyclopedic Dictionary of Managerial Economics
Edited by Robert McAuliffe

The Blackwell Encyclopedic Dictionary of Organizational Behavior
Edited by Nigel Nicholson

The Blackwell Encyclopedic Dictionary of International Management
Edited by John O'Connell

The Blackwell Encyclopedic Dictionary of Finance
Edited by Dean Paxson and Douglas Wood

The Blackwell Encyclopedic Dictionary of Human Resource Management
Edited by Lawrence H. Peters, Charles R. Greer and Stuart A. Youngblood

The Blackwell Encyclopedic Dictionary of Operations Management
Edited by Nigel Slack

The Blackwell Encyclopedic Dictionary of Business Ethics
Edited by Patricia Werhane and R. Edward Freeman

The Blackwell Encyclopedic Dictionary of Operations Management

Edited by Nigel Slack

Warwick University

Copyright © Blackwell Publishers Ltd, 1997, 1999
Editorial Organization © Nigel Slack, 1997, 1999

First published 1997
Reprinted 1998

First published in paperback 1999

Blackwell Publishers Inc.
350 Main Street
Malden, Massachusetts 02148, USA

Blackwell Publishers Ltd
108 Cowley Road
Oxford OX4 1JF
UK

Library of Congress Cataloging-in-Publication Data

The Blackwell encyclopedic dictionary of operations management /
edited by Nigel Slack.
     p.   cm.
    Includes bibliographical references and index.
    ISBN 1–55786–905–7 (acid-free paper) — ISBN 0–631–21082–2 (Pbk: acid-free paper)
    1. Production management–Dictionaries.   I. Slack, Nigel
TS155.B525   1996   96–30369
658.5′003—dc20   CIP

British Library Cataloguing in Publication Data
A CIP catalogue record for this book is available from the British Library.

Typeset in 9½ on 11pt Ehrhardt by Page Brothers, Norwich
Printed in Great Britain by T.J. International Ltd, Padstow, Cornwall

This book is printed on acid-free paper

Contents

—— Preface ——

Operations management is the set of tasks which manages the arrangement of resources in an organization which is devoted to the production of goods and services. This is a broad definition of the subject which has an application to all types of organization. However, this was not always the case. At one time it seemed that the glory days of operations management (or factory management as it would probably then have been called) were from the post-war period through to the 1960s. This was when the problems of supplying markets hungry for manufacturing products was clearly an important issue and, furthermore, subject to systematic, and often mathematical analysis. Few richer grounds existed for the application of these quantitative models whose development roughly coincided with the same period. Indeed, up until the early 1970s, operations management was barely distinguishable from operations research and management science. It was a collection of techniques, methods and models, a sort of all-purpose tool-box for the solution of complex manufacturing problems. Essentially, operations management was merely an aggregation of these models that focused on the provision of prescriptive solutions for such 'problems' as stock control, quality control, facilities layout, replacement of machine parts, maintenance and repair policies and so on.

In reality, this influx of quantitative models was overlaying an earlier set of models developed during the emergence of mass industrialization in the late nineteenth century. These models and methods were formalized during the (with hindsight naive) scientific management movement. In fact, the scientific management era had already laid the foundations of work–study and industrial engineering-based techniques upon which the quantitative modellers built.

Given its preoccupation with technique-related problem solving, it is not surprising that by the 1970s operations management was sometimes looking uninspired, irrelevant, or both. It was a subject largely devoid of intellectual excitement, seen as closer to the technical minutiae of engineering than to management, and having little to say on the emerging issues of competitiveness and strategic positioning.

But no longer. Twenty years can make a lot of difference and operations management is once more at the forefront of management thought and fashion. From what was once the neglected function in management studies, it has regained a position such that academics, students, and consultants are willing to take it seriously. So what has changed? What has impacted on the subject and so radically enhanced its status? In truth, no single development can be held responsible for the transformation. Rather it was the coincidence of a number of factors, the implications of which have influenced this encyclopaedic dictionary.

'Operations' Has Extended Beyond Its Conventional Boundaries

Increasingly, operations management is seen as involving consideration of resource management beyond the limits of the core transformation system. In the limited sense, this involves extending the definition of operations management to include all value stages, including initial design of products and services, the purchasing of bought-in materials, and the logistics considerations involved in transporting products and services to customers. Beyond organizational boundaries, it involves setting internal operations in the context of a larger supply network. The entries on supply chain management, design chain management and design for manufacture, for example, all reflect this influence.

Operations Has Become More Strategic

There is clearly a distinction, now well accepted, between *'operations'* and *'operational'*. The former is concerned with the management of resources for the creation of products and services. The latter implies short-term, detailed, and localized decisions. Thus, operations management is not necessarily operational management. The implication of this is that the concept of 'operations strategy' is not the contradiction it once seemed. Thus, the entries on operations strategy, manufacturing strategy, service strategy, for example, would not have even been included in a work of this kind until relatively recently.

Operations Includes the Production of Services as well as Products

Even though in most developed nations the largest part of GDP has for decades been accounted for by service industries, the serious study of how services are produced dates only from the 1970s. Now, by contrast, operations management is deemed to include all those issues pertinent to the creation of either products or services. Indeed, it is widely accepted that most organizations produce a bundle of products and services, and while the tangible or intangible may predominate, relatively few businesses are solely concerned with the production of either products or of services alone. The entries on service operations, service innovation and service processes all reflect this shift.

Operations Includes Both Concepts and Techniques

Building a set of concepts which allow us to articulate the similarities and differences between various types of operations is a task which has dominated much of the academic development in the subject over the last few years. Some of these concepts attempt to bind together seemingly disparate operations. For example, the entry on transformation models reflects this desire. Others reflect a particular approach to the management of operations. Many of these latter concepts, although radical when first introduced, have now, at least partly, been subsumed within the constituent elements of operations management. The entries on just-in-time and total quality management are typical of these concepts.

Operations Has Relevance in all Parts of a Business

Any function or department within a business can be viewed as having two types of task – a technical task that involves exploration of the underlying logic of the decisions it is making, and an operations task that involves the production of its internal services. So for example, within the marketing function, technical decisions involve such things as pricing policy, promotional strategy, market positioning and so on. These are clearly not directly the concern of operations management as such. However, its other set of tasks are concerned with the production of plans which embody these technical decisions. In doing so it is, in effect, producing services for internal customers, hopefully to an appropriate level of quality, responsiveness, reliability, flexibility, and cost. As such the marketing (or any other) function can be judged as an operation. For example, the entry on business process re-engineering is a reflection of this idea.

Inevitably, when a subject reaches the stage of development which operations management has, there are different ideas as to how it should move forward. Some see the subject becoming subsumed within concepts they regard as larger scale, such as supply chain management. Others see developments in strategic management, such as resource based theories of the firm, as creating alternatives to the more strategic aspects of operations management. Yet others hold that only by creating a centre of study for service management independent of either operations (or any other conventional functional study for that matter) can the differences between manufacturing and service businesses truly be explored. This work represents a compromise. We hope that all major topics within the subject are addressed and apologize if some topics, regarded as important by some readers, have been missed out because of lack of space. Some of the entries are relatively short, little more than extended definitions, others are several thousand words long. These longer entries could have been broken down into their constituent parts. However, the judgement of the contributors was that this would reduce the coherence necessary for a reasonable understanding of the topic. Hopefully, with judicious use of the 'see also' sections at the end of each entry and the index the reader should be able to find their way to whatever aspect of the topic interests them.

Nigel Slack

—— Contributors ——

Colin Armistead
TheBusiness School, Bournemouth University

David Bennett
Aston Business School, Aston University

John Bessant
Centre for Research in Innovation Management, University of Brighton

Peter Burcher
Aston Business School, Aston University

Stuart Chambers
Warwick Business School, University of Warwick

David Collier
College of Business, Ohio State University

Barrie Dale
Manchester School of Management, UMIST

Christine Harland
University of Bath

Alan Harrison
Cranfield School of Management, Cranfield University

John Heap
Leeds Metropolitan University

Robert Johnston
Warwick Business School, University of Warwick

Ralph Levene
Cranfield School of Management, Cranfield University

John Mapes
Cranfield School of Management, Cranfield University

Andy Neely
University of Cambridge

Felix Schmid
Advanced Railway Research Centre, University of Sheffield

Michael Shulver
Warwick Business School, University of Warwick

Rhian Silvestro
Warwick Business School, University of Warwick

Nigel Slack
Warwick Business School, University of Warwick

Mike Sweeney
Cranfield School of Management, Cranfield University

David Twigg
Warwick Business School, University of Warwick

Christopher Voss
London Business School

A

ABC analysis *see* PARETO ANALYSIS

acceptance sampling *see* STATISTICAL
QUALITY TECHNIQUES

advanced manufacturing technology Advanced manufacturing technology (AMT) is an umbrella term used to describe a wide range of automation and related technologies which have emerged during the past two decades as a consequence of developments in information technology (IT). The label "advanced" derives from the perception in the 1970s that IT applied in manufacturing would open up radically different ways of doing things and would require a different approach to its management. It was widely expected that such a "revolution" in manufacturing technology would have an equally powerful impact on productivity and performance – and as a result there was strong pressure on firms to adopt this new generation of technology.

Underpinning this was the growing recognition that the emergence of IT would accelerate developments along three important paths in manufacturing:

- It would open up dramatic new possibilities in the automation of manual tasks.

- It would facilitate the integration of such automation.

- It would be applicable across a wide range of manufacturing sectors.

Originally mechanization was aimed at substituting manual labor with mechanical equipment; as the pace of industrialization grew so did the attempt to take this one stage further and replace the monitoring and control activities in manufacturing by some form of automatic device. This trend was limited by the availability of suitable technology until the emergence of electronics. Experiments during the Second World War gave a considerable boost to automation, and the development of digital computers in the 1960s enabled a new generation of automatic control. These systems were originally applied only in large, capital-intensive industries, but diffused more widely as computing power became more easily available. With the development of the microprocessor it became feasible to automate individual machines and functions. Diffusion of such automation accelerated rapidly during the 1980s, and spread across from large capital-intensive firms through to very small and specialized applications and sectors. For some, microelectronics-based automation became something of a solution looking for a problem.

From the late 1970s the trend towards integration began to accelerate. There were distinct limits to what could be integrated mechanically, but the potential of IT to communicate in a common language of electronic signals enabled the emergence of integrated systems for monitoring and controlling industrial applications. At first this was confined to simple integration of functions within a particular item of equipment; then it spread to linked applications within a sphere of activity, after which it began to open up integration between functional areas and beyond. Significantly this moved the emphasis from what might be termed "substitution innovation" (doing what had always been done but a little better, for example faster or more accurately), towards doing completely new things or doing old things in radically new ways. This opened up the possibilities for using AMT strategically, for

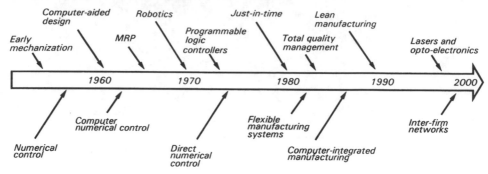

Figure 1 Convergent streams in AMT

example, in making the business more flexible, faster, or more customer responsive.

IT offers radical improvements in the processing, storage, retrieval, and communication of information. Because much of manufacturing involves information activity there is considerable scope for improvement through IT. Recognition of the huge possibilities in applying IT led to its being seen as heralding a new Industrial Revolution, with electronics playing the role which steam power had done in the eighteenth century.

Nature of AMT

AMT is not simply the application of IT but its combination with several other technologies to enable a particular set of applications. It can be usefully represented as a convergent stream which continues to develop, as shown in Figure 1. Characteristic of these component technologies is a three-stage process, moving from discrete automation of individual tasks, through increasing integration of functions to a final stage in which the basic configuration is adapted and extended to suit widely different applications.

The emergence of AMT can be seen through considering some particular elements which illustrate these trends.

FLEXIBLE MANUFACTURING SYSTEMS (FMS) are the archetypal manifestation of AMT, at least in engineering-based manufacture, although their component parts are themselves applied much more widely in other industries. ROBOTICS are used to manipulate parts, tools and materials, AUTOMATED GUIDED VEHICLES (AGVs) are used to transport mater-

ials or assemblies, and PROGRAMMABLE LOGIC CONTROLLERS (PLCs) are used to monitor and control most types of process. All can be integrated to different levels of sophistication (*see* COMPUTER-INTEGRATED MANUFACTURING) (CIM). Other applications of AMT, which demonstrate the same pattern of evolution from discrete automation and "substitution" innovation towards integrated and more strategic innovations, include COMPUTER-AIDED DESIGN (CAD) and computer-aided production management systems, based on versions of MATERIAL REQUIREMENTS PLANNING. Other elements in the AMT convergent stream include "mechatronics" (the convergence of mechanical and electronic systems), laser and other optical technologies, and the increasing use of new materials and forming processes.

Managing AMT

AMT appeared to represent a perfect marriage between technological potential and the manufacturing challenges of the late twentieth century. Industrial experience in a variety of applications confirmed the powerful advantages which could be used technically and also strategically. But in the late 1980s ,evidence began to accumulate about problems with achieving these advantages. In a few extreme cases the considerable investment made in AMT failed completely; but in most cases what was reported was a general feeling of expectations not being fully met. It became clear that unlocking the full potential offered by AMT involved more than simply adopting the technology.

Several studies showed that two key features are associated with successful implementation of AMT. The first is that the investment needs to be made within the context of a clear strategic framework. Rather than selecting and investing in CIM because it is fashionable, successful firms have a clear understanding of their business, knowing where they want to be in the marketplace and how they plan to compete, and the implications this has for manufacturing. They also know their present strengths and weaknesses within their manufacturing operations (in terms of equipment, facilities, experience, and skills) and can plan a step–by–step strategy which builds up to highly integrated automation in a series of stages rather than in a single step. This underlines the importance of MANUFACTURING STRATEGY as a precursor to investment in AMT.

The second key point is that successful firms recognize that they need to make significant and far-reaching changes to the way production is organized and managed. Using a "revolutionary" technology such as CIM requires a similarly radical degree of organizational change along a number of dimensions, including the skills profile, the functional and hierarchical structure, the philosophy of management and control, and the underlying culture of the organization. The nature of the organizational changes required depends on the scale of technological shift (small changes can often be absorbed with only slight variations on the existing pattern, whereas larger shifts require a fundamental rethink of the way the organization operates). Equally, technologies which span more than one functional boundary are likely to pose problems of organizational integration; for example, one of the major requirements in effective CAD/CAM utilization is the organization of the multidisciplinary, multifunctional design process to enable close co–operation and integration.

The dimensions of such change vary with each application but there is a general trend towards a new model for manufacturing organization. This includes elements such as more emphasis on skills and on training, more team working, more decentralized autonomy, flatter structures, and closer integration between different functional areas. AMT provides a catalyst for moving towards this kind of model

since it is unlikely to deliver its full benefits without such changes.

The lists below indicate typical dimensions of change in organization design (Bessant et al., 1992).

Work organization:
(1) from single skill to multiskill developments;
(2) from high division of labor to integrated tasks;
(3) from long skill lifecycle to short skill lifecycle;
(4) from skill life = employee life to skill life < employee life;
(5) from individual work/accountability to team work/accountability;
(6) from payment by results to alternative payment systems;
(7) from supervisor-controlled to supervisor-supported;
(8) from low work discretion to increased flexibility/autonomy.

Changes in management organization:
(9) from sharp line staff boundary to blurred boundaries;
(10) from steep pyramid to flat structure;
(11) from vertical communication to network communication;
(12) from formal control to "holographic adjustment";
(13) from functional structures to product-/project-/customer-based;
(14) from differentiated status to single status
(15) from rigid and non-participative to flexible-participative.

Inter-organization relationships:
(16) from tight boundaries between firms to blurred boundaries;
(17) from "arm's length dealing" to co-operative relations
(18) from short-term to long-term relationships;
(19) from confrontational to co-operative relationships/partnerships;
(20) lack of customer involvement to "customer is king."

Significantly, much of the evolution of this alternative model for manufacturing organization took place in parallel with the emergence of AMT. Concepts like JUST-IN-TIME, TOTAL QUALITY MANAGEMENT, and cellular manufacturing were applied with increasing frequency and it became clear that many of the benefits offered by AMT could also be realized (at lower cost and with less organizational disruption) through the adoption of new organizational forms. A key theme in lean manufacturing (see just-in-time) is that many of the differences between "best practice" plants and others lie in work organization and production management, rather than in levels of AMT being deployed.

The emerging prescription for successful AMT implementation is one which combines the two themes of technological and organizational change, and employs AMT to augment rather than supplant a skilled workforce organized around high quality, customer-focused, flexible teams. There is no conflict but rather a complementarity; the nature and direction of organizational change (new LAYOUT patterns, new WORK ORGANIZATION, new organization structures, etc.) are precisely those which are needed to support more advanced and capital-intensive applications of AMT. This model should be seen not simply as the extension of technical integration but rather as the convergence of two streams (new IT-based equipment and systems and new approaches like just-in-time and total quality management). Rather than simply computer-integrated manufacturing, perhaps a better term would be "total integrated manufacturing."

See also **process technology; service innovations; human-centered CIM**

Bibliography

Bessant, J. (1991). *Managing advanced manufacturing technology: The challenge of the fifth wave.* Oxford/Manchester: NCC-Blackwell.

Bessant, J., Smith, S., Tranfield, D. & Levy, P. (1992). Factory 2000: organisation design for the factory of the future. *International Studies of Management and Organisation,* **22.**

Diebold, J. (1964). *Beyond automation: Managerial problems of an exploding technology.* New York: McGraw-Hill.

Ettlie, J. (1988). *Taking charge of manufacturing.* San Francisco: Jossey-Bass.

Jacobsson, S. & Edquist, C. (1986). *Flexible automation.* Oxford: Basil Blackwell.

Jaikumar, R. (1986). Post-industrial manufacturing. *Harvard Business Review,* **64**, 6.

Majchrzak, A. (1988). *The human side of factory automation.* San Francisco: Jossey-Bass.

JOHN BESSANT

after-sales service   *see* CUSTOMER SUPPORT OPERATIONS

aggregate capacity management   Aggregate capacity management is the activity of setting the capacity levels of an organization in the medium term. The important characteristic of capacity management here is that it is concerned with capacity measured in aggregated terms. Thus aggregate plans may assume that the mix of different products and services will remain relatively constant during the planning period (*see* CAPACITY MANAGEMENT).

Typically, in aggregate capacity management, operations managers are faced with a forecast of demand which is unlikely to be either certain or constant. They will also have some idea of their own ability to meet this demand. Nevertheless, before any further decisions are taken they must have quantitative data on both capacity and demand. So step one will be to measure the aggregate demand and capacity levels for the planning period. The second step will be to identify the alternative capacity plans which could be adopted in response to the demand fluctuations. The third step will be to choose the most appropriate capacity plan for their circumstances.

Measuring Demand and Capacity

Demand forecasting is a major input into the capacity management decision. As far as capacity management is concerned there are three requirements from a demand forecast. The first is that it is expressed in terms which are useful for capacity management, which means it should give an indication of the demands that will be placed on an operation's capacity, and expressed in the same units. The second is that it is as accurate as possible, and the third that it should give an indication of relative uncertainty, so that operations managers can make a judgment between plans that would, at one extreme, virtually guarantee the operation's ability to meet actual demand, and, at the other, plans that minimize costs.

In many organizations aggregate capacity management is concerned largely with coping with seasonal demand fluctuations. Almost all products and services have some seasonality of demand and some also have seasonality of supply.

The Alternative Capacity Plans

There are three "pure" options for coping with supply or demand variation:

- Ignore the fluctuations and keep activity levels constant (level capacity plan).

- Adjust capacity to reflect the fluctuations in demand (chase demand plan).

- Attempt to change demand to fit capacity availability (demand management).

In practice most organizations will use a mixture of all of these "pure" plans, although often one plan may dominate.

In a level capacity plan, the processing capacity is set at a uniform level throughout the planning period, regardless of the fluctuations in forecast demand. This means that the same number of staff operate the same processes and should therefore be capable of producing the same aggregate output in each period. Where non-perishable materials are processed, but not immediately sold, they can be transferred to finished goods inventory in anticipation of sales at a later time period. This can provide stable employment patterns, high process utilization, and usually also high productivity with low unit costs. Unfortunately, it can also create considerable inventory. Nor are such plans suitable for "perishable" products, products which are tailor-made against specific customer requirements, or products susceptible to obsolescence.

Very high underutilization levels can make level capacity plans prohibitively expensive in many service operations, but may be considered appropriate where the opportunity costs of individual lost sales are very high, for example, in high-margin retailing. It is also possible to set the capacity somewhat below the forecast peak demand level in order to reduce the degree of underutilization. However, in the periods where demand is expected to exceed planned capacity, customer service may deteriorate.

The opposite of a level capacity plan is one which attempts to match capacity closely to the varying levels of forecast demand. Such pure "chase" demand plans may not appeal to operations which manufacture standard, non-perishable products. A pure chase demand plan is more usually adopted by operations which cannot store their output such as service operations or manufacturers of perishable products. Where output can be stored the chase demand policy might be adopted in order to minimize or eliminate finished goods inventory.

The chase demand approach requires that capacity is adjusted by some means. There are a number of different methods of achieving this, although all may not be feasible for all types of operation.

Overtime and idle time.   Often the quickest and most convenient method of adjusting capacity is by varying the number of productive hours worked by the staff in the operation. The costs associated with this method are overtime, or in the case of idle time, the costs of paying staff who are not engaged in direct productive work.

Varying the size of the workforce.   If capacity is largely governed by workforce size, one way to adjust capacity is to adjust the size of the workforce. This is done by hiring extra staff during periods of high demand and laying them off as demand falls. However, there are cost, and possibly also, ethical implications to be taken into account before adopting such a method. The costs of hiring extra staff include those associated with recruitment as well as the costs of low productivity while new staff go through the LEARNING CURVES. The costs of lay-off may include possible severance payments, but might also include the loss of morale in the operation and loss of goodwill in the local labor market.

Using part-time staff.   A variation on the previous strategy is to recruit staff on a part-time basis, that is for less than the normal working day. This method is extensively used in service operations such as supermarkets and fast food restaurants, but it is also used by some manufacturers to staff an evening shift after the normal working day. However, if the fixed costs of employment for each employee, irrespective of how long he or she works, are high, then using this method may not be worthwhile.

Subcontracting.   In periods of high demand an operation might buy capacity from other organizations. Again, though, there are costs associated with this method. The most obvious one is that subcontracting can be expensive because of the subcontractor's margin. Nor may a subcontractor be as motivated to deliver on time or to the desired levels of quality.

Many organizations have recognized the benefits of attempting to manage demand in various ways. The objective is to transfer customer demand from peak periods to quiet periods. This is usually beyond the immediate responsibility of operations managers, whose primary role is to identify and evaluate the benefits of demand management, and to ensure that the resulting changes in demand can be satisfactorily met by the operations system. One method of managing demand is to change demand by altering part of the "marketing mix," for example by changing prices or promotional activities to make them more attractive in off-peak periods. A more radical policy may be to create alternative products or services to fill capacity in quiet periods.

Choosing an Aggregate Capacity Management Approach

An operation must be aware of the consequences of adopting each plan. For example, a manufacturer, given an idea of current capacity and given a demand forecast, must calculate the effect of setting an output rate at a particular level. A method which is frequently cited as helping to assess the consequences of adopting capacity plans is the use of cumulative representations of demand and capacity. The most useful consequence of this is that, by plotting capacity on a cumulative graph, the feasibility and consequences of a capacity plan can be assessed. Some impression of the inventory implications can also be gained from a cumulative representation by judging the area between the cumulative production and demand curves. This represents the amount of inventory carried over the period.

The cumulative representation approach succeeds in indicating where operations managers can plan to provide the appropriate level of capacity required at points of time in the future. However, in practice, the management of capacity is a far more dynamic process which involves controlling and reacting to actual demand and actual capacity as it occurs. This aggregate capacity control process can be seen as a sequence of partially reactive capacity decision processes.

See also **bottlenecks; capacity strategy; inventory management**

Bibliography

Vollmann, T. E., Berry, W. L. & Whybark, D. C. (1992). *Manufacturing planning and control systems.* 3rd edn. Boston, MA: Irwin.

NIGEL SLACK

analytical estimating   Analytical estimating is a structured, estimating technique, often used in WORK MEASUREMENT, in which a task is analyzed into its basic component operations or elements. Standard times, where available from another source, are applied to these elements. Times are applied to the remainder, where no prior data are available, by estimating based on experience of the work under consideration. The estimating is carried out by a skilled and experienced worker who has had additional training in the process of estimating and who simply estimates the time that would be required by a fully competent and experienced worker, working at a defined level of performance. The analysis into elements is a key factor in producing reliable times, since, while time estimates for individual elements may be "inaccurate," any errors are random and will compensate for each other. Additionally, since the technique is normally used for assessing workloads over a reasonably long planning period, errors in individual tasks will also cancel each other out.

Bibliography

Whitmore, D. (1991). Systems of measured data: PMTS and estimating. In T. J. Bentley (Ed.), *The management services handbook.* 2nd edn. London: Pitman.

JOHN HEAP

automated guided vehicles Automatic guided vehicles (AGVs) are small, independently powered vehicles which move materials to and from value-adding operations. They are usually guided by cables buried in the floor of the operation and receive instructions from a central computer. Variations on this arrangement include AGVs which have their own on-board computers or optical guidance systems.

In addition to any cost advantages gained by substituting labor with technology, the use of AGVs can help promote just-in-time delivery of parts between stages in the production process (JUST-IN-TIME). In some industries they are also used as mobile work stations to replace the more traditional conveyor systems; for example, truck engines can be assembled on AGVs, with the AGV moving between assembly stations. The ability to move independently reduces the pacing effect on each stage in the process and allows for variation in the time each stage takes to perform its task. AGVs are also used to move materials in non-manufacturing operations such as warehousing, libraries, offices, and hospitals.

NIGEL SLACK

allowances   *see* WORK MEASUREMENT

anthropocentric manufacturing systems *see* HUMAN-CENTERED CIM

assembly lines   *see* PRODUCT LAYOUT

autonomous groups   *see* GROUP WORKING

availability   *see* FAILURE MEASURES

B

backward scheduling *see* SCHEDULING

balancing *see* LINE BALANCING

batch processes *see* MANUFACTURING PRO-
CESSES

blueprinting *see* SERVICE DESIGN

benchmarking Benchmarking is the creation
of a "standard" or a reference point. Such a
standard or reference point could, in a business
management context, be a measure of current
product or process performance or it could be
used as a target for future performance. If
benchmarks are to be used for either or both of
these purposes then they can be considered as
catalysts for CONTINUOUS IMPROVEMENT.
Therefore, benchmarking should be considered
as an element of the TOTAL QUALITY MANAGE-
MENT approach to improved customer satisfaction.

A formal definition of benchmarking is the
continuous process of measuring products,
services and practices against the toughest
competitors, or those companies renowned as
industry leaders, in order to achieve superior
performance.

To accomplish such a goal requires, in the
first instance, an in-depth understanding of the
procedures or practices of one's own organization and the competitive strengths and weaknesses of its products and services. Careful
selection of the appropriate measure of competitiveness will be needed to ensure a meaningful
comparison. Through such a comparison with
"the best" will come knowledge of what can be
achieved. However, the essence of benchmarking is also gaining an understand of *how*

superior standards of performance can be
achieved.

Camp (1989) suggests that there are four
types of benchmarking activities that can be
used by organizations to improve the performance of their products, services or processes:
these are competitive, internal, functional, and
generic benchmarking.

(1) Competitive benchmarking is comparing
the performance of one's own products
and, if possible, the work processes operating within the company with those of a key
competitor in order to reverse engineer
them for improvement.
(2) Internal benchmarking is the continuous
attempt to establish good practice uniformly
and company-wide by regularly comparing
the procedures adopted for all the same
operations of a business and changing them
to emulate the practices of the best.
(3) Functional benchmarking compares the
activities of specific functions with the best
in industry and the best in class. It only
relates to a specific function and a functional
performance improvement may not necessarily result in a performance improvement
in other operations within the business.
Examples of purely functional process are
invoicing or production scheduling.
(4) Generic benchmarking encompasses most
processes of a business. These are the
processes that are cross-functional and
they are usually more complex than functional processes. An example is new product
development. Generic benchmarking therefore compares the performance of this
activity with companies that excel at this
task.

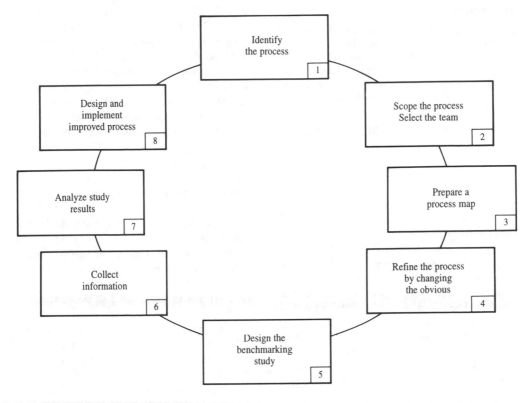

Figure 1 The Corning "Wheel"

There are two commonly used methodologies for the implementation of benchmarking. Camp (1989) recommends a ten-step process, as follows:

(1) Identify what is to be benchmarked.
(2) Identify comparative companies.
(3) Determine data collection method and collect data.
(4) Determine current performance levels.
(5) Project future performance levels.
(6) Communicate benchmark findings and gain acceptance.
(7) Establish functional goals.
(8) Develop action plans.
(9) Implement specific actions and monitor progress.
(10) Recalibrate benchmarks.

An alternative model has been developed and used by the Corning Glass Company of America. This is shown in Figure 1.

The particularly significant feature of this model is the attention paid to the need to prepare a map of a process which is necessary to understand the practices currently used. Often, as a consequence of doing this, a process can be improved before benchmarking it against best practice.

Benchmarking requires the careful selection of a best practice partner and the training of the process owners to use TOTAL QUALITY MANAGEMENT techniques to brainstorm what changes should be made and how they will be implemented.

Benchmarking is a relatively new management tool and little research has been carried out to evaluate its costs and benefits. The barriers to effective benchmarking have been investigated (Sweeney, 1994), but much still remains to be researched to determine whether the application of benchmarking generally delivers the benefits claimed by its proponents.

Bibliography

Camp, R. C. (1989). *Benchmarking: The search of industry best practices that lead to superior performance*. Milwaukee, WI: Quality Press.

Sweeney, M. T. (1994). Benchmarking for strategic manufacturing management. *International Journal of Operations and Production Management*, 14, 9, 4–15.

MICHAEL SWEENEY

bill of materials   The bill of materials (BOM) is a file or set of files which contains the "recipe" for each finished product assembly in a MATE-RIAL REQUIREMENTS PLANNING system. It consists of information regarding which materials, components and sub-assemblies go together to make up each finished product, held on what is often known as a product structure file. Associated data about each item, such as part number, description, unit of measure and lead time for manufacturing or procurement are held on a part or item master file.

For each finished product, a bill of materials is originally created from design and process planning information. The designs might be developed internally or be supplied by the customer. They will initially be in the form of drawings and material lists. The process planning information may be in the form of assembly charts. Together with information on the relevant lead times, these form the basis of the inputs to the BOM.

While most MRP systems can cope with part numbers allocated at random, it is necessary for all items within the organization to be given a unique part number. Clearly the information on the BOM needs to be accurate, since inaccuracies can lead to incorrect items or incorrect quantities of items being ordered. This accuracy needs to be audited. However, in many operating environments, there are continual changes to the BOM in the form of product modifications. These modifications may originate from many sources, such as safety legislation, production process changes, improvements for marketing purposes or value analysis exercises. The control of the implementation of modifications can be a time-consuming task, especially since factors such as the depletion of unmodified stocks and the timing of combined modifications have also to be considered.

There is an accepted numbering system for BOM levels which allocates level 0 to the finished product and increases the level number as the raw material stage is approached. Items that appear at several levels in a BOM, for example in the final assembly as well as in sub-assemblies, are usually assigned the lowest level code at which the item occurs. This ensures that when MRP processing proceeds from one level code down to the next, all gross requirements for the item are accumulated before continuing any further (*see* NETTING PROCESS IN MRP).

The number of levels of assembly breakdown is determined by the complexity of the product; however some BOMs are unnecessarily complicated by including too many sub-assembly stages, and many companies have made determined efforts to flatten their BOM structures.

Bills of materials for hypothetical products are sometimes created to help in the forecasting and MASTER PRODUCTION SCHEDULE of products which could have an extremely wide variety of saleable end items. These are referred to as planning BOMs, and may take the form of modular BOMs or BOMs which separate out common items from optional items and features. For example, in car production, there may be thousands of items common to each model; there may also be optional items such as air conditioning assemblies and features such as an automatic gearbox or a manual gearbox. If forecast ratios of the take-up of these optional and feature sub-assemblies can be determined, then a planning BOM can be created using these ratios as the "quantity per" parent hypothetical finished product. It is these planning BOMs that are then used for master production scheduling in this environment.

See also **manufacturing resources planning; design**

Bibliography

Clement, J., Coldrick, A. & Sari, J. (1992). *Manufacturing data structures: Building foundations for excellence with bills of material and process information*. Essex Junction, VT: Oliver Wight.

Vollmann, T. E., Berry, W. L. & Whybark, D. C. (1992). *Manufacturing planning and control systems.* New York: Irwin.

PETER BURCHER

bottlenecks   Bottlenecks are the parts of an operation which are the constraints on its capacity. Bottlenecks are an important issue in operations management because most operations attempt to maximize the output from a given set of resources, and maximizing output means minimizing capacity "leakage," and improving throughput efficiency, which depends on understanding bottlenecks.

The question which arises for operations managers is the extent to which bottlenecks are fixed or moveable as the variety or mix of products or services alters. There are two main approaches to managing bottlenecks. The first is to try to eliminate the bottleneck, recognizing that this will create another bottleneck step in the process. The alternative is to manage the bottleneck so that it is never unnecessarily idle by ensuring that resources needed at the bottleneck are always available (perhaps by using buffers), and ensuring that change overs cause minimum loss of capacity. Managing a bottleneck means ensuring that its utilization is as high as possible. If the bottleneck is fairly stable there is also the need to make sure subsequent stages in the process after the bottleneck do not become bottlenecks themselves, otherwise the important work at the main bottleneck may be wasted. The theory of constraints gives simple rules for managing bottlenecks when they are reasonably stable in a process (*see* OPTIMIZED PRODUCTION TECHNOLOGY).

The rules are:

(1) Balance flow not capacity.
(2) The level of utilization of a non-bottleneck resource is not determined by its own potential (capacity) but by some other constraint (i.e. bottleneck) in the system.
(3) Making a resource work (activation) and utilization of the resource are not the same.
(4) An hour lost at a bottleneck is an hour lost for the total system.
(5) An hour saved at a non-bottleneck is a mirage, unless resources can usefully be employed elsewhere.
(6) Bottlenecks govern both throughput and buffer stocks.
(7) The size of the batch we move between stages may be less than the process batch size at one stage. This allows us to prevent bottleneck stages running short of material.
(8) The process batch should be variable not fixed allowing us to influence lead time and throughput efficiency.
(9) Schedules should be established by looking at all constraints simultaneously. Lead times are a result of the schedule.

See also **capacity management; material requirements planning; product layout; line balancing**

Bibliography

Goldratt, E. M. & Cox, J. (1984). *The goal.* New York: North River Press Inc.

COLIN ARMISTEAD

blueprinting   *see* SERVICE DESIGN

breakthrough improvement   The "breakthrough" approach to improvement (or innovation-based improvement) sees the main vehicle of improvement as major and dramatic changes in the way an operation works. The impact of these improvements is relatively sudden, abrupt, and represents a step change in practice (and, it is hoped, performance). Such improvements often call for high investment of capital, often disrupting the on-going workings of the operation, and frequently involving changes in the product, service, or process technology. The approach is often contrasted with that of CONTINUOUS IMPROVEMENT but may be combined with it.

See also **business process redesign**

NIGEL SLACK

buffer stock   *see* INVENTORY MANAGEMENT

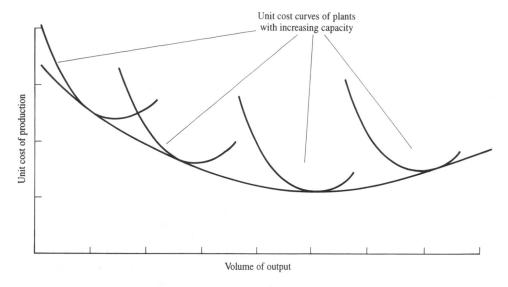

Figure 1 Unit cost of output curves for plants of varying capacity

disruption if one part of the organization fails (*see* FAILURE MEASURES).

The Increment of Capacity Change

Large units of capacity also have some disadvantages when the capacity of the operation is being changed to match changing demand. If an operation where forecast demand is increasing, seeks to satisfy all demand by increasing capacity using large capacity increments, it will have substantial amounts of overcapacity for much of the period when demand is increasing, which results in higher unit costs. However, if the company uses smaller increments, although there will still be some overcapacity it will be reduced. This results in higher capacity utilization and therefore lower costs.

The inherent risks of changing capacity using large increments can also be high. For example, if the rate of change demand unexpectedly slows, the capacity will only be partly utilized. However, if smaller units of capacity are used the likelihood is that the forecast error would have been detected in time to delay or cancel the capacity adjustment, leaving demand and capacity in balance.

A related concept is that of the "capacity cushion." This is the amount of planned capacity which is above the forecast level of demand in a period. Companies may deliberately plan for a capacity cushion so that they can cope with aggregated demand even if it turns out to be greater than forecast. Alternatively they might judge that extra capacity might be needed to absorb the inefficiencies caused by an unplanned mix of demands on the operation, even if the aggregated level of demand is as expected.

The magnitude of any capacity cushion is likely to reflect the relative costs to the organization of having either over- or undercapacity. The costs of overcapacity relate to the financing of the capital and human resources which are not being used to produce revenue. The cost of undercapacity is either the opportunity cost of not supplying demand or the extra cost of supplying demand by unplanned means such as overtime or subcontracting. One suggested approach to quantifying this concept (Hayes and Wheelwright, 1984) is to make the size of any capacity cushion proportional to the following ratio:

$$(C_s - C_x)/C_s$$

where C_s = the unit cost of shortage and C_x = the unit cost of excess capacity.

It is suggested that if this ratio is greater than 0.5 then a capacity cushion is appropriate; if it is

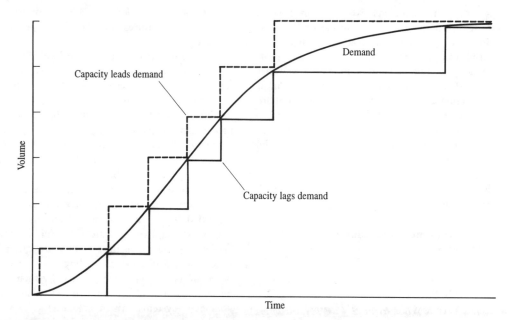

Figure 2 Capacity leading and capacity lagging strategies

less than 0.5 a "negative cushion" is appropriate. So when C_x is large (as in capital-intensive industries) capacity cushions, if they are justified at all, will tend to be small, whereas in industries where C_s is large (because of large profit margins) and C_x is small (because of low capital intensity) a relatively large capacity cushion is likely to be justified.

The Timing of Capacity Change

An operation also needs to decide when to bring new capacity on stream. In deciding when the new capacity is to be introduced an organization must choose a position somewhere between the two extreme strategies of capacity leading demand (timing the introduction of capacity in such a way that there is always sufficient capacity to meet forecast demand), and capacity lagging demand (timing the introduction of capacity so that demand is always equal or greater than capacity). Figure 2 shows these two extreme strategies, though in practice organizations are likely to choose a position somewhere between the two extremes. Each strategy has its own advantages and disadvantages.

Capacity leading strategies have the advantage of always being able to meet demand, therefore revenue is maximized and customers satisfied. Most of the time there is also a "capacity cushion" which can absorb extra demand or help if there are start-up problems with new plants. However, utilization of capacity is relatively low, therefore costs will be high. There are also risks of even greater (or even permanent) overcapacity if demand does not reach forecast levels, and the capital spending on plant is required relatively early.

Capacity lagging strategies always have sufficient demand to keep the plants working at full capacity, therefore unit costs are minimized. Furthermore, overcapacity problems are minimized if forecasts prove to be optimistic, and the capital spending on the plants is later than in a capacity leading strategy. However, there will, for long periods, be insufficient capacity to meet demand fully, resulting in reduced revenue and dissatisfied customers. Also there would be little or no ability to exploit short-term increases in demand, and the under supply position might be even worse if there were start-up problems with new plants.

A strategy on the continuum between pure leading and lagging strategies can be implemented so that no inventories are accumulated, so that all demand in one period is satisfied (or not) by the activity of the operation in the same period. For operations which cannot store throughput there is no alternative to this. However, for those operations which can, output can be stored for use in the next period. Capacity may be introduced in such a way that demand can always be met by a combination of production and inventories, with capacity more likely to be fully utilized. Because demand is always met and capacity is usually fully utilized, the profitability of the operation is likely to be high. However, the cost of carrying the inventories will need to be funded and the risks of obsolescence and deterioration of stock are introduced.

See also **content of manufacturing strategy; volume; cost**

Bibliography

Hayes, R. H. & Wheelwright, S. C. (1984). *Restoring our competitive edge: Competing through manufacturing*. New York: Wiley.
Manne, A. S. (1967). *Investments for capacity expansion*. London: Allen and Unwin.

NIGEL SLACK

cause and effect diagrams   *see* TOOLS OF QUALITY MANAGEMENT

cell layout   The usual basic options for laying out facilities are FIXED POSITION LAYOUT, PROCESS LAYOUT and PRODUCT LAYOUT. A cell layout is actually a hybrid facility arrangement based on combining some of the principles of fixed position and product layouts. A cell layout involves grouping together a number of dissimilar machines or processes according to the design of the product being made or the operations required for its production. In this respect a cell layout is similar to a product layout. The main difference, however, is that in a cell layout the operation sequence and flow direction can be varied. Another important difference is that the workers in a cell are usually multiskilled and can operate more than one machine or process, whereas in a product layout they tend to be dedicated to just one task on one work station.

In this respect, therefore, a cell layout draws on one of the features of the fixed position approach.

As with product layouts, a cell layout can be used in high-product volume situations, but its use is probably better established in intermittent batch operations. In this case the cell is used to produce product families rather than a single product and is based on the principles of "group technology." Here the cell (or group of processes) and associated family (or group) of products/parts can be identified using a number of techniques. Among these are coding and classification, where products and parts are identified by a numerical or alphanumeric coding system, then classified into families and allocated to cells according to their design and processing requirements. Coding systems can be of two types: "universal" systems, which can be applied to all production situations or "bespoke" systems, which are specifically tailored to the needs of a particular organization (*see* PRODUCT FAMILIES). An alternative approach to cell design is to use "production flow analysis," where operation route sequence data are analyzed to identify the appropriate combination of product families and processes. However, this technique has the disadvantage of being based on existing products and processes. The ideal approach would be to design all new products specifically for production using a cell layout; this should produce a more efficient overall result.

Originally, cell layouts were associated with the processing of component parts. However, they are increasingly becoming regarded as an appropriate type of layout in connection with assembly work. In this case they are often used for higher product volumes which would otherwise necessitate using a product layout. The use of cells overcomes many of the disadvantages associated with product layouts. For example, the wider operator skill requirements provide greater JOB ENRICHMENT which can result in less absenteeism, lower labor turnover, and easier recruitment. Many of the physical problems associated with product layouts can also be overcome using assembly cells; a reduction in work station interdependency makes the overall system more reliable and the assembly of different product variants is easier with cells than with conventional "line"-

type product layouts. Cell layouts for assembly also avoid the need for LINE BALANCING, and SYSTEM LOSS.

A further aspect to be considered regarding cell layouts is the use of automation for materials handling and production operations. In cells for producing component parts industrial robots (*see* ROBOTICS) are frequently used for loading, unloading and the transfer of material between machines. The processes within a cell can also be automated and CNC machine tools are often incorporated in production cells. Sometimes the complexity of such cells is such that they can be defined as FLEXIBLE MANUFACTURING SYSTEMS. In assembly cells an increasingly common form of materials handling device is the automated guided vehicle (AGV), which can transport products both within and between cells under automatic control. Robots are also starting to be developed with the necessary dexterity, flexibility, and intelligence to carry out the type of assembly operations which at one time could only be done manually.

The concept of the "cellular" arrangement of facilities has also been used in service operations. For example, some retail operations might cluster goods in one area, not because the goods are similar in their function but because they conform to a theme recognizable to customers. A sports goods area in a department store sells types of goods, which might all be available elsewhere in the store, but are clustered around the "sports" theme. This cell-like arrangement is sometimes called the "shop within a shop" concept.

Two additional points which warrant discussion in relation to manufacturing cell layouts are concerned with production control and the payment of workers. As far as production control is concerned cells have the benefit of being a single "planning point," which means that the central planning and control function only needs to be concerned with the cell level rather than the level of each individual machine and process. The cells themselves will have their own individual controllers, which can be computerized or manual, and will interface with the central planning and control function. In this way the cell can be largely regarded as an autonomous production unit or a focused factory. The degree of autonomy involved and the multiskill requirements of cells also demand a more appropriate payment system than that used in other types of situation. Typically such a payment system will include different elements designed to reflect the characteristics of work carried out in cells.

See also **group working; focus; job design**

Bibliography

Burbidge, J. L. (1978). *The principles of production control.* 4th edn. London: Macdonald and Evans.
Green, T. J. & Sadowski, R. P. (1984). A review of cellular manufacturing assumptions and advantages and design techniques. *Journal of Operations Management*, 4, 2.
Kirton, J. & Brooks, E. (1994). *Cells in industry.* London: McGraw-Hill.

DAVID BENNETT

closed loop MRP Closed loop MRP is a system which grew out of MATERIAL REQUIREMENTS PLANNING and which primarily allows plans to be checked against capacity to determine whether they are realistic and achievable. The main plan to which this refers is the MASTER PRODUCTION SCHEDULE. Also incorporated are the other planning functions of sales and operations, including production planning, resource requirements planning, rough cut capacity planning and capacity requirements planning. The closing of the loop at the planning stage refers to the checking of the various plans against appropriate resources and feeding back any alterations that may be necessary to the plans.

Once these planning phases are complete, the execution functions come into play. These include the manufacturing control functions of input–output measurement, detailed SCHEDULING and dispatching, as well as anticipated delay reports from manufacturing and suppliers. The closing of the loop at these stages involves the feedback from these execution functions so that the planning can be kept valid at all times.

Closed loop MRP is the intermediate stage between MATERIAL REQUIREMENTS PLANNING (MRPI) and MANUFACTURING RESOURCES PLANNING (MRPII).

The production plan is a top-level statement of the planned rate of production expressed in aggregate terms, usually by product family. The units may be physical units of product, standard hours of production, tonnes, gallons, or, most often, sales values of product families. Typically the time periods are months or quarters, and the planning horizon may be two to ten years. The principal purposes of the production plan are, first, to provide authorization to disaggregate the production plan into specific end items in the master production schedule; second, to provide the input to resource requirements planning so that decisions can be made on long lead time changes in resources such as plant expansion or acquisition of special purpose equipment. The third purpose may be to stabilize production and employment where demand is subject to seasonal or other variation.

Resource requirements planning is the capacity system at the production planning level. It may make use of historical ratios to determine the resources required to meet the production plan. These might include person hours per unit or sales value of product family, square meters of space required in final assembly as a function of the production rate, cubic meters required in stores per unit of finished product, and so forth. Assumptions must be made concerning the mix of products within families, average sales value per item per product family or typical products may be chosen as a basis for projecting required resources. If resource requirements planning arrives at an acceptable plan for providing the capacity to produce the production plan, the production plan becomes firm. If this cannot be resolved, the production plan and possibly the long-term business and marketing plans, will have to be modified.

Analysis of the resources required by the master production schedule (MPS) is carried out by rough cut capacity planning (RCCP). Under RCCP, a set of load profiles is maintained for each item scheduled in the MPS. The profiles show the amount of critical resources required to make one unit of the product. The critical resources may be, for example, person power, machine hours, or floor space in certain departments or work centers. These resource requirements are spread by time period over standard lead times.

Once a tentative master production schedule is developed, it is input to rough cut capacity planning to determine whether it is compatible with available planned capacity. Load profiles are extended by order quantities, set-up hours are added, and the totals are summed across products by time period. If the schedule calls for more capacity than will be available, either plans must be made for increasing the capacity by such means as hiring, overtime, or subcontracting, or the schedule must be reduced. If the schedule calls for less capacity than will be available, the capacity can be reduced by planning for such actions as lay-offs, shortened work weeks, or transfer of employees. When inconsistencies between the MPS and planned capacity are resolved, the MPS is made firm.

The rough cut capacity planning is approximate in that it is only concerned with critical resources and does not take into account changes in work in process or component inventories. However, normally rough cut capacity planning is sufficient to avoid major inconsistencies between the master production schedule and available capacity, and remaining problems can be handled at the materials requirements planning (MRPI) or operation scheduling levels. "What if" scenarios can be investigated with changes to the master production schedule using "simulated" rather than live data. The effect of such changes will be reflected in the rough cut capacity plan.

Capacity requirements planning refers to the intermediate range of planning and is confined to the timespan covered by material requirements planning (MRPI). It is the process of determining how much labor and machine resources are required to accomplish the tasks of production. Open shop orders and planned orders in the material requirements planning (MRPI) system are input to capacity requirements planning, which translates these orders into hours of work by work center by time period by back scheduling from the net requirements due date through the elements of the lead time.

These work loads may be for person power (direct labor load), machine or assembly loads, or indirect labor loads. Analysis of load reports may indicate needed corrections to shop floor capacity. This might entail make or buy decisions, the planning of alternative routings, subcontracting over long periods of time, the reallocation of the workforce, changing the workforce where feasible, and adding additional tooling. If sufficient resources cannot be found at this stage of planning, closing the loop entails feeding back to material requirements planning (MRPI) and the master production schedule to alter the plans which have caused the overload. This type of capacity planning is referred to as infinite capacity planning since no automatic action is taken to keep within finite resource limits.

Input–output control is the basis for monitoring the capacity plans. Planned work input and planned work output at a work center can be compared to the actual work input and output. This allows the identification of load per work center or group of work centers and any changes to that load. In order to control work in progress levels and hence lead times, the idea is to not release work that cannot be done, but to hold the backlog in the production and inventory control department.

The final stage in closed loop MRP is the detailed scheduling and dispatching on the shop floor. This usually entails the management of queues at the various work centers by means of priority rules which take account of due dates and the work content of orders.

See also **capacity management; JIT/MRP; planning and control in operations**

Bibliography

Luscombe, M. (1993). *MRPII: Integrating the business.* Oxford: Butterworth Heinemann.

Vollmann, T. E., Berry, W. L. & Whybark, D. C. (1992). *Manufacturing planning and control systems.* New York: Irwin.

Wight, O. (1984). *Manufacturing resource planning: MRPII.* Essex Junction, VT: Oliver Wight.

PETER BURCHER

computer-aided design Computer-aided design (CAD) systems provide the computer-aided ability to create and modify product drawings. These systems allow conventionally used shapes (called entities) such as points, lines, arcs, circles, and text, to be added to a computer-based representation of the product. Once incorporated into the design these entities can be copied, moved about, rotated through angles, magnified, or deleted. The system can usually also "zoom in

and out" to reveal different levels of detail. The designs thus created can be saved in the memory of the system and retrieved for later use. This enables a library of standardized drawings of parts and components to be built up. Not only can this dramatically increase the productivity of the process but it also aids the standardization of parts in the design activity. Some CAD systems come already supplied with their own libraries of standard parts.

CAD systems can be configured in various ways. These range from using large mainframe computers down to single PC-based systems. CAD systems first of all need some kind of input device: these include joy sticks, light pens, electronic tablets, a mouse, or even the keyboard itself. The processing unit includes the central processing unit (CPU) and the software. The data storage part of the system usually includes either disk or magnetic tape storage. The display unit is usually a graphic terminal, while the output device can either be a printer or a plotter.

The software used in CAD systems varies in its degree of sophistication and modeling ability. The simplest type models only on two dimensions. This produces plans and elevations of the design in a similar way to a conventional engineering "blueprint." More sophisticated systems can model products in three dimensions. This can be done in very basic form by "extruding" the two-dimensional image to give thickness to different parts of the two-dimensional shape. However, this approach is not capable of modeling complex products: it is often known as the two and half dimension approach. True three-dimensional software is capable of presenting an object accurately in full three-dimensional form. It may do this either by representing the edges and corners of the shape (known as a wire frame model) or as a full solid model. The advantage of wire frame modeling is that it demands considerably less computer power because an object is represented only by its outline. However, for complex objects wire frame models can be confusing.

The most obvious advantage of CAD systems is that their ability to store and retrieve design data quickly as well as their ability to manipulate design details can considerably increase the productivity of the design activity. In addition to this, however, because changes can be made rapidly to designs, CAD systems can considerably enhance the flexibility of the design activity, enabling modifications to be made much more rapidly. Further, the use of standardized libraries of shapes and entities can reduce the possibility of errors in the design. Perhaps most significantly, though, CAD can be seen as a prototyping as well as a drafting device. In effect the designer is modeling the design in order to assess its suitability prior to full production.

See also **advanced manufacturing technology; flexible manufacturing systems; computer-integrated manufacturing; process technology; robotics; design**

NIGEL SLACK

computer-integrated manufacturing Integration of PROCESS TECHNOLOGY prior to the development of ADVANCED MANUFACTURING TECHNOLOGY have usually taken place within particular functional areas of manufacturing. For example, improvements in machining systems have mostly been confined to the factory floor. Integration based on AMT, however, enables further blurring of the lines between areas and functions, for example, in the case of COMPUTER-AIDED DESIGN (CAD) and manufacturing (CAD/CAM), where the electronic information created and manipulated in designing a product is then passed automatically to the computer controlled machinery required for producing it. This type of integration forms the basis of computer-integrated manufacturing (CIM) which can be defined as:

> the integration of computer based monitoring and control of all aspects of the manufacturing process, drawing on .a common database and communicating via some form of computer network.

Such integration need not stop at the boundaries of the firm. Integration via electronic means can also extend backwards along the supply chain (with, for example, shared design processes or electronic components ordering linked to INVENTORY MANAGEMENT computers) or forwards into the distribution chain, using "electronic data interchange" (EDI) to speed the flow of products to outlets, while also minimizing the inventory held within the chain (*see* SUPPLY CHAIN MANAGEMENT).

At its heart CIM brings together two key aspects of manufacturing activity: materials processing and information processing. Automation has already had a major impact on many of the physical transformation processes. CIM moves the emphasis towards indirect activities, many of which involve information processing or communication. The application of IT in these areas is beginning to contribute significant improvements in performance, although the degree to which CIM can have an impact depends upon reconfiguring both technological and organizational systems. The application of BUSINESS PROCESS REDESIGN is an important enabler of this.

Most models of CIM involve some form of stepwise or hierarchical arrangement of control, from low levels where individual elements (machine controllers, data collectors, etc.) operate autonomously but also communicate information to the next level which is responsible for the overall monitoring and control of a level (for example, a manufacturing cell). Further up, a plant controller would handle the activities of several cells, co-ordinating their use of resources and monitoring their overall performance. Level four would involve the integration of other key functional areas, for example, design and marketing, and would represent a shared information system of the kind represented by MANUFACTURING RESOURCES PLANNING (MRPII). Level five would be an overall business systems integration, in which the financial and sales information would be linked into the manufacturing system, and level six would be the overall board level strategic view which includes long- and short-term perspectives, etc.

A key enabling technology in all of this is the computer network which has the important architectural property that information can be shared throughout the system. Changes anywhere in the system will update the rest of the information in the system; thus the entire operation can be seen to behave as if it were a single, enormously complex machine. This is not, however, simply a centralizing and concentrating process; the key property of the networks which form the "nervous system" for

CIM is the ability to be simultaneously highly centralized and highly decentralized. Thus the economies of shared resources and information can be added to those of local autonomy and flexibility in uncertain environments.

CIM exemplifies the distinction between "substitution" innovation and more radical and strategic innovation. CIM applications do not just offer considerable improvements in traditional ways of making things; they also open up completely new and often highly integrated options. CIM also differs from other technologies in having potential impact on indirect cost areas as well as direct costs. It contributes to better co-ordination; it tightens the linkages between previously separate elements in a production chain; it brings powerful planning and monitoring tools to bear upon the problems of production control; and it reduces the amount of paperwork required to maintain even a simple manufacturing system. Thus many of the traditional areas of overhead cost (which can often account for 40 percent or more of total product costs) can be reduced, adding further to the competitive benefits offered by CIM.

See also **advanced manufacturing technology; flexible manufacturing systems; process technology; robotics**

Bibliography

Adler, P. (1989). CAD/CAM: managerial challenges and research issues. *IEEE Transactions on Engineering Management*, **36**.

Ayres, R. (1992). CIM: a challenge to technology management. *International Journal of Technology Management*, **7**.

Bessant, J. (1991). *Managing advanced manufacturing technology: The challenge of the fifth wave*. Oxford/Manchester: NCC-Blackwell.

JOHN BESSANT

Concurrent engineering *see* SIMULTANEOUS DEVELOPMENT

condition-based maintenance Conditioned-based maintenance (CBM) is an approach to maintaining physical facilities which intervenes in the facilities to either repair or replace parts based on some form of ongoing monitoring

activity. CBM thereby attempts to perform MAINTENANCE only when the facilities require it. This approach becomes particularly effective where the facilities or equipment need to be run for long periods in order to achieve high utilization. The machinery used in high volume or continuous processes especially can benefit from CBM since stopping the equipment when it is not strictly necessary to do so could take it out of action for long periods and reduce utilization.

CBM can involve monitoring any characteristic of the equipment which might indicate its condition. For example, vibration might indicate the wear characteristics of a machine tool, especially when the vibration is measured near bearing positions. The lubrication oil in machines might be sampled and tested spectrographically for particle contamination in order to indicate the likelihood of failure in the immediate future. Temperature in electric motors might indicate the efficiency, and therefore condition, of the motors.

Typically the results of this monitoring are then analyzed and used to decide whether the equipment should be stopped and repair effected. However, the principle of condition-based monitoring extends beyond technology-based equipment. Simple routine inspection of furniture or floor coverings at leisure facilities, for example, could be regarded as CBM if the results of such inspections were used to take the decision as to whether to replace facilities.

See also **reliability-centered maintenance; total productive maintenance; preventive maintenance**

MICHAEL SHULVER

content of manufacturing strategy The content of MANUFACTURING STRATEGY is the collection of policies, plans, and behaviors which an organization chooses to pursue in its manufacturing function. It is the definition of how the company expects to use its manufacturing resources to contribute to its strategic direction. The content of manufacturing strategy is usually contrasted with the PROCESS OF MANUFACTURING STRATEGY FORMULATION which is the way in which content is determined.

Content decisions can be classified in several ways according to the classification of OPERATIONS ACTIVITIES which is adopted. The most common is to distinguish between the strategic-level decisions which determine the operation's structure (sometimes called process decisions) and those which determine its infrastructure. Typical structural decisions include the amount, timing, and type of capacity, the size, type, and location of facilities, the type of process technology to develop and the direction, extent and balance of vertical integration. Typical infrastructural decisions include determining the development of the workforce, the organization of quality policy, the type of production planning and materials control, and the organization structure of the manufacturing function (Hayes and Wheelwright, 1984).

See also **operations objectives; vertical integration; capacity management; product–process matrix; planning and control in operations; quality management systems; job design**

Bibliography

Hayes, R. H. & Wheelwright, S. C. (1984). *Restoring our competitive edge: Competing through manufacturing*. New York: Wiley.

NIGEL SLACK

continuous improvement   Continuous improvement is an approach to improving the performance of operations which promotes frequent, regular, and possibly small incremental improvement steps. Although continuous improvement is not concerned with promoting small improvements *per se*, it does see small improvements as having a significant advantage over large ones in that they can be followed relatively easily by other small improvements. Large steps in improvement, on the other hand, usually require a pause for consolidation between steps.

Continuous improvement is also known as *kaizen*, a Japanese word meaning "improvement. Moreover it means improvement in personal life, home life, social life and work life. When applied to the workplace *kaizen* means continuing improvement involving

everyone – managers and workers alike" (Imai, 1986).

In continuous improvement it is not the size of each step which is important. Rather it stresses the likelihood that improvement will be on-going. Put another way the rate of improvement is less important than the momentum of improvement. What matters is that some kind of improvement has actually taken place.

Continuous improvement as a philosophy is often contrasted with BREAKTHROUGH IMPROVEMENT. Breakthrough improvement places a high value on creative solutions. It encourages free thinking and individualism. It is a radical philosophy in as much as it fosters an approach to improvement which does not accept many constraints to what is possible. "Starting with a clean sheet of paper," "going back to first principles," and "completely rethinking the system," are all typical breakthrough improvement principles. Continuous improvement, on the other hand, is less ambitious, in the short term. It stresses adaptability, team work and attention to detail. It is not radical, as such; rather it builds upon the wealth of accumulated experience within the operation itself, often relying primarily on the people who operate the system to improve it. A frequently quoted analogy is the difference between the sprint and the marathon. Breakthrough improvement is a series of explosive and impressive sprints, whereas continuous improvement, like marathon running, does not require the short-term strength required for sprinting; but it does require persistence and perseverance.

Notwithstanding the differences between breakthrough and continuous improvement, it is now widely held that it is possible to combine the two, albeit at different times. Large improvements can be implemented as and when they seem to promise significant gains, but between such occasions the operation can continue making its quiet and less spectacular *kaizen* improvements.

See also **business process redesign; total quality management; just-in-time; PDCA cycle**

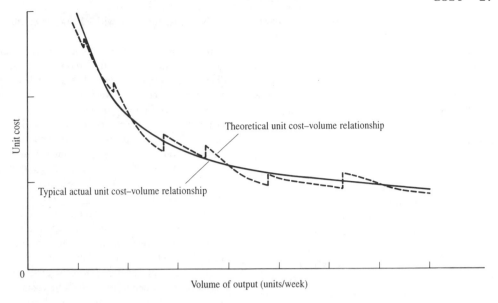

Figure 1 *Unit cost of output varies as volume of output varies*

Bibliography

Imai, M. (1986). *Kaizen: The key to Japan's competitive success.* McGraw-Hill.

NIGEL SLACK

continuous review system   *see* INVENTORY CONTROL SYSTEMS

control   *see* PLANNING AND CONTROL

control charts   *see* STATISTICAL QUALITY TECHNIQUES

cost   The cost incurred by an operation as it produces goods and services is always regarded by both academics and practitioners as one of its significant OPERATIONS OBJECTIVES. It is closely related to PRODUCTIVITY, but whereas productivity is concerned with the way in which inputs are transformed into outputs, cost is taken to refer to the monetary value of the resources used to produce goods or services. Two major management issues are of concern to most operations managers; how to measure costs associated with particular goods or services, and what decisions and activities will influence the costs of the goods and services which are produced. The first issue lies clearly within the province of management accounting. It is with the second issue that this entry is largely concerned.

The Strategic Influences on Cost

VOLUME has always been seen as having an important influence on costs. It is therefore surprising that many operations managers have little real idea of how costs vary with volume. Partly this is because the exact relationship between volume and cost is rarely clear. In the shorter term, volume effects are largely a matter of higher levels of throughput spreading the fixed costs of the operation over a larger number of products or services produced. In theory the effects of this are straightforward. Figure 1 shows how average costs are supposed to reduce as volume increases, according to the formula

Average cost
= total cost/output
= fixed costs/output + variable costs/output
= fixed costs/output + variable cost/unit

In some operations such as some process industries cost–volume curves do approach that shown in Figure 1. However, for most operations this is a simplification, since operations usually accommodate changes in volume through a series of relatively small discontinuities in the cost curve, for example shedding labor and subcontracting when output reduces or starting up production lines as output increases. Further, nominal capacity is not usually the definite cut-off point implied by Figure 1. Capacity is rarely so well balanced between every part of the production process that it all reaches its limit at the same level of output, so BOTTLENECKS occur as demands are placed on some parts of the operation more heavily than on others. This means that each part of the operation has to incur fixed cost steps as it attempts to balance capacity. The result is that in most operations the volume–cost curve is neither smooth nor entirely predictable because there is some management discretion as to when to commit the operation to fixed cost breaks.

In the longer term the volume of output may allow changes in the way an operation either uses its existing technology, or acquires new types of technology. Opportunities in the way technology is used derive from the effective VARIETY placed on parts of the operation. As volume increases, the tendency is for variety per unit volume to decrease, so each part of the operation has fewer different tasks to perform per time period. This is likely to reduce the number of change-overs necessary, which will in turn release the capacity previously spent changing from one activity to the next, and avoid the quality problems associated with change-over. More significantly, it may allow more dedicated technology to be developed where economies derive from focused specialization on a narrow set of tasks (see FOCUS).

Variety is often a less well understood driver of cost than volume. High product or service variety often means high parts variety, process variety, and routing variety, behind which is the complexity which is the root cause of variety-related costs. First, high variety requires more complex technology, or alternatively makes it more difficult to develop the dedicated technology which may keep costs low. Second high variety loaded onto plant and equipment usually leads to higher capital and operating costs because of the increased complexity of control systems, materials handling and adjustment

mechanisms, together with change-over downtimes.

In the same way as for volume-driven costs, the relationship is neither smooth nor static. There are often "variety breaks" where an incremental increase in variety cannot be borne by existing technology, although this is less true for many newer process technologies, which are changing some aspects of the relationship between variety, flexibility, and cost (see ADVANCED MANUFACTURING TECHNOLOGY).

Variation, which is the degree to which the demand placed on the whole operation fluctuates over a period of time, also affects an operation's costs. One way of understanding the variation–cost relationship is to imagine a perfectly steady demand. All customers demand exactly the same level and mix of products or services every week of the year. The costs saved under such an ideal, and hypothetical, condition are the costs associated with variation. The exact source of these variation-driven costs will depend on how an individual operation chooses to treat fluctuations in demand. The choices available are part of the AGGREGATE CAPACITY MANAGEMENT activity.

The Operational Influences on Cost

The benefits of achieving high levels of performance in the other performance objectives of QUALITY, speed (see TIME-BASED PERFORMANCE), DELIVERY DEPENDABILITY, and FLEXIBILITY, can be viewed as having both external and internal aspects. Externally, performance is valued by customers for the enhanced levels of product or service specification, or levels of services it brings. Internally, high levels of performance bring benefits which are seen primarily in terms of their effect on cost.

A higher quality performance reduces cost, where "quality" is used to mean conformance to specification. Fewer errors within the operation directly reduces rework, scrap and waste as well as resulting in fewer unplanned activities, which in turn leads to greater internal dependability. Further, error-free operation enhances an operation's ability to reduce throughput time, which in turn reduces costs.

Fast throughput reduces cost because material information or customers which move quickly through an operation spend less time in inventory, attract fewer overheads and make forecasting easier. Fast throughput also encourages dependable delivery since small deviations from schedule can be accommodated faster.

Internal delivery dependability reduces cost because it reduces the level of uncertainty in the operation. If all materials information and customers transferred within the operation exactly as planned, the overhead devoted to monitoring and progressing late deliveries is eliminated, as is all the effort of rescheduling resources in order to accommodate the late delivery. Also without internal dependability there is little chance of success in trying to speed up throughput.

Finally, greater flexibility often can reduce costs directly by letting the operation change from producing one product or service to another with little loss of output (for example, by increasing change-over flexibility (see SET-UP REDUCTION), and indirectly, by reducing throughput time which, in turn, reduces costs. Flexibility can also increase internal dependability, by allowing an alternative process route to bypass a breakdown for example, which in turn reduces cost.

Bibliography

Eilan, S. & Gold, B. (1978). *Productivity measurement.* Oxford: Pergamon Press.

New, C. C. & Myers, A. (1986). *Manufacturing operations in the UK.* London: British Institute of Management.

Skinner, W. (1985). The productivity paradox. *Harvard Business Review*, 63.

NIGEL SLACK

critical incident technique The critical incident technique (CIT) is a technique found predominantly in the service quality literature. CIT attempts to identify critical incidents in order to be able to understand customer-perceived quality (see SERVICE QUALITY) and to help managers develop approaches to its improvement. CIT was originally developed during the Second World War by psychologist John Flanagan and was used to determine the reasons for the high rate of pilot failure during training. The analysis of his tests provided the basis for selection tests that achieved a substantial reduction in failure rate.

Critical incidents are events that contribute to, or detract from, perceived service or product performance in a significant way. For an incident to be defined as critical it must deviate significantly, either positively or negatively, from what is normal or expected. The CIT instrument usually comprises two questions. The first question asks customers to think of a time when they felt very pleased and satisfied with the service/product received and to describe, in a few sentences, the situation and why they felt so happy. The second question requires customers to think of a time when they were unhappy and dissatisfied with the service/product they received and to describe, in a few sentences, why they felt this way.

The outcomes correspond to delight and dissatisfaction outcomes (see SERVICE QUALITY). CIT oes not identify incidents which might be associated with the neutral satisfied state (see ZONE OF TOLERANCE).

This technique is quite unlike scale item questionnaires which usually measure perceptions against predetermined factors. CIT allows customers to express their own views without prejudice. Thus, the critical incident technique provides an understanding of quality from a customer's point of view (customer-perceived quality). As the technique collects the interpretation of events by customers, in their own words, the anecdotes may be a valuable source of information to help managers understand how they might improve service quality.

There are three key disadvantages in using this technique. First, the incidents may have taken place some time before the collection of the data and so they may have been reinterpreted in the light of further events. Second, CIT requires customers to take more time and effort than, for example, ticking boxes, so the response rate tends to be quite low. And, third, the classification and interpretation of data can be a considerable task.

Bibliography

Edvardsson, B. (1992). Service break-downs: a study of critical incidents in an airline. *International Journal of Service Industry Management*, 3, 4, 17–29.

Johnston, R. (1995). The determinants of service quality: satisfyers and dissatisfyers. *International Journal of Service Industry Management*, 6, 5, 53–71.

ROBERT JOHNSTON

critical path method   *see* NETWORK TECH-NIQUES

critical success factors   *see* OPERATIONS OBJECTIVES

Crosby   Before gaining his reputation as a quality consultant, Philip Crosby served in the navy, became quality manager on the first Pershing missile program, and was ITT's corporate vice-president with responsibility for quality. Crosby's approach to quality improvement was popularized through his book *Quality is Free*, so entitled because Crosby's contention was that it is not producing high-quality goods and services that is costly, but rather failing to produce goods and services right first time.

Crosby's philosophy is encapsulated in his four "absolutes of quality":

(1) Quality is defined as conformance to requirements, where requirements are defined by the customer.
(2) The system for causing quality is prevention, not appraisal.
(3) The performance standard must be zero defects.
(4) The measurement of quality is the price of non-conformance (PONC).

Crosby estimates that the cost of non-conformance is typically between 25 and 40 percent of operating costs and promotes the measurement of PONC as a necessary step towards quality improvement. He argues vehemently against the concept of "acceptable quality levels," which can lead to acceptance of poor quality and undermine the performance standard of zero defects. He also proposes a 14-step approach to quality improvement, recommending that implementation be led by a steering group of senior managers, and be realized through the activities of cross-functional quality improvement teams.

See also **total quality management; quality; service quality**

Bibliography

Crosby, P. (1979). *Quality is free: The art of making quality certain*. New York: McGraw-Hill.
Crosby, P. (1984). *Quality without tears*. New York: McGraw-Hill.
Crosby, P. (1988). *The eternally successful organisation*. New York: McGraw-Hill.

RHIAN SILVESTRO

customer support operations   Customer support operations, sometimes called customer service and support operations, provide the activities which support customers in the use of products and also provide the means by which equipment is serviced. Customer service and support used to be known as after-sales service and was often regarded by companies in this form as a "necessary evil" to satisfy warranty requirements. Manufacturing companies would now regard customer service and support as a key business process which lies within SUPPLY CHAIN MANAGEMENT, interacting if not integrated with a LOGISTICS activity. The elements of customer service and support typically involve the use of telephone response centers from which customers can gain help and advice and from which resources can be dispatched to assist customers. This off-site provision of assistance to customers for repair or collection of equipment is performed by a field service team. The management of spares is a necessary part of the customer service and support activity. The management of other services which can be categorized as field service operations have similarities with customer service and support. In this group are emergency service including fire, ambulance, police services, and relief agencies including the Red Cross.

The Role of Customer Service and Support

The role of customer service and support is mistakenly seen by some firms as being relevant after a sale has been made. However, customer service and support is influenced by, and should influence, earlier stages in the contact with customers and the design and production of products. This philosophy is one of a consistency of service for customers by means of a designed and built-in serviceability of products.

The need for customer service and support for a product is driven by three factors; its initial purchase price, the cost of failure to customers, and its reliability index. The latter is the inverse of the number of times the product will fail during its economic lifetime. Products which are regarded as disposable have an index of one. Where the initial price and cost of the customer of downtime for equipment are both high, the role of customer service and support is to provide accessible and rapid response, and to influence the design of products to increase reliability and serviceability (*see* FAILURE ANALYSIS).

The provision of customer service and support and the role it plays within a firm should be an integral part of the service strategy. Different firms display different strategies for customer service and support depending on the nature of the product and the type of customer. Customer service and support may be viewed within a range of simply providing spares to customers through to the provision of an integrated service and support operation. The actual role for customer service may depend on the industry. For example, the provision of spares to customers is more common for capital goods manufacturers who deal solely with industrial customers. Alternatively, the role may be determined by a strategic decision to compete on aspects of service and support.

The Elements of Customer Service and Support

The major areas for customer service and support may be grouped under the four categories related to:

(1) products;
(2) service and repair;
(3) support for the customer;
(4) process issues associated with "how" the customer is dealt with.

Product-related issues are connected with design and the capture of information relating to the use of products and the relay of this information in a timely manner so that it influences the design of the next generation of new products or upgrades of existing products. The mean time between failures (MTBF) is a key measure of reliability for products which will influence the nature of the service and support activity (*see* FAILURE MEASURES).

Service-related issues are to do with elements of timing, speed of response, the nature of the response, and what is expected by customers. These expectations may be influenced by specific promises contained within a product service agreement.

Service, repair, and support are influenced by the initial response. The aims of initial response are to enable customers to make contact easily with people who can help them. They should provide a meaningful response within the time expected if this cannot be completed during the time of the initial contact.

Process issues are similar to those of the design of SERVICE OPERATIONS. Some specific aspects of the nature of customer service and support are the appropriateness of timings; the availability of the service and support provision; the presence of service engineers on customers' premises; and the need often to train customers in the use of equipment.

The Use of Technology in Customer Service and Support

Technology can play a central role in changing the customer service and support process. Its influence is felt in three main areas: customer support, remote sensing of equipment, and control of field resources.

A main means of providing support is through telephone response centers. Technology allows customers to gain access to information from the service provider without direct human contact. Access may be through the use of a telephone and the use of voice recognition or telephone key pad or through computer links. When personal contact is needed the support staff are enabled by the construction of the databases to be able to provide individual service and respond to complex requests for support.

Remote sensing and possible repair of essential equipment is often possible where life may be threatened or the customer values the service. Computer installations may be remotely monitored, and software and hardware faults corrected remotely.

The use of technology for the control of field resources includes making information immediately accessible to engineers through computer links by land-based or radio links, and the tracking and tracing and redirection of engineers, and the redirection of materials.

Bibliography

Armistead, C. G. & Clark, G. (1992). *Customer service and support: Implementing effective strategies.* London: Financial Times Pitman Publishing.

Armistead, C. G. & Clark, G. (1994). *Outstanding customer service: Implementing the best ideas from around the world.* New York: Financial Times Irwin Professional Publishing.

Mathe, H. & Shapiro, R. D. (1993). *Integrating service strategy in the manufacturing company.* London: Chapman and Hall.

COLIN ARMISTEAD

D

delivery dependability Delivery dependability is one of the commonly quoted OPERATIONS OBJECTIVES which define the performance of the operations function. Delivery dependability is generally taken to mean keeping delivery promises. It can be viewed as the other half of delivery performance along with delivery speed (*see* TIME-BASED PERFORMANCE).

Although speed and dependability are the two halves of delivery performance they are fundamentally different in as much as speed is usually quoted and defined as part of the specification for the order. Customers may make some attempt to specify dependability also (by the use of penalty clauses for late delivery, for example), but this remains a performance objective which becomes important when a history of performance, good or bad, is established.

Dependability has a number of attributes in common with QUALITY. It is a "conformance" measure, but conformance to time rather than specification. It is also an attribute which influences customer satisfaction over the longer term rather than one which necessarily ensures an immediate sale.

Measuring Delivery Dependability

In principle dependability is a straightforward concept, where

$$\text{Dependability} = \text{due delivery date} - \text{actual delivery date}$$

When delivery is on time the equation will equal zero; a positive measure means delivery is early and negative means delivery is late.

However, measurement is not always so straightforward. For example, the "due date" can mean the date originally requested by the customer or the date quoted by the operation. Also there can be a difference between the delivery date scheduled by the operation and that which is promised to the customer. Nor are delivery dates immutable; they can be changed, sometimes by customers but more often by the operation. If the customer requests a new delivery date this may be used to calculate delivery performance.

The Benefits of Delivery Dependability

It is worth distinguishing between the external benefits of delivery dependability (how the outside customer views dependability), and its internal benefits (what internal customers gain), and how it benefits the whole operation.

Delivery dependability is often seen as a "qualifying" (*see* ORDER-WINNERS AND QUALIFIERS) performance objective. However, this may not be the case. Although it is an attribute judged over the longer term by customers, that is not the same as being a qualifier. The key questions is, "Can an operation win more business directly by being more dependable?" Partly this is a consequence of customers becoming more sophisticated in their purchasing behavior.

The most significant internal benefit of dependability is the stability it gives. In a highly dependable operation relatively little is wasted on coping with unexpected events. Perhaps more significant is the reduction in the fragmenting effects of continuing interruptions to routine operations and the absence of a lack of trust in the internal working of the operation. Operations managers can "keep their eye on the ball."

From this stability can come other benefits, most notably less inventory. Part of the reason for the build up of inventory between stages in an operation is that it buffers each stage from the output variation of its neighbors. In-process inventory is often justified on the basis that internal deliveries might not be on time and therefore inventory is required to protect the operation. However, with increased dependability there is no need for the "insurance" of buffer inventory.

Improving Delivery Dependability

A number of prescriptions have been advocated as to how the external and internal dimensions of delivery dependability may be improved. Most commonly a link is drawn between dependable delivery and dependable technology. The effectiveness of any operations MAINTENANCE practices will clearly affect internal, and therefore external, dependability. Other prescriptions include the following.

- *Plan ahead*: often when a delivery is late the root cause will be some occurrence which was unexpected by the operation. Frequently the unexpected event could have been predicted with some internal mechanism which looks forward for indications of possible trouble.

- *Do not overload capacity*: loading an operation above its operational capacity often results in missed internal delivery dates. The consequences of excess load may be a lack of control and overlooked due dates.

- *Flexibility can localize disruptions*: certain types of FLEXIBILITY can service to localize disruptions when they do occur, by providing alternative processing capability. However, flexibility does not prevent disruption; although it can limit its effects.

- *Monitor progress closely*: a common cause of lateness seems to be overlooked internal delivery dates. Every day that internal lateness is not recognized is a day less in which to do something about it. An internal monitoring system may become self-reinforcing because when internal dependability increases and flow becomes more predictable, it is easier for internal customers to signal late deliveries.

- *Emphasize internal supplier development*: initially the role of internal customers may be to monitor the delivery performance of their suppliers. Later it may be a matter of improving communications, for example, holding joint improvement team meetings and so on.

See also **cost; lifecycle effects**

Bibliography

Ferdows, S. K. & De Mayer, A. (1990). Lasting improvement in manufacturing performance: In search of a new theory. INSEAD Working Paper. Fontainebleau: INSEAD.

New, C. C. & Sweeney, M. T. (1984). Delivery performance and throughput efficiency in UK manufacturing industry. *International Journal of Physical Distribution Management*, **14**, 7.

NIGEL SLACK

demand response   The demand response of an operation refers to the extent it chooses to produce its goods or services ahead of a firm customer order.

In broad terms the activities necessary to produce products (and some services) are:

- the design of the product or service;

- the procurement of the resources from which the products or services are produced (the transformed resources);

- the procurement of the resources which are used to produce the products or services (the transforming resources);

- the production of the parts from which the products or services are assembled;

- the assembly of the finished products or services;

- the delivery of the finished products or services.

(*See* TRANSFORMATION MODELS,, DESIGN CHAIN MANAGEMENT, and SUPPLY CHAIN MANAGEMENT.)

Some operations do not undertake any of these activities prior to customer order. Each product or service is designed for a specific customer need; the resources to produce it are acquired, as are the resources from which it is made. Such operations are usually called resource to order operations, even when some of the resources are already within the operation (usually the transforming resources).

Most operations do possess at least their transforming resources prior to customer order but many operations do not design their products or services until they have discussed specific customer needs. These are called design to order operations or, when the extent of customer-specific design is not extensive, customize to order operations. Design to order operations may or may not also be resource to order. Make to order operations produce pre-designed products only when they receive a firm customer order.

Operations which produce relatively standardized products or services may create a relatively wide variety of offerings from a smaller set of standard "parts" or service elements. They may choose to produce these parts prior to customer orders but only assemble them when they have a specific order. These are usually termed assemble to order operations.

Operations which have a standard range of products may choose to produce them prior to any firm customer order and store them. They are called make to stock operations. By the nature of most service operations, which precludes storage, they cannot usually respond to customer demand entirely "from stock" but may be able to do so partially.

See also **P:D ratios; runners, repeaters, and strangers**

NIGEL SLACK

Deming   W. Edwards Deming became highly influential as a consultant in Japan in the 1950s, when he was invited to lecture at the Japanese Union of Scientists and Engineers (JUSE) on QUALITY control methods. By the 1980s his methods had achieved widespread recognition in the West.

Deming called into question the traditional view that there exists a trade-off between quality and productivity (*see* TRADE-OFFS). He argued that improved quality leads to reduced rework, fewer delays, better utilization of resources, and hence improved market share and long-term business survival. Although defining quality in terms of uniformity and dependability, Deming

was emphatic about the importance of focusing the whole organization on customer needs. He identified two key contributors to process variability: "common causes," which relate to weaknesses in the management systems, and "special causes" arising from individual machines or operations. He promoted the use of statistical methods to identify the special causes, analyze, and improve production processes, while his renowned "14 points for management" were intended to address the common causes (see Table 1). He identified seven common obstacles to quality improvement ("the seven deadly diseases"), and argued that 94 percent of quality problems are caused by poor management rather than incompetence on the part of workers.

Table 1   Deming's 14 points for management

1	Create constancy of purpose toward improvement of product and service
2	Adopt the new philosophy. We can no longer live with commonly accepted levels of delays, mistakes, defective materials and defective workmanship
3	Cease dependence on inspection. Require, instead, statistical evidence that quality is built in
4	End the practice of awarding business on the basis of price tag
5	Find problems. It is management's job to work continually on the system
6	Institute modern methods of training on the job
7	Institute modern methods of supervision of production workers. The responsibility of foremen must be changed from sheer numbers to quality
8	Drive out fear, so that everyone may work effectively for the company
9	Break down barriers between departments
10	Eliminate numerical goals, posters, and slogans for the workforce, asking for new levels of productivity without providing methods
11	Eliminate work standards that prescribe numerical quotas
12	Remove barriers that stand between the hourly worker and his right to pride of workmanship
13	Institute a vigorous program of education and retraining
14	Create a structure in top management that will push every day on the above 13 points

Deming stressed the importance of never-ending, CONTINUOUS IMPROVEMENT. His improvement cycle, based on earlier work by the statistician Dr W. Shewart, consisted of four stages: plan (identify goals and performance measures), do (implement the plan), check (review progress against plan), and act (*see* PDCA CYCLE).

See also **total quality management; service quality**

Bibliography

Deming, W. E. (1986). *Out of crisis.* Cambridge, MA: MIT Center of Advanced Engineering Study.
Deming, W. E. (1982). *Quality, productivity and competitive position.* Cambridge, MA: MIT Center of Advanced Engineering Study.

RHIAN SILVESTRO

dependent and independent demand The classification of demand into dependent demand and independent demand is used to indicate how the operation's PLANNING AND CONTROL activity accommodates orders.

Dependent demand is demand which is relatively predictable because it is dependent upon some factor which is known. For example, an operation that produces parts which go into an assembled product will not treat demand as a totally random variable. The process of demand in this case is relatively straightforward. It will consist of examining the manufacturing schedules for the assembled product and deriving the demand for the part from these. For every finished assembly which is to be manufactured on a particular day, it is simple to calculate that the number of parts which will be demanded by the assembly plant on that day is the number of assemblies produced, multiplied by the number of parts per assembly. Demand is dependent on a known factor, and the demand for every part in the assembly will be derived from the assembly schedule for finished assemblies. Manufacturing instructions and purchasing requests will all be dependent upon this figure.

Dependent demand planning and control concentrates on the consequences of the demand within the operation. MATERIAL REQUIREMENTS PLANNING is one such dependent demand approach.

Independent demand is demand which is not exactly predictable because the causes from which it is derived are not fully understood. Demand is treated as, to some extent, random. When demand is of this type operations have little choice but to take decisions on how they will supply demand without having any firm forward visibility of customer orders. They must make planning and control decisions based on demand forecasts and in the light of the risks they are prepared to run of being unable to supply demand. Independent demand planning and control makes "best guesses" concerning future demand, attempt to put the resources in place which can satisfy this demand, and attempt to respond quickly if actual demand does not meet forecasts. Conventional INVENTORY MANAGEMENT systems are usually based on an assumption of independent demand.

See also **demand response; P:D ratios**

NIGEL SLACK

design There is no universally recognized definition of "design" in operations management, different authorities use sometimes quite different definitions. One view of the meaning of design is captured by Finneston (1987):

> In my definition, design is the conceptual process by which some functional requirement of people, individually or en masse, is satisfied through the use of a product or of a system which derives from the physical translation of the concept. As examples of individual products which satisfy a public or a market need there are the motor car, the television set and the radio, the ·fridge and the dishwasher, shoes and socks and baby nappies but also the painting, the sculpture, the musical score and the other manifold realized expressionism of the artist etc., and as to systems there are the telephone and the railway, the motorway and the supermarket, the orchestra, the provision of utilities (gas, water and electricity), and so on.

As far as operations managers are concerned the important points which can be extracted from this description of design are: first, that the purpose of the design activity is to satisfy the needs of customers; second, that the design activity applies both to products (or services) and systems or processes; third, that the design activity is itself a transformation process (*see* TRANSFORMATION MODELS); and fourth, that design starts with a concept and ends in the translation of that concept into a specification of something which can be created.

Often the operations management literature treats the design of products and services on one hand, and the design of the processes which make them on the other as though they were separate activities. Yet in practice they are clearly interrelated, and many authorities are concluding that the design of products and services, and the design of processes, should be considered as overlapping activities. In manufacturing especially, considerable effort has recently been put into examining this overlap (see SIMULTANEOUS DEVELOPMENT). There are probably two reasons for this. First is a growing recognition that the design of products has a major effect on the cost of making them. Second, the way overlap between product or service design and process design is managed has a significant effect on the time between the initial concept for the product and service and eventually getting it to market (*see* TIME TO MARKET).

The benefits of integrating the activities of "product" design and process design hold good whether the operation is producing products or services. However, the overlap between the two activities is generally greater in operations which produce services, because many services involve the customer being part of the transformation process. The nature and form of the service, as the customer sees it, cannot be separated from the process to which the customer is subjected. However, not all the processes in a service operation will involve the customer. The back office part of the operation will have processes which can be designed, to some extent, separately from the design of the service itself. However, for the most part the design of a service is difficult to separate from the process which produces it.

See also **design–manufacturing interface; service design; design chain management; quality function deployment; value engineering; Taguchi methods; organization of development**

NIGEL SLACK

design chain management   Design chains (sometimes called development chains) can be viewed as a specific form of supply chain that relates to the transfer of information between organizations in the pursuit of product design and development. Whereas SUPPLY CHAIN MANAGEMENT focuses on the manufacture and distribution relationships of a business or industry, design chain management can be defined as the management of the participants, both internal and external to a focal firm, who contribute the capabilities (knowledge and expertise) necessary for the design and development of a product which, on completion, will enable full-scale manufacture to commence. The chain involves all participants from the concept of a product, to prototype manufacturer, and beyond.

Not all authorities separate the closely related concepts of development chains and supply chains. The latter have often been viewed as involving operations that add value to goods and services, and therefore include the development of the product or services as being implicit to the process of supply. This does not explicitly define product development as part of the supply chain, rather it focuses on the processes that add value.

Many organizations "trade" in design. In the same way that the manufacture of a product requires inputs, the design and development of a product requires the accumulation and codifying of information such as customer requirements, advances in technology, manufacturing process knowledge, and so forth. These inputs may be internalized by the firm in the form of VERTICAL INTEGRATION, which has been a traditional form of design work. "Previously design had been conceived as an activity always undertaken within the vertically integrated enterprise as in the case of Ford... However, design may be subcontracted and bought in, or designers may subcontract supply and assembly while retaining control over aspects of distribution" (Clark and Starkey, 1988).

Thus, there is a range of alternative design capabilities available to a firm. At one extreme of this continuum, a firm may retain all the necessary design capabilities in house, while at the other end a firm may outsource design work and act as a focal point for the co-ordination of the design process. Between these extremes, there exist options with varying degrees of internal and external design capabilities.

Since the capabilities with which a firm wishes to compete do not remain static, the design capabilities retained or outsourced by a firm may reflect its response to the competitive environment. The increased use of technology and new materials in the product, and the concentration toward core capabilities, means that the identification and management of external design capabilities has grown in importance. In the case of complex products an extensive network of external sources of information may be necessary, which contribute knowledge and expertise to the design and development of the product (see DO OR BUY).

One sector at the forefront of managing design chains is the automotive industry. The process of designing and developing an automobile resembles a complex web of organizations interacting and contributing to a chain of activities, through concept to manufacture, and beyond into the after market. The traditional nature of the manufacturer–supplier relationship was dominated by suppliers who supplied a finished component, often from engineering designs supplied by the vehicle manufacturer or, designed by the supplier from specified requirements. However, increasingly, suppliers are contributing to design and engineering work much earlier in the process, so that they are more than purely manufacturing sites. During the various stages of product development several organizations may thus be involved. At concept stage, design houses may contribute to the design; at the detailed engineering stage, large multinational component system suppliers may contribute proprietary "black box" designed parts; and, at the process engineering stage, manufacturing knowledge will be necessary, often relying upon the expertise of toolmakers, equipment manufacturers, and raw materials suppliers.

Hence, in aggregate terms, the involvement of suppliers in engineering activities may be more than half of the total procurement cost of engineering. In automotive engineering, for example, 10 percent of engineering procurement costs is for supplier proprietary parts (for example, off-the-shelf items, such as tyres or batteries), 40 percent is for "black box" items (for example, systems or modules designed and developed to customer specifications by primary suppliers), and the remaining 50 percent is designed and developed in-house by vehicle manufacturers. What these figures do not demonstrate, however, is the increasing "gray box" element where suppliers may sit in with a vehicle manufacturer and provide process knowledge for product design work. Similarly, these figures do not emphasize the design house contributions at concept stage. Such organizations provide design and development expertise as a professional service and may provide prototype parts; however, they do not manufacture parts.

See also **design; simultaneous development; organization of development; time to market**

Bibliography

Clark, K. B. & Fujimoto, T. (1991). *Product development performance*. Boston, MA: Harvard Business School Press.

Clark, P. & Starkey, K. (1988). *Organization transitions and innovation design*. London: Pinter.

DeBresson, C. & Amesse, F. (1991). Networks of innovators: a review and introduction to the issue. *Research Policy*, **20**, 5, 363–79.

DAVID TWIGG

design for manufacture   Design for manufacture (DFM) is concerned with the relationship between product design decisions and the effectiveness of the manufacturing system which produces the products. The purpose is to optimize jointly the effectiveness of the design of the product and the performance of the manufacturing system.

The interest in DFM is based on considerable empirical evidence that failure to consider production requirements at the design stage can lead to products which are either of poor quality or high cost, or both. Without proper consideration of manufacturing process constraints and opportunities during design, features may be incorporated which either fall outside the range of economically or technically feasible manufacture or, less obviously, fail to capitalize upon the capabilities of process technology which may themselves suggest design changes. Attempting to rectify such failures later in the design process usually involves inconvenience and extra cost.

DFM is a general term which includes more specific examples of the relationship between design and manufacturing processes, for example design for fabrication (DFF) which deals with basic metal forming, shaping or jointing processes, or design for assembly (DFA) which deals with assembly processes. It is related to, but distinct from, SIMULTANEOUS DEVELOPMENT, which implies active development of manufacturing processes concurrently with product design development. DFM does not necessarily imply any full concurrent development of both product and process design. It is also related to VALUE ENGINEERING, but whereas value engineering is primarily concerned with the cost of providing "function," DFM is closer to the concept of "producibility engineering" which is concerned with assuring that parts can be manufactured and assemblies made and tested to meet specifications with available or potentially available techniques, tooling and test equipment at costs compatible with the product's selling price (Howell, 1982). DFM, however, goes further than producibility engineering in bringing full consideration of manufacturing capabilities into play at the design stage.

The success of design efforts using DFM principles can be quantified using one of several available techniques, the best known of which is the Boothroyd–Dewhurst method. The most obvious benefit of using such methods is usually held to be that alternative designs can be assessed in a systematic and quantified manner in order to select the most easily manufactured design which at the same time fulfills its functional purpose. However, a more general benefit is that such methods codify the previously described set of design principles which encourage manufacturable design. In doing so they train designers in good design practice. Similar benefits are ascribed to the computer-aided DFM packages used to assist designers.

See also design; design–manufacturing interface; time to market; design chain management; quality function deployment; Taguchi methods

Bibliography

Boothroyd, G. & Dewhurst, P. (1983). *Assembly: A designer's handbook*. Amherst, MA: Department of Mechanical Engineering, University of Massachusetts.

Howell, V. W. (1982). Are producibility and productivity correlated? SME Technical paper AD82-153 Dearborne, MI: Society of Manufacturing Engineers.

Stoll, H. W. (1986). Design for manufacture: an overview. *Applied Mechanics Reviews*, **39**, *9*, 1356–64.

NIGEL SLACK

design–manufacturing interface Product (engineering) design has traditionally been seen as a function separate from manufacturing. Increasingly, however, there are arguments for viewing the two as a single unit in their potential for developing competitiveness. Orders are not won in the marketplace from the individual efforts of the various functions, they are won through the joint efforts and capabilities of both product engineering and manufacturing. The operational capability to win orders and gain competitive advantage does not come from manufacturing alone, but from a broad range of sources. The manufacturing function is only part of a wider set of interlinked functions.

Because of the complexity of both manufacturing and product technologies the engineering function often requires a manufacturing input during the design process, and manufacturing requires engineering input during the early stages of product ramp up and production. A concern for companies is the degree to which and how they choose to integrate or couple the product engineering and manufacturing functions. Successful firms in many market sectors are introducing close coupling between product engineering and manufacturing. High coupling between engineering and manufacturing is essential when the market based priorities include fast product development times (*see* SIMULTANEOUS DEVELOPMENT), TIME TO MARKET and the ORGANIZATION OF DEVELOPMENT).

Integration between functions can be seen as problem solving, the greater the complexity and urgency of the problem, the greater the need for and intensity of two-way information flows. This in turn depends on the ability of people to be able to work together, to solve problems, and to combine their knowledge. The integration between product engineering and manufacturing can be put in place through various means, such as the use of cross-functional organizations and information management. The use of common databases can provide rapid transfer of information and problem solving. They also enable projects to be managed with a wide geographical spread, leading to "virtual" project organizations. Computer-aided design linked to computer-aided manufacturing (*see* ADVANCED MANUFACTURING TECHNOLOGY) allows companies to integrate closely design and manufacture.

The nature of linkage and the information flows will depend on the customer specificity of an order. Where orders are placed in manufacturing, such as in make-to-stock and make-to-order environments, products are developed prior to being sold to customers. Transfer of new products to manufacture in this context should be a controlled and discrete process. Where orders are placed on engineering, such as design or concept to order, the development process begins in the customer and continues through to manufacturing, sometimes as a continuous process. A hybrid between these is where products are tailored to customer preferences; in high-volume products this is often known as mass customization. Here the integration between product engineering and manufacture is intense, requiring sophisticated systems of design and communication. This integration may also extend to the customer (*see* DEMAND RESPONSE).

A company has many choices in how it chooses to exploit these combined capabilities of engineering and manufacturing. It can focus on the capability to design to customer order, having flexible processes, and closely coupled information flows. It can seek to respond rapidly to changes in customer needs and markets through fast development of new products. It can develop a system capable of customizing products through developing capabilities to configure rapidly products which meet customer needs. Finally, it can focus on design for mass production, with an emphasis on design for manufacture and quality, and on short product development cycles. Such positioning is not static; as companies change the way they conduct their business and relate to customers, they need to reflect this in matching changes to their engineering/manufacturing organization and systems.

See also **project leadership**

Bibliography

Clark, K. & Fujimoto, T. (1991). *Product development performance*. Boston, MA: Harvard Business School Press.

Leonard-Barton, D. (1992). The factory as a learning laboratory. *Sloan Management Review*, **34**, *1*, 23–38.

Pine, B. J., Victor, B. & Boynton, A. C. (1993) Making mass customization work. *Harvard Business Review*, **71**, September–October 108–19.

CHRIS VOSS

design organization   *see* ORGANIZATION OF DEVELOPMENT

division of labor   Division of labor means dividing a total task down into smaller parts, each of which is accomplished by a single person. It is an idea which has been evident in job design from the earliest times of organizational activity (arguably back to Greece in the fourth century BC), though it was first formalized as a concept by the economist Adam Smith in his *Wealth of Nations* in 1746.

Smith said labor should be divided because the process of division made tasks simpler, easier to learn, and enabled them to be carried out more quickly. Through the division of labor the output of a given number of people in a given time could be greatly increased. One of the most dramatic demonstrations of the division of labor principle was provided by Eli Whitney who, during the American War of

Independence, fulfilled a government contract to supply muskets to the army by coupling the principle with the idea of parts standardization. This represented a radical departure from established practice for arms production, where every item was crafted and individual products were unique.

Today the division of labor principle is still popular, particularly in batch and line processes (*see* MANUFACTURING PROCESSES) where tasks are carried out repeatedly on batches of products or continuously on a line. The continuing popularity of the idea is because, in spite of its drawbacks, there are some advantages in division of labor principles.

- It promotes faster learning. It is easier to learn how to do a relatively short and simple task than a long and complex one.

- Automation becomes easier. Dividing a total task into small parts raises the possibility of automating some of those small tasks.

- It reduces non-productive work. This is probably the most important benefit of division of labor and goes some way to explaining why highly divided jobs still exist. In large complex tasks the proportion of time spent picking up tools and materials, putting them down again and finding, positioning and searching can be relatively high. None of these "non-productive" activities contributes directly to making the product; they are there because of the way the job has been designed. When jobs are short and repetitive individual operatives are concentrating only on one piece of the job, specialist equipment and materials handling devices can be devised to help them carry out their job more efficiently, and non-productive work can be considerably reduced.

All these benefits contributed to the wide adoption of division of labor principles as industrialization took hold in the developed economies of the early twentieth century. Henry Ford described his use of the principles for the manufacture of the flywheel magneto of the Model T in 1913 (Ford and Crowther, 1924):

> We had previously assembled the flywheel magneto in the usual method. With one workman doing a complete job he could turn out from thirty-five to forty pieces in a nine hour day, or about twenty minutes to an assembly. What he did alone was then spread into twenty-nine operations; that cut down the assembly time to thirteen minutes ten seconds. Then we raised the height of the line eight inches – this was in 1914 – and cut the time to seven minutes. Further experimenting with the speed that the work should move at cut the time down to five minutes. In short, the result is this; by aid of scientific study one man is now able to do somewhat more than four did only a comparatively few years ago. That line established the efficiency of the method and we now use it everywhere.

However there are also serious drawbacks to highly divided jobs:

- Monotony: the shorter the task, the more often operators will need to repeat the task. As well as any ethical objections to deliberately designing monotonous jobs, there are other objections to jobs which induce boredom such as the increased likelihood of absenteeism, staff turnover, the increased likelihood of error, and sabotage.

- Physical injury: the continued repetition of a very narrow range of movements, as well as being monotonous, in extreme cases leads to physical injury. This is sometimes called repetitive strain injury (RSI).

- Low flexibility: dividing a task up into many small parts often gives the job design a rigidity which is difficult to change. Small product changes may mean changing every operator's set of tasks, which can be a long and difficult procedure.

- Poor robustness: highly divided jobs imply materials passing between several stages (*see* PRODUCT LAYOUT). If one of these stages fails the whole operation is affected.

See also **job design; work organization; learning curves; "scientific" management; job enrichment; job enlargement; job rotation**

Bibliography

Ford, H. & Crowther, S. (1924). *My life and work.* Revised edn. London: Heinemann.

DAVID BENNETT

do or buy   Originally termed "make or buy," a broader and more appropriate term is "do or buy" because the underlying issue is whether a firm would "do" an activity itself or whether it should pay a supplier or subcontractor to do it. This concerns more than purely manufacturing activities. Outsourcing is becoming increasingly popular in all business sectors. Outsourcing is on option in the "do or buy" decision where a company decides it will not do something itself but instead will use an external firm to provide products or services. The decision can be viewed as a micro version of the more strategic VERTICAL INTEGRATION decision.

Utilization is an important motivation when firms outsource. Businesses often find it difficult to fully utilize their capacity to perform some tasks. For example, maintenance and repair engineers may be extremely busy during plant shutdowns but may have periods with less work when the plant is running. One way to avoid such variable loading would be to outsource the work. In effect this pools the demand from all the supplier's customers and allows for high utilization, the efficiency benefits of which may be passed on to customers.

The principle of focusing on a limited, manageable set of tasks at which a firm can become expert, leaving others to focus on a different set, may also be an issue. Specialist suppliers can usually concentrate their expertise to provide enhanced services (*see* FOCUS).

Firms may decide to "do" rather than "buy" because of a desire to maintain secrecy, the unreliability of suppliers, a lack of quality in suppliers, the desire to retain their workforce rather than cause redundancy, confidence in stable market conditions, and the desire to keep abreast of developments in that market for competitive reasons.

Firms may decide to "buy" rather than "do" because of a belief in the specialization developed by suppliers, patent protection owned by the supplier, the desire to retain flexibility in uncertain market conditions, small volume requirements which do not justify in-house processes, or conversely, large, lumpy orders which may not be manageable in house and are best provided by a large supplier, and a desire to gain economies of scale benefits from the supplier.

Ford and Farmer (1986) and Ford et al. (1993) identified three different approaches to do or buy decisions. First, an operational, cost-based approach is where cost savings are balanced against the operational implications on a case by case basis. Second, a business approach where multifunctional teams continually review do or buy decisions in relation to potential suppliers. Third, and increasingly common in recent years, is a policy approach where assessment of the do or buy decision is made more on strategic direction and focus.

See also **supply chain management; purchasing and supply management**

Bibliography

Ford, D. & Farmer, D. (1986). Make or buy: a strategic issue. *Long Range Planning*, 19, 5, 54–62.
Ford, D., Cotton B., Farmer, D., Gross, A. & Wilkinson, I. (1993). Make or buy decisions and their implications. *Industrial Marketing Management*, 22, 217–24.

CHRISTINE HARLAND

diseconomies of scale   *see* CAPACITY STRATEGY

distribution   *see* PHYSICAL DISTRIBUTION MANAGEMENT

E

economic order quantity When placing an order for materials with a supplier the economic order quantity is the quantity for which the sum of total annual ordering and stockholding costs will be a minimum. If a large order is placed then orders need to be placed less frequently so that annual ordering costs are less. On the other hand, the material ordered must be stored until it is required and so the larger the order the larger the stockholding costs. The relationship between total annual costs and order quantity is shown graphically in Figure 1. The most convenient way of calculating the economic order quantity (EOQ) is to use the following formula:

$$Q = \sqrt{\frac{2SD}{IV}}$$

where Q is the economic order quantity in units, S is the cost of raising a single order, D is the annual demand in units, I is the annual stockholding fraction (annual stockholding cost expressed as a fraction of average stock value), and V is the value of one unit of stock.

Although the EOQ formula is a useful starting point for setting order quantities it does have a number of limitations.

Limitations of the EOQ Formula

(1) The ordering cost, S, and the stockholding fraction, I, are very difficult to estimate accurately. Fortunately the total cost curve is fairly flat for values of Q near to the economic order quantity. Consequently small errors in S and I have little effect on total costs.
(2) Mechanical application of the formula may generate order quantities for some items representing several years' usage. This is

normally dealt with by setting an upper limit on the order quantity.
(3) Unit value is assumed to be constant and unaffected by order quantity so that no account is taken of bulk discounts. This is a fairly major omission as the size of the bulk discount may be far in excess of any of the costs considered earlier. However, methods of allowing for bulk discounts in calculating the economic order quantity are available.
(4) Rigorous application of the formula to every single stock item may require an unacceptable change in the size of the purchasing department or in the amount of storage space needed. Bearing in mind the uncertainties about the values of S and I it is understandable that managers are a little nervous of using the formula if its use will require the construction of two additional warehouses or the laying off of half the staff in the purchasing department.
(5) Manufacturing decisions on batch size have more to do with balancing capacity than balancing set-up and stockholding costs. When demand is less than capacity then any reduction in the number of set-ups just increases idle time. The effect of this on total costs will be minimal. It therefore makes sense to reduce batch sizes until set-up times plus run times equal time available, perhaps leaving a small amount of spare capacity in case of unplanned lost time.

Economic Manufacturing Quantity

If the stock item is manufactured within the company instead of being ordered from an outside supplier then the approach described earlier will need modifying. The cost of placing

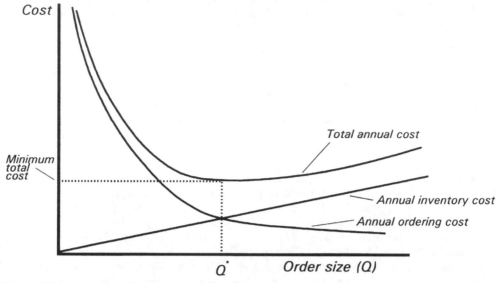

Figure 1 Variation of total annual cost with order size

an order will be replaced by the cost of setting up the plant to manufacture the product. This set-up cost will need to include the cost of shutting down the previous product and the opportunity cost of the production lost while the plant is idle and during the start-up period when the plant is building up to full output. The units will be produced at a daily rate based on plant capacity rather than being delivered as a single quantity. The formula for calculating the economic manufacturing quantity is:

$$Q = \sqrt{\frac{2SD}{IV} \times \frac{p}{p - d}}$$

where Q is the economic manufacturing quantity in units, S is the cost of setting up plant or changing over from the previous product, D is the annual demand in units, I is the annual stockholding cost expressed as a fraction of average stock value, V is the value of one unit of stock, p is the daily production rate in units, and d is the daily demand in units.

See also **inventory management; lot sizing in MRP; set-up reduction; materials management; just-in-time**

JOHN MAPES

empowerment   Empowerment is an extension of the autonomy job characteristic prominent in the behavioral approach to JOB DESIGN. However, it is usually taken to mean more than autonomy. Whereas autonomy means giving people the ability to change how they do their jobs, empowerment means giving people the authority to make changes to the job itself as well as how it is performed. This can be designed into jobs to different degrees, "suggestion involvement," "job involvement," or "high involvement" (Bowen and Lawler, 1992).

Suggestion involvement, although not really empowerment in its true form, does "empower" people to contribute their suggestions for how the operation might be improved. However, people do not have the autonomy to implement changes to their jobs.

Job involvement goes further to the extent that it empowers people to redesign their jobs. However, there must be some limits on the way each individual makes changes which could impact on other staff and on the performance of the operations as a whole. People may be formed into design teams to make sure that redesigned jobs fit together in a way which meets operational objectives. The implication of this is that the managerial mechanisms which control and support the job must be adapted to reflect empowered staff. For example, training and development must give the problem solving skills necessary to improve operations. More importantly, managers need to take on facilitating rather than controlling roles.

High involvement means including all people in the strategic direction and performance of the whole organization. This the most radical type of empowerment and there are as yet few examples. However, the degree to which individual staff of an operation contribute towards, and take responsibility for, overall strategy can be seen as a variable of job design which, for some operations, could be beneficial.

See also **job enrichment**

Bibliography

Bowen, D. & Lawler, E. (1992). Empowerment. *Sloan Management Review*, April.

NIGEL SLACK

economies of scale   *see* CAPACITY STRATEGY

efficiency   *see* CAPACITY MANAGEMENT

ergonomics   Ergonomics is the study of how the human body reacts to its immediate workplace and environment. Ergonomics may also be termed "human factors engineering" or just "human factors." It is concerned primarily with the physiological aspects of JOB DESIGN and WORK ORGANIZATION in two areas. The first is concerned with how people relate to the physical aspects of their workplace such as machines, seats, desks, etc. The second is concerned with how people relate to the environmental conditions of their immediate work area such as temperature, lighting, noise, etc.

Both aspects of ergonomics have two common characteristics. First, there is the implicit assumption that there must be a fit between people and the jobs they do, and second, that making job design decisions must be on a basis of data collection and experimentation. Data on how people react to their workplace or immediate environment should be collected on a probabilistic basis which allows for the naturally occurring variation in individual reactions.

Ergonomic Work Place Design

The design and LAYOUT of a workplace depends on the nature of work being undertaken, and its sequencing, and this in turn depends on the process of which the work is a part. The design must include the spatial arrangements of the various components of the work process, such as equipment, tools, and furniture. Key factors are the degree of variability in the tasks undertaken in the workplace, and the degree to which one work station is decoupled from others in the same workplace. Variability affects the level of prescription of the layout and may affect the range of fixtures, fittings, tools, and equipment that must be accommodated within the workplace. Decoupling affects the degree of temporary storage of incoming and outgoing materials that must be provided – in a highly coupled environment, no such storage is necessary since the work flows through the workplace without delay from one work station to the next (*see* PRODUCT LAYOUT).

The aim of the design of workplaces and individual work stations is to provide for effective and efficient working which can allow for the defined flexibility of the manufacturing process and for differences in operator characteristics (height, reach, etc.) and for differences in their preferred working positions (standing, seated). This increases the flexibility of the workplace and reduces the fatigue induced by a constant body position. The PRINCIPLES OF MOTION ECONOMY provide a starting point for the ergonomic design of work stations and workplaces, but a more comprehensive, albeit basic, knowledge of anthropometry, and access to anthropometric data, is required. Anthropometric data are data which detail the body dimensions and properties of people, usually classified by gender and age. They are usually expressed in percentile terms. The analysis of work required to support ergonomic workplace design requires a high level of detail and may include analysis down to the level of operator motion patterns. For example, the design of controls, warning, and safety devices must insure their rapid and effective use. The design of the workplace should promote, and certainly not hinder, safe ways of working and should take place alongside ergonomic work environment design.

A number of specific charts and diagrams have been developed to aid the recording and analysis of workplace and work station layouts. These include PROCESS CHARTS, charts which specifically record travel and movement, and those such as MULTIPLE ACTIVITY CHARTS designed to record the interrelationships over time between teams of workers or between workers and equipment. It is common to make use of plans and drawings which represent the work area and to experiment with layouts using templates and models. The aims are to insure first that movements within a process are minimized (both in number and then in distance), and then that necessary movements take place by the most appropriate method. Once the schedule of movement is fixed, individual work stations can be placed on the layout and then designed as ergonomic stations.

Ergonomic Work Environment Design

The work environment is a generic term used to describe the sum of a variety of factors – principally temperature, ventilation, noise, illumination, vibration, and exposure to harmful substances. As a minimal position, organizations must comply with statutory legislation. The working environment is an important determinant of worker health, safety, and well-being, and as a result directly affects worker (and therefore organizational) performance. For all the factors, it is possible to establish a range of exposure intensity under which it is reasonable to expect a worker to give good performance without undue short- or longer-term ill effects. For some of the factors, especially temperature and illumination, the range is bounded by unsatisfactory intensity levels on either side – too much heat or light is as harmful as too little. Knowledge on acceptable exposure intensities changes as understanding of each factor improves, and as observation of actual results extends. Thus, the impact of exposure to noise on hearing loss is better understood with regard to the effects of intermittent as distinct from continuous noise levels. The situation is further complicated since the various factors interrelate, and measures taken to alleviate the effects of one factor may result in increased sensitivity to another. As an example, clothing designed to

protect from radiation exposure will significantly affect the worker's ability to withstand exposure to heat. Although work environments are designed for "average workers," it is also important to be aware of, and make allowances for, variation in the sensitivities of different personnel.

The factors which make environmental conditions severe and/or harmful can be complex. In the case of vibration, for example, a worker is affected according to the intensity of the vibration, the frequency of vibration, the duration, the posture of the worker while exposed to the vibration and the manner by which the vibration is transmitted. The nature of the work being undertaken will influence whether vibration has an immediate and/or significant effect on performance.

Where the environment is considered unsatisfactory in some way, it is essential to consider protection in the form of special clothing or apparatus. Where this is not possible, a work–rest regime which permits the worker to recover from the effects of the environment must be implemented. (Note that recovery from an unsatisfactory regime need not be spent in relaxation; it can be spent performing other work in a satisfactory, or even beneficial, environment.)

In WORK MEASUREMENT, it is usual to make additions to job completion times to compensate for the effects of an adverse environment. Such additions are normally based on one of a set of published tables which may have some currency within a particular country or industry. However, the research that underpins the derivation of these tables is at best incomplete, and it is wise to consider them as empirical guides with no official status.

Bibliography

Kanawaty, G. (Ed.) (1992). *Introduction to work study.* 4th edn. Geneva: International Labour Organisation.

Oborne, D. J. (1995). *Ergonomics at work.* 3rd edn. Chichester: John Wiley.

JOHN HEAP

ethics in operations management   There are ethical implications in almost every operations management activity, and although ethical judgments are not always straightforward, there is an emerging agenda of such issues. Sensitization of operations managers to ethical issues includes the identification of the groups to whom an ethical duty is due. These groups can be categorized as the organization's customers, its staff, the suppliers who provide it with materials and services, the community in which the environment operates, and the shareholders and owners who invest their capital in the business.

Customers' welfare is directly affected by many operations management activities. The most obvious effect is that their safety might be compromised. If a product is badly assembled, or if the equipment used in a service (such as a rail transport system) is not maintained, customers may come to harm. However, customer safety is influenced by more than this; it could also be affected by the degree to which an operation discloses the details of its activities, for example in the case of an airline admitting that it has received bomb threats, or the full disclosure of all the components or ingredients in a product (which may prevent allergic reactions). At a less serious level the ethical framework of operations decisions can affect the equity and fairness with which customers are treated (for example, whether a bank should or should not discriminate between different customers in order to give priority to those from whom they can make more profit).

Staff are constantly exposed to the ethical framework of the organization throughout their working lives. Organizations are generally accepted as having a duty to their staff to prevent their exposure to hazards at work. In addition to preventing catastrophic physical injuries, this also means that organizations must take into account the longer-term threat to staff health from, say, repetitive strain injury (RSI) due to short-cycle repetitive work motions. A more subtle ethical duty is the organization's responsibility to avoid undue work place stress, caused, for example, through not providing employees with the information which allows them to understand the rationale and consequences of operations decisions, or expecting staff to take decisions for which they are not equipped.

Suppliers are often the source of an ethical dilemma for the operation; for example, is it legitimate to put suppliers under pressure not to trade with other organizations? Should organizations impose their own ethical standards on suppliers (in the case of not wishing to exploit workers in developing countries)? The transparency in relations which is increasingly expected from suppliers also poses ethical dilemmas. If suppliers are expected to be transparent in opening up their costing calculations, should customers be equally transparent?

The community in general also has ethical expectations. At its most evident organizations have a direct impact on levels of environmental pollution in the community. All manufacturing processes have waste emissions of some sort, often governed by legislation, although organizations often have some discretion over their responsibility to minimize their pollution-causing activities on one hand, and the cost of doing this on the other. The ethical dilemma is similar for a company's products after sale. The extent to which an organization should insure that its products are easily disposed of, or recycled, or made sufficiently durable that they do not need replacing, has clear ethical implications.

Finally, shareholders and owners are regarded as being owed some ethical duties. They are entitled to a reasonable return on their investments, although what constitutes "reasonable," and whether the return should be judged in the short term or long term, are both open to interpretation.

Bibliography

Hopfenbeck, W. (1992). *The green management revolution: Lessons in environmental excellence.* London: Prentice-Hall.

Thompson, A. & Strickland, A. J. (1992). *Strategic management, concepts and cases.* 6th edn. Homewood, IL: Irwin.

NIGEL SLACK

European Quality Award *see* QUALITY AWARDS

experience curves   *see* LEARNING CURVES

F

fail-safing The concept of fail-safing has emerged since the introduction of Japanese methods of operations improvement. Called *poka-yoke* in Japan (from *yokeru*, to prevent, and *poka*, inadvertent errors) the idea is based on the principle that human mistakes are, to some extent, inevitable. The important issue, therefore, is to prevent them becoming defects. *Poka-yokes* are simple and preferably inexpensive devices or systems which are incorporated into a process to prevent inadvertent operator mistakes resulting in a defect.

Typical *poka-yokes* are such devices as limit switches on machines which allow the machine to operate only if the part is positioned correctly, gauges placed on machines through which a part has to pass in order to be loaded onto, or taken off, the machine, incorrect size or orientation stopping the process, digital counters on machines to insure that the correct number of cuts, passes, or holes have been machined, checklists which have to be filled in, either in preparation for, or on completion of, an activity, and light beams which activate an alarm if a part is positioned incorrectly.

More recently, the principle of fail-safing has been applied to service operations. Service *poka-yokes* have been classified as those which "fail-safe the server" (the creator of the service) and those which "fail-safe the customer" (the receiver of the service).

Examples of fail-safing the server include color coding cash register keys to prevent incorrect entry in retail operations, the McDonalds french fry scoop which picks up the right quantity of fries in the right orientation to be placed in the pack, trays used in hospitals with indentations shaped to each item needed for a surgical procedure – any item not back in place at the end of the procedure might have been left in the patient – and paper strips placed round clean towels in hotels (the removal of which helps housekeepers to tell whether a towel has been used and therefore needs replacing).

Examples of fail-safing the customer include the locks on aircraft lavatory doors, which must be turned to switch the light on, beepers on ATMs to ensure that customers remove their cards, height bars on amusement rides to insure that customers do not exceed size limitations, outlines drawn on the walls of a child care center to indicate where toys should be replaced at the end of the play period, and tray stands strategically placed in fast-food restaurants to remind customers to clear their tables.

See also **maintenance; failure in operations; service recovery; failure analysis**

Bibliography

Chase, R. B. & Stewart, D. M. (1994). Make your service fail-safe. *Sloan Management Review*, Spring, 35–44.

NIGEL SLACK

failure analysis Failure analysis is the activity of identifying the root cause of a failure in order to understand why the failure occurred and to take steps to try to prevent it happening again. For some organizations this may be a large-scale exercise, for others, though the consequences may be less catastrophic, it is a daily activity.

Finding the root cause of failures provides two important opportunities for organizations. First, the identification of a failure and its cause is an opportunity to improve the products or services by turning this knowledge into learning for the organization in order to help better train its employees and improve its processes and procedures (*see* CONTINUOUS IMPROVEMENT). Second, an organization's response to a failure can have a significant effect on perceived quality. In many situations, customers may well accept that things do go wrong and so the failure itself does not necessarily lead to dissatisfaction. It is usually the organization's response, or lack of it, that leads to dissatisfied customers.

Organizations sometimes may not be aware that the system has failed and thereby lose the opportunity both to put things right for the customer, and to learn from the experience.

Many mechanisms are available to seek out failures in a proactive way. These include in-process checks where employees check that the service is acceptable during the process itself (though in some situations this form of failure detection can detract from the service itself). Machine diagnostic checks involve testing a machine by putting it through a prescribed sequence of activities designed to expose any failures or potential failures. Computer servicing procedures often include this type of check. Point of departure interviews are used at the end of a service where staff may formally or informally check that the service has been satisfactory and try to solicit problems as well as compliments. Phone surveys can be used to solicit opinions about products or services. Focus groups are groups of customers who are asked together to focus on some aspects of a product or service. These can be used to discover either specific problems or more general attitudes towards the product or service. Complaint cards or feedback sheets are used by many organizations to solicit views about the products and services; the problem here is that very few people tend to complete them. However, it may be possible to identify the respondents and so follow up on any individual problem. Finally, questionnaires may generate a slightly higher response than complaint cards. However, they may generate general information within which it is difficult to identify specific individual complaints.

Several tools and techniques are available to identify and analyze failures once they have occurred. One of the most frequently used techniques is complaint analysis. The advantage of using complaints is that they are usually a cheap and readily available source of information about errors. On the other hand they may not be consistent with the opinions of all the customers. However, complaints are usually taken seriously as they may represent a great amount of "hidden" customer dissatisfaction from customers who do not complain. Complaint analysis involves tracking the actual number of complaints over time, which can in itself be indicative of developing problems. By factor analyzing the content of the complaints, managers may be better able to understand the nature of the problem as perceived by the customer. PARETO ANALYSIS and cause and effect analysis, using "fishbone" (cause–effect) diagrams for example, can then be used to identify the most important problems and their causes (*see* TOOLS OF QUALITY MANAGEMENT).

Unlike complaints, which are usually unsolicited, the CRITICAL INCIDENT TECHNIQUE actively solicits customer-perceived problems. The two main advantages of this technique are, first, that it proactively seeks out problems, and second that it may identify "problems" before they become "failures."

Other tools and techniques are usually associated with trying to identify and analyze failures before they occur. Blueprinting is a way of systematically documenting and evaluating processes which enables potential process problems to be identified and their causes investigated before the process is used. In particular, it may help identify potential fail points, allow "what if" scenarios to be discussed and may help identify where monitoring devices are best installed (*see* SERVICE DESIGN). Similarly, failure mode and effect analysis (FMEA) is a checklist procedure usually used in the design stage of products. This technique is used to identify the potential problems, assess their likelihood and the consequences of failure (*see* FAILURE MODE AND EFFECT ANALYSIS). Alternatively, system redundancy can be used to reduce the impact of failure. Redundancy is the building in of back-up systems or components in case of failure. The back-up systems then take over when a failure occurs in the main system. However, this can be an expensive solution and is generally used only when the system or component breakdown will have a critical impact.

See also **failure measures; service recovery; fault tree analysis**

Bibliography

Chase, R. B. & Stewart, D. M. (1994). Make your service fail-safe. *Sloan Management Review,* Spring, 35–44.

Feinberg, R. A., Widdows, R., Hirsch-Wyncott, M. & Trappey, C. (1990). Myth and reality in customer service: good and bad service sometimes leads to repurchase. *Journal of Consumer Satisfaction, Dissatisfaction and Complaining Behavior,* 3, 112–14.

Hart, C. W. L., Heskett, J. L. & Sasser, W. E. (1990). The profitable art of service recovery. *Harvard Business Review,* 68, 4, 148–56.

ROBERT JOHNSTON

failure in operations   Failure is the state that occurs when the performance standard of an intended function of a process, product or service is not met. The converse of failure is "reliability." Reliability is the probability that a product, piece of equipment or system performs its intended function for a stated period of time under specified operating conditions. Failures occur because of lack of reliability.

Not all failures are equally serious. Organizations therefore need to discriminate between failures and pay particular attention to those which are critical either in their own right or because they may jeopardize the rest of the operation. A prerequisite for this is some understanding of the reasons for failures and an ability to measure the effects of the failure.

Two dimensions of failure determine the way in which failure is treated by operations managers. If the probability of a particular failure occurring in an operation is high and the impact of that failure is also high, it is unlikely that the operation itself will be viable. Conversely, when both the probability and impact of a failure is low, the very issue of failure will be relatively trivial. It is the spectrum between the two poles of low impact failures occurring relatively frequently, and high impact events occurring infrequently, which is of most interest. The types of failure which occur relatively frequently but which individually may not have a catastrophic effect on an operation, may be seen as the concern of QUALITY MANAGEMENT,

whereas the less frequent but more significant failures are usually seen as the subject of failure management.

Causes of Failure

Although failure in an operation can occur for many different reasons, it is convenient to classify failures as belonging to one of the following three classes:

- those which are caused by faults in the material or information inputs to the operation;

- those which have their source inside the operation, because its overall design was faulty, or because its individual facilities (machines, equipment, and buildings) or staff fail to operate as they should;

- those which are caused by the actions of customers.

Any failure in the input of goods and services into an operation can cause failure within the operation, either directly because of the non-availability of the function which they are supposed to perform through delivery or quality failures, or indirectly because of their eventual "failure in service." The more an operation relies on suppliers of materials or services, the more it is liable to failure which is caused by missing or substandard inputs.

The overall design of an operation can also prove to be the root cause of failure. Some design failures occur because a characteristic of demand was overlooked or miscalculated, so that although there was no unexpected demand placed on the operation, it was unable to cope because of straightforward errors in translating the requirements of demand into an adequate design. Other design-related failures occur because the circumstances under which the operation has to work are not as expected. Yet although the demands placed on the operation were unexpected at the point of design they may still be regarded as design failures. Adequate design includes identifying the range of circumstances under which the operation has to work, and designing accordingly.

As well as failure due to overall design, operations may become ineffective because of the failure of their technical and human resources. Failures which are directly due to staff are of two types: errors and violations. Errors are mistakes in judgment; with hindsight, a person should have acted in some way differently and the result is some significant deviation from normal operation. Violations are acts which are clearly contrary to defined operating procedure.

Customers can also cause failure by their misuse of the products and services which the operation has created. However, even if it is the inattention or incompetence of customers which has been the cause of failure, most organizations will accept that they have a responsibility to educate and train customers and to design their products and services so as to minimize the chances of failure.

Notwithstanding this categorization of failure, the origin of all failures can be viewed as some kind of internal human failure. The implications of this are, first, that failure can, to some extent, be controlled, and second, that organizations can learn from failure and modify their behavior accordingly. The realization of this has led to what is sometimes called the "failure as an opportunity" concept. Rather than identifying a "culprit" who is held to be responsible and blamed for the failure, failures are regarded as an opportunity to examine why they occurred, and to put in place procedures which eliminate or reduce the probability of them reoccurring.

In practical terms, operations managers have three sets of activities which relate to failure. The first is concerned with understanding what failures are occurring in the operation and why they are occurring (see FAILURE ANALYSIS). Once the nature of any failures are understood, the second task of operations managers is to examine ways of either reducing the chances of failure or minimizing the consequences of failure (see FAIL-SAFING) and MAINTENANCE). The third task is to devise plans and procedures which help the operation to recover from failures when they do occur (see SERVICE RECOVERY). The first of these tasks is, in effect, a prerequisite for the other two.

Bibliography

Chowdhury, A. R. (1985). Reliability as it relates to QA/QC. *Quality Progress*, 18, *12*, 27–30.

Evans, J. R. & Lindsay, W. M. (1993). *The management and control of quality*. 2nd edn. St Paul, MN: West.

NIGEL SLACK

failure measures   There are three main ways of measuring failure, failure rate (how often a failure occurs), reliability (the chances of a failure occurring) and availability (the amount of available useful operating time. "Failure rate" and "reliability" are different ways of measuring the same thing, that is the propensity of an operation, or part of an operation, to fail. Availability, on the other hand, is one measure of the consequences of failure in the operation.

Failure Rate

Failure rate (FR) is calculated as the number of failures over a period of time. For example, the number of security breaches per year at an airport, or the number of failures over a defined operating time for an aircraft engine. Failure rate (FR) is usually calculated from examining actual operating or test data. It can be measured either as a percentage of the total number of products tested or as the number of failures over time:

$$FR = (\text{number of failures/total number of products tested}) \times 100$$

or

$$FR = \text{number of failures/operating time}$$

Failure, for most parts of an operation, is a function of time. At different stages during the life of anything the probability of it failing will be different. The probability of a piece of equipment failing is relatively high when it is first used. Any small defect in the material from which the equipment was constructed, or in the way it was assembled might cause it to fail. If the equipment survives this initial stage it could still fail at any point, but the longer it survives, the more likely its failure becomes. Most physical parts of an operation behave in a similar manner. The curve which describes failure probability of this type is called the "bath tub" curve. It comprises of three distinct stages. The "infant" mortality or "early life" stage is where early failures occur caused by defective parts or improper use. During the "normal life" stage the failure rate is usually low and reasonably constant, and caused by normal random factors. The "wear out" stage when the failure rate increases as the part approaches the end of its working life and failure is caused by the aging and deterioration of parts.

Reliability

Reliability measures the ability of a system, product or service to perform as expected over time. The importance of any particular failure is determined partly by the effect it has on the performance of the whole operation or system. This in turn depends on the way in which the parts of the system which are liable to failure are related. If components in a system are all interdependent, a failure in any individual component will cause the whole system to fail.

So, for example, if an interdependent system has n components each with their own reliability $R_1, R_2 \ldots R_n$, the reliability of the whole system, R_s, is given by:

$$R_s = R_1 \times R_2 \times R_2 \times \ldots R_n$$

where R_1 = reliability of component 1, R_2 = reliability of component 2, etc.

The more interdependent components a system has, the lower its reliability will be. So for a system with 400 components (not unusual in a large automated operation) even if the reliability of each individual component is 99 percent the whole system will be working for less than 5 percent of its time.

An alternative (and common) measure of failure is the mean time between failure (MTBF) of a component or system. MTBF is the reciprocal of failure rate (in time), so,

$MTBF$ = operating hours/number of failures

Availability

Availability is the degree to which the operation is ready to work. An operation is not available if it has either failed or is being repaired following failure. There are several different ways of measuring availability depending on how many of the reasons for not operating are included. Lack of availability because of planned maintenance or change overs could be included, for example. However, when "availability" is being used to indicate the operating time excluding the consequence of failure, it is calculated as follows:

Availability $(A) = MTBF/(MTBF + MTTR)$

where $MTBF$ is the mean time between failure of the operation and $MTTR$ is the mean time to repair, which is the average time taken to repair the operation, from the time it fails to the time it is operational again.

See also **failure analysis; failure mode and effect analysis; failure in operations; maintenance**

NIGEL SLACK

failure mode and effect analysis The objective of failure mode and effect analysis (FMEA) is to identify the product or service features that are critical to various types of failure. It is a means of identifying failures before they happen by providing a checklist procedure which is built round three key questions.

For each possible cause of failure:

● What is the likelihood that failure will occur?

● What would the consequence of the failure be?

● How likely is such a failure to be detected before it affects the customer?

Based on a quantitative evaluation of these three questions a risk priority number (RPN) is calculated for each potential cause of failure. Corrective actions, aimed at preventing failure, are then applied to those causes whose RPN indicates that they warrant priority.

This is essentially a seven-step process:

Step 1: identify all the component parts of the products or service.

Step 2: list all the possible ways in which the components could fail (the failure modes).

Step 3: identify the possible effects of the failures (down time, safety, repair requirements, effects on customers).

Step 4: identify all the possible causes of failure for each failure mode.

Table 1   Severity and detection of failure

Description	Rating	Possible failure occurrence
Remote probability of occurrence	1	0
It would be unreasonable to expect failure to occur		
Low probability of occurrence	2	1 : 20,000
Generally associated with activities similar to previous ones	3	1 : 10,000
with a relatively low number of failures		
Moderate probability of occurrence	4	1 : 2,000
Generally associated with activities similar to previous		
ones which have resulted in occasional	5	1 : 1,000
	6	1 : 200
High probability of occurrence	7	1 : 100
Generally associated with activities similar to ones which	8	1 : 20
have traditionally caused problems		
Very high probability of occurrence	9	1 : 10
Near certainty that major failures will occur	10	1 : 2

Severity of failure

Description	Rating	
Minor severity		
A very minor failure which would have no noticeable effect	1	
on system performance		
Low severity		
A minor failure causing only slight customer annoyance	2	
	3	
Moderate severity		
A failure which would cause some customer	4	
dissaatisfaction, discomfort or annoyance, or	5	
would cause noticeably deterioration in performance	6	
High severity		
A failure which would engender a high degree	7	
of customer dissatisfaction	8	
Very high severity		
A failure which would affect safety	9	
Catastrophic		
A failure which may cause damage to property,	10	
serious injury or death		

Detection of failure

Description	Rating	
Remote probability that the defect will reach the customer.	1	0 to 15%
It would be unreasonable to expect such a defect to go		
undetected during inspection, test or assembly		
Low probability that the defect will reach	2	6 to 15%
the customer	3	16 to 25%
Moderate probability that the defect will reach	4	26 to 35%
the customer	5	36 to 45%
	6	46 to 55%
High probability that the defect will reach the	7	56 to 65%
customer	8	66 to 75%
Very high probability that the defect will reach		
the customer	10	86 to 100%

Step 5: assess the probability of failure, the severity of the effects of failure and the likelihood of detection. Rating scales which can be used to quantify these three factors are shown in Table 1.

Step 6: calculate the RPN by multiplying all three ratings together.

Step 7: instigate corrective action which will minimize failure on failure modes which show a high RPN.

See also **failure in operations; failure analysis; reliability-centered maintenance; fail-safing**

NIGEL SLACK

fault tree analysis   This is a logical procedure that starts with a failure or a potential failure and works backwards to identify all the possible causes and therefore the origins of that failure. The fault tree is made up of branches connected by two types of nodes, AND nodes and OR nodes. The branches below an AND node all need to occur for the event above the node to occur. Only one of the branches below an OR node needs to occur for the event above the node to occur. In this manner a cause–effect "map" of the causes of failure is constructed. In use the benefits of using this type of analysis is largely in codifying a common understanding of the intrinsic logic of failure possibility. It does not either predict failure or directly solve failure problems. Nevertheless it does provide the basis for further action.

See also **failure in operations; failure analysis; failure measures; maintenance**

NIGEL SLACK

Feigenbaum   A. V. Feigenbaum, who was head of quality at General Electric, originated the concept of total quality control (TQC). His book *Total Quality Control*, first published in 1951 under a different title, defines total quality as follows:

> "The underlying principle of the total quality view ... is that to provide genuine effectiveness, control must start with identification of customer quality

requirements and end only when the product has been placed in the hands of a customer who remains satisfied. Total quality control guides the co-ordinated actions of people, machines, and information to achieve this goal" [Feigenbaum, 1983].

Feigenbaum introduced the concept of the "hidden plant," which he defines as the proportion of plant capacity expended on the rework of defective parts and goods and which, he claims, typically represents between 15 and 40 percent of plant capacity. He identifies four categories of quality costs: cost of prevention, cost of appraisal, cost of internal failure and cost of external failure; and argues that by investing in prevention, failure and eventually appraisal costs will decline, resulting in a significant reduction of total quality costs (*see* QUALITY COSTING).

Perhaps most notably Feigenbaum made a direct attack on the view that responsibility for TQC lies solely with the quality assurance or quality control function, arguing that it must be shared by all functions in the organization since they all have an impact upon the costs of quality. He describes organizational functions such as marketing, engineering, manufacturing, purchasing, installation and service as being stages in the "industrial cycle," maintaining that improved quality in every stage of the cycle leads to cheaper quality costs in the long term.

See also **total quality management; quality; service quality**

Bibliography

Feigenbaum, A. V. (1983). *Total quality control.* 3rd edn. New York: McGraw-Hill.
Feigenbaum, A. V. (1988). Total quality developments in the 1990s: an international perspective. In R. Chase, (Ed.), *Total quality management: An IFS briefing.* IFS Publications.

RHIAN SILVESTRO

finite and infinite loading   Loading is the process of allocating tasks and activities to work centers. There are two main approaches to loading operations, finite and infinite loading.

Finite loading is an approach which only allocates work to a work center up to a set limit. This limit is the estimate of capacity for the work center (based on the times available for loading). Work over and above this capacity is not accepted and so the work center is not allowed to exceed the capacity limit. Finite loading is particularly relevant for operations where it is possible to limit the load, and it is necessary to limit the load, and the cost of limiting the load is not prohibitive.

Infinite loading is an approach to loading which does not limit accepting work, but instead tries to cope with it. The load on each work center may therefore exceed its theoretical capacity constraints. Infinite loading is relevant for operations where it is not possible to limit the load, or it is not necessary to limit the load, or the cost of limiting the load is prohibitive.

In complex planning and control activities where there are multiple stages, each with different capacities and with varying mix arriving at the facilities, such as a machine shop in an engineering company, the constraints imposed by finite loading may make loading calculations complex and not worth the considerable computational power which would be needed.

See also **planning and control in operations; capacity management; scheduling**

Bibliography

Vollman, T. E., Berry, W. L. & Whybark, D. C. (1992). *Manufacturing planning and control systems.* 3rd edn. Burr Ridge, IL: Irwin.

NIGEL SLACK

fixed position layout A fixed position layout is one of the three basic options for laying out facilities to produce goods or deliver services, the other options being a PROCESS LAYOUT or PRODUCT LAYOUT. A fourth alternative, the CELL LAYOUT, is actually a hybrid facility arrangement which combines some of the principles of fixed position and product layouts.

The term "fixed position" implies that the product remains (more or less) stationary and all materials, equipment, labor, instructions, etc. are brought to the place of work. The service

equivalent might be where the "customer" remains stationary and the various elements of the service are delivered to the point where the customer is located. The labor resource can comprise an individual worker or might involve GROUP WORKING. Fixed position layouts are usually a feature of batch production, or jobbing operations. They offer a number of advantages, the most important of which is product FLEXIBILITY. This is achieved because the machines and equipment used in fixed position layouts are mostly of a general purpose nature, the workers are usually multiskilled and several different products (or services) can be produced simultaneously and in parallel.

In some cases, use of a fixed position layout is unavoidable as a result of the sheer size and nature of the product being made (e.g. construction of an oil rig) or because the product will remain stationary in the position it was made (e.g. a bridge). In other cases, however, there is a genuine choice of layout and a fixed position approach is taken because of the advantages it offers. For example, motor vehicle assembly sometimes uses a fixed position layout, coupled with group working, because it enables a large variety of finished products to be produced more easily. Also the multiskilling and greater autonomy of the workforce, together with a focus on the entire product rather than a small part of it, can provide the motivation to improve quality and labor efficiency. In service provision a fixed position layout (where the customer remains stationary) has the advantage of offering greater convenience to customers. For example, office workers may use a sandwich delivery service to save the time of going out to lunch, while telephone home banking avoids the need for customers to visit their local branch.

See also **manufacturing processes; job design**

DAVID BENNETT

flexibility Three reasons have been put forward to explain the increase in interest in flexibility. First is the need to cope with turbulent trading conditions. Second is the significant advances in process technology (*see* ADVANCED MANUFACTURING TECHNOLOGY). Third, the developments in processing technology have been promoted by suppliers as contributing to flexibility, and the resulting debate has widened the scope of operations objectives to include flexibility.

Three sets of issues have occupied researchers in the area. The first concerns how the concept of flexibility can be defined and the various types of flexibility classified. The second concerns the stimuli which promote operations managers to enhance the flexibility of their processes. The third concerns how the flexibility of manufacturing processes can be measured.

Types of Flexibility

Much of the early interest in flexibility concerned how the different types of flexibility should be characterized and resulted in several typologies of flexibility. These typologies usually classify flexibility at one of four levels of analysis.

- The level of the firm, where flexibility issues concern the ability of the whole organization.

- The level of the operations function or total system, where flexibility issues concern the ability of the operations function to change the nature, volume and timing of its outputs.

- The level of the cell or small system (*see* CELL LAYOUT), where flexibility issues concern, for example, the variety of products able to be made, or the time taken to change from the manufacture of one product to another.

- The level of the resources of operations, where flexibility issues again concern the variety of tasks which individual machines or people perform and the nature of changing tasks.

Most typologies relate to the two intermediate levels of analysis. Browne et al.'s (1984) typology is the most comprehensive of the typologies at the cell level. It defines flexibility as a set of eight capabilities.

(1) *machine flexibility*: the ability to replace or change tools in a tool magazine, and mount the required fixtures, without interference or long set-up times. It is the ease of the system in making changes required to produce a given set of part types;

(2) *process flexibility*: the ability to vary the stages or activities necessary to complete a task. This allows several different tasks to be completed in the system, using a variety of machines;

(3) *product flexibility*: the ability to change over to produce a new product, within the defined parts range, economically and quickly (*see* SET-UP REDUCTION);

(4) *routing flexibility*: the ability to vary machine activity sequences, for example, to cope with breakdowns, and to continue producing the given set of part types. This ability exists when there are several viable processing routes or when each operation can be performed on more than one machine;

(5) *volume flexibility*: the ability to operate a cell or system cost effectively at different production volumes (*see* AGGREGATE CAPACITY MANAGEMENT);

(6) *expansion flexibility*: the capability of building a system and expanding it as needed, easily and modularly;

(7) *process sequence flexibility*: the ability to interchange the ordering of several operations for each part type;

(8) *production flexibility*: the ability to vary the part variety quickly and economically for any product that a cell can produce. A cell does not attain production flexibility until all the other flexibilities have been achieved.

At the operations function or total system level different typologies become more appropriate. One such distinguishes between four types of flexibility:

(1) *product flexibility*: the ability to introduce and produce novel products or services or to modify existing ones;

(2) *mix flexibility*: the ability to change the range of products or services being made by the operation within a given time period;

(3) *volume flexibility*: the ability to change the level of aggregated output;

(4) *delivery flexibility*: the ability to change planned or assumed delivery dates.

Somewhat separate from the typologies of flexibility is the distinction drawn between the meaning of the word "flexibility." One dictionary definition has it as "the ability to be bent." This translates into operational terms the ability to adopt a range of states. So one production system is more flexible than another if it can exhibit a wider "range" of states or behavior; for example, produce a greater variety of products or services, operate at different output levels or delivery lead times. This is the "range" dimension of flexibility. However, the range of states an operations system can adopt does not totally describe its flexibility. The ease with which it moves from one state to another, in terms of cost, time or organizational disruption, is also important and can be termed the "response" dimension of flexibility.

The stimuli for flexibility. Flexibility can be seen as a response to two types of stimuli – VARIETY and uncertainty. Variety indicates the necessity for processes to adopt a range of operating conditions. For example, to cope with the existing range of service parts, components or products, to adapt products or services to varying customer requirements, to be able to adjust output levels to cope with seasonality, or to be able to expedite orders to different levels of priority. Uncertainty can refer to either relatively short-term conditions which cannot be predicted exactly, such as the ability to cope with machine breakdowns (*see* FAILURE IN OPERATIONS), to adjust output to demand levels different from forecast, or to cope with the failure of internal and external suppliers, or it can refer to longer-term conditions such as the process attributes necessary to produce future generations of products or services, or levels of physical capacity needed.

Flexibility is frequently cited as the appropriate operational response to variety. It is seen as the "antidote" to variety because it mitigates the effects of variety on cost. The negative effects on an operation's cost base are held by practitioners to be good reasons to avoid variety in its many forms. The frequent introduction of new or modified products and services, a wide range of products and services, a wide range of output levels, and frequent changes in delivery dates, are all manifestations of variety and all are held to increase cost. The implicit paradigm here is that there are TRADE-OFFS between variety and cost.

The two ideas of perceived uncertainty and operational flexibility have been brought together by several authors. The most influen-

tial proposition is that organizations are open systems faced with uncertainty and ambiguity yet require certainty and clarity to operate in a rational manner. The management of the organization's operations function therefore needs to reduce uncertainty so as to maintain operational objectives. Several strategies have been proposed which management can use to cope with uncertainty, among which is "adapting" to environmental changes. Some authors propose the adoption of flexible technology. However, this does draw attention to the paradox that the introduction of flexible process technologies intended to cope with long-term uncertainty could very well introduce extra uncertainty to the organization's operations function during its adoption and implementation.

Some empirical support for the importance of flexibility as a response to uncertainty does exist. For example Swamidass and Newell (1987) explore the relationship between manufacturing strategy, environmental uncertainty and performance. Among the "dimensions of manufacturing strategy ... flexibility offers the capability to cope with environmental uncertainty." In this context, coping with environmental uncertainty means that performance is unaffected by environmental uncertainty. Their analysis shows that the higher an organization's flexibility, the higher its performance, no matter what kind of process is involved. Gerwin and Tarondeau (1989) connect particular types of uncertainty to particular types of flexibility.

Measuring Flexibility

There are two main arguments for formally assessing flexibility needs. The first is that resources need to be developed in those areas where they can best contribute to company competitiveness. To gain the maximum benefit, therefore, resources need to be developed against an understanding of current flexibility. Second, evidence from organizations which have been through some flexibility assessment exercise indicates some benefits.

Because flexibility is a concept which is difficult to operationalize, it is therefore difficult to measure. Some authors argue that it is unprofitable to attempt to measure flexibility directly for a number of reasons:

- Flexibility is a multidimensional concept; each dimension of which is influenced by many context-dependent variables.

- Range and response aspects of flexibility would need to be measured on very different scales and are manifested by different characteristics of an operation.

- The dimensions of flexibility are interdependent and difficult to reconcile; for example, to have simultaneously the goal of coping effectively with machine failures, while at the same time trying to cope with frequent product mix changes. The former may be solved by machine versatility, the latter by reducing set-up times. Yet these objectives frequently conflict.

- Flexibility is different from other aspects of operations performance because it is an indication of potential. It does not have to be demonstrated to be real. It may be that an operation really does have the ability to change its operations in a particular manner if required to do so, but that as yet it has not been required to do so.

Two approaches attempt to overcome these difficulties. The first is to measure the flexibility of some aspect of an operation directly by using both range and response dimensions simultaneously. This involves charting the degree of change possible within an operation at different timescales. These "range–response" curves can be used to chart, for example, the degree of increase (or decrease) in output levels which can be achieved at different times from when the decision is made to adjust output levels. The other approach is to measure flexibility indirectly by assessing the impact or worth of changed flexibility on some other aspect of operations performance. One advantage of this is that it allows a comparison of the cost of having flexibility with the benefits derived. This involves assessing the worth of flexibility in terms of enhanced quality, faster customer response, more dependable operations, a wider range of product or service offerings and the cost of producing them.

See also **operations objectives; lifecycle effects; product–process matrix; cost**

Bibliography

Browne, J. & Dubois, D. et al. (1984). Classification of flexible manufacturing systems. *The FMS Magazine*, **2**, *2*, 114–17.
Gerwin, D. & Tarondeau, J. C. (1982). Case studies of computer integrated manufacturing systems: a view of uncertainty and innovation processes. *Journal of Operations Management*, **2**, *2*.
Gupta, Y. P. & Goyal, S. (1988). Flexibility of manufacturing systems: concepts and measurements. *European Journal of Operations Research*, **43**, 119–35.
Slack, N. (1983). Flexibility as a manufacturing objective. *International Journal of Production management*, **3**, *3*, 4–13.
Slack, N. (1990). Flexibility and managers see it. In M. Warner, et al. (Eds), *New technologies and manufacturing management*. Wiley.
Swamidass, P. M. & Newell, W. T. (1987). Manufacturing strategy, environmental uncertainty and performance: a path analytic model. *Management Science*, **33**, *4*, 509–24.

NIGEL SLACK

flexible manufacturing systems Flexible manufacturing systems (FMS) are computer-controlled configurations of semi-independent work stations connected by automated materials handling and machine loading (Voss, 1986).

The first machine tool for metalworking a lathe was invented by Maudsley in 1800 at the height of the Industrial Revolution and possessed a high degree of flexibility. Its invention signaled a move away from the era in which a product was carefully and individually crafted to suit a customer, and towards more systematic production in a factory context.

Maudsley's basic design became the basis for the development of other machine tools. It was followed by developments which offered new responses to the challenge of large scale, high volume manufacturing, such as PROCESS LAYOUT, and the notion of the "mechanization of work." One part of this process was a gradual substitution of machines for men. However, there were limits to this substitution until the development in the 1950s of numerical control.

In the engineering industry numerical control (NC) technology for machine tools evolved out of a program in the US air force in the late 1940s. This offered a way of describing the entire complex process of producing a part in terms of a mathematical expression. The major innovation here was reprogrammability. In the NC system changes in the products to be produced no longer required extensive physical changes to the machine set-up but only a change in the control program. For the first time, the flexibility of general purpose machinery could be combined with the precision and accuracy of special purpose equipment.

While the principles of NC were established in the 1950s the technology did not diffuse widely until the 1970s. The major limiting step was the cost of the technology; with the emergence of the microprocessor it became possible to reduce the costs of a controller by up to 50 percent, and thus diffusion accelerated rapidly from the mid-1970s. Low-cost computer numerical control (CNC) of this type also enabled other functions, such as tool change or part manipulation, to be automated and integrated within the same control system. Technical development at this time was characterized by a rapidly increasing integration of functions associated with the machine tool, leading to highly sophisticated, multipurpose machining centers complete with a range of support functions such as tool change, head change, transport and manipulation.

From this it was a short step to the idea of direct (or distributed) numerical control (DNC), in which more than one tool (plus associated functions) could be grouped into a manufacturing cell under the overall control of a bigger, supervisory computer responsible for work scheduling, routing of products and parts, monitoring status, feeding in new programs and so on. Such integration brought together many different machines into a configuration in which they behaved as if they were a single, complex and highly integrated machine. Flexible manufacturing systems (FMS) emerged as a result of this trend.

It is generally accepted that the first FMS for metal working was developed by Theo Williamson in 1962 for the Molins Company, a small batch manufacturer of machinery for the tobacco industry. His System 24 was able to machine blocks of aluminum into a variety of parts with short set-up and change-over times. But it was not until the development of cheaper and more powerful control options and the emergence of concepts like DNC that the technology of flexible manufacturing really came into its own.

FMS technology has diffused widely and it is now possible to see variants of this concept in many different industries. Much depends on the particular types of flexibility required; for example, the high-volume industries are looking for equipment which will carry out long production runs but which can be changed quickly to making something new by reprogramming. The advantage here is that traditionally they would have been forced to replace the line whereas now they can reconfigure it. By contrast, a small engineering contractor may have a requirement to make very small production runs and sometimes single prototype parts for a wide range of clients. Here the requirement is for rapid change over between different jobs.

With this proliferation of variety have come different terms to describe FMS configurations; a rough typology of FMS might be as follows:

- flexible manufacturing system (FMS): a combination of more CNC machine tools under supervisory computer control via some form of DNC linkage;

- flexible manufacturing cell (FMC): a combination of two or more CNC machine tools but not under DNC linked control;

- flexible manufacturing unit (FMU): a single, multifunction CNC machine tool;

- flexible transfer line (FTL): a multimachine layout including several CNC machine tools and other specialist pieces of equipment all under supervisory computer control, used in high-volume industries like vehicle manufacture as an alternative to a dedicated transfer line.

An important feature of the emergence of FMS was the recognition that organizational change – in planning, supporting organizational structure, skills and training, etc. – was essential to success. A key theme in this restructuring was the emergence of cellular manufacturing (see CELL LAYOUT), often based on specific PRODUCT FAMILIES, which provided the most appropriate context for successful exploitation of FMS.

An important development in FMS has been the increasing use of ROBOTICS in providing manipulation of parts and tools within a manufacturing cell. Experiments have been underway for some time to develop flexible assembly systems based upon robots; although these have been used with some success in the assembly of products such as electric motors and power tools, their diffusion is still limited by some of the cost and control constraints in robotics technology.

Although much early interest was focused on engineering industries as prime users of FMS the technology has evolved to find applications in many other sectors including clothing and footwear, ceramics and furniture manufacturing. The main motives driving its adoption have centered on increasing throughput and reducing work-in-progress inventory through faster change over, on capital saving (integrated systems replace many discrete machines) and space saving; labor saving is rarely seen as significant.

See also **advanced manufacturing technology; computer-integrated manufacturing; process technology; robotics**

Bibliography

Jaikumar, R. (1986). Post-industrial manufacturing. *Harvard Business Review*, November-December.
Tidd, J. (1989). *Flexible automation*. London: Frances Pinter.
Voss, C. (1986). Managing new manufacturing technologies. Operations Management Association. Monograph 1.

JOHN BESSANT

focus   The concept of focused (manufacturing) operations was first described by the American academic Wickham Skinner (1974). Based on his empirical research, Skinner claimed that:

> A factory that focuses on a narrow product mix for a particular market niche will outperform the conventional plant which attempts a broader mission. Because its equipment, supporting systems, and procedures can concentrate on a limited task for one set of customers, its

costs, and especially its overheads are likely to be lower than those of a conventional plant.

He added that while such operations are relatively rare in practice, they do offer the opportunity to gain competitive advantage because the entire operation is focused on accomplishing the objectives required by the company's overall business and marketing strategies. Skinner's work on focus has been a major influence on manufacturing strategy methodology developments in which different market requirements are recognized and reflected in the design of the operations system.

There are a number of ways that focus can be designed into operations. One approach is to restrict the range (variety) of products or services offered, so that only higher volume requirements have to be produced. Although this can restore some economies of scale and reduce overhead costs, it is based on the view that the retained markets will be sufficiently large, and provide adequate return on investment. Most organizations decide to retain all or most of the existing product and market coverage, and so can only advance focus within the operations function. This is achieved either by reallocation of the products within the existing operation facilities, or redesign of the facilities, usually by division, to allow the development of smaller, more focused operations.

A number of approaches to focus have been identified.

• Focus by volume: this approach involves the allocation of products or services to separate facilities on the basis of their volumes. The high-volume operations can then concentrate on exploiting the economies of scale, while one or more lower volume facilities develop other competencies such as flexibility or speed. Many operations have always used this approach, for example, to separate prototype production from mainstream production. Focus by volume implies that products should move between facilities at different stages of their lifecycles, which some writers believe to be disadvantageous as it involves potential duplication of processes and tooling, and the need to transfer product knowledge between facilities.

• Focus by process: where the production of specific products or services involves the use of specialized skills, or capital-intensive technologies, it may be preferable to form process-based focused facilities, thereby avoiding unnecessary duplication of resources, and maintaining high utilization levels. One form of this type of focus uses PRODUCT FAMILIES within a CELL LAYOUT, where the transformation resources are brought together for products with similar processing requirements.

• Focus by market: separation of facilities by market (or customer) creates the opportunity to provide specialized resources and infrastructure for the exact requirements of that market. This dedication of resources should provide enhanced responsiveness to customers' needs and priorities; opening up the opportunity for them to communicate directly with the operations function. However, this approach requires an agreed and sustained level of demand so that capacity can continue to be used effectively. Market-focused operations may lose flexibility in terms of volume and mix, and may require considerable duplication of resources and dilution of technical skills.

• Focus by product: an extreme case of focus is where a single product or a group of similar products or services is produced in a dedicated facility. In effect, this combines the advantages of focus by market *and* process; conflicts of objectives are eliminated and resources can be used to enhance quality conformance, and reduce costs. Where volumes are sufficiently high, dedicated high-volume processes can be employed, exploiting the economies of scale. Focusing by product, however, can create inflexibility; new product introductions may be more difficult, and such systems are vulnerable to volume and mix variations. This approach to focus seems to be most appropriate in stable, high-volume environments.

• Focus by market requirements (order-winning criteria): Skinner (1974) contended that a focused factory should encompass a consistent and limited set of market demands, and one set of internally consistent, non-compromised criteria for success. Other types of focus may only partially satisfy this requirement. For example, even within one market, the exact customer requirements, or ORDER-WINNERS AND QUALIFIERS criteria may vary widely. Where possible, focus should be planned around grouping together sets of products which have similar order-winning criteria, such as the speed, quality or cost requirements of the market. This also creates the greatest potential for creating appropriately designed (effective) and efficient infrastructures to support each focused unit, thereby minimizing overheads. A significant problem with focus by order-winning criteria is that these usually change as a product progresses through its lifecycle, and so products and tooling must be moved from plant to plant. Where volumes are expected to remain high for a period, product focus may be preferred as this can give the lowest costs for low-variety products.

• Focus by geography: for many organizations it is necessary to conduct operations in close proximity to the geographic location of the customer. This is particularly the case where value is added through direct interaction with the customers, as with many services. Equally, for products where the logistic costs are greater than the economies of scale benefits, there can be advantages of focusing manufacturing on the requirements of the location within economic transport distance of the site.

• Focus in practice: in practice, organizations may decide to use a combination of focused operations; for example, product focus for high volume, repetitive products or services; a market focus for specific customers or groups of customers with similar operational requirements; focus by volume for other products; and focus by order-winners where there are some specific requirements for fast delivery or special quality specifications.

Although most academic literature is based on manufacturing operations, the concepts and principles of focus apply equally to SERVICE OPERATIONS. For example, some very successful services in diverse sectors are based on product focus: a narrow range of services provided by simple, low-overhead facilities and infrastructures, designed to exactly meet the needs and expectations of the customers.

It is widely accepted that the main sources of the benefits of focus derive from clarity of mission, repetitive operations tasks, and the reduction in conflict between objectives which results in complexity and ineffectiveness. Some writers also claim that significant benefits come from better matching of product and process technologies to each other and to market requirements, enhanced asset management (particularly of inventory), and improved interfunctional communication and performance.

There is relatively little conclusive research evidence to support the claims for benefits of focus. However, the concept has widespread intuitive support among academics and practitioners. Some research evidence, provided by the Boston Consulting Group, is reported by Hayes and Wheelwright (1984). For example:

● In one industry, researchers found a significant inverse relationship between the number of product lines produced and the operating margin achieved.

● Within a seven-site process-intensive business, the highest margin achieved was at the sites where there was the narrowest product range, and the fewest customers served.

● Within one plant, as product range was progressively reduced, and average product volume was increased over time, the standard cost reduced significantly.

The lack of factual evidence for the benefits of focus can be attributed to the difficulties of collecting such evidence. Claimed benefits include greater efficiency, increased effectiveness and enhanced market orientation; therefore cost comparisons alone could be misleading. More significant are the benefits which should manifest themselves in long-term profitability, but this is difficult to assess conclusively in fluctuating business cycles. Alternatively, inter-company or inter-plant comparisons could be useful, but depend heavily on exact comparability of their measurement systems.

The concept of focus can be applied at various levels within organizations, and has its parallels in other subjects. Much of the strategic management literature supports moves towards better corporate focus, claiming that businesses that try to cover too wide a field are likely to be disadvantaged compared to those that have focused on the needs of niche segment(s). Most literature on focus is appropriate at plant level. However, focus can also be achieved by the physical division of plants into smaller, relatively self-contained smaller units, often known as "plants within plants" (PWP). Ideally, these PWPs should include most of the processes and supporting functions to enable them to work independently and to interface directly with suppliers and customers. Similarly the concept of cellular manufacture could be regarded as an extension of focus at the micro level of operations.

See also **volume; manufacturing strategy; service strategy; trade-offs**

Bibliography

Hayes, R. H. & Schmenner, R. W. (1978). How should you organize manufacturing? *Harvard Business Review*, 56, *1*, 105–18.

Hayes, R. H. & Wheelwright, S. C. (1984). *Restoring our competitive edge.* New York: Wiley.

Hill, T. J. (1994). *Manufacturing strategy: Text and cases.* Burr Ridge, IL: Irwin.

Lee, Q. (1992). *Manufacturing focus: A comprehensive view.* In C. A. Voss (Ed.), *Manufacturing strategy: Process and content.* London: Chapman and Hall.

Schmenner, R. (1976). Before you build a big factory. *Harvard Business Review*, 4, 100–4.

Skinner, W. (1974). The focused factory. *Harvard Business Review*, 52, *3*, 113–21.

STUART CHAMBERS

G

Gantt chart   A Gantt chart is a simple device, first devised by H. L. Gantt in 1917, which represents time as a bar, or channel, on a chart. Often the charts themselves are made up of long channels into which colored pieces of paper can be slotted to indicate what is happening with a job or a work center, these may be called schedule boards. The start and finish times for activities can be indicated on the chart and sometimes the actual progress of the job is also indicated on the same chart.

Gantt charts provide a simple visual representation of what should be happening and what actually is happening in an operation, and can be used to "test out" alternative schedules, especially when using moveable pieces of paper. However, the Gantt chart is in no way an optimizing tool. It merely facilitates the development of alternative schedules by communicating them effectively.

See also **scheduling**

NIGEL SLACK

generic manufacturing strategies   To describe a MANUFACTURING STRATEGY as "generic" implies that a single and unique type of manufacturing strategy has generally been adopted by a substantial number of manufacturing businesses. This may, at first, seem improbable given the considerable diversity of manufacturing companies and the variety of products that they produce.

To assess the probability of the existence of a small number of generic manufacturing strategies, consideration must be given to how a manufacturing strategy is designed. Skinner (1969), in his pioneering research of the manufacturing strategy management process, recommends that the manufacturing capabilities of an organization should be congruent with the competitive strategy of a firm. Porter (1980) claims that organizations of all types implement generic competitive strategies; it therefore seems logical that their implementation would induce the establishment of a common set of generic manufacturing strategies.

The concept of generic manufacturing strategies fulfilling an ideological fit with generic competitive strategies is helpful to the creation of a vision of how the manufacturing capabilities of a firm should be developed. A framework that links generic competitive strategies with generic manufacturing strategies would therefore provide an aid to the manufacturing manager when planning the long-term development of the manufacturing capabilities of a company.

For these reasons, a considerable amount of research has been carried out to investigate whether generic manufacturing strategies can be identified and what competitive advantages are enabled by their implementation.

Stobaugh and Telesio (1983) carried out a study and review of a hundred case studies. They found three groups of international manufacturers – cost driven, technology driven, and market driven. Miller and Roth (1994) used American Manufacturing Futures data to determine empirically a taxonomy of manufacturing strategies. From their statistical analysis they distinguished three groups of manufacturing strategies, which they named caretakers, marketeers, and innovators. Their definitions of these manufacturing strategy groupings were as follows:

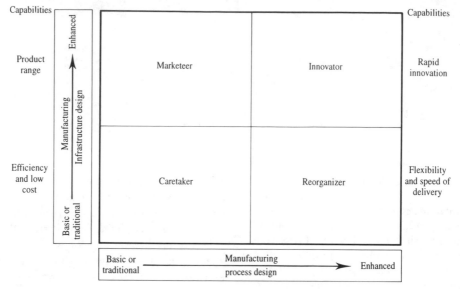

Figure 1 Generic manufacturing strategies

(1) Caretakers tend to compete on price but they were notable for the low levels of importance that they ascribe to manufacturing capabilities and improvement programs.
(2) Marketeers seek to obtain broader distribution, to offer broader products lines, and to be responsive to changing volume requirements. Marketeers plan on strengthening their manufacturing operations through infrastructural change.
(3) Innovators place emphasis on their ability to make quick changes to product design and focus on providing high-performance products.

Miller and Roth found that although the taxonomy they propose is influenced by industry type, it is not dominated by it, and it applies to a broad number of competitive circumstances.

De Meyer (1992) carried out a similar empirical study. The data source for this research was the 1987 and 1988 European Manufacturing Futures Survey. De Meyer also identified three clusters of organizations with similar emphasis given to their competitive priorities and manufacturing action plan. His general conclusion was that the European manufacturing innovators coincide to a certain extent with the North American innovators. The second group, which he defined as the marketing-oriented group, was described as "having quite a number of analogies with the North American caretakers, but has in its priorities something of the marketeers." The third group De Meyer labeled as the high-performance products group. This group was defined in the following way:

The third group of focused manufacturers emphasize the performance of their products. They seem to be a bit more oriented towards the deployment of technology in their emphasis on computer-aided design and FLEXIBLE MANUFACTURING SYSTEMS, and strive for a good production process characterized by worker safety.

Concurrent with these empirical research studies, Sweeney (1993) was developing a conceptual framework linking generic competitive strategies with their equivalent manufacturing strategies which derived from case studies. This conceptual framework is shown in Figure 1. The figure shows four generic manufacturing strategies, three of which are those created by Miller and Roth. The fourth, the reorganizer strategy, is intended to convey that a change to the production process to increase FLEXIBILITY and delivery speed is a key priority for those implementing this strategy.

Bibliography

De Meyer, A. (1992). An empirical investigation of manufacturing strategies in European industry. In C. A. Voss, (Ed.), *Manufacturing strategy: process and content.* London: Chapman and Hall.

Miller, J. G. & Roth, A. (1994). A taxonomy of manufacturing strategies. *Management Science*, **40**, *3*, 285–304.

Porter, M. (1980). *Competitive strategy: Techniques for analysing industries and competitors.* New York: Free Press.

Skinner, W. (1969). Manufacturing: missing link in corporate strategy. *Harvard Business Review*, **47**, *3*, 136–45.

Stobaugh, R. & Telesio, P. (1983). Match manufacturing policies and product strategy. *Harvard Business Review*, *2*, 113–20.

Sweeney, M. T. (1991). Towards a unified theory of strategic manufacturing management. *International Journal of Operations and Production Management*, **11**, *8*, 6–22.

Sweeney, M. T. (1993). Strategic manufacturing management: restructuring wasteful production to world class. *Journal of General Management*, **18**, *3*, 57–76.

MICHAEL SWEENEY

group working Group working is a type of WORK ORGANIZATION which has emerged as an alternative to other forms, using individual working, which are based on DIVISION OF LABOR and specialization. Organizing work on a group, rather than an individual, basis is not an entirely new idea. Many traditional craft-based industries have always used group working because of the benefits it brings in terms of better communications and control of the process. This in turn has been found to influence product quality, one of the most important factors in such industries.

With the advent of "SCIENTIFIC" MANAGEMENT, work organization became less craft based and increasingly fragmented and controlled. Industries using the traditional forms of organization became the rarity and differentiation and predetermination emerged as the principal characteristics of industrial work.

More recently, however, there has been a significant reversal in thinking. Problems have been encountered with types of work organization based on differentiation, such as task-orientated work on lines and process-orientated work in functional workshops. These problems result from the alienation of people who work in these types of system. As a result there is often high labor turnover, recruitment problems, high absenteeism rates, and quality can suffer. Sometimes workers have even been known to sabotage equipment or products as a way of demonstrating their frustration and boredom brought on by the monotony associated with repetitive, differentiated, work.

Using group working as an alternative was first put forward in countries where industrial workers had a better standard of education, principally in Scandinavia. The effect of these higher education standards was a demand for more fulfilling work. Norway, for example, experimented with group working in the steel and paper making industries during the 1960s and Sweden's experiments in the automotive industry during the 1970s are well known. Today, group working is well established and complete production plants have been designed and built using the concept, whereas earlier examples were based on reorganizing the work within existing facilities.

To be effective, group work should be supported by a technical system which will allow a high degree of task flexibility and autonomy. Where this has been achieved the term "autonomous work group" is sometimes used. Such technical systems will be based on the principle of parallel, rather than sequential, work stations. Sometimes the work can be carried out while the product is stationary in what is known as a "dock" system. The material handling equipment will also allow workers to control the pace, and even the routing, of products. Automated guided vehicles (or AGVs) are often used rather than fixed speed conveyors.

A particular consideration with group working is the need for an appropriate system of payment for this type of work organization. Conventional payment systems, particularly those based on an individual financial incentive, are usually inappropriate since they do not take account of the interdependence of group members. A better payment system would probably comprise several components depending on the nature of work organization and the motivational and reward factors being emphasized.

Some of the more relevant features might be an individual element based on job evaluation (taking into account factors such as education, training, range of acquired skills, extra responsibilities, timekeeping record, etc.), a group element based on delegated responsibilities (these might include production planning, quality responsibility, cost accounting, administration, and social responsibilities such as not rejecting other group members), and a results-related element which is possibly paid on a plant-wide basis (this might take into account the total cost of production workers, cost of staff, number of rejects, amount of rework, use of operational supplies and tools, added material, store value, and a quality index).

See also **cell layout; job design; job enrichment**

Bibliography

Sandberg, T. (1982). *Group working and autonomous groups*. Liber Verlag.

DAVID BENNETT

H

hierarchy of operations Each part of an operation can be viewed as part of an interconnecting hierarchy of TRANSFORMATION MODELS. Inside most operations there are units or departments, which themselves act as smaller versions of the whole operation. The total operation is sometimes termed a macro operation, while its departments are termed micro operations. These micro operations have inputs, some of which will come from outside the macro operation but many of which will be supplied from other internal micro operations. Similarly, each micro operation will produce outputs of goods and services for the benefit of customers, though again, some of each micro operation's customers will be other micro operations. The hierarchy of operations concept can be extended further. Within each micro operation there are likely to be sections or groups which also can be considered as operations in their own right. These sections or groups might also take much of their input from, and give much of their output to, other sections or groups, both within their own micro operation and outside it. Thus any operations function is considered to be a hierarchy of operations, perhaps extending down as far as the individual staff member taking inputs, carrying out a transforming process and producing outputs.

Closely related to the hierarchical concept of macro and micro operations is the systems-theory-based idea of emergent properties. Emergence is founded on the observation that each level in the operations hierarchy possesses properties which cannot be found at lower levels in the hierarchy. Put another way, the total operation is more than the sum of its parts. The implication of this idea is that for an operation to perform to its full potential, the activities of the operation as a whole must be considered at some point. This, in turn, has important implications when the hierarchy of operations is used to formalize the concept of INTERNAL CUSTOMER–SUPPLIER RELATIONSHIP.

See also **operations management; continuous improvement; business process redesign**

NIGEL SLACK

human-centered CIM Human-centered computer-integrated manufacturing (CIM) is a development of conventional COMPUTER-INTEGRATED MANUFACTURING which incorporates the concept of "human centeredness." The concept of human-centeredness and the ideas that underlie the approaches were first developed and formulated by Hower Rosenbrock in the early 1980s. The phrase human-centered is often replaced by the term anthropocentric. The concept of human-centered design goes along with, and includes, many principles well known in the field of human work design: personality promotion, skill-based manufacturing and complementary design of man–machine systems.

In general, a human-centered technology is one which extends human skill and its application to real-life situations. The technology itself must be designed so as to optimize the synergy between human skill and computer power. The work within the factory must be organized in such a way that in all areas people are able to apply a substantial range of their skills rather than just a small "useful" part. Individual skill and competence should be increased through a balanced combination of learning by doing, and formal training and education.

In a human-centered system traditional design and manufacturing skills are used to their fullest extent. The range of activities for which each operator is responsible is maximized to include, for example, production work as well as quality and planning-related duties. As a result, each person will develop a general knowledge of the whole production process, and must be given the freedom and opportunity to comment on any aspect of it. Such input must be taken into consideration when upgrading and modifying the system.

Bibliography

Rosenbrock, H. H. (1983). Flexible manufacturing systems in which the operator is not subservient to the machine. *Research Project Mimeo*. Manchester, UK: UMIST.

Rosenbrock, H. H. (1990). *Machines with a purpose*. Oxford.

Schmid, F., Hancke, T. & Wu, B. (1993). The human-centred approach to the implementation of computer integrated systems in control and dynamic systems. *Computer aided manufacturing: Computer integrated manufacturing (CAM/CIM)*. San Diego: Academic Press.

FELIX SCHMID

importance–performance matrix One of the most significant activities in the operations strategy formulation process is the derivation of a list of competitive factors prioritized in terms of their relative importance. Typically such a list ranks or rates those factors which the operations function contributes to the competitiveness of the organization. So, for example, quality may be regarded as more important than product or service range but less so than price, and so on. PROCESS OF MANUFACTURING STRATEGY FORMULATION models may also include an attempt to assess the operations performance against its competitors. This allows the gap between relative importance and performance to be compared in order to prioritize improvement efforts.

In the service operations/marketing area one gap-based method is that proposed by Martilla and James (1977), who suggested an importance–performance matrix. The utility of such a matrix lies in its ability to bring together both customers (importance) and competitor (performance) perspectives to judging the relative improvement priorities which need to be applied to competitive criteria. One suggested form of the matrix is shown in Figure 1 (Slack, 1994). It is divided into zones representing different improvement priorities. There is a "lower boundary of acceptability" shown as line *AB* in Figure 1, representing the boundary between acceptable and unacceptable performance relative to importance. Below this line there is a need for improvement: above it there is no immediate urgency for any improvement. However, not all competitive factors falling below the minimum line have the same degree of improvement priority. A boundary approximately represented by line *CD* represents a distinction between an urgent priority zone and

a less urgent improvement zone. Similarly, above the line *AB*, not all competitive factors are regarded as having the same characteristics. The line *EF* can be seen as the approximate boundary between performance levels which were regarded as "good" or "appropriate" on the one hand and those regarded as "too good" or "excess" on the other. Segregating the matrix in this way results in four zones which imply different treatments.

The "appropriate" zone is bounded on its lower ledge by the "minimum performance boundary," that is the level of performance which the company, in the medium term, would not wish the operation to fall below. Moving performance up to, or above, this boundary is likely to be the first-stage objective for any improvement program. Competitive factors which fall in this area should be considered satisfactory, at least in the short to medium term. Any competitive factor which lies below the lower bound of the "appropriate" zone will be a candidate for improvement. Those lying either just below the bound or in the bottom left-hand corner of the matrix (where performance is poor but it matters less) are likely to be viewed as non-urgent cases. They need improving, but probably not as a first priority. This is the "improve" zone.

More critical will be any competitive factor which lies in the "urgent action" zone. These are aspects of operations performance where achievement is so far below what it ought to be, given its importance to the customer, that business is probably being lost directly as a result. The short-term objective must therefore be to raise the performance of any competitive factors lying in this zone at least up to the

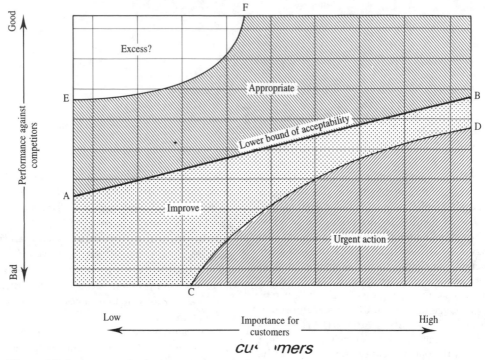

Figure 1 Priority zones in the importance–performance matrix

"improve" zone. In the medium term they would need to be improved to beyond the lower bound of the "appropriate" zone.

The "Excess?" zone lies in the top left-hand area of the matrix. If any competitive factors lie in this area their achieved performance is far better than would seem to be warranted. This does not necessarily mean that too many resources are being used to achieve such a level, but it may do so. It is only sensible, therefore, to check if any resources which have been used to achieve such a performance could be diverted to a more needy factor.

See also **manufacturing strategy; operations objectives; order-winners and qualifiers; performance measurement**

Bibliography

Martilla, J. A. & James, J. C. (1977). Importance–performance analysis. *Journal of Marketing*, January.

Slack, N. (1994). The importance–performance matrix as a determinant of improvement priority. *International Journal of Operations and Production Management*, 4, 5, 59–75.

NIGEL SLACK

industrial engineering   Industrial engineering is an engineering discipline which is concerned with increasing the effectiveness of manufacturing and service operations. In one sense it is equivalent in its scope to OPERATIONS MANAGEMENT, but in practice has a more operational (as opposed to strategic) approach. It is also more concerned with modeling and techniques rather than the management of operations. However, its roots, like operations management, are in the "SCIENTIFIC" MANAGEMENT movement of the early twentieth century.

See also **transformation model; manufacturing systems engineering**

NIGEL SLACK

internal customer–supplier relationships The terms internal customer and internal supplier can be used to describe those micro operations (*see* HIERARCHY OF OPERATIONS) which take outputs from, and give inputs to, any other micro operations. Each micro operation is therefore at the same time both an internal supplier of goods and services and an internal customer for the other micro operation's goods and services.

The internal customer–supplier concept is regarded by some as one of the most powerful aspects to emerge from TOTAL QUALITY MANAGEMENT. It is a recognition that everyone is a customer within the organization and consumes goods or services provided by other internal suppliers, but at the same time is an internal supplier of goods and services for other internal customers. The implication of this is that errors in the service provided within an organization will eventually affect the product or service which reaches the external customer. It follows that if external customers are to be satisfied, every part of the organization must contribute to external customer satisfaction by satisfying its own internal customers. This is done primarily by defining as clearly as possible what their own and their customer's requirements are. In effect this means defining what constitutes "error-free" service, the QUALITY, speed, dependability, and FLEXIBILITY required by internal customers. The exercise replicates what should be happening with the macro operation and its external customers.

As well as helping to embed the quality imperative in every part of the operation, the internal customer concept is useful because it affects the "upstream" parts of the internal supply network. These parts of the organization, especially those which provide internal services, can be the origin of errors which do not always become evident until later in the process.

It is generally recognized that internal customers and suppliers cannot be treated in exactly the same way as external customers and suppliers. External customers and suppliers usually operate in a free market. If an organization believes that in the long run that it can get a better deal by purchasing goods and services from another supplier, it will do so. Similarly, the organization would not expect its customers

to purchase its own goods and services unless it could in some way offer a better deal than its competitors. Internal customers and suppliers, however, cannot operate like this. They are not (in the short term) in a "free market" and they usually cannot look outside to either purchase input resources or sell their output goods and services.

However, notwithstanding the differences between internal and external customers, the concept is useful in the sense that it provides a model to analyze the internal activities of an operation. If the macro operation is not working as it should, the error can be traced back along the internal network of customers and suppliers.

Some organizations bring a degree of formality to the internal customer concept by encouraging (or requiring) different parts of the operation to agree "service level agreements" (SLAs) with each other. SLAs are formal definitions of the dimensions of service and the relationship between two parts of an organization. The type of issues which would be covered by such an agreement could include response times, the range of services, dependability of service supply and so on. Boundaries of responsibility and appropriate performance measures could also be agreed.

Criticisms of the concept largely center around its implicit acceptance of the existing organizational structure of an organization. By contrast approaches such as BUSINESS PROCESS REDESIGN take a more radical stance which would be difficult using the internal customer supplier concept.

See also **quality; service quality**

NIGEL SLACK

international location The international location decision is one which is concerned with the LOCATION of facilities at the highest level. It is a decision that needs to be made by any organization involved in international operations. Such organizations can include subsidiaries of multinational enterprises, international joint ventures, licensees or franchising operations. They may be involved in a range of different activities such as local assembly, offshore manufacturing or the complete production of goods for global markets. International organizations are also increasingly becoming involved in the delivery of services, particularly since the barriers preventing them being transferred across national boundaries are progressively being removed.

In many respects the international location decision is similar to any decision regarding the location of facilities for a domestic organization. Tangible factors can be taken into account, such as the cost of land, cost of buildings, labor costs, transport costs, etc. Similarly there are intangible factors to be considered, such as environmental constraints and ease of communications.

Perhaps the main thing that distinguishes an international location decision from a domestic one is its strategic dimension. Many organizations choose a particular international location with a view to exploiting the long-term possibilities offered and not simply to meet short-term objectives. Therefore, many of the established techniques for evaluating alternative locations or determining an "optimum" location are only of partial relevance.

The actual method used to determine the location of an international operation will tend to vary according to its type.

Local assembly normally takes place where tariff barriers exist on imported goods, or the assembly costs in the parent company are high, thereby making the products too expensive in the local market. The solution is therefore to use local labor to assemble CKD (complete knock down) or SKD (semi-knock down) kits, thereby avoiding import tariffs or taking advantage of lower local labor costs. Location decisions in this case need to consider the logistics of supplying parts and the availability of suitable low-cost labor.

Offshore manufacturing is where products are made in a foreign country to the design of, and often using parts supplied by, an original equipment manufacturer (or OEM), then reexported to the country of the OEM or to third countries. Therefore it is often restricted to assembly operations with the purpose of exploiting one or more of the local advantages such as reduced labor costs, specialized skills or lower overheads. Where there is a tariff on imported materials this is often overcome by locating in an "export processing zone," which is a tariff free area for export-oriented companies. Location decisions in such situations are influenced by the local costs of production, the incentive and taxation regime, and the ease with which materials, parts and finished goods can be transported into and out of the country in question.

Complete production of goods for the global market is the approach to international operations commonly encountered in multinational corporations. It is often chosen because it offers the opportunity of achieving good economies of scale since production for every market takes place at just one single location and is fully integrated. Here, the location decision involves finding the best place to manufacture the product, taking into account a wide range of factors such as design capability, engineering competence and availability of low-cost productive resources, as well as the need to minimize transport costs. This last factor is not too easy to determine because the materials, parts and finished goods can come from, and go to, an enormous number of other countries. The distribution of finished goods can also present difficulties because of the ever changing nature of the market in terms of customer location and product mix.

An alternative and overlapping approach to international location is to consider the configuration of a company's network at an international level. Four configuration strategies have been identified.

Home Country Configuration

The simplest strategy for an organization trading around the world is not to locate plants outside its home country and to export its products to foreign markets. The reason for this might be, for example, that the technology employed in the product is so novel that it needs to be manufactured close to its research and development headquarters. Alternatively the home location of the company might be part of the attraction of a product (e.g. high fashion garments from Paris).

Regional Configuration

An alternative strategy is to divide the company's international markets into a small number of regions and make each region as self-contained as possible. So, for example, the Pacific region's market would be served by an operation or operations, in that region. Companies might adopt this strategy because their customers demand speedy delivery and prompt after-sales service. If products or services were created outside the region it might be difficult to provide such a level of service without regional warehouses and service centers.

Global Co-ordinated Configuration

The opposite of the regional strategy is the global co-ordinated configuration. Here each plant concentrates on a narrow set of activities and products and then distributes its products to markets around the world. So, for instance, a company might take advantage of low labor costs in one region and the technical support infrastructure in another in order to seek to exploit the particular advantages of each site or region. However, by doing so it does place a co-ordination requirement on the headquarters of the company. All product allocations, operations capacities and movement of products are planned centrally.

Combined Regional and Global Co-ordinated Configuration

The regional strategy has the advantage of organizational simplicity and clarity, the global co-ordinated strategy of well exploited regional advantages. Firms often attempt to seek the advantages of both by adopting a compromise between them. Under such a strategy regions might be reasonably autonomous, but certain products could still be moved between regions to take advantage of particular regional circumstances.

See also **manufacturing strategy; capacity strategy; supply chain management**

Bibliography

Dicken, P. (1992). *Global shift*. London: Paul Chapman.

DuBois, F. C. & Oliff, M. D. (1992). International manufacturing configuration and competitive priorities. In C. A. Voss (Ed.), *Manufacturing strategy: Process and content*. London: Chapman and Hall.

DAVID BENNETT

inventory accuracy   In order to properly control inventory levels and reduce the risk of stockouts it is important that stock records accurately reflect physical stock levels. As soon as any difference is discovered the stock records should be adjusted to reflect the physical stock available and a corresponding adjustment made to accounting records. In order to monitor stock accuracy each item of stock must be physically counted at regular intervals. Two methods are available for doing this: periodic inventory counting, and cycle inventory counting. Periodic inventory counting involves physically counting every item of stock at the same time, usually once a year. Cycle inventory counting involves physically counting a few items of stock each day or week so that at the end of a specified time interval all items have been counted.

Periodic inventory counting is the auditing of the physical stock on hand for every item of stock over a short period of time at regular intervals. It is usually carried out on an annual or semi-annual basis. It requires all operations to be closed down during the period of stock taking and so it can be extremely disruptive. Because of the need to complete the audit as rapidly as possible, non-specialist staff are usually brought in to help and this can lead to errors. It also results in a large number of adjustments and write-offs occurring at the same time, placing a considerable load on the departments concerned.

Cycle inventory counting is the auditing of a few items at a time on a continuous basis throughout the year. It can be carried out by stores personnel as part of their normal duties and so it tends to be more accurate and less disruptive. It also provides a continuous measure of inventory accuracy. If the level of accuracy is unacceptable, action can be taken to identify the causes of errors and eliminate them. One of the attractions of this method is its flexibility. High usage items can be counted more frequently than low usage items. Items can be counted when stocks are likely to be at their lowest, for example when a replenishment order has just been received. Items can be counted when an error might be critical, for example when a replenishment order is about to be placed or stock records show a zero or negative stock level.

See also **inventory management; inventory-related costs; inventory valuation; inventory performance measures**

Bibliography

Burch, J. D. (1981). Cycle counting and inventory accuracy. *Production and Inventory Management Review and APUICS News*, 1, 9, 66.

Backes, R. W. (1980). Cycle counting: a better way of achieving accurate stock records. *Production and Inventory Management*, 21, 2, 36–44 .

JOHN MAPES

inventory control systems In most organizations the amount of capital tied up in inventory is likely to be quite substantial. It is therefore important that suitable methods of inventory control are employed in order to ensure that inventories are kept at the minimum level consistent with maintaining continuity of supply to meet the needs of external customers and users within the business.

The inventory control system must provide answers to the following two questions for each item stocked:

(1) When should the stock be replenished?
(2) What quantity should be ordered at that time? (*See* ECONOMIC ORDER QUANTITY.)

In very broad terms there are two categories of inventory control systems. There is the continuous review system (also called the perpetual inventory system) where the inventory level is monitored continuously. As soon as the inventory level falls below a predetermined level then an order is placed for the reorder quantity. The alternative system is the periodic review system. Here the inventory level is only checked at fixed intervals, say once a month. An order is then placed of sufficient size to bring total inventory up to a specified maximum level.

The periodic review system has the advantage of not requiring inventory levels to be monitored all the time. It also enables the user to decide the time when an order is placed. This prevents peaks and troughs in the work load of the ordering department and enables all items from a given supplier to be ordered at the same time. The disadvantage of the periodic review system is that it increases the period of time

during which a stockout can occur. In the case of a reorder point system a stockout can only occur during the period between placing an order and receiving the goods. If an increase in demand occurs outside this period then the next replenishment order will be placed earlier. With the periodic review system a stockout could occur at any time. An increase in demand immediately after one inventory review would not be picked up until the following inventory review. Even then there would still be the risk of a stockout during the period between the review and delivery of the goods ordered. As a consequence, for a given stockout risk the average investment in inventory for the periodic review system must be higher than the average investment in inventory for the reorder point system.

The Continuous Review System

In the continuous review system of inventory control, a fresh order is placed as soon as the inventory level falls to a level equal to the expected lead time demand plus a safety stock to allow for those occasions when lead time demand is higher than expected. The size of the safety stock depends on the desired stockout risk and the variability in lead time demand. The most common measure of variability in lead time demand is the standard deviation. Various statistical methods are available to determine what multiple of the standard deviation is necessary as safety stock in order to achieve the required stockout risk.

The Periodic Review System

The main drawback of the reorder point system is that continuous review of inventory levels is implied. This, in turn, means that posting of stock movements has to be kept up to date, and inevitably an unpredictable work load is to be expected, particularly for the purchasing department. This can be avoided using the period review system. In the pure form of the periodic review system, the inventory level is reviewed at regular intervals, and a replenishment order is placed at each review.

The basic periodic review system involves regular reviews of all stock items, although the frequency and time of review will not necessarily be the same for all stock items. In general, items with large annual requirement values will be reviewed frequently and items with low annual requirement values will be reviewed infrequently. At each review, an order is placed sufficient to bring total inventory up to a maximum level equal to expected demand during the review period and lead time, plus a buffer stock to cover above average demand during this period. This can lead to orders being placed for very small numbers of items, but it becomes very attractive when a large number of different stock items can be ordered from the same supplier at the same time.

See also **inventory management; inventory performance measures; inventory accuracy**

JOHN MAPES

inventory management   All goods and materials which are held by an organization for future use or sale are called inventories or stocks. The terms inventory and stock tend to be used interchangeably. Inventory management involves planning and controlling these inventories with the objective of meeting the materials requirements of the organization at the lowest possible cost (*see also* MATERIALS MANAGEMENT).

Ideally supplies of materials would always exactly match requirements. Raw materials would be delivered just as they were required for use. Finished products would be manufactured just as they were required for dispatch to customers. In practice this is rarely possible. In order to ensure efficiency of operation, materials are ordered or produced in advance of actual requirements and held as inventory. By holding inventory of raw materials the operations manager is able to continue manufacturing at a steady rate even when supplies are delivered late. Inventories of finished goods enable the sales manager to continue to meet orders promptly even when there is an unexpected surge in demand. Inventories of part completed work between processes enable machine operators to carry on working even when there is a slowdown or stoppage at the previous stage of production.

However, holding inventories of materials costs money. Not only is there the investment in the stocks themselves, there is the cost of storage space, materials handling equipment, and warehouse staff. If the holding of stocks is to be justified then there must be benefits in the form of increased sales or reduced costs which exceed the cost of holding the stocks. An important aspect of materials management is the trading off of the costs of holding inventory against the benefits resulting from holding inventory. The consequences of poor inventory management can be extremely serious. Profits are affected, both by the costs incurred in holding too much of some items and by the lost sales resulting from holding insufficient of other items.

Categories of Stock

From an accounting point of view there are four categories of stock: raw materials, spares and supplies, work in progress, and finished goods.

Raw materials are those items obtained from outside the organization to be used directly in the production of finished goods. Raw materials include not only things like sheet metal and chemicals but also bought-in assemblies like gear boxes and cathode ray tubes.

In addition to raw materials, organizations must also stock spare parts for the machinery and equipment in use within the organization. Also there are supplies, items which are consumed by the organization but do not form part of the finished product. Supplies will include typewriter ribbons, cleaning materials, and electric batteries.

At any given time there will be materials which have been issued from raw materials stocks but have not yet been fully converted to finished goods. These materials will either be on the shop floor being worked on or queuing between processes or they may be in the stores in the form of sub-assemblies, waiting until they are required for conversion into finished products.

Finally, there are stocks of the finished product which have not yet been sold to customers. Some of these stock may have already been allocated to specific customer orders but until ownership is legally transferred to the customer these form part of finished goods stocks.

While it is useful to know how much of total stock is in the form of raw materials, work in process and finished goods, it is also important to categorize stock in terms of why it is there, that is, the purpose for which the stock is held. Using this approach the following categories can be identified.

(1) *Transit inventories*: at a given point in time there will be materials in transit between different parts of the system, either between factories or between the finished goods warehouse and the customer. These inventories are called transit or pipeline inventories (*see* PHYSICAL DISTRIBUTION MANAGEMENT).

(2) *Lot size inventories*: when ordering materials from an outside supplier there is a fixed cost associated with placing and expediting the order, which is independent of the quantity ordered. It is therefore sensible to spread this fixed cost over a number of items by ordering in fairly large quantities at infrequent intervals (*see* LOT SIZING IN MRP, and ECONOMIC ORDER QUANTITY). A further benefit of ordering in large quantities may be the availability of bulk discounts. The quantities ordered will take some time to be consumed and will in the meantime have to be held as stock. These stocks are referred to as lot size or cycle inventories. Lot size inventories can also arise for items manufactured internally as a result of long production runs in order to spread the fixed cost of machine set-up over a large number of items.

(3) *Fluctuation inventories*: the time between placing an order with a supplier and receiving the goods is called the supplier lead time. If the usage rate and supplier lead time for each item could be forecast exactly, then replenishment orders could be timed so that just as the last item in stock was being issued staff would be restocking the shelves with items which had just been delivered. In practice both the usage rate and the supplier lead time are subject to unpredictable fluctuations. Basing the timing of replenishment orders on forecast demand and lead time would therefore lead to a stockout whenever actual demand during the lead time was higher than forecast, either as a result of underestimating demand or as a result of under-

estimating lead time. This would occur on approximately half of all orders placed and is unlikely to be acceptable. To give protection against unexpected fluctuations a safety (or buffer) stock is held. A replenishment order is placed as soon as stocks fall to a level equal to forecast lead time demand plus safety stock. A stockout then only occurs when lead time demand is so much higher than forecast that all of the safety stock is consumed before the new delivery arrives (*see* PURCHASING AND SUPPLY MANAGEMENT).

(4) *Anticipation inventories*: when demand shows pronounced seasonal variation it is often difficult for a manufacturing company to justify providing enough capacity to meet peak demand. Instead stocks are built up during periods of low demand and held until needed during the seasonal peak. Inventories which are deliberately built up in this way for consumption at a later date are called anticipation inventories (*see* AGGREGATE CAPACITY MANAGEMENT).

(5) *Decoupling inventories*: in manufacturing processes involving a number of linked stages then a delay at one stage can lead to delays at later stages in the process as they run out of work. To reduce the chances of this happening, decoupling stocks (also called buffer stocks) are placed between the stages. When a delay at one stage occurs, succeeding stages can continue producing by drawing items from the decoupling stock (*see* PRODUCT LAYOUT).

In recent years major changes have taken place in the inventory management task. Initially the emphasis was on cost minimization. Mathematical techniques were developed to determine the optimum stock levels necessary to provide an acceptable risk of stock non-availability at minimum cost. As computers became more widely available MATERIAL REQUIREMENTS PLANNING systems were developed capable of rapidly translating product requirements into a detailed schedule of time-phased orders for raw materials, components and sub-assemblies. While this enabled significant reductions in stock levels it did not deal with many of the underlying problems which make it necessary to hold inventory. The next

$$\text{Stock turn} = \frac{\text{value of materials used over a period}}{\text{average stock value over the period}}$$

Another measure which is sometimes used is a week's usage:

$$\text{Week's usage} = \frac{\text{average stock value over a period}}{\text{average stock value of materials used per week during the period}}$$

Figure 1

development was JUST-IN-TIME management. This approach emphasized the identification and elimination of the inefficiencies which result in high stock levels. Such inefficiencies include long set-up times, late delivery from suppliers, unreliable machines, and inflexible production processes.

See also **inventory-related costs; inventory control systems**

Bibliography

Fogarty, D. W. & Blackstone, J. H. (1991). *Production and inventory management*. Cincinnati: South-Western Publishing.

Greene, J. H. (1987). *Production and inventory control handbook*. 2nd edn. New York: McGraw-Hill.

Jessop, D. & Morrison, A. (1994). *Storage and supply of materials*. 6th edn. London: Pitman.

Mather, H. (1984). *How to really manage inventories*. New York: McGraw-Hill.

Plossl, G. W. (1985). *Production and inventory control: Principles and techniques*. 2nd edn. Englewood Cliffs, NJ: Prentice-Hall.

Vollman, T. E., Berry, W. & Whybark, D. C. (1988). *Manufacturing planning and control systems*. Homewood, IL: 2nd edn. Richard D. Irwin.

JOHN MAPES

inventory performance measures Measures of inventory performance consist of two main types. The first is concerned with how well inventory levels are being controlled and the most common measure is inventory turnover.

The second is concerned with how good a service the inventory function is providing to users. The most common measure of this is customer service level.

Although all organizations monitor the total value of stocks held, this figure is not very useful when viewed in isolation. It needs to be related to the value of material usage. The most common measure used to do this is inventory turnover. This gives an indication of the number of times the inventory has been consumed or turned over during a specified period, usually a year (Figure 1).

The two measures are just different ways of presenting the same information. Each can be derived from the other.

Customer service level is a measure of the percentage of customer requirements which have been met during a given period. There is a wide variety of different ways in which customer service level can be measured depending on how customer requirements are defined. If the emphasis is on measuring inventory performance then a typical measure of customer service level might be as shown in Figure 2.

See also **inventory management; inventory accuracy; inventory control systems**

JOHN MAPES

inventory valuation In order to control stock effectively a consistent method of assessing its value is needed. This is important from an accounting viewpoint as inventory usually constitutes a significant proportion of total assets and so the stock valuation method adopted can

$$\text{Customer service level} = \frac{\text{value of orders met immediately from stock during a period}}{\text{total value of orders during the period}}$$

Figure 2

affect the company's apparent worth. Also the value assigned to stock withdrawals helps determine the cost of goods sold which in turn affects the profit during a period. From a materials management point of view, inventory decisions and policies must be based on a method of valuing stock which is consistent and realistic. Stock valuation is complicated by the fact that stocks of each item are continually being used up and replenished and the unit price is likely to be different for each replenishment. The following methods are the ones most commonly used for valuing stock.

First In, First Out (FIFO)

Here it is assumed that the items are used in strict chronological order of receipt. When an item is withdrawn from stock the unit price used is that of the earliest order from which the item could have come. For most items, particularly those with a limited shelf life, FIFO corresponds with the actual order in which items are issued. Calculation of prices is fairly simple and the value of stock remaining approximates to its current value as it is based on the prices of those items purchased most recently. However, during periods of inflation the cost of goods sold will be lower than would be the case if current material costs were used.

Last In, First Out (LIFO)

Here it is assumed that the most recently received items are issued first. When an item is withdrawn from stock the unit price used is that of the most recent order from which the item could have come. LIFO is unlikely to correspond with the order in which items are actually issued from stores. Its aim is to take a more conservative view of profits during periods of rising prices, reflecting the fact that stocks consumed have to be replenished at current prices. During inflationary periods this leads to lower tax liability and more cash in hand. It also results in a lower valuation of stock remaining which can distort the balance sheet.

Average Cost

This method attempts to achieve a compromise between the extremes of LIFO and FIFO. Once an item enters stock it is assumed to be identical to all other items of the same type and they are all valued at the same average price. This average price is then used as the valuation for all withdrawals from stock until the next order is received and a new average price calculated. The advantage of averaging is that it smoothes out fluctuations in purchase prices. This carried with it the disadvantage that when prices are consistently rising or falling then the average price lags behind current prices.

Specific Cost

For large, expensive items each item can be given an identification number and the purchase price recorded. Then when the item is used it can be valued at the specific price paid for it. While this is the most realistic method of valuation it involves a considerable amount of record keeping. For the majority of items the benefits gained do not justify the recording cost.

Choosing a Valuation Method

There is no one method which is superior to the other methods in all respects and so the choice of method tends to be based on individual preference and administrative convenience. Once a method of valuation has been decided upon it is important that the method is applied consistently and is not changed. Otherwise comparisons of the value of stock at different locations and at different times can be very misleading.

See also **inventory management; inventory-related costs; inventory accuracy**

JOHN MAPES

inventory-related costs The costs associated with inventory can be divided into four categories.

(1) the purchase cost of the items;
(2) the cost of ordering the items;
(3) the cost of holding the items in stock;
(4) the costs arising due to items not being available when required.

Purchase Cost

Purchase prices will usually be affected by the quantity ordered. For large quantities bulk discounts can usually be negotiated. The purchase price is also likely to vary over time so that timing of the order may affect the price paid. Building up stocks prior to a known price increase may be financially advantageous even after taking into account the resulting increase in stockholding costs. The prices of many commodities show marked fluctuations over time so that average unit prices can be reduced by building up stocks when prices are low and running down stocks when prices are high.

Ordering Costs

Whenever an order is placed with an outside supplier there is the cost of selecting a vendor, agreeing a price, processing the paperwork, transporting the goods, and arranging for payment. Most of these costs will be independent of the actual quantity ordered and so total ordering costs can be reduced by ordering less frequently in larger quantities. When an order is raised for a product or component to be manufactured internally there is the cost of raising the paperwork and setting up the machine.

Inventory Holding Costs

Inventory holding costs are all of the costs that are incurred as a result of an item being held in stock. They include the cost of the capital tied up, the warehouse space occupied, warehouse staff, insurance, damage, deterioration, and obsolescence. The cost of holding an individual item in stock is quite difficult to measure and so annual stockholding costs for all items are usually expressed as a set percentage of their average stock value.

Stockout Costs

When an item is required which is out of stock then the costs incurred will depend on the circumstances. In some cases it may be possible to obtain the items from another site or from an outside supplier sufficiently rapidly to still meet the requirement. The costs incurred will include the costs of locating the items, arranging special delivery, and perhaps paying a premium on the normal price for the items. In other cases a back order may be possible, if the customer is willing to wait until the item is available. The costs will include the additional paperwork and labor costs involved in processing the back order and notifying the customer. If the customer is not willing to wait, then a lost sale will result. Not only will there be the lost profit on the sale but there will also be goodwill costs. The customers may decide to place future orders elsewhere, they may make adverse comments to other customers and so on.

See also **inventory management; inventory valuation; inventory accuracy**

JOHN MAPES

J

JIT tools and techniques Supporting the JUST-IN-TIME (JIT) philosophy is a set of tools and techniques. Many of these techniques are not new, and some had Western rather than Japanese origins, although JIT proponents hold that it is the combined effect that is significant, rather than the individual techniques themselves.

Bicheno (1991) divides up JIT techniques into "JIT stage 1" (mainly simplifying techniques) and "JIT stage 2" (mainly integrating techniques). Stage 1 techniques are applicable in all operations environments, whereas stage 2 techniques build on stage 1, and often require progress in stage 1 before they can be started. However, it is not intended that stage 1 must be completed before stage 2 starts. Nor are all the techniques exclusive to a JIT view of manufacturing; yet they have been embraced by practitioners as embodying the basic philosophies of JIT.

JIT Stage 1 Techniques

- DESIGN FOR MANUFACTURE: the JIT emphasis on simplicity in manufacture is complemented by design approaches with similar aims (*see also* VALUE ENGINEERING and SIMULTANEOUS DEVELOPMENT).

- Focus: the concept of FOCUS is that the operations task has been limited to a simple, consistent, and achievable set of goals. Again this approach enhances the simplicity of operational practice. Product focus is a major feature of many of the best JIT companies.

- The use of small machines: the principle here is that several small machines are used in preference to a single, large one. Small machines are held to be less prone to BOTTLENECKS, lengthy MAINTENANCE, and the build up of inventories.

- Simple layout and flow: this approach involves using LAYOUT principles to achieve a drive towards shorter routings by moving machines and processes closer together whenever the opportunity arises. This reduces wasted effort in the transport of materials.

- TOTAL PRODUCTIVE MAINTENANCE (TPM): the principle here is to assure maximum equipment up-time at minimum cost, but just as important to contribute to the general JIT principle of dependability in the operation.

- SET-UP REDUCTION: cutting down the time it takes to change equipment over from producing one batch to the next is key to improving flexibility without losing capacity. In turn, this helps to reduce inventories and throughput times.

- Team preparation: assigning people to product work areas within a developing TQ climate is the start of team preparation. It continues with developing operators who are multiskilled and multifunctional, so that they can carry out all processes, conduct routine maintenance, are responsible for quality, and are involved in improvement activities (*see* GROUP WORKING, and EMPOWERMENT).

JIT Stage 2

- Flow scheduling: the principle here is to keep materials moving. Keeping machines and people busy is less important. Parts and sub-assemblies are kept moving throughout the operations system to the "direction" of the factory assembly schedule. The analogy to water is often used in JIT literature, in this case clear the river bed of rocks and obstructions and straighten its path to shorten and even the flow of the river and its tributaries (*see* LEVELED SCHEDULING).

- Inventory reduction: JIT is not an inventory reduction program *per se*; however, inventory reduction is often one of its most visible benefits. It is accomplished by reducing batch sizes and buffer stocks following improvements in set-up times, productive maintenance, and flow scheduling.

- Visibility: a JIT-influenced factory is often recognizable from the charts and checksheets which are on show to record the status of operations processes and improvement projects, and from the light and/or sound indicators that monitor running conditions. Such relatively simple devices are much favored in JIT philosophy both for their simplicity (hence robustness) and their transparency of operation (contributing to a culture of shared information and objectives).

- Enforced improvement: this approach is intended to further identify and reduce waste. Enforced improvement is concerned with deliberately creating pressure for change. As each improvement project is implemented, the question is asked "what further improvement does this enable us to do now?" For example, set-up reduction may help to reduce batch sizes and buffer stocks. In turn, this helps to improve layout because processes can be placed closer together, which in turn improve visibility, and so on.

- Co-makership: a recognition of the dependencies of the links within SUPPLY CHAIN MANAGEMENT can lead to joint development programs, partnership agreements, integrated systems, and to mutual investments.

See also **design chain management;** *kanban*

Bibliography

Bicheno, J. R. (1991). *Implementing JIT*. Bedford: IFS Publications.

Harrison, A. S. (1992). *Just-in-time manufacturing in perspective*. Hemel Hempstead: Prentice-Hall.

Schonberger, R. J. (1992). *Operations management: Serving the customer*. Homewood, IL: Irwin.

Vollman, T. E., Berry, W. L. & Whybark, D. C. (1992). *Manufacturing planning and control systems*. Homewood, IL: Irwin.

Wickens, P. (1987). *The road to Nissan*. Basingstoke: Macmillan.

ALAN HARRISON

JIT/MRP   JIT/MRP is a combination of two popular approaches to operations planning and control, namely JUST-IN-TIME (JIT), and MATERIALS REQUIREMENTS PLANNING (MRP). Although seen as alternative approaches for some years after the popularization of JIT in the 1980s, the two approaches are now seen as being, to some extent, complementary. Certainly just-in-time is seen as having much to contribute to the strengthening of conventional MRP systems. Two major aspects of JIT philosophy especially, simplification and the elimination of waste, can be applied to the improvement and focusing of MRP design.

JIT concepts help to address a number of potential weaknesses in the way that MRP is designed and executed. These include the following:

- Although MRP can be seen as a pull system (*see* PUSH AND PULL PLANNING AND CONTROL) driven by the MASTER PRODUCTION SCHEDULE, the way it is used is actually as a push system. Inventory is driven through the factory in response to detailed, time-phased plans by part number.

- MRP is usually operated as a computer-based system which may require substantial investment in hardware, software, and systems support. It has a complex, centralized structure which may result in the operation losing sight of customer needs.

- MRP depends on a large amount of data, from bills of material to routing and stock records. This makes it particularly vulnerable to problems of data accuracy.

- Understanding MRP is a lengthy process for users, therefore training may be expensive and time consuming.

- MRP assumes fixed lead times. Batches of parts are moved from one operation to the next according to these set lead times. This, to some extent, disguises the real performance of the operation. It is easy to become preoccupied with improving the planning and control system performance (data accuracy, etc.) at the expense of more fundamental improvements.

• Because of the lengthy processing time to update MRP records, it is often run in batch mode on a weekly basis. Many versions today have "net change" options which enable records for selected parts to be updated daily. MRP is therefore only responsive on a daily or weekly basis, thus records are often out of step with reality.

Perhaps most significantly, while MRP excels at planning and co-ordinating materials, it is relatively weak in its control of the timing of material movements and the complexity of MRP may become a liability at shop floor level, where control systems are comparatively cumbersome and unresponsive. Yet the comparative simplicity resulting from such JIT techniques as LEVELED SCHEDULING and KANBAN can greatly help to simplify shop floor control of parts, especially those which are made at regular intervals, sometimes termed "runners" and "repeaters" (see RUNNERS, REPEATERS, AND STRANGERS). Further, JIT concepts can be used to attack many of the wasteful assumptions which are often built into MRP, such as fixed reorder rules and scrap allowances.

There are a number of ways in which the overall control of complex operations through MRP and the improvement-oriented simplicity of JIT can be combined at a technical level. Two general approaches to this are particularly influential.

The first is to use different planning and control systems for different products. Using the runners, repeaters, and strangers terminology, pull scheduling using *kanbans* can be used for "runners" and "repeaters," while MRP is used for "strangers." For "strangers," works orders are issued to explain what must be done at each stage and the work itself is monitored to push materials through manufacturing stages. One advantage of this approach is that by increasing responsiveness and reducing inven-

tories of runners and repeaters, it encourages operations to increase their number by design simplification.

The other approach is to use MRP for overall control and JIT for internal control. So, for example, MRP is used for the planning of supplier materials to ensure that sufficient parts are available to enable them to be called off "just-in-time." The master production schedule is broken down by means of MRP for supplier schedules (forecast future demand). Actual material requirements for supplies are signaled by means of *kanbans* to facilitate JIT delivery. Within the factory, all material movements are governed by *kanban* loops between operations.

The relative complexity of product structures (gauged by the number of levels in the BILL OF MATERIALS, and of process routing (gauged by the number of processes through which parts must travel), both have an important influence on which PLANNING AND CONTROL system is used. Where there are simple structures and routings, internal material control merits simple systems such as JIT-based systems. As complexity increases, so the power of the computer is needed to break down forecast demand into supplier schedules through MRP, but much internal control can still be carried out by means of pull scheduling. As structures and routings become more complex, so the opportunities for pull scheduling reduce, and MRP is needed to co-ordinate material movements. Network planning and control systems are needed for the most complex structures and routings.

Bibliography

Karmarkar, U. S. (1989). Getting control of just-in-time. *Harvard Business Review*, **67**, 5.

Vollman, T. E., Berry, W. L. & Whybark, D. C. (1992). *Manufacturing planning and control systems*. Homewood, IL: Irwin.

ALAN HARRISON

job design   Job design is a general term given to the aspect of operations system design which relates to the way in which jobs are structured and workers motivated. The activity of job design has been influenced by several concepts. In chronological sequence these are, DIVISION OF LABOR, "SCIENTIFIC" MANAGEMENT, ERGO-

NOMICS, and more recently approaches to job design based on theories of motivation such as JOB ENRICHMENT, JOB ENLARGEMENT, JOB ROTATION, and EMPOWERMENT.

The term "job design" is sometimes taken to refer only to this latter influence which originates from the Hawthorne studies which were carried out in the Hawthorne Works of the Western Electric Company in the USA. Intended originally to be a straightforward investigation into the effect of different lighting levels on output, the studies developed into a series of experiments which increasingly demonstrated that human behavior was an important factor affecting operating system performance and which had, up to that time, been grossly underestimated by managers. This recognition that the design of jobs was important was later refined by considering the issue of workers who were organized into groups. This work was carried out in the 1950s by the Tavistock Institute of Human Relations in London and used the coal mining industry as its research base. It demonstrated that informal structures and relationships were just as significant as the informal ones. The Tavistock work led to a whole new area of job design, that of "socio-technical systems" design. This new approach was based on the fact that it is frequently impossible to separate the design of jobs from that of the physical, or technical, system.

In general terms, job design can be categorized into two broad approaches: those which are based on "horizontal job loading" and those based on "vertical job loading."

Horizontal job loading, more commonly known as job enlargement, means that jobs are extended horizontally. That is to say that the workers' length of tasks are increased or further similar tasks are added. Alternatively the variety of products with which the worker is involved can be increased. A variation on this idea is job rotation where workers move from one job to another as a way of extending the scope of tasks.

Vertical job loading, more commonly known as job enrichment, means that jobs are extended vertically. More satisfying jobs are created by adding work of a different level. For example, tasks of greater complexity can be carried out or

further responsibilities can be assigned such as production planning, material ordering, quality control, or maintenance.

The "output" of the job design activity can be seen as a set of interrelated decisions, including the following:

- the tasks which are to be allocated to each person in the operation;

- the sequence of tasks to be established as the approved manner to do the job;

- the location of the job within the operation;

- who else should be involved in the job;

- the interface with the facilities and equipment used in the job;

- the environmental conditions which should be established in the workplace;

- the degree of autonomy to include in the job;

- the skills to develop in staff.

Recently, job design has received increased attention, particularly as a result of the problems which have arisen with some of the more conventional production systems. These problems are probably most acute in line operations (see MANUFACTURING PROCESSES) where cycle times are short and tasks are highly repetitive, which leads to monotonous jobs with little to motivate the worker.

Increasingly this situation has led to radical measures being taken to redesign jobs with entirely new types of production system being designed based on CELL LAYOUT or using GROUP WORKING. In these systems work cycles are extended and groups can, within reason, organize their own work, which brings the benefits of job enlargement, job rotation, and job enrichment mentioned above.

See also **method study; principles of motion economy**

Bibliography

Benders, J., De Haan, J. & Bennett, D. (Eds) (1995). *The symbiosis of work and technology.* London: Taylor and Francis.

DAVID BENNETT

job enlargement   Job enlargement is an approach to JOB DESIGN which provides a way of increasing job satisfaction and motivation. It is also known as horizontal job loading, which means that jobs are extended horizontally. That is to say the length of workers' tasks is increased or further similar tasks are added. Alternatively the variety of products with which the worker is involved can be increased. A variation on this idea is JOB ROTATION, where workers move from one job to another as a way of extending the scope of tasks.

The essential point about job enlargement is that a greater amount of work is carried out as a way of increasing worker involvement, but the level of work remains unchanged. This can lead to greater job satisfaction and, as a result, higher performance and better quality of output, but the degree to which it provides greater self-actualization is limited. For this reason an alternative approach is often used known as JOB ENRICHMENT, or vertical job loading, in which tasks of greater complexity are carried out or further job responsibilities are assigned.

DAVID BENNETT

job enrichment   Job enrichment is an approach to JOB DESIGN which provides greater self-actualization than JOB ENLARGEMENT or JOB ROTATION. It is also known as vertical job loading, which means that jobs are extended vertically rather than horizontally. That is to say more satisfying jobs are created by adding work of a different level instead of merely increasing the amount of work carried out.

To provide job enrichment, tasks of greater complexity can be carried out or further responsibilities can be assigned such as production planning, material ordering, quality control, or maintenance. In this way it gives greater responsibility to workers and, as a consequence, improves their motivation. This can result in a more flexible and adaptable workforce, which is particularly appropriate within the context of modern operations systems.

Job enrichment programs are often coupled with other production system redesign measures to maximize the benefits they can offer.

These include creating cellular layouts and GROUP WORKING, which provide the structural mechanisms for vertically extending jobs.

Bibliography

Hackman, J. R. & Oldham, G. (1975). A new strategy for job enrichment. *California Management Review*, 17.

DAVID BENNETT

job rotation   Job rotation is a variation on JOB ENLARGEMENT, which itself is an approach to JOB DESIGN for increasing job satisfaction and motivation. Job rotation means that workers move from one job to another as a way of extending the scope of tasks so it is a form of horizontal job loading. This means that jobs are extended horizontally but the level of work remains unchanged.

The essential point about job rotation is that a greater variety of work is carried out as a way of reducing the monotony associated with carrying out repetitive tasks continuously. It is most commonly used in line operations where other job design approaches are more difficult to implement due to the restrictions of the physical system. It can lead to greater job satisfaction and, as a result, higher performance and better quality of output, but the degree to which it provides greater self-actualization is limited. To overcome this drawback it is sometimes linked with team working, where members of the team can organize their own work assignments and achieve a greater sense of responsibility.

DAVID BENNETT

Juran   Joseph Juran, like DEMING, established his reputation as a consultant in QUALITY management during the 1950s when he was invited to give a series of lectures on the subject at the Japanese Union of Scientists and Engineers (JUSE).

Juran's definition of quality as "fitness for purpose or use" from the customer's perspective focused management attention on the needs of both internal and external customers. Stressing the importance of commitment from senior management in improving quality, he ascribed over 80 percent of quality problems to poor management rather than poor workmanship.

Juran also contributed the concept of the quality trilogy: quality planning, control, and improvement. He advocates the use of statistical methods of quality control, while warning against acceptance of "chronic waste." He recommends the following breakthrough procedure:

(1) Convince others that a breakthrough is needed.
(2) Identify the vital few projects.
(3) Organize for a breakthrough in knowledge.
(4) Conduct an analysis to discover the cause(s) of the problem.
(5) Determine the effect of the proposed changes on the people involved, and find ways to overcome resistance to these changes.
(6) Take action to institute the changes, including training of all personnel involved.
(7) Institute the appropriate controls that will hold the new, improved quality level but not restrict continued improvement.

He also stresses the importance of preventive maintenance, but differs from other exponents of TOTAL QUALITY MANAGEMENT in that his model of optimum quality costs implies that as defect levels decrease, failure costs are reduced, while the costs of appraisal and prevention increase; thus accepting an implicit trade-off between quality and cost.

See also **trade-offs; quality characteristics; service quality**

Bibliography

Juran, J. M. (1964). *Managerial breakthrough.* New York: McGraw-Hill.
Juran, J. M. & Gryna F. M, Jr. (1980). *Quality planning and analysis.* 2nd edn. New York: McGraw-Hill.
Juran, J. M. (1986). The quality trilogy. *Quality Progress,* **19,** *8,* 19–24.

RHIAN SILVESTRO

just-in-time   The term "just-in-time" (abbreviated to JIT) is the Western embodiment of a distinctive approach to operations, the foundations of which were developed by Japanese companies in the 1950s and 1960s. While the origins are somewhat clouded, one of the "founding fathers" was the industrial engineer, Shigeo Shingo. Shingo's (1989) view is that many of the basic ideas of JIT were developed in electrical, shipbuilding, and automotive industries. The company most widely quoted for advancing JIT is the Toyota Motor Company. In the company's production philosophy, known as the Toyota Production System (TPS), JIT is one of two "pillars" which support "excellence in manufacture." The other is *jidoka* (see below).

According to Taiichi Ohno (1988), one of the originators of the TPS, the primary objective of JIT is to make the time between customer order and the collection of cash as short as possible. Only the customer is free to place demand when he or she wants: after that the JIT system should take over to assure the rapid and co-ordinated movement of parts throughout the system to meet that demand. JIT is operationalized by means of *heijunka* which is the leveling and smoothing of the flow of materials (*see* LEVELED SCHEDULING), the use of KANBANS which signal to the preceding process that more parts are needed, and *nagare*, which are layout principles which aim to achieve a smooth flow of materials.

Jidoka is the Toyota concept aimed at describing humanization of the man/machine interface. This concept is based on the belief that in mass production (*see* MANUFACTURING PROCESSES) the pacing effect of the assembly line and the stopwatch drive people's efforts. The philosophy behind *jidoka*, however, is that people remain free to exercise judgment, while the machine serves their purposes. *Jidoka* is operationalized by means of machine *jidoku*, which are fail-safe devices on machines to stop defects from being made, human *jidoka* meaning "fixed position stops" which allow operators to stop the process in the event of a problem, and visual control, which is the means of assessing, at a glance, the status of production processes and the visibility of process standards.

The concept of just-in-time has been used loosely in the West to cover some or all of these aspects. In particular, interpretation of the concept has often paid scant attention to the *jidoka* element. Limiting the concept of JIT to mean only improvements in material control has been referred to as "little JIT" (Chase and Aquilano, 1994). "Little JIT" has been presented in numerous forms, such as pull scheduling, *KANBAN* and CELL LAYOUT. The extended role of JIT to mean an operations strategy which starts with a holistic philosophy of cutting out waste and improving quality across the business and its supply chain, is referred to by the same authors as "big JIT." In turn, "big JIT" has also been referred to in a variety of ways, such as world class manufacturing and lean production. In this entry, we use the term "JIT" in the broad sense (*see* MANUFACTURING STRATEGY).

Respect for Human System

One of the key differences between big JIT and little JIT is the attitude to human resources (HR). Concern for HR does not feature in little JIT and the term "Japanization" has been used to focus on the social aspects of work organization which little JIT is held to cause. It has been argued that JIT works in a Japanese context because of its appeal to the Japanese characteristics of discipline and team working.

Further, employment practices in major Japanese firms emphasize other characteristics which would be problematic to copy in the West, such as lifetime employment and single company trades unions. In the West, it is necessary to adapt HR thinking to make little JIT work. It is therefore likely that JIT will in fact take on many different forms. As a result JIT is often linked with TOTAL QUALITY MANAGEMENT initiatives which are aimed at changing the organization's culture. There is some disagreement in academic literature as to whether JIT is essentially people-building, or whether it intensifies work and concentrates more power in the hands of capital (Oliver and Wilkinson, 1992).

The JIT Philosophy

A central precept of JIT concerns doing the simple things within operations well and then gradually doing them better, squeezing out waste at every step. Waste is here defined as any activity that does not add value. Wasteful activities include inspection, producing defective goods; transport, producing more than is needed, and storing products. Waste often shows up as various forms of inventory, which is why the reduction of inventory can act as a measure of progress in the reduction of waste. One well-known analogy is of the "ship and the rocks" which sees problems as rocks in the water. Traditionally, problems have been covered by the water of inventory. It is only by deliberately lowering the level of water that operations managers can start to understand and prioritize the problems (rocks) which have lain hidden. Further progress demands that the rocks are systematically removed through enforced problem solving.

Simplicity is another recurrent theme in JIT philosophy. One of the first books to popularize JIT in the West was Schonberger's *Japanese manufacturing techniques: Nine hidden lessons in simplicity* (1982), the last chapter of which was entitled "Simplicity: the natural state." Complexity, clutter, and excessive paperwork are seen as alien to the excellent company. JIT TOOLS AND TECHNIQUES are deployed to transform previously complex, cluttered, and variable tasks into simple and clear tasks with increasingly low levels of variability and high levels of accuracy. These tools and techniques themselves tend to be relatively simple to understand, unlike the more complex, system-based techniques such as MATERIAL REQUIREMENTS PLANNING.

Many Japanese companies use the concept of the "4S" to start operationalizing JIT philosophy: these are *seiri*, meaning "sort things out," by separating materials, etc. into those which are really needed and those which are not, and disposing of those not wanted. *Seiton*, meaning "put into order," involves storing materials so that they are immediately available when wanted. *Seiso*, meaning "keep things clean," is also seen as a form of inspection. *Seiketsu*, meaning "keep things neat and tidy," implies maintaining cleanliness and clarity of work areas to provide safe working conditions. The 4Ss are intended to promote the discipline of cleanliness and tidiness as a set of shared values throughout the organization. If one cannot do the simple things right, the argument goes, then how can one do the more difficult things?

Another theme of much JIT writing is the use of absolute standard. For example, the goals of JIT are often expressed as a set of absolutes, such as:

● zero paper;

● zero inventory;

- zero downtime;
- zero delay;
- zero defects.

Such absolutes form a fixed concept of manufacturing ideals. The ideals embody a vision of an excellent company, and act as a focus for improvement activities. While real organizations may be far from achieving such an exalted state, the JIT argument is that they can get closer to these ideals over time if all company members follow the shared vision. Such visioning forms a key part of JIT philosophy, it provides goals to aim for and to measure progress against, it co-ordinates improvement efforts, and it communicates purpose. CONTINUOUS IMPROVEMENT (the Japanese word is *kaizen*) is concerned with making never-ending progress towards such goals. The *kaizen* process is led by team work: natural work teams who use simple problem solving tools to identify and solve problems which affect their work. These may be supplemented by small-group improvement activities, which are cross-functional teams aimed at specific problems which demand a broader base to solve.

JIT philosophy is sometimes summarized as the quest for superior performance manufacturing through three broad approaches. First is the use of some specific techniques, many of which are intended to identify and reduce all sources and causes of waste. However, techniques are secondary to the general beliefs, principles, and philosophies of JIT; they are simply seen as being instrumental. It is the combined effect of applying many techniques alongside its supporting philosophy which can make JIT so effective. Second is the inclusive concept of everyone being involved. JIT is regarded as a "total" approach to manufacturing. It holds that if only some of the people in the organization are involved, then only some of the problems can be solved. Third, continuous improvement is seen as working towards the goal of perfection, which although it can never be fully achieved, each improvement takes the operation a step closer.

The Evolution to Lean Production

JIT thinking has not remained within the confines of the manufacturing function. Any concept embodying a "war on waste" inevitably leads to the study of related non-manufacturing processes which are themselves a source of improvement. First, suppliers may be included. The principles of *heijunka*, *kanban*, and *nagare* can be applied throughout the supply chain. Suppliers can also be involved in joint development programs for new products, and generally more closely integrated into business strategy. Second, distribution may be included. Closer co-ordination with actual customer demand can be achieved through such approaches as tightly coupled logistics with customer processes and just-in-time delivery. Third, design may be included. It is estimated that 80 percent of manufacturing costs for engineered products are determined at the design stage. A specially rich source of improvements is therefore designing products for ease and low cost of manufacture. (*See for example* VALUE ENGINEERING, QUALITY FUNCTION DEPLOYMENT and TAGUCHI METHODS.)

This extended use of JIT principles is sometimes termed lean production. The term lean production was introduced by Krafcik and McDuffie (1989) to interpret how JIT thinking had radically altered the stakes in relation to traditional Western concepts of mass production:

> It uses less of everything compared with mass production – half the human effort in the factory, half the manufacturing space, half the investment in tools, half the engineering hours to develop a product in half the time. Also, it requires keeping far less than half the needed inventory on site, results in many fewer defects, and produces a greater and ever-growing variety of products.

See also **planning and control; push and pull planning and control; trade-offs**

Bibliography

Chase, R. B. & Aquilano, N. J. (1992). *Production and operations management.* Homewood, IL: Irwin.

Harrison, A. S. (1992). *Just-in-time manufacturing in perspective.* Hemel Hempstead: Prentice-Hall.

Krafcik, J. F. & McDuffie, J. P. (1989). *Explaining high performance manufacturing: The international automotive assembly plant study.* Cambridge, MA: IMVP, MIT Press.

Ohno, T. (1988). *Toyota production system: Beyond large scale production.* Cambridge, MA: Productivity Press.

Oliver, N. & Wilkinson, B. (1992). *The Japanisation of British industry.* Oxford: Blackwell.

Schonberger, R. J. (1982). *Japanese manufacturing techniques: Nine hidden lessons in simplicity.* New York: Free Press.

Shingo, S. (1989). *A study of the Toyota production system from an industrial engineering viewpoint.* Cambridge, MA: Productivity Press.

Womack, J. P., Jones, D. T. & Roos, D. (1990). *The machine that changed the world.* New York: Rawson Associates.

ALAN HARRISON

K

kanban *Kanban* is the Japanese word for card or signal. In JUST-IN-TIME production it is the means by which a customer (or succeeding operation) instructs a supplier (or preceding operation) to send more parts. *Kanban* is also the means by which part movements are synchronized during the course of manufacture. In a repetitive manufacturing environment, there is often no requirement to schedule parts to be made in batches in response to a central instruction (as in MATERIAL REQUIREMENTS PLANNING (MRP)). Instead, the aim is to orchestrate part movements only as needed in response to a "rate-based" schedule. The rate is derived from the short-term factory assembly schedule which regulates part movements throughout the production system. A *kanban* is the mechanism by which this is communicated from one operation to another. The same thinking can apply to suppliers, so that *kanban*s may be used to regulate supplier deliveries. The concept which the use of *kanban*s helps to promote is often described as a series of "invisible conveyors" which deliver parts just-in-time to the succeeding operations.

Kanban is a simple to operate, visible control system which offers the opportunity to delegate routine material control transactions to the shop floor. Many transactions can be removed from MRP altogether (*see* JIT/MRP). The aim is to facilitate close, evolving linkages between steps in the production process. Regularity at the front end is translated into a consistent distribution of work at all preceding processes.

The scheduling system is referred to as pull scheduling because the emphasis is on each process pulling more parts from the preceding process(es) in line with demand (*see* PUSH AND PULL PLANNING AND CONTROL).

Types of Kanban

There are three basic types of *kanban*, classified by their intended purpose.

A conveyance *kanban* is used to signal to a previous stage that material can be withdrawn from inventory and transferred to a specific destination. This type of *kanban* would normally have details of the particular parts name and number, the place where it should be taken from, and the destination to where it is being delivered. A production *kanban* is a signal to a production process that it can start producing a part or item to be placed in an inventory. The information contained on this type of *kanban* usually includes the particular part's name and number, a description of the process itself, the materials required for the production of the part, and the destination to which the part or parts need to be sent when they are produced. A vendor *kanban* is used to signal to a supplier to send material or parts to a stage. In this way it is similar to a conveyance *kanban* but it is usually used with external suppliers.

Whichever kind of *kanban* is being used the principle is always that the receipt of a *kanban* triggers the conveyance, or production, or supply of one unit or a standard container of units. If two *kanban*s are received it triggers the conveyance, production, or supply of two units or standard containers of units and so on.

There are also numerous variants of *kanban*. Some of the more popular are as follows:

- *Kanban* cards: cards or tokens are sent from customer to supplier to indicate that more parts are needed. A fresh supply of parts is accompanied by the *kanban* card or token-which triggered the movement. The card or token is then available for reuse, and the cycle repeats.

- Messages and golf balls: the customer processes signals that more parts are needed by telephone, by electronic message, or by simply shouting "send me some more!" An internal variant is to roll color-coded balls (color referring to the required part number) down a tube. An external variant is the "faxban" (the use of a fax to transmit signals).

- Priority *kanban*s: tokens may be color coded to indicate priority: red for top, amber for moderate, and green for normal. Parts are pulled in the order green, amber, red and made in reverse order.

- Container as *kanban*: the empty container which holds a given number of parts of a given type is returned to the preceding process after it has been exhausted. It acts as the instruction to the preceding process to make more.

- Colored squares can act to limit the amount of inventory that is permitted in the system. Once a square is full, work at the preceding process must stop.

- Packaging: parts are stored in two bins. As the first is emptied, it is placed at the back of the rack to act as a signal that it must be replaced.

- Sequence: where there are many possible variants of a given sub-assembly or part, it is necessary to give specific instructions using product cards or "broadcast" systems, which launch sub-assemblies in the exact sequence to meet a given product requirement.

There are two procedures which can govern the use of *kanban*s. These are known as the single card system and the dual card system. The single card system is most often used because it is by far the simplest system to operate. It uses only conveyance *kanban*s (or vendor *kanban*s when receiving supply of material from an outside source). The dual card system uses both conveyance and production *kanban*s, and, although the more complex procedure, gives tighter control.

Kanban Operation

The rules for the use of *kanban*s are simple but most JIT authorities stress that they must be strictly adhered to:

- Each container must have a *kanban* card which shows the part number and description, user and maker locations, and quantity.

- Parts are always pulled by the succeeding process.

- No parts are pulled without a *kanban* card.

- All containers hold exactly their stated number of parts.

- No defective parts may be sent to the succeeding process.

- The preceding process may only make enough parts to replace those withdrawn.

- The number of *kanban*s should be progressively reduced over time so as to minimize the amount of inventory between production stages.

Such rules help to create great orderliness in an operating environment. Each container must have its set number of parts, there must be a set number of containers in any situation, and each must have an allocated position. A high level of discipline is promoted on the shop floor, and part count accuracy is naturally improved, because of which stocktaking becomes fast, simple, and accurate.

The number of *kanban*s in a given loop is governed by the part cost, the replacement lead time, the risk of running out and transport considerations (weight, volume, etc.). The aim, when determining the number of *kanban*s, is to balance the overall stockholding level against the value, risk and number of inventory related transactions. Some items might be replenished in larger quantities than others because they are low value and/or used in large quantities. Where there is seasonality in demand, then the number of *kanban*s may be flexed in line with expected variations by using MRP to make the necessary prediction of the overall required output rate.

Where manufacture is not repetitive, then *kanban*s become less appropriate. It would be counterproductive to maintain *kanban* containers of seldom used parts (*see* JIT/MRP). A further potential limitation is disruptions like breakdowns and absenteeism. *Kanban* models an orderly, regulated environment where customer demand is met instantaneously. At best, disruptions result in excessive stock: at worst, the system becomes inoperable.

See also **JIT tools and techniques; inventory management**

Bibliography

Harrison, A. S. (1992). *Just-in-time manufacturing in perspective*. Hemel Hempstead: Prentice-Hall.
Karmarkar, U. S. (1989). Getting control of just-in-time. *Harvard Business Review*, **67**, 5.
Vollman, T. E., Berry, W. L. & Whybark, D. C. (1992). *Manufacturing planning and control systems*. Homewood, IL: Irwin.

ALAN HARRISON

L

layout The term layout is used to mean the physical location of an operation's facilities, (machines, equipment, and staff) within the operation. It determines the way in which the transformed resources of the operation (the materials, information, and customers) flow through the operation. This, in turn, can affect the costs and general effectiveness of the operation. The term LOCATION is more usually applied for the positioning of facilities geographically.

Layout is often a lengthy and difficult task because of the physical size of the transforming resources being moved, even when size is not an issue. The relayout of an existing operation can disrupt its smooth running, leading to customer dissatisfaction or lost production. Furthermore, if the layout is poorly designed, it can lead to over-long or confused flow patterns and inventories of materials or customer queues building up in the operation. It is the combination of these two points which gives the layout activity its character. Changing a layout can be difficult and expensive to execute so operations managers are reluctant to do it frequently, yet the consequences of any misjudgments in an operation's layout will have a considerable, and usually long-term, effect on the operation.

There are many different ways of arranging physical facilities. But most practical layouts are derived from only three basic layout types: FIXED POSITION LAYOUT, PROCESS LAYOUT, and PRODUCT LAYOUT. A fourth type, CELL LAYOUT, is usually regarded as a hybrid of product and process layout.

Bibliography

Apple, J. M. (1977). *Plant layout and materials handling*. New York: Wiley.

NIGEL SLACK

learning curves Learning curves are the functions which predict the reduction of labor input per unit of manufactured output. The concept can be applied at both micro and macro levels.

At the micro level when a worker is first trained to carry out a specific task, the performance on that task will naturally be poor. As the worker gains experience and develops the work-specific skills, performance will improve. The rate at which such improvement is made will depend on a number of factors such as the complexity of the work, the cycle time of the work, the ability of the workers, and their experience of similar work. However, in all cases, the rate of improvement will decrease over time as the worker becomes more proficient. A learning curve is a graphical representation of the improvement in performance and for most work follows a general asymptotic pattern. The graph normally relates performance (measured as job completion time) either to time on the job, or to the number of job cycles completed.

Where WORK MEASUREMENT is used to establish the standard time for a job, it is possible to plot on the curve the desired end-point of an induction or training period and to measure operator performance over time against this end-point. Where a learning curve has been established by prior observation of a range of workers adjusting to the same work, it is possible to measure the progress of a new worker to the present time, and then to predict further rates of progress from the shape of the curve. Where a payment system based on individual performance is in use, it is common to add a "learner allowance" to the standard time to form an "allowed time" for a trainee. Similarly, where a payment system is based on team or group performance, it is common to compensate the team for the poor performance of new members of the team. If learning curves are available for the work, any allowance or compensatory payments can be adjusted over time as the trainee moves along the curve.

At the macro level learning curves can be used to relate the total cost per unit (or value added per unit) to the cumulative output. At this level they are often called "experience curves." The relationship between cost and output usually assumes that costs decrease by the reciprocal of some function of cumulative output. This is often expressed as the amount cost decreases for each doubling of cumulative output. So, for example, an 80 percent experience curve means that costs reduce to 80 percent of their value when cumulative output doubles. For simplicity this relationship can be drawn on logarithmic scales which will show a straight line relationship.

See also cost; volume

Bibliography

Abernathy, W. J. & Wayne, K. (1974). Limits to the learning curve. *Harvard Business Review*, **52**, *8*, 109–19.

JOHN HEAP

leveled scheduling In PLANNING AND CONTROL IN OPERATIONS it is possible to consider the leveling of scheduled material movements so that each movement is co-ordinated with the others when work cycles repeat. "Co-ordination" here refers to the timing and volumes of material movements. This consideration can be extended from the factory to suppliers and customers so that material movements are co-ordinated throughout the supply chain. Leveled scheduling is an important aspect of JUST-IN-TIME philosophy, and plays a key role in the Toyota production system, where it is referred to as *heijunka*.

According to the RUNNERS, REPEATERS, AND STRANGERS classification, runners and repeaters are prime candidates for leveled scheduling. Strangers must be scheduled by alternative means, such as MATERIAL REQUIREMENTS PLANNING (*see* JIT/MRP).

Leveled scheduling involves distributing volume and mix evenly over a given production timespan. Output thereby matches customer demand as closely as possible at any instant during that timespan. The development of leveled scheduling is illustrated in Figure 1. Suppose that we begin with a weekly production schedule for a range of three products A, B, and C which runs at 200 of product A, 120 of B, and 80 of product C. Assume that the customer for these products is using them evenly across the product range. Then producing them in large batches according to weekly usage will create inventories of finished product, and lead to production peaks which impose excessive work on one team at a time in preceding processes. Instead, it is better to level the finished product schedule as much as possible, and to downdate that leveling to production of sub-assemblies and components as well. To begin, the batch sizes could be reduced to five of product A followed by three of product B followed by two of product C. But even greater leveling of "runners" can be produced by scheduling in the sequence AABABCABCA. This is called a mixed-model assembly sequence, and achieves maximum repetition in the shortest cycle. Mixed model assembly allows close tracking of changes to mix in demand for the products, and finished product inventory should be at a minimum. However, mixed model assembly is the most extreme approach to leveled scheduling in terms of set-ups. Therefore, it only becomes possible as SET-UP REDUCTION leads to short set-up times. Also, mixed model assembly places increased pressure on operators, who must cope with constantly changing product mixes. Use of error-proof devices (*see* FAIL-SAFING) to make it impossible to produce non-conforming products therefore becomes a necessary feature of this approach.

Leveled scheduling places a number of demands on a production system. Operators must be capable of switching quickly between different product mixes, transferring between areas of high demand and areas of low demand,

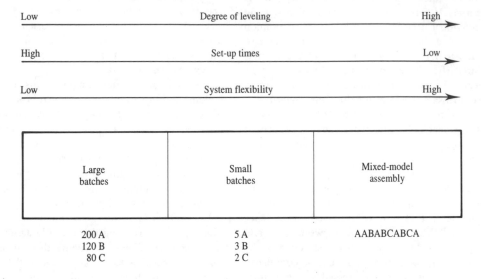

Figure 1 Leveled scheduling

and taking on different tasks. The processing capacity of each machine also needs to be harmonized. A frequent temptation is to use the capacity of a machine to the fullest, but leveled scheduling principles indicate that the output of each process should be leveled to whatever is needed to produce the required output. This often means that machines are "derated," inasmuch as the output from them is deliberately reduced so that it is co-ordinated with other processes.

A related concept is that of the "band width" (Vollman et al., 1992) of a production system, which is a measure of its surge capacity to handle changes in volume and mix across a given range. If the objective of leveled scheduling is to be able to make any product in any sequence with no disruption, many processes only need to meet full surge capacity occasionally. Such processes are therefore usually run below capacity, and may often be shut down.

Bibliography

Schonberger, R. J. (1982). *Japanese manufacturing techniques: Nine hidden lessons in simplicity.* New York: Free Press.

Shingo, S. (1988). *Non-stock production: The Shingo system for continuous improvement.* Cambridge, MA: Productivity Press.

Shingo, S. (1989). *A study of the Toyota production system from an industrial engineering viewpoint.* Cambridge, MA: Productivity Press.

Vollman, T. E., Berry, W. L. & Whybark, D. C. (1992). *Manufacturing planning and control systems.* Homewood, IL: Irwin.

ALAN HARRISON

lifecycle effects   One way of generalizing the relative importance of OPERATIONS OBJECTIVES is to link them to the lifecycle of the products being produced. Lifecycle theory holds that a product passes through several distinct stages, introduction, growth, maturity, and decline. Products require different marketing, financial, manufacturing, purchasing, and personnel strategies, in each stage of their lifecycle.

This last point is particularly important for all operations managers. It implies that the way in which operations should be managed and the objectives they should set themselves will change as a product ages in its market. When a product or service is first introduced it is likely to be presented to the market on the basis that it is novel in some way. Because the number of customers are few and their needs are not perfectly understood, the design of the product or service could be subject to frequent change.

The operations management of the company can best contribute to competitiveness by developing the FLEXIBILITY to cope with changes in the specification of the product or service and possibly also in its output volume. At the same time they will also need to maintain QUALITY levels so as not to undermine the performance of the product/service.

If products survive their introduction to the market they will begin to be more widely adopted, and VOLUME starts to grow. The design of the product or service could start to standardize. Supplying demand could prove to be the main preoccupation of organizations which have products or services in this part of the lifecycle. Rapid and dependable response will help to keep demand buoyant, while ensuring that the company keeps its share of the market as competition starts to increase (*see* TIME-BASED PERFORMANCE and DELIVERY DEPENDABILITY).

After a period of rapid growth, products "mature." Demand starts to level off and the designs of the products or services may also stabilize to a few standard types. Competition will almost certainly move to emphasize price or value for money, although individual companies might try to prevent this by attempting to differentiate themselves in some way. This increasingly price-conscious environment means that operations will be expected to improve its COST performance, either to maintain profits or to allow price cutting, or both. Therefore cost and PRODUCTIVITY issues, together with dependable supply, are likely to be the operation's main concerns.

When the product has been in the market for some time, the need which it was filling will eventually be largely met and sales will decline. For companies left with the old products or services there might be a residual market but, if capacity in the industry lags demand, the market will continue to be dominated by price competition. Operations objectives will therefore still be dominated by cost.

See also **manufacturing strategy; performance measurement; order-winners and qualifiers**

Bibliography

Hayes, R. H. & Wheelwright, S. C. (1984). *Restoring our competitive edge: Competing on manufacturing.* New York: Wiley.

NIGEL SLACK

line balancing Line balancing is a technique used in connection with the design of PRODUCT LAYOUT or "lines." The term "balancing" is used because one of its main objectives is to minimize the idle time and spread it as evenly as possible across the work stations.

When balancing a line the following factors need to be taken into account:

- the required output rate or cycle time (which depends on the demand for the product);

- precedence constraints (these are restrictions on the order in which tasks can be done; in other words certain tasks will have "predecessor tasks" which must be done first);

- zoning constraints (these are restrictions on where certain tasks or combinations of tasks should, or should not, take place);

- whether there is a need for work station duplication or replication (this would be the case when any task takes longer than the available cycle time).

The line balancing problem comprises two aspects: determination of the required number of stations, and the assignment of tasks to each station with the objective of maximizing efficiency (by minimizing idle time and spreading it evenly across work stations).

The effectiveness of the balance decision is measured by the "balance loss" of the line. The balance loss is the time invested in making one product which is lost through imbalance, expressed as a percentage of the total time investment. For a paced n stage line the time lost through imbalance is the cumulative difference between the stations' allocated work times and the cycle time allowed by the pacing of the line. For unpaced lines it is the cumulative difference between each stage's work time and that of the stage with the largest work time (this effectively governs the cycle time of the whole line) (*see* BOTTLENECKS).

A very simple line balancing problem may be solvable by "trial and error." Most practical problems, however, are extremely complex, requiring thousands of tasks to be assigned across hundreds of work stations and with numerous precedence and zoning constraints to be taken into account.

To solve such problems a large number of heuristic algorithms have been developed, such as the Kilbridge and Wester method and the ranked positional weights technique. Being based on heuristics, or "rules" which have been tested empirically, such techniques can provide good, though not necessarily optimal, results. More recently, simulation has grown in popularity as an approach to balancing lines and a visual interactive simulation can allow the line designed to immediately see the effect of any modifications made.

Product layouts have traditionally been used to produce highly standardized products, but today the demand is for a greater variety of products or models. Therefore two types of line are now in widespread use and require a modification to the traditional line balancing approach. These are multimodel lines, where the line is reorganized periodically to produce different models or variants, and mixed model lines, where the line is designed to allow simultaneous production of any model or variant without reorganization.

The aim in multimodel line balancing should be to minimize total production cost, taking account of the additional factor of change-over costs. For very large batches the problem degenerates into the successive application of single model line balancing.

The main costs of an operator changing from one product to another are connected with reallocation of inventory and equipment to work stations and LEARNING CURVES of operatives in new jobs. To reduce these the number of stations and location of equipment should be constant whenever possible, and work elements common to more than one model should always be performed by the same operator. Since work content and production requirements vary between models the cycle times are the best factors to manipulate in reducing idle time, but balancing efficiency may be sacrificed for compatibility. The total balance loss will be the average per model, weighted in proportion to production ratios. A sensible ploy is to balance the line for the most popular model and to adjust this basic arrangement by empirical methods for the other models. If this is unsatisfactory, the steps may be repeated but centered on the model of second highest production volumes, etc.

For very small batches the problem is akin to the mixed model line. Here, achieving a good long-term balance is more difficult and depends on the sequencing of model types proceeding down the line. One approach is to balance the line using a range of task times for each activity.

Bibliography

Wild, R. (1972). *Mass production management.* London: Wiley.

DAVID BENNETT

location Facility location is the physical positioning of an organization's operations geographically. Because of the usually long-term nature of the decision the facility location decision is important to any organization, regardless of whether it is making goods or delivering services.

Facility location can take place at a number of different levels. At one extreme there is the highest level INTERNATIONAL LOCATION decision where a global or pan-national organization makes a choice of region or country in which to locate a manufacturing or service facility. After choosing a country, the area, town or city might be chosen, after which an individual site is selected.

There are a number of different objectives that an organization can seek to achieve when making a location decision:

● minimization of operating COSTS;

● minimization of material and goods transportation;

● maximization of sales revenue;

● minimum movement of people (staff and/or customers);

● minimum movement of machinery and equipment;

● maximization of profit.

As far as the factors influencing location are concerned these can be classed as either tangible or intangible. Tangible factors include the cost of land, the cost of buildings, labor costs (direct and indirect), transport costs (of materials and goods), and cost of power. Intangible factors associated with location include, community attitudes, environmental constraints, ease of communications, competition for skills, industrial relations, and weather conditions. A third group of factors will include those that can be manipulated by national and local governments or other authorities, such as regional assistance for industry, taxation and tariff regimes, and market subsidies.

Although organizations often claim to base their location decisions on objective criteria, it is generally accepted that subjectivity is a major component of the decision-making process, particularly where it is dominated by intangible factors. Many location decisions are made by managers on the basis of a hunch or personal preference.

Where a location decision is being made based on objective criteria there are two basic approaches: the evaluation of pre-selected alternative locations, and the determination of the optimum location. Although these two approaches differ in terms of the way they define the location problem they are not mutually exclusive. For example, the second approach might not yield a single "optimum" and a secondary assessment may be required to choose the preferred location based on supplementary criteria.

The methods for evaluating alternative locations include simple comparison of cost factors (based on fixed volumes), analysis of fixed and variable costs (based on different volumes), and transport cost minimization for alternative additional sites.

Two methods are commonly used for determining the optimum location, the transport cost equilibrium model, and the market equilibrium model.

Bibliography

Finch, B. J. & Luebbe, R. L. (1995). *Operations management*. Fort Worth, TX: The Dryden Press.

DAVID BENNETT

logistics   There are many different definitions of logistics. The US Council of Logistics Management defines it as "the process of planning, implementing and controlling the efficient flow and storage of goods, services and related information from point of origin to point of consumption for the purpose of conforming to customer requirements" (Christopher, 1993). However, it is not clear from this definition whether "origin" refers to original source of material (in which case the definition is very similar to one definition of SUPPLY CHAIN MANAGEMENT) or whether it refers to the material and information flow associated with finished products (in which case logistics is more akin to PHYSICAL DISTRIBUTION MANAGEMENT. Other authorities see the logistical process of a firm as cutting across every internal organizational unit and reaching out to encompass customers and suppliers (which is more akin to another definition of supply chain management as management of the internal supply chain).

Most of the written work in logistics has been performed by ex-marketing or ex-physical distribution management authors; therefore they naturally tend to consider planning, control, and distribution of finished products. There is little evidence of the term logistics being used to include operations further upstream into the supply network.

See also **vertical integration; materials management**

Bibliography

Bowersox, D. J., Daugherty, P. J., Droge, C. L., German, R. N. & Rogers, D. S. (1992). *Logistical excellence: It's not business as usual*. Digital Press.
Christopher, M. G. (1992). *Logistics and supply chain management*. London: Pitman.

CHRISTINE HARLAND

lot sizing in MRP   Lot sizing (or batching) in MRP refers to the modification of the net requirement quantities before they are translated into planned orders in a MATERIAL REQUIREMENTS PLANNING (MRP) system (*see* NETTING PROCESS IN MRP).

If net requirements were translated directly into planned orders, it would result in manufacturing component schedules and purchasing schedules which did not take any account of the cost of machine set-ups or the cost of ordering. In other words, making the requirements as they occur on a period by period basis, otherwise known as the lot-for-lot policy, may certainly reduce overall stockholding costs, depending on the size of planning period chosen, but may increase costs incurred through excessive set-up and ordering activities for small batches.

To take account of the total costs of managing the materials, that is holding costs and ordering or set-up costs, batch sizing rules or ordering policies may need to be applied to the net requirements to produce planned orders for the manufacturing or purchasing of items.

There are basically three different groups of methods of batching requirements together. These are fixed quantity batching rules, fixed period coverage batching rules, and dynamic batching rules.

Fixed quantity batching rules essentially state that every time an item is manufactured or bought it is done so in batches of minimum size X, or multiples of X. The fixed multiple batch size may be determined by a physical constraint of a manufacturing process, for example furnace or oven size, by considering the quantity that would normally be produced in one shift or in one week, or, most frequently, by the size of container that is used to transport the item.

The minimum fixed quantity batch size is usually determined by some form of economic calculation. This could take account of price breaks or discounts for quantity or it might use the so-called ECONOMIC ORDER QUANTITY (EOQ) formula as used in traditional INVENTORY MANAGEMENT approaches. However, it should be noted that in a MRP system environment, the assumptions upon which the EOQ calculation is based are not valid, that is; a continuous review inventory system is not in operation and there may not be continuous demand and a gradual depletion of the stock of the item (*see* INVENTORY CONTROL SYSTEMS). Consequently, although the EOQ may be a guide to the best batch size, it cannot be guaranteed that its implementation will result in minimizing total inventory operating costs.

Fixed period coverage batching rules calculate a batch size by batching together the net requirements for the next y periods ahead. The coverage period may be chosen to fit in with a cycle scheduling approach to shop loading where, for example, machined components may be manufactured on a three weekly repeated cycle with one third of components starting in week one, one third in week two and so on. If the choice is not determined by this constraint, an economic coverage period may be calculated by relating the economic order quantity calculation to an equivalent number of time periods' coverage.

With dynamic batching rules, the computer uses an algorithm which attempts to arrive at a batching schedule which minimizes inventory operating costs. Dynamic rules include the following: least unit cost, least total cost (part period algorithm), McLaren's order moment and Wagner-Whitin.

As an example, the least total cost (part period) algorithm consists of computing the cumulative holding costs and stopping at the batch size just short of the point where cumulative holding costs exceed the set-up cost. It makes the cost comparison by first calculating the ratio of the set-up cost to the holding cost per period known as the part period value (PPV), i.e. how many parts may be held for how many periods whose holding cost will equate to the set-up cost. For example, if the set-up cost for an item was $500 and the holding cost was $0.3 per period, the PPV would be 500/0.3, which equals 1667 part periods.

Each type of batching rule has its own advantages and disadvantages. The fixed quantity rule is easily understood and may fit in well with manufacturing process constraints or suppliers' standard order sizes. However, it suffers from the drawbacks of generating orders at irregular intervals and, compared to,the other methods of batching, it generates higher stock levels. In a non-repetitive manufacturing environment it can also generate extra stocks which may become obsolete. Since the fixed period coverage rule is directly related to the future period's requirements it is more economical in terms of the overall stock level generated and, as mentioned previously, it may fit in well with the balancing of the workload on the shop floor.

However, it may result in sizes of batches which fluctuate considerably, especially if there are periods with zero net requirements. Theoretically the dynamic batching rules are superior to the other two methods of batch sizing in the reduction of costs. However, they suffer the disadvantages of not being understood as easily and of generating differing batch sizes at uncertain time intervals which, in turn, may lead to difficulties in shop loading.

Bibliography

Vollman, T. E., Berry, W. L. & Whybark, D. C. (1992). *Manufacturing planning and control systems.* New York: Irwin.

PETER BURCHER

M

maintenance Maintenance is the term used to cover the activities and decisions by which organizations try to avoid failures in their operations by caring for their physical facilities. It is an important part of most operation's activities, especially those whose physical facilities play a central role in creating its goods and services, such as power stations, hotels, airlines, and petrochemical refineries. In such operations maintenance activities typically will account for a significant proportion of operations management's time, attention, and resources.

Maintenance activities, however, are not the only influence on the failure performance of physical facilities, the two indicators of which are generally taken to be the "mean time between failure" (MTBF) and the "mean time to repair" (MTTR) (*see* FAILURE MEASURES). MTTR is influenced by the ease with which facilities can be repaired which includes such factors as ease of fault diagnosis, ease of access, and ease of repair or replacement. MTBF is influenced by the way in which facilities are used by staff and/or customers, the intrinsic robustness of the facilities design, and the care regime used for the facilities. Different approaches to maintenance take different views of the extent to which all these factors come within the legitimate scope of the subject. A minimalist approach such as "run to breakdown" intervenes only when failure occurs, whereas TOTAL PRODUCTIVE MAINTENANCE encompasses all the above factors.

The benefits of maintenance are generally taken to include some, or all, of the following:

- enhanced safety, in that well-maintained facilities are less likely to behave in an unpredictable or non-standard way, or fail outright, all of which could pose a hazard to staff;

- increased reliability, which in turn leads to less time lost while facilities are repaired, less disruption to the normal activities of the operation, less variation in output rates and more reliable service levels;

- higher quality because badly maintained equipment is more likely to perform below standard and cause quality errors;

- lower operating costs since many process technologies run more efficiently when regularly serviced;

- longer life-span of equipment because regular care, cleaning, or lubrication can reduce the (perhaps small) problems whose cumulative effect causes wear or deterioration;

- higher end value since well-maintained facilities are generally easier to dispose of.

In practice an organization's maintenance activities will consist of some combination of the three basic approaches to the care of its physical facilities. These are run to breakdown (RTB), PREVENTIVE MAINTENANCE (PM), and CONDITION-BASED MAINTENANCE (CBM). As its name implies, run to breakdown maintenance involves allowing the facilities to continue operating until they fail. Maintenance work is performed only after failure has taken place. Preventive maintenance attempts to eliminate or reduce the chances of failure by servicing (cleaning, lubricating, replacing, and checking) the facilities at pre-planned intervals. Condition-based maintenance attempts to perform maintenance only when the facilities require it. Some characteristics of the line (such as vibration) would be monitored and the results of this monitoring would then be used to decide whether an intervention is needed.

Each approach to maintaining facilities is appropriate for different circumstances. RTB is often used where repair is relatively straightforward (so the consequence of failure is small), or where regular maintenance is very costly (making PM expensive), or where failure is not at all predictable (so there is no advantage in PM because failure is just as likely to occur after repair as before). PM is used when the cost of unplanned failure is high (because of disruption to normal operations) and where failure is not totally random (so the maintenance time can be scheduled before failure becomes very likely). CMB is used where the maintenance activity is expensive, either because of the cost of providing the maintenance itself, or because of the disruption which the maintenance activity causes to the operation. However, many operations adopt a mixture of these approaches because different elements of their facilities have different characteristics.

See also **reliability-centered maintenance**

NIGEL SLACK

manufacturing processes Manufacturing operations are made up of transformation processes (*see* TRANSFORMATION MODELS) which are conventionally classified according to their VOLUME and VARIETY characteristics. Some operations produce products of a single type in very large volumes with little or no choice of design or product range. At the opposite extreme, operations may provide unique or highly customized outputs which exactly meet the specific requirements of individual customers. In practice, most operations fall between these extremes, producing some range of designs of products or services in a variety of volumes, and usually having to respond to changes in mix of outputs as market requirements vary.

The necessity for some classification of processes derives from the assumption that no single manufacturing process could ever be appropriate for all circumstances. For example, processes designed to produce efficiently high volumes of single products will usually have little FLEXIBILITY, in that it would be both expensive and time consuming to adapt them to make other products. Conversely, processes designed for low volume, high variety products or services are designed to achieve fast, low-cost change-overs from one product type to another. From this it is intuitively reasonable to suppose that different generic designs of manufacturing process (the term process choice is commonly used) for products with different volume and variety characteristics will be required.

The names adopted for these general manufacturing process types can have slightly different meanings in different parts of the world. In particular, North American terminology uses some classifications which are different to those in Europe. Similarly, the colloquial use of these process names may also in practice differ between individual industries or plants. The underlying principle of all process classifications, however, is that transformation processes should be designed to best match the volume and variety characteristics of the required outputs.

In order of increasing volume and decreasing variety the conventional manufacturing process types are as follows:

- project processes;
- jobbing processes;
- batch processes;
- line processes;
- continuous processes.

Project

In addition to representing an emerging sub-category of operations management as a whole, the term "project" is also used to describe an extreme form of process (*see* PROJECT MANAGEMENT). At one time those processes which were categorized as "projects" were associated with the construction industry and large, complex engineering tasks. The general characteristics of these projects are that they have a relatively large work content, a diverse and complex set of inputs, and a long timescale often extending over years from design to completion. These types of project may be physically large, necessitating a FIXED POSITION LAYOUT.

More recently, it has become accepted that the use of project processes and principles has spread beyond these industries, to encompass both services and complex, but more "portable" products. Examples include software development, international marketing campaigns, privatization projects by government, and television program production. However, all project processes deal with very low volume and high variety.

Jobbing

Like project processes, jobbing processes produce products or services tailored to suit the requirements of individual orders, in very small quantities, in a form that is not expected to repeat. However, smaller scale, reduced work content, and lower complexity of jobbing often allows the work to be completed in fewer stages. Because transport of the product is possible, all stages of manufacture can be undertaken by a single operative at specialized work stations or machines which are often arranged in a PROCESS LAYOUT, although fixed position layouts may also be used. As a result, the operatives will usually possess wide skills (to operate a range of technologies) and may be given considerable responsibility in planning and executing their tasks.

Jobbing is used in most sectors to satisfy customers who want specially made products or services, but usually cost is higher than more standardized products because of higher labor cost and lower equipment utilization compared to higher volume processes. Jobbing businesses, therefore, usually compete by providing high levels of flexibility, quality, or responsiveness. Jobbing businesses or departments are sometimes referred to as job shops, but in North America this term may also encompass batch processes.

Batch

Most operations are designed to provide an ongoing output of repeating products to satisfy their markets, at such a level of demand which cannot be economically satisfied by jobbing processes. Batch processes are frequently used to cover this middle ground of volume and variety so that labor and general-purpose equipment are shared across the range of products. This involves the transformation together of predetermined quantities of a product, known as a batch or lot (hence the name batch process). Usually the stages of manufacturing are clearly separated, and may be located in separate specialized areas, usually in a PROCESS LAYOUT form, although at the higher volume end of batch manufacturing PRODUCT LAYOUT may be used.

Each of the stages of manufacture begins by setting up the equipment in preparation for the processing of the complete batch of the product. Because these set-ups take time and cost money, operations will usually plan to transform many items at a time, to minimize the unit cost (*see* ECONOMIC ORDER QUANTITY) and SET-UP REDUCTION).

The operatives at each processing stage may be skilled only in one part of the process, and because all the items in a batch are processed at separate stages, periods of added value processing are separated by periods of non-added value movement and delay. This results in the intermittent flow of materials and is associated with high levels of work-in-progress. The ratio of total added value processing time to total time in the system (throughput efficiency) is characteristically very low in batch manufacturing. This may be considered unacceptable where markets require fast response from order to delivery (*see* TIME-BASED PERFORMANCE).

Despite this, batch processing remains the most common form of process in manufacturing. The main advantages are that this approach has the flexibility to allow a very wide range of outputs to be produced in differing volumes, while simultaneously maintaining high levels of utilization.

Line

Where volumes are sufficiently high, line processes (sometimes referred to as "flow" or "mass" processes) are often preferred, particularly where high volume involves repetitive but large work content tasks such as the assembly of complex automotive, electrical, or electronic products.

The underlying principles of line processes is that transformation is divided into steps which can be completed in similar times (*see* LINE BALANCING) which are then usually arranged as a PRODUCT LAYOUT. When operating, the transformed resources are moved progressively along the stages of the process (sometimes known as stations). For much of the time in the process, value is being added to products and so throughput efficiency can be high, work-in-progress inventory low, and output consistent and predictable. There is a smooth flow of movement through the process. In its classic form, line process produce only one product type at a consistent rate, regardless of fluctuations in market demand which must be provided through the use of inventory. Because variety is low, set-ups are infrequent.

Line processes may be highly capital intensive, comprising many dedicated technologies and materials movement systems. In these cases, the rate of transformation is usually predetermined and controlled by the technology. Such systems, known as machine-paced lines, are often highly automated, but where human effort is required, each task must be completed within the cycle time.

Other types of line process are designed to allow operators some control over the output rate: these are known as unpaced or worker paced. In some cases, this simply gives the team of operators control over the speed of the technology, such as the conveyors in assembly lines; in other cases, there is less use of technology, and the transformation is largely manned, with materials being passed from operator to operator by hand.

Continuous Process

High volume processing of bulk standard materials such as powders and liquids, requires dedicated equipment, configured in a product layout to complete the task in a fixed sequence. Such processes are termed continuous processes. They are often dominated by the technology of transformation with little labor input and little contact between the operatives and the materials. Labor may be predominantly used for the control and monitoring of the process, often through computer systems. This implies that some technical skills and knowledge will be needed.

Rather confusingly this type of manufacturing is sometimes referred to simply as process manufacturing, and some industries are referred to as process industries. This can be misleading, as they often involve the batch production of liquid or powder products, without the degree of dedication and absence of set-ups which is associated with continuous processes.

Process Choice

A key concept in the classification of manufacturing processes is that each process type occupies an overlapping but distinct position on a volume–variety continuum from low volume – high variety through to high volume – low variety. The volume–variety characteristics of a process type then imply a set of properties which define the design, planning, and control of the process. This is the basis of process choice which, at one level, can be seen as a predictive instrument inasmuch as it indicates the nature of operations management as being contingent upon the process type used. So, for example, as processes move from project through to continuous, material flow goes from intermittent to continuous, process technology goes from general purpose to dedicated, staff skills go from task oriented to system oriented, planning decisions go from being concerned with timing issues to being concerned with volume issues, control goes from detailed to aggregated, and so on. At another level, process choice can be seen as a diagnostic tool which detects inconsistency in operations management practice. So if an operation is charted in terms of its properties and activities, they should all be at the same point on their continuum which characterizes the spectrum from project to continuous processes. Any deviation implies a lack of internal coherence in the operation.

See also **volume; variety; transformation models; operations activities; layout; service processes**

Bibliography

Hill, T. J. (1991). *Production/operations management.* 2nd edn. London: Prentice-Hall.

STUART CHAMBERS

manufacturing resources planning Manufacturing resources planning (MRPII) is a structured approach to manufacturing management in which an integrated business system is used for the effective closed loop planning of all the resources of a manufacturing company. It is a direct outgrowth of CLOSED LOOP MRP which in turn is an extension of MATERIAL REQUIRE-MENTS PLANNING (MRPI).

It is made up of a variety of functions, each linked together, sharing much information on a central common database. These functions include all those incorporated in closed loop MRP such as: business planning, sales planning, production planning, resource requirements planning, MASTER PRODUCTION SCHEDULE, rough cut capacity planning, material requirements planning (MRPI), capacity requirements planning, input–output control, SCHEDULING, and dispatching. The extra functions which are included in MRPII are primarily the commercial, financial, and costing systems such as sales order processing, invoicing, purchase, sales and nominal ledgers, standard costing, actual product costing, and estimating/quoting.

MRPII systems provide information that is useful to all functional areas and encourage interdepartmental interaction. MRPII supports sales and marketing by providing an order-promising capability. This allows sales staff to have accurate information on product availability and gives them the ability to give customers accurate delivery dates. MRPII supports financial planning by converting material schedules into capital requirements. MRPII can be used to simulate the effects of different master production schedules on material usage, labor, process capacity, and capital requirements. MRPII provides the purchasing department with long-range planned order release schedules for developing long-range buying plans. Data in the MRPII system are used to provide accounting with information on material receipts to determine accounts payable. Shop floor control information may be used to track workers' hours for payroll purposes.

Other reports that can be produced from MRPII systems include full product costings at standard or actual cost, profit plans, cash flow plans, costed purchase commitments, shipping budgets, and inventory projections in value terms. Manufacturing resources planning (MRPII) can be viewed as a total approach to managing a business.

Over the years much has been written and a lot of research has been carried out into the reasons for success and failure in the implementation of MRPII systems. Among the main conclusions drawn are the need for a thorough understanding of the philosophy and discipline underlying MRPII, top management support, maintaining stability around the implementation and committing resources to support education and training. The Oliver Wight organization, which specializes in MRPII education and consultancy, developed an ABCD checklist in order to provide a universal measure of success in MRPII implementation. The original ABCD checklist was a questionnaire covering some of what the Oliver Wight Organization considered to be the key aspects of MRPII. These included the functionality of the software being used, the accuracy of the data held within the system, the way in which management was using the system, the extent of the training program undertaken, and a selection of operational performance measures. A grade was awarded to the company depending on the answers given. The ultimate accolade was to achieve Class A status.

Bibliography

Luscombe, M. (1993). *MRPII: Integrating the business.* Oxford: Butterworth Heinemann.

Wight, O. (1984). *Manufacturing resource planning: MRPII.* Essex Junction, VT: Oliver Wight Ltd.

Wilson, F., Desmond, J. & Roberts, H. (1994). Success and failure of MRPII implementation. *British Journal of Management*, 5, 221–40.

PETER BURCHER

manufacturing strategy   The need for manufacturing decisions to be made in a strategic context has been recognized for many years. The first developments in what is now known as manufacturing strategy took place at Harvard in the 1940s and 1950s. Researchers started looking at industries and began to see that there were many different ways in which companies were choosing to compete within particular industries. These in turn were accompanied by different choices concerning production technology and production management. From this developed a series of industry-based casebooks. These contained notes on the industry and its technological choices as well as case studies of different companies in the industry. Success and failure could be explained in many cases by the choices that the companies made and the alignment of these choices to competitive strategies. In many ways these early manufacturing strategy approaches presaged the development of the industry-based strategy approaches of economists.

Vital to the widespread dissemination of manufacturing strategy as a key area of concern was the pulling together of the lessons learnt in this industry-based study and teaching. This was done by Wickham Skinner in his two seminal articles: "Manufacturing: the missing link in corporate strategy" (1969) and "The focused factory" (1974). The first article set out the importance of explicit linkages between manufacturing choices and the firm's environment and corporate strategy. The second article developed the concept of focus and of internal as well as external consistency. The framework in the missing link article was very thorough, and much subsequent work has focused on parts of the framework, simplifying, and explaining rather than expanding.

A common way of viewing manufacturing strategy has been to separate the PROCESS OF MANUFACTURING STRATEGY FORMULATION from the CONTENT OF MANUFACTURING STRATEGY.

Since the early work of Skinner, writing and practice in manufacturing strategy has developed on several different fronts. The first of these can be characterized as competing through manufacturing. This is achieved through aligning the capabilities of manufacturing with the competitive requirements of the marketplace. The second is the approach based on internal and external consistency between the business and product context and the choices in the content of the manufacturing strategy. This is effectively a contingency-based approach. Finally there are approaches based on the need to adopt best practice, characterized by, for example, "world class manufacturing." We will explore each of these in turn.

Competing through Manufacturing

At its simplest this approach to manufacturing strategy argues that the role of manufacturing in competitive strategy is that the firm should compete through its manufacturing capabilities, and should align its capabilities with the key success factors, its corporate and marketing strategies, and the demands of the marketplace (*see* OPERATIONS ROLE).

The theme of deciding "how we are to compete" recurs repeatedly in many forms in manufacturing strategy literature. Cost, quality, dependability, and flexibility (*see* OPERATIONS OBJECTIVES) have become widely used as statements of the competitive dimensions of manufacturing. One of the best formulated approaches is that of Hill (1993) who developed the concept of ORDER-WINNERS AND QUALIFIERS. His "order-winning criteria" include price, delivery, quality, product design, and variety. Similar sets of criteria or priorities have been developed by most writers in manufacturing strategy. Hill also argues that although companies "win orders" based on particular criteria, this does not mean that other criteria are not important. He develops the idea of "qualifying" criteria, performance criteria that a company must meet if it is to be in a market, even if they do not win orders. He suggests methodologies for identifying order-winning and qualifying criteria.

The choice of competitive priorities and international comparisons of different countries has also been widely studied. Such approaches are consistent with the business strategy concepts of writers such as Porter. His generic strategies of cost leadership, differentiation, and focus can be considered as business priorities directing manufacturing choice and management. A number of authors have defined GENERIC MANUFACTURING STRATEGIES: one such group comprises cost-, technology-, and market-driven strategies; others have developed taxonomies of manufacturing strategies.

The underlying argument of this paradigm is that aligning the capabilities of manufacturing with the key success factors will maximize the competitiveness of a firm. This can involve, for example, choosing manufacturing technology to achieve particular desired capabilities, or developing capabilities to develop and launch new products rapidly.

Hayes and Wheelwright (1984), propose a four-stage development of a businesses ability to compete through manufacturing (*see* OPERATIONS ROLE). To be able to do this they argue that companies should go beyond looking to align capabilities with the marketplace. Manufacturing should seek to influence corporate strategies and to proactively develop and exploit manufacturing capability as a competitive weapon.

There has been wide-ranging work on identification, development, and measurement of manufacturing capability. For example, much attention has been paid to the area of time-based competition, and the technologies and capabilities needed to achieve it. Others have examined the role of FLEXIBILITY in manufacturing. More recent work has tried to link the views of manufacturing capability with resource-based theories of strategy (Powell, 1995).

A further element of this paradigm is the argument that through clear articulation of corporate missions and strategies a company's vision will be shared by its managers and other employees. In the manufacturing area, this approach is frequently espoused in the quality literature. For example, the Malcolm Baldrige National Quality Award and the European Quality Award both emphasize the role of leadership in creating a shared vision, and the concept of "policy deployment" is used to describe this process (see QUALITY AWARDS). A shared vision is not confined to quality, but can encompass a wide range of capability and market dimensions.

Strategic Choices in Manufacturing Strategy

The second paradigm is based on the need for internal and external consistency between choices in manufacturing strategy. Skinner (1969) proposed that the key choice areas in manufacturing strategy consisted of plant and equipment, production planning and control, labor and staffing, product design and engineering, and organization and management. These are commonly considered in terms of two sets of choices; process (or "structure") and infrastructure (Hill, 1993); (see CONTENT OF MANUFACTURING STRATEGY). These are in effect contingency-based approaches, as they argue that choices made are contingent on context and strategy. Many other authors have followed this approach.

A central concern has been the choice of manufacturing process, first put forward by Hayes and Wheelwright (1984) in their PRODUCT-PROCESS MATRIX. They viewed process both in a static and in a dynamic mode. In a static mode they argued that the choice of

process was contingent on the context of manufacture, in particular the VOLUME and VARIETY. They showed how misalignment could lead to poor manufacturing and business performance. They also argued that as markets evolved and changed, so too did the required process. Finally, they also related this to more complex environments such as multiprocess, multiproduct environments where there was a need for focused plants.

The process choice concept has been taken and developed by many authors, taxonomies of process have been developed relating the newer manufacturing technologies such as FMC and FMS to the traditional processes used by Hayes and Wheelwright. From this has developed the concept of mass customization. Pine et al. (1993) argue that process is not only a choice but there is also an optimal route from one process to another. Process choice is not confined to manufacturing process, but can be extended to include choices of processes and infrastructure in engineering. The strategic choice paradigm is essentially a contingent approach, with many authors using terms such as internal and external consistency. Hill's approach in particular has a strong contingent basis. He argues that choice of process is dependent on both the market strategy (expressed in similar terms to Hayes and Wheelwright's volume and variety) and on the order-winning criteria.

Strategic choices also apply to infrastructure. Hill (1993) argues that all the other (infrastructure) choices are contingent on the choice of process. A number of authors have examined the relationship with manufacturing strategy of various individual infrastructure areas such as manufacturing planning and control systems, middle management, and organizational culture. These approaches naturally lead to the operationalization of the concept of FOCUS. They define for a given context the dimensions and choices on which a factory should be focused.

In summary, the paradigm based on strategic choices is based around the need to attain internal and external consistency, and is a contingency-based approach. Failure to match with external business, product, and customer factors can lead to a mismatch with the market. Also emphasized is the importance of internal consistency between all the choices in manufacturing. Failure to do so can result in a mismatch between the various choices in manufacturing which will severely impair a company's ability to be competitive.

Best Practice

Best practice is probably the most recent of the three paradigms to become prominent in manufacturing strategy, though it can be argued that concern for best practice has been with humankind ever since the emergence of the first craft in pre-history.

In recent years, writing on best practice has been dominated by Japanese manufacturing practice. However, best practice has come from many sources: MRP from the USA, OPT from Israel, FMS from the UK, group technology from Russia, to name but a few. In recent years best practice literature has included JUST-IN-TIME manufacturing, which has evolved into lean production; TOTAL QUALITY MANAGEMENT, and concurrent engineering (*see* SIMULTANEOUS DEVELOPMENT). This approach is supported by research that shows strong linkages between adoption of best practice and operating performance. Companies with best practice perform better than those without.

Three particular stimuli have brought best practice to greater prominence. The first has been the outstanding performance of Japanese manufacturing industry. This has led to a continuous focus in the West on identifying, adapting, and adopting Japanese manufacturing practices. The second is the growth of business process based approaches and BENCHMARKING. This has led companies to identify their core practices and processes and to seek out best in class practice. Finally there has been the emergence of awards such as the Malcolm Baldrige National Quality Award and the European Quality Award. These have brought a high profile to best practice in certain areas.

Much of the best practice school of manufacturing strategy has been brought together in the concept of world class manufacturing. This is commonly taken to be the aggregation of best practice in a wide range of areas of manufacturing. The concept of competing through world class manufacturing was developed by Hayes and Wheelwright (1984) and the term was widely adopted after the publication of Schonberger's (1986) book. World class can be seen as

having best practice in areas such as total quality, concurrent engineering, lean production, manufacturing systems, logistics, and organization, and in achieving operational performance equaling or surpassing best international companies.

The underlying assumption of this paradigm is that best (world class) practice will lead to superior performance and capability. This in turn will lead to increased competitiveness. To summarize, this paradigm focuses on the continuous development of best practice in all areas within a company. Failure to match industry best practice can remove the competitive edge from manufacturing.

The Three Paradigms

Each paradigm has a particular set of strengths and weaknesses. The competing through manufacturing approach can lead to very high visibility for manufacturing strategy in an organization. The visible focus on competing on a limited coherent set of factors can be a uniting force within an organization. It can lead to employees and managers sharing a common vision and has the potential of creating a debate between manufacturing, marketing, and corporate strategists. The focus on capability can lead to management attention being paid to the development and exploitation of competitive capabilities in manufacturing, potentially leading to Hayes and Wheelwright's stage four (*see* OPERATIONS ROLE).

There are, however, questions and limitations. If not carried out properly, this approach can lead to just a bland mission statement. If not backed up by consistent decisions and action it risks leading to little more than management by rhetoric. It is also clearly not sufficient for development of a complete manufacturing strategy. No matter how good the focus and commitment of the company to meet a particular goal is, it will fail if there are inappropriate processes, or a misaligned infrastructure. Unbounded choice has also been questioned by several authors. In particular, Ferdows and de Meyer (1990) propose that there is a natural sequence of priorities. They describe this in the SANDCONE MODEL OF IMPROVEMENT. They argue that there is a need to build a strong foundation of quality before proceeding to focus on other priorities.

Strategic choice is potentially the most powerful of the manufacturing strategy approaches. It can provide a clear view of a wide number of choices that a company has. Its contingency-based approaches can lead to matching the whole of the operations strategy to the market positioning. This can result in strong internal as well as external consistency. To succeed it requires an effective process of manufacturing strategy development, which can be difficult to install. However, once developed it can not only put manufacturing on the top management agenda, but also imbed strategic approaches to manufacturing within a company. The correct choices can lead to focused manufacture, from which superior performance will be derived. However, it can be argued that it is possible to have internal and external consistency in manufacturing without having good practice. Consistency approaches do not in themselves lead to the adoption of new and different practices. As a result, step changes resulting from this may be missed.

The visible success of Japanese companies has led many companies to seek best practice as the basis of their manufacturing strategies. However, the evidence is that this can cause major problems, particularly in companies who are far from best practice. First, best practice usually comes in small isolated pieces such as just-in-time, MRPII, FMS, TQM, concurrent engineering and business process re-engineering. These approaches are often used in an isolated manner by companies. In addition, they are often treated as the means of solving all of a company's problems, "if only we had this we would become competitive." There is often a lack of perspective. Questions such as "is this appropriate for us?" and "would adoption support our key competitive needs?" often fail to be asked. Research has shown that there are sharp differences between companies and countries, with some having most good practice in place, and others with relatively little. For those already with substantial good practice, searching for and incrementally adopting best practice becomes a routine task. However, for those far from best practice the problems are compounded by difficulty in knowing where to start. A firm will have limited capability to adopt new practices. The question of "what will we do first?" will dominate. It is for these companies

that linking programs of adoption of best practice to competitive needs becomes crucial. Another agenda in best practice approaches becomes implementation. Best practice will not by itself guarantee improved performance. All reports of best practice show that there is a substantial failure rate in the implementation of each practice.

The three different paradigms should not be treated in isolation, and indeed many authors and experts bring at least two of them together. There are clear links between "competing through manufacturing" and "strategic choices" approaches. Hill directly links priorities (order-winning criteria) to contingency approaches (choice of process), and sees them as a single linked framework. For example, competing on cost leads to a particular process choice and in turn infrastructure. Writers on flexibility and mass customization also stress the link between process choice and competitive priorities.

Similarly there is also a clear link between "competing through manufacturing" and best practice. Hill implicitly argues that best practice programs should be matched to order winning criteria. However, the implicit assumption that priorities and hence manufacturing tasks are orthogonal has been questioned. The relationship between quality and costs is a good example. Increasingly, quality is now recognized as a major contributor to cost reduction. Thus in a cost competitive environment, quality programs may be the most appropriate response rather than cost reduction programs. Empirical evidence from Japanese companies suggests that the best companies have very high productivity and high quality, and that these companies also have fast product development times. Writers have questioned whether this means that TRADE-OFFS in manufacturing strategy no longer exist. On the one hand, the traditional trade-offs such as cost versus quality are no longer valid. On the other, it is difficult to be best in class in a large number of criteria simultaneously.

The link between best practice programs and strategic choice is less clear. First, there is the issue of whether some best practices are universal, and as such are independent of context. Proponents of TOTAL QUALITY MANAGEMENT would strongly argue this. On the other hand some "best" practices such as *kanban* or MRPII are clearly not applicable in certain contexts. The phrase "best in class" frequently used in BENCHMARKING may reflect the need to link best practice to context or "class."

The above discussion has focused on the different paradigms of content of manufacturing strategy. The PROCESS OF MANUFACTURING STRATEGY FORMULATION is equally important as content. Until recently, most attention had been paid to the content rather than the process of manufacturing strategy.

PERFORMANCE MEASUREMENT is a concern that underlies different manufacturing strategy paradigms. It has frequently been argued that measurement must match the companies' strategic needs, and to respond to this "balanced scorecard" approaches have been developed. The study of manufacturing strategy has developed in the context of single countries. Increasingly, manufacturing strategy must be set in the context of global business. Manufacturing process and infrastructure choices must reflect the additional set of economics and issues arising from managing in multiple countries. These must in turn reflect the local culture, and resources, practices.

All three paradigms of manufacturing strategy have their strengths and weaknesses, and each partially overlaps the other. Any company needs a strategic vision, as without one the other actions may fail. This is the logical starting point and needs to be revisited at regular intervals. The strategy for competing through manufacturing will lead to the need to make key strategic choices. These in turn will require the development of world class performance in the areas chosen and, by necessity, the development of best in class practices. The choice and focus of these will be guided in part by the previous approaches. The CONTINUOUS IMPROVEMENT and development of process and practice will lead to developing the company's capabilities. These in turn may enhance or change the way it chooses to compete through manufacturing.

See also **service strategy; importance–performance matrix; lifecycle effects; operations strategy**

Bibliography

Anderson, J., Cleveland, G. & Schroder, R. G. (1989). Operations strategy: a literature review. *Journal of Operations Management*, **8**, 2.
Ferdows, K. & De Meyer, A. (1990). A lasting improvement in manufacturing. *Journal of Operations Management*, **9**, 2, 168–84.
Hayes, R. H. & Wheelwright, S. C. (1984). *Restoring our competitive edge*. New York: Wiley.
Hayes, R. H., Wheelwright, S. C. & Clark, K. (1988). *Dynamic manufacturing*. New York: Free Press.
Hill, T. J. (1993). *Manufacturing strategy: The strategic management of the manufacturing function*. 2nd edn. Basingstoke: Macmillan.
Miller, J. G. & Roth, A. V. (1994). A taxonomy of manufacturing strategies. *Management Science*, **40**, 3, 285–304.
Pine, B. J., Victor, B. & Boynton, A. C. (1993). Making mass customization work. *Harvard Business Review*, September–October, 108–19.
Powell, T. C. (1995). Total quality management as competitive advantage: a review and empirical study. *Strategic Management Journal*, **16**, 15–37.
Schonberger, R. J. (1986). *World class manufacturing*. Free Press.
Skinner, W. (1969). Manufacturing: the missing link in corporate strategy. *Harvard Business Review*, **47**, 3.
Skinner, W. (1974). The focused factory. *Harvard Business Review*, **52**, 3.
Voss, C. A. (Ed.) (1992). *Manufacturing strategy: process and content*. London: Chapman and Hall.

CHRIS VOSS

manufacturing systems engineering Manufacturing systems engineering (MSE) is a multi-disciplinary engineering approach which takes a broad view of the disciplines of production engineering by studying the manufacturing process as a whole. It is different to the traditional forms of engineering concerned with production. Manufacturing systems engineers are required to have the knowledge and skills related to the technology, control, programming and monitoring of single machines and interconnected systems of machines. In addition, however, they must also have an understanding of systems approaches to the design and operation of total manufacturing systems, so that they can correctly incorporate advanced manufacturing techniques into manufacturing systems which support the wider objectives of the business. MSE spans the gap between traditional production engineering and production management.

See also **operations management; industrial engineering; operations activities**

Bibliography

Parnaby, J. & Donnovan, J. R. (1987). Education and training in manufacturing systems engineering. *IEE Proceedings*, **10**, 1354.

NIGEL SLACK

master production schedule The master production schedule (MPS) is a management commitment to produce certain volumes of finished products in particular time periods in the future. The MPS "drives" MATERIAL REQUIREMENTS PLANNING (MRPI).

Depending on the market environment, an MPS is created for each finished product using either known customer orders, sales forecasts, or a combination of both. The MPS must also take account of the longer-term production plan, any finished product stock or overdue orders, and management policies and goals. It should be realistic and achievable and hence checked against the manufacturing capacity of the key resources of the business (*see* CLOSED LOOP MRP).

The length of the planning horizon for the master production schedule is determined by calculating the longest cumulative lead time for the finished product and possibly adding a period of time to give the purchasing department visibility over future requirements so that they are able to take advantage of bulk purchasing discounts.

Since the further ahead a forecast is made, the less accurate it is likely to be, it would be unrealistic to allow no changes to the MPS, particularly as forecasts are revised and orders are taken which consume the forecast. There are, however, increasing difficulties in making changes to the MPS the closer that the beginning or "front end" of the schedule is approached.

One method of controlling the changes to the MPS is to split the planning horizon into time zones, each of which has different constraints on the type of change which can be made.

Essentially, that period of the schedule which represents finished products which are currently being assembled are usually only changed in emergency situations, since parts and sub-assemblies will have already been manufactured to the original schedule. This is often referred to as the "frozen zone." In that part of the planning horizon which represents parts currently being manufactured, it may be possible to alter the sequence of the finished products already scheduled, bearing in mind material and capacity availabilities. In the period which represents orders for materials that have been placed on suppliers, it may be feasible to alter the quantities of finished products on the MPS if it is possible to make the consequent alterations of material quantities on the open orders with suppliers. In the last section of the planning horizon, or "back end" of the schedule, which represents forward information for the purchasing department, it is usually possible to make alterations to both the sequence and volume of finished products scheduled, presuming, of course, that checks have first been made with the purchasing department regarding any major bulk material purchases which may have been made on the basis of the original information.

Apart from the sales of finished products, a company might also be concerned with the supply of spares in the form of components or sub-assemblies. These independent demands can be incorporated into an MRP system by inputting them into the MPS, thus ensuring that they are added to the generated dependent demands for the items in the relevant time periods.

The time periods used in the master schedule will be a result of the degree of control required in the overall production planning and control system, and for most companies it is accepted that time periods in excess of one week do not give sufficient control for the setting of priorities for manufactured components and their subsequent progressing.

Some companies have tackled the problem of the choice of time period or time "bucket" by adopting variable length periods across the planning horizon, which give the possibility of greater control of the final assembly operations and less detailed control for the bulk purchasing of materials. Many companies are now using daily periods or so-called "bucketless" systems where MPS quantities are associated with specific calendar dates using an internal manufacturing calendar.

In some market environments it may be particularly difficult or impossible to forecast every possible saleable finished product because of the combinations of options and extras which might be offered. In such cases it is not usually the finished product which is master scheduled but items at a level below the saleable product. This is achieved by utilizing planning bills of material (see BILL OF MATERIALS).

See also capacity management; manufacturing resources planning

Bibliography

Luscombe, M. (1993). *Integrating the business.* Oxford: Butterworth Heinemann.
Vollmann, T. E., Berry, W. L. & Whybark, D. C. (1992). *Manufacturing planning and control systems.* New York: Irwin.
Wight, O. (1984). *Manufacturing resource planning: MRPII.* Essex Junction, VT: Oliver Wight Ltd.

PETER BURCHER

material requirements planning   Material requirements planning (MRP) is a computer-based set of planning techniques which looks at a future requirement for a finished product in terms of a MASTER PRODUCTION SCHEDULE and uses this, together with the BILL OF MATERIALS, inventory status data and lead time information, to generate the requirements for all the sub-assemblies, components, and raw materials which go to make up a finished product. It suggests the release of replenishment orders for material and, since it is time phased, it makes recommendations to reschedule open orders when due dates and need dates are out of phase. In essence, MRP has been designed for a dependent demand environment with the objective of providing the right parts at the right times.

Material requirements planning is also abbreviated to MRPI to distinguish it from the later development, MANUFACTURING RESOURCES PLANNING, which is abbreviated to MRPII.

The first computer programs which attempted to carry out material requirements planning calculations were produced in the late 1950s and early 1960s in the USA, at a time when business computing was in its infancy. Early pioneers were Oliver Wight and Joe Orlicky, whom many authorities regard as the fathers of modern MRP. During the 1970s, the American Production and Inventory Control Society (APICS) undertook its MRP Crusade which tried to persuade US manufacturing companies that MRP was the way to plan and control materials. During the same decade, many MRPI software packages were produced and sold, mostly based on the early programs which had been developed inside manufacturing corporations. Very quickly it became apparent that other resources in businesses needed planning as well as materials and MRP evolved into CLOSED LOOP MRP and, eventually, with the linking to the other main business planning and control functions, into manufacturing resource planning (MRPII) systems. MRPI still forms the central module of the majority of commercially available production control software packages and has been referred to as the "engine" of such systems.

MRPI is concerned with the manufacture of multicomponent assemblies and relies on the fact that the demands for all sub-assemblies, components, and raw materials are dependent upon the demand for the finished product itself. They are said to have dependent demands.

There may also be some items which have independent demands, that is, the demand for them does not depend on the demand for any other item. Notably, the finished product itself usually has an independent demand in that it depends solely on the customer purchasing the product. Components and sub-assemblies may also have independent demands in the form of spare parts sales requirements. In a purely independent demand environment, items could be satisfactorily controlled using classical inventory approaches such as continuous and periodic review inventory systems (see INVENTORY CONTROL SYSTEMS), but in a predominantly dependent demand situation, these independent demands would be the inputs to the master production schedule in terms of forecasts and orders that would then be processed by the MRPI system.

For dependent demand items, MRPI offers considerable advantages over classical inventory approaches by trying to ensure that all the parts for the assembly of the product are available at the right time. In doing so, it can reduce overall stockholding costs while improving the service that the stock is providing.

The MRPI calculation process involves exploding the master production schedule on a level by level basis through the bills of material. At each level the gross requirements for the items are first calculated, then the effect of any projected stock and open orders are taken account of to produce the net requirements, and finally, using the lead time, the net requirements are offset in time to produce the suggested or planned orders (see NETTING PROCESS IN MRP). The planned orders may need to be batched together to take account of physical material handling or process constraints or the costs associated with ordering or setting up processes (see LOT SIZING IN MRP). Also, safety factors may need to be built into the calculation process to allow for problems in supply, unreliability of processes or short-term changes in demand (see SAFETY STOCKS IN MRP).

The master production schedule needs to be as realistic and achievable as possible and, to this end, it needs to have been checked out against the capacity of the key processes in the business (see CLOSED LOOP MRP). The bill of materials needs to be accurate for each product, an objective that is easier to achieve in the standard product, repetitive production type of industry than in the custom built environment. Inventory records also need to be accurate, which implies good procedures, regular stock checking and possibly the use of on-line stock recording systems (see INVENTORY ACCURACY).

MRPI can be operated in one of two modes. The first is referred to as regenerative, and involves the complete recalculation of all the planned orders for every item on the database for every time period into the future that has been specified. This often takes place in organizations at the end of a week or over a weekend and is thus relatively inflexible in a fast-moving business environment. To overcome this infrequent updating scenario, most MRP systems have been adjusted to allow for the recalculation and rescheduling of requirements and orders based upon determining the effect on only those items that have been affected by a change. This mode of operation is referred to as net-change MRP and is usually run, as requested, during the working day or, at the minimum, at the end of a shift.

In a manufacturing resource planning system, MRPI provides the input to various capacity planning and shop floor scheduling systems.

See also **optimized production technology; just-in-time; JIT/MRP**

Bibliography

Luscombe, M. (1993). *MRPII: integrating the business.* Oxford: Butterworth Heinemann.

Orlicky, J. (1975). *Material requirements planning.* New York: McGraw-Hill.

Vollmann, T. E., Berry, W. L. & Whybark, D. C. (1992). *Manufacturing planning and control systems.* New York: Irwin.

Wight, O. (1984). *Manufacturing resource planning: MRPII.* Essex Junction, VT: Oliver Wight Ltd.

PETER BURCHER

materials management   There are many definitions of materials management. Lee and Dobler (1977) identified that there was little agreement, at that time, on what functions were involved in materials management, LOGISTICS and PHYSICAL DISTRIBUTION MANAGEMENT. They define materials management as "an integrated management approach to planning, acquisition, conversion, flow and distribution of production materials from the raw materials state to the finished product state." Implicitly their definition refers to finished products within one firm, rather than the flow of materials through the entire supply chain down to the ultimate consumer (see SUPPLY CHAIN MANAGEMENT). More recently some authorities have defined materials management as the cost and control of materials, incorporating all functions involved in obtaining and bringing materials into the plant; this appears to exclude movement through the plant and from the plant. However, others define materials management as including purchasing, inbound transport, storage, materials handling, inventory control, and production scheduling.

The definition of materials management appears now to be covered by the phrase SUPPLY CHAIN MANAGEMENT.

Underlying all the definitions is that materials management is a cross-functional, integrative approach to managing materials and information associated with materials. Cross-functional management of the materials flow from the supply end of the business to the demand end of the business is intended to yield the following benefits:

- *Increased speed of material flow*: which results in reduced lead time; this enables shorter lead times to be quoted to customers which, in speed oriented businesses, can provide the business with a competitive advantage (*see* TIME-BASED PERFORMANCE).

- *Greater flexibility and ability to respond to change*: integrating the materials flow allows the organization to respond customer volume changes or range changes as examples.

- *Reduced cost*: managing materials through the organization rather than in functional departments allows business wide visibility of inventories, allowing inventory reduction (*see also* BUSINESS PROCESS REDESIGN).

- *Greater dependability*: the integrated processes under materials management compared to separated functional processes can make material and order tracking easier in the organization, ensuring greater dependability (*see* DELIVERY DEPENDABILITY).

- *Improved quality*: in an organization that integrates the materials flow processes, quality problems are visible and made more visible to all parts of the materials flow. This also means that there is less waste in the organization arising from poor quality (*see* QUALITY MANAGEMENT SYSTEMS).

Bibliography

Cavinato, J. (1984). *Purchasing and materials management*. St Paul, MN: West Publishing.
Lee, L. & Dobler, D. (1977). *Purchasing and materials management*. New York: Tata McGraw-Hill.
Zenz, G. (1994). *Purchasing and the management of materials*. 7th edn. New York: Wiley.

CHRISTINE HARLAND

method study Method study is the process of subjecting work activity to systematic, critical scrutiny in order to make it more effective and/or more efficient. It was originally designed for the analysis and improvement of repetitive, manual work but it can be used for all types of activity at all levels of an organization. The process is often seen as a linear, described by its main steps of:

- select (the work to be studied);

- record (all relevant information about that work);

- examine (the recorded information);

- develop (an improved way of doing things);

- install (the new method as standard practice);

- maintain (the new standard proactive).

Although this linear representation shows the underlying simplicity of method study, in practice the process is much more one of iteration around the above steps with each dominating at a different stage of the investigation. The cyclic process often starts with a quick, rough pass in which preliminary data are collected and examined, before subsequent passes provide and handle more comprehensive and more detailed data to obtain and analyze a more complete picture.

Work is selected for method study on the basis of it being an identified problem area or an identified opportunity (resulting from a systematic review of available data, normal monitoring or control processes, high levels of dissatisfaction and complaint or as part of a management-derived change in policy, practice, technology or location), and usually because it meets certain conditions of urgency and/or priority.

Before any method study investigation is begun, it is necessary to establish clear terms of reference which define the aims, scale, scope, and constraints of the investigation. This should also include an identification of who "owns" the problem or situation and ways in which such "ownership" is shared. This may lead to a debate on the aims of the project, on the reporting mechanisms and frequencies, and on the measures of success. This process is sometimes introduced as a separate and distinct phase of method study, as the "define" stage. It leads to a plan for the investigation which identifies appropriate techniques, personnel, and time-scales.

The recording stage of method study is to provide sufficient data (in terms of both quality and quantity) to act as the basis of evaluation and examination. A wide range of techniques are available for recording; the choice depends on the nature of the investigation and the work being studied, and on the level of detail required. Many of the techniques are simple charts (such as PROCESS CHARTS) and diagrams, but these may be supplemented by photographic and video recording, and by computer-based techniques. Especially with "hard" (clearly defined) problems, method study often involves the construction and analysis of models, from simple charts and diagrams used to record and represent the situation to full, computerized simulations. Manipulation of and experimentation on the models leads to ideas for development. The recorded data are subjected to examination and analysis; formalized versions are critical examination and systems analysis. The aim is to identify, often through a structured, questioning process, those points of the overall system of work that require improvement, and where such improvements may be made. The examination stage merges into the development stage of the investigation as more thorough analysis leads automatically to identified areas of change. The aim here is to identify possible actions for improvement and to subject these to evaluation in order to develop a preferred solution. Sometimes, it is necessary to identify short-term and long-term solutions so that improvements can be made (relatively) immediately, while longer-term changes are implemented and come to fruition.

At this stage it is often necessary to present interim results (which might include a number of options which are only partially appraised) to the project sponsor. Thus, presentation and communication techniques are an important part of the method study "toolbag." The sponsor may at this stage make comments or requests that lead to further data collection and examination as part of the iterative process. Eventually the process will lead to an identified and agreed solution which has to be implemented.

A method study can only be considered a success when the situation changes to solve the identified problem or take advantage of the identified opportunity, in such a way as to meet the aims of the project identified in the original terms of reference. The installation phase may be a major project in itself since it may involve changes in location, technology, equipment, fixtures, fittings, and tools in addition to or as part of system and procedural change. It may involve significant testing or prototyping of the proposed method and will, almost certainly, involve consultation with, and training of, the personnel involved. For larger projects involving major change, it may involve phased implementation or parallel running of old and new systems. The aim is to balance the speed of the change with the reliability and the security of the system, recognizing that both these have a bearing on the cost of the change. However, the most important part of making the change is often identifying and dealing with any resistance to change by personnel. It is important to fully prepare and support people through the period of change if they are to make the new method work.

After the new method has been operating for some time, there should be a check to ensure that the planned changes have been adopted and maintained. Working methods can be subject to a process of "drift," by which they move away from the previously defined, standard working practices. Although such drift may be beneficial to an organization (where it improves on the method), it may also be responsible for unsafe working practices, poor quality production or sub-optimization of production – where processes at different stages of an overall cycle become unbalanced. The process of monitoring and review may be a part of a formal methods audit or systematic review, or part of the remit of supervisors.

One criticism of method study is that it is inappropriate for "soft" problems, which are vague and less easily understood, cannot be represented by simple models and often involve high "people content." Alternative methodologies (such as soft systems methodology) have been developed to cope more effectively with such circumstances, although these may be regarded simply as application of the method study procedure with a different emphasis.

See also **work study; ergonomics; "scientific" management; multiple activity charts; principles of motion economy; work measurement**

Bibliography

BS3375. (1993). Part 2: Management services. Part 2: Guide to method study. London: British Standards Institution.
Heap, J. P. (1991). Method study: the principles. In T. J. Bentley, (Ed.), *The management services handbook*. 2nd edn. London: Pitman.

JOHN HEAP

multiple activity charts Multiple activity charts are used to show the interrelationships of individuals in teams of workers, or the relationships between workers and equipment, usually during the record stage of METHOD STUDY. The activities of each subject (whether worker or equipment) are recorded, normally as blocks in columnar form, against a common timescale. It is not usual, or necessary, to include a high level of detail but it is necessary to distinguish between components of work where subjects are working in an independent way (such as a worker carrying out a manual task while a machine carries out an automatic process) or in an interconnected way (such as a worker setting up or operating a machine). The resulting chart clearly shows both interdependence and interference between subjects, and their effects in terms of creating delays and unoccupied time periods. They serve as useful devices to assist in the redistribution and balancing of work loads.

Bibliography

BS3375. (1993). Part 2: Management services. Part 2: Guide to method study. London: British Standards Institution.

JOHN HEAP

N

netting process in MRP The MRP netting process is the way MATERIAL REQUIREMENTS PLANNING carries out calculations on a level by level basis down through a BILL OF MATERIALS which converts the MASTER PRODUCTION SCHEDULE of finished products into suggested or planned orders for all the sub-assemblies, components, and raw materials. These calculations or requirements generation runs are likely to be carried out on the computer every week, or more frequently on a net change basis.

At each level of assembly breakdown, MRP undertakes three steps in its calculations before continuing to the next lower level. These steps are as follows:

(1) It generates gross requirements for the item by "exploding" the "planned order" quantities of the next higher level assembly, by reference to the bill of material structure file. For example, for a finished product A which requires six components X; a "planned order" of 200 As in week 15 would be exploded to give gross requirements of 1,200 Xs in week 15.

(2) The gross requirements are amended by the amount of inventory of that item that is expected to be available in each week, i.e. on hand from previous week plus scheduled receipts. This information is obtained from the inventory status file and the amended requirements are called the net requirements. For example, if in week 15 a total of 800 Xs are expected to be available, the gross requirement of 1,200 is amended to give a net requirement of 400 Xs in week 15.

(3) The net requirements are then offset by the relevant lead time for the item to give planned orders for initiating the manufac-

ture or purchase of the item. For example, if the lead time for the Xs is 4 weeks, the net requirements of 400 Xs in week 15 are offset as in Figure 1.

To summarize, in its simplest form, material requirements planning would calculate the requirements and planned orders for Xs for each period of the planning horizon as in Figure 2. This calculation assumes that the only use of X is in the assembly of A. If this were not the case, and if its usage was common to other products assembled by the organization, then the gross requirements for X would have been the aggregated requirements generated from the planned orders of all the assemblies using X. This simplified approach to the calculation of requirements has, so far, assumed that the net requirements would be translated directly into planned orders, resulting in manufacturing component schedules and purchasing schedules which do not take any account of the cost of machine set-ups or the cost of ordering. It may therefore be necessary to modify the net requirements by the application of batching rules or ordering policies (*see* LOT SIZING IN MRP). Similarly, no account has been taken of the need for any unplanned occurrences or short-term changes in supply or demand. In such cases it may be necessary to incorporate safety factors into the MRP calculations (*see* SAFETY STOCKS IN MRP).

Bibliography

Luscombe, M. (1993). *MRPII: Integrating the business.* Oxford: Butterworth Heinemann.
New, C. (1973). *Requirements planning.* Epping: Gower Press.

Part no. *A*

Week no.	10	11	12	13	14	15	16
Master schedule	400	300	200	200	300	200	400

Part no. *X* (BOM = 6 per item *A*)   Lead time = 4 weeks

Week no.	10	11	12	13	14	15	16
Gross requirements	2400	1800	1200	1200	1800	1200	2400
Scheduled receipts		6000					
Projected stock	3200	800	5000	3800	2600	800	0	0
Net requirements							400	2400
Planned orders		400	2400				

Figure 1 An example of offsetting

Vollmann, T. W., Berry, W. L. & Whybark, D. C. (1992). *Manufacturing planning and control systems.* New York: Irwin.

PETER BURCHER

network techniques In PROJECT MANAGE-MENT the scope of work is best determined using a structured approach such as creating a WORK BREAKDOWN STRUCTURES. This then provides a starting point to develop an effective plan of work. Project network techniques are designed to determine the sequence of carrying out the activities and thus their scheduling. The techniques are known by a number of names sometimes used incorrectly: network analysis, critical path method (CPM) and PERT (program evaluation review technique) are all terms used to describe the process by which the constituent activities of a project are assembled into a model and then analyzed by time and (potentially) resource. The model usually takes the form of a diagram which represents the

Week no.	11	12	13	14	15	16
Net Requirements					400	
Planned Orders	400					

Figure 2 An example of calculating requirements

logical relationship between activities and thus the way in which the project will be carried out.

The diagram (plan) is sometimes confused with the schedule which is derived from the plan by analysis of the timings associated with the activities. The schedule is often shown diagrammatically as a time-scaled chart – a bar chart or GANTT CHART. A schedule can also be represented as a list of activities with associated start and finish dates (or times). Milestones can also be identified within a plan and, as events, will only have a single date associated with them.

The essential steps in producing an analyzed plan are:

(1) determine all the activities required to complete the project;

(2) produce a diagram that models their logical sequence;

(3) assign durations to each activity;

(4) calculate the total duration of the project and the timings of each activity (see below).

The longest path through the project network is the minimum project duration and its critical path. Further scheduling taking into account resource needs and limitations can be carried out.

An acceptable plan may often be the result of several cycles of the steps shown above. The initial plan should represent the "best" way to carry out the project. Often the calculated end date does not match the business need. Alternative ways of executing the project can be explored, as can the possibility of using more resources. The final plan will represent the input and consideration of the project team and its stakeholders and should be widely communicated.

Producing an acceptable plan is crucial to the future success of the project. Assembling the activities of the project and their sequence is often done together at a planning meeting. This is frequently a consensus process involving the project team; in this way they "own" the plan, although a project planner is often responsible, in larger projects, for its formation and maintenance.

Durations rely for their estimation on both expert opinion and historical data. Poor estimates of duration often result from time pressures and lack of care during the estimating process.

The subsequent calculations required are simple in principle and can be done by hand; but they can become very complex in practice when different work patterns are involved within the network plan. Computer software is readily available to do the calculations economically and conveniently. The calculations involved in resource scheduling are complex and the use of a computer is essential.

When the project is under way the activities on the critical path must run to schedule at the time calculated for each of them. If an activity on the critical path is delayed all subsequent activities on its path will also be delayed and the project will take longer than the minimum time, unless remedial action is taken. Activities on the other paths have spare time known as "slack" or "float," and these can be scheduled to make best use of the available resources. The project plan is updated regularly throughout the project with activity progress and reanalyzed to produce a revised schedule.

Network Diagrams

The network represents the logical sequence of activities. Two diagrammatic standards exist; both achieve the same purpose in modeling the project and are both widely used throughout the world. They are known as "arrow" (or "activity on arrow," AOA) and "precedence" (or "activity on node," AON) diagramming methods. Over the last 20 years the "precedence" method has become the most commonly used form and is described below. Arrow diagrams handle milestones more easily, while the more complex interactivity relationships are modeled better in the precedence form. Details of the arrow method are extensively described in the literature.

Precedence Diagrams

The diagram is drawn conventionally from left to right, i.e. the start will be at the left-hand side of the diagram.

● Activities: each individual activity is represented conventionally as a rectangle and is also referred to as a node.

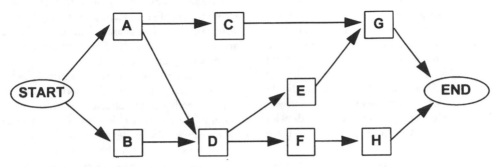

Figure 1 Example of precedence diagram

- Constraints: relationships between activities are known as constraints and are shown by an arrow drawn between activities indicating preceding and succeeding activities.

- Milestone activities: nodes can also be used to show important points in the plan, e.g. the START and END, although no work takes place and no time is consumed. They are often drawn using a different shape as a means of easy identification.

The diagram — an example. The following activities need to be completed for a kitchen refurbishment project. Unique start and end nodes are included as good practice (see Figure 1).

(A) upgrade and install services (water and electricity);
(B) order and deliver new kitchen units (frames and doors);
(C) install appliances (cooker, refrigerator, etc.);
(D) fit new units (frames);
(E) fit worktops;
(F) fit doors to units;
(G) tile walls;
(H) lay flooring.

It is important when creating the logical sequence, that any resource limitations are ignored; only the logic should be considered. Resource needs and availability are taken into account when scheduling the activities as part of the subsequent analyses.

Delays between activities can be imposed deliberately to stagger one activity in relation to another activity, e.g. allowing paint to dry.

This is best done by assigning a duration to the constraint between activities, although the reason for the delay should be made clear in the schedule.

Other constraints. Although most relationships will be between the completion of one activity and the start of a succeeding one (FS), it is sometimes necessary to use other relationships. In the following example, A is the preceding activity and B the succeeding activity:

- Start to start (SS) constraints: as soon as A can start, so can B.

- Finish to finish (FF) constraints: B cannot finish until A has finished.

- Start to finish (SF) constraints: B cannot finish until A has started.

Durations can also be associated with these constraints, for example to show that activity B starts two days after A starts, there would be a start to start (SS) constraint between A and B with a duration of two days. It is common practice to place the abbreviation of the relationship type above the constraint if it is SS, FF, or SF.

Activity identity. Each node should have a unique number or code for reference and easy location in a large project network. It is conventional to number progressively from left to right and, in practice, codes often are designed to incorporate other information such as a department code or even a grid system.

Good practice in drawing network diagrams.. The first diagram is often untidy and this draft is frequently redrawn many times before publication. There is frequent use of removable sticky pieces of paper, to accelerate the assembly of the plan. It is sometimes appropriate to plan the project in outline form and increase the level of detail as it becomes available through the project. Most project management software packages provide graphical facilities for drawing the network, making it easier to amend and change.

Calculation of project duration and time analysis. The calculation process requires the durations of all activities; the process is carried out in two phases the forward and backward passes. In the forward pass, the early start and finish dates (or times) are calculated for each activity; in the backward pass the latest dates are calculated. In most cases the early and late dates will be the same for critical activities unless target dates have been imposed on the network. The spare time or "float" (or "slack") available to each activity is the difference between its early and the late dates. The critical path has zero float, so that no activity on the critical path can be delayed without it affecting the project. Where target dates are imposed on the project the critical path will be that with minimum float.

The effect of resources. Insufficient resources will obviously delay the project. The extent of any delay will depend on the shortfall between resources needed and those available. The project manager is interested not only in the following extremes but trade-off positions in between:

(1) How long will the project take if there are not enough resources?
(2) What resources are needed to complete the project in the minimum time?

The resource needs for each activity are determined, as is the overall level of availability for each resource through the project duration. The resource scheduling process then takes into account a number of factors including activity float, criticality, and analyzed times in order to produce a new schedule. This is ideally carried out as a computerized process.

Sophisticated project management software systems allow the use of priority rules to schedule activities and allocate resources. Some graphical-based packages also allow manual manipulation of activities to show the effect of placement of activities on the resource loads.

The schedule will be changed by the effect of limited resources; this resource-limited plan can now form the basis for the rest of the project. It is often frozen as the project baseline plan (or original plan). Progress will be measured against the baseline. Each activity progress can be measured as either the time remaining at the status date or as its percentage time complete. The statused plan is rescheduled with the data provided and either the plan is updated as needed or recovery plans are formulated.

In summary, the project can be represented by a logic diagram showing the interrelationship between activities; the assignment of durations and resources to the activities is then used to calculate a schedule that can be realistically achieved. It can then be used as a basis for monitoring as the project proceeds.

See also **scheduling; project control**

Bibliography

Lockyear, K. & Gordon, J. (1991). *Critical path analysis and other project network techniques.* London: Pitman.

Moder, J. J., Phillips, C. R. & Davis, E. W. (1983). *Project management with CPM/PERT and precedence diagramming.* New York: Van Nostrand Reinhold.

RALPH LEVENE

O

operations activities Operations activities are the clusters of tasks and decisions which form the core responsibilities of operations managers. A distinction is usually drawn between activities on one hand, and the techniques of operations management on the other. Techniques are models, approaches, and guide rules intended to help decision making in operations management. A single technique may be used to support more than one activity. Although the terms "activities" or "tasks" are common when discussion operations management at an operational level, the term "decision areas" is more widely used in operations strategy.

There are two main approaches to clustering the tasks and activities of operations management. The first is to cluster activities as they affect the various resources under the control of operations managers. The second takes a roughly chronological approach and clusters activities in terms of the sequence of tasks which operations managers must address.

Typical of the approach which clusters operations activities around resources is that used by Muhlemann et al. (1992). They divide operations activities into those concerning, respectively, product- (or service-) related decisions such as design, quality, and reliability, plant-related decisions such as location, layout, and maintenance, process-related decisions such as industrial engineering and quality control, program-related decisions such as forecasting, operations planning, and control, inventory management, project management and purchasing, and people activities such as job design and health and safety management. A more common approach and one which is almost universally used in the operations strategy area is that which distinguishes between structural and infrastruc-

tural activities (Hayes and Wheelwright, 1984). Structural decisions are those which shape the "building blocks" of the operation; they define its overall tangible shape and architecture. Infrastructural decisions, on the other hand, affect the people, systems, and culture which lubricate the decision making and control activities of the operation. The distinction between structural and infrastructural is sometimes characterized as analogous to that between hardware and software in computer-based systems. Although there is some ambiguity as to which decisions are structural and which are infrastructural, structural decisions are normally taken to include those concerned with capacity, facilities and plant, technology, and vertical integration, whereas infrastructural decisions include those concerned with planning and control, quality management, new product or service development, and performance measurement.

The second approach to grouping operations activities is that which takes a broadly chronological sequencing. At its simplest level this involves grouping activities into those which concern design, those which concern planning, and those which concern control. Sometimes planning and control are grouped together. Design activities would include such tasks as product or service design, layout of physical facilities, job design, and technology choice. Planning and control activities would include such tasks as capacity planning and control, inventory management, scheduling, quality control, and plant maintenance. More recently this approach has been extended to include improvement activities to follow design and planning and control activities. A more explicit chronological approach is taken by Chase and Aquilano (1992), who classify activities under the headings of design, systems start–up, steady-state activities, and improvement activities. Design activities include product and service design, design for total quality management, capacity and location decisions, facilities layout, and job design. Start-up includes project planning and control activities. Steady-state decisions include aggregate capacity planning, inventory management, scheduling, and materials management. Improvement activities include managing the continuous improvement process and revising operations strategy.

See also **operations management; operations role; manufacturing strategy; service strategy; content of manufacturing strategy**

Bibliography

Chase, R. B. & Aquilano, N. J. (1992). *Production and operations management: A life cycle approach.* Homewood, IL: Urwin.

Hayes, R. H. & Wheelwright, S. C. (1984). *Restoring our competitive edge: Competing through manufacturing.* New York: Wiley.

Hayes, R. H., Wheelwright, S. C. & Clark, K. (1988). *Dynamic manufacturing.* New York: Free Press.

Muhlemann, A., Oakland, J. & Lockyer, K. (1992). *Production and operations management.* 6th edn. London: Pitman Publishing.

Slack, N., Chambers, S., Harland, C., Harrison, A. & Johnston, R. (1995). *Operations management.* London: Pitman Publishing.

NIGEL SLACK

operations management Operations management (OM), also known as production/operations management (POM), is concerned with the task of managing the arrangement of resources in an organization which are devoted to the production of goods and services. Organizationally, the function which is responsible for producing goods and services is called the "operations function." Every organization has an operations function because every organization produces some type of goods and/or services. However, not all types of organization will necessarily call the operations function by this name. Note that the shorter terms "the operation" or "operations" and, at times, the "operations system" may be used interchangeably with the "operations function."

"Operations managers" are the staff of the organization who have particular responsibility for managing some, or all of the resources which comprise the operations function. In some organizations operations managers could be called by some other name. For example, they might be called fleet managers in a distribution company, administrative managers in a hospital, or store managers in a retail operation. "Operations management" is the term which is used for the activities, decisions, and responsibilities of operations managers (*see* OPERATIONS ACTIVITIES).

The term "operations management" is used to imply one or both of two distinctions from the narrower subject of "production management." The first distinction is that operations management, even in manufacturing organizations, is seen as including more than solely its core manufacturing activities. Other activities associated with the total set of material transformation processes are also included, such as purchasing and distribution. Even broader definitions of operations management in a manufacturing context would also include associated activities such as process engineering, design engineering and some management accounting activities.

The second distinction is that operations management is used to indicate production activities in both manufacturing and non-manufacturing organizations. It is this latter distinction which has also led to the concept of operations management being seen as relevant in organizational areas other than the core production or service producing "operation."

Many of the issues, methods, and techniques which apply to the core operations function also have meaning for each unit, section, group, or individual within the organization. For example, a marketing function can be viewed as an operations system (*see* TRANSFORMATION MODEL) with inputs of market information, staff, computers, and outputs of marketing plans, advertizing campaigns, and sales force organizations. Thus, all organizational functions can be viewed as operations themselves because they are there to provide goods or (more usually) services to the other parts of the organization. Each function will have its "technical" knowledge. For example, in marketing this is the expertise in designing and shaping marketing plans, in finance it is the technical knowledge of financial reporting. Each will also have an operations role of producing plans, policies, and reports and service. This means that every manager in all parts of an organization is to some extent an operations manager. It is therefore possible to distinguish between two meanings of "operations": operations as a function, meaning the part of the organization which produces the goods and services for the organization's external customers, and operations as an activity, meaning any transformation of input resources in order to produce goods and services, either for internal or external customers.

The Development of the Subject

It is not surprising then that "We in the field of operations management consider our field to be one of the oldest in business schools pre-dating the emergence of finance and accounting by decades. In those times it was known as 'factory management'" (Meredith and Amoako-Gyampah 1990). Factory management developed with the onset of the industrial revolution during the period when factories were created. The main efficiency creators were the substitution of external energy sources for manpower and changes in the planning and organizing of work, for example the DIVISION OF LABOR, and "SCIENTIFIC" MANAGEMENT. It has been claimed that scientific management was the major historical landmark for the field. Taylor's approach to the planning and control of the activities of the workforce resulted in techniques such as METHOD STUDY, TIME STUDY, planning and progress charting, pay incentives, and standardization of practices. These are the ancestors of many of the principles of modern operations management.

The most rapid development of the concepts, theories, and techniques of operations management took place during the Second World War. At this time operations research techniques were being applied to military problems. The implementation of many of the "new" techniques, for example PERT/CPM, INVENTORY MANAGEMENT, simulation and queuing theories, although seemingly efficient, tended to lead to the optimization of sub-systems. Any gains were then often lost in other parts of the system.

During the 1950s a broader system view was introduced which led to a wider application of systems thinking in management, much of which has been embodied in more recent operations texts.

Modern operations management did not come into its own until probably the late 1950s," with a plethora of texts covering what are now widely recognized as standard topics, such as PLANNING AND CONTROL IN OPERATIONS, LAYOUT, MATERIALS MANAGEMENT, CAPACITY MANAGEMENT, and QUALITY MANAGEMENT SYSTEMS. From this time texts adopted an approach clearly influenced by systems thinking, and also recognized the limitations of the "scientific" approach.

See also **service operations; operations role; transformation model; hierarchy of operations; ethics in operations management**

Bibliography

Buffa, E. S. (1969). *Modern production management.* New York: Wiley.

Chase, R. B. & Aquilano, N. J. (1973). *Production and operations management: A life cycle approach.* Homewood, IL: Irwin.

Johnston, R. (1994). Operations: from factory to service management. *International Journal of Service Industry Management,* 5, *1,* 49–63.

Meredith, J. R. & Amoako-Gyampah, K. (1990). The genealogy of operations management. *Journal of Operations Management,* 9, *2,* 146–67.

Starr, M. K. (1972). *Production management, systems and syntheses.* Englewood Cliffs, NJ: Prentice-Hall.

NIGEL SLACK

operations objectives The term operations objectives is usually used to refer to the specific attributes of performance which the operations function can influence in some way and which directly or indirectly impact on the operation's customers. However, they do not usually include either long-term strategic goals, such as return on investment or market share, and nor are they the same as the general role or aspirations which the operations function may have (*see* OPERATIONS ROLE), rather they relate to the way in which the operation performs in the short and medium term. Operations objectives provide the dimensions against which operations performance may be measured. For this reason they are sometimes called performance objectives (*see* PERFORMANCE MEASUREMENT).

The purpose of defining a set of operations objectives is that it is a necessary step in translating longer-term business aspirations into a specific performance-related language which can give guidance to how the resources of an operation are managed. There should therefore be a clear logic which links long-term business strategy with operations objectives which in turn clearly link with day-to-day operations decisions (*see* MANUFACTURING STRATEGY).

In fact the term operations objectives is used in two different ways. It is used to relate to the external direct customer related factors which are seen as affecting the likelihood of winning specific business (*see* ORDER-WINNERS AND QUALIFIERS). Hill (1993), for example, cites such factors as price, delivery reliability, delivery speed, quality, product range, the intrinsic design of a product (both the performance of the design and the novelty of the design), branding, technical liaison, after sales support, and being an "in" supplier.

Two things are noticeable about this list. First, not everything on it is a direct responsibility of the operations function. It includes factors which are primarily influenced by research and development, marketing, and distribution. Second, the list is generated primarily with an external focus. The organization's customers would recognize each of these factors as influencing their propensity to purchase the goods or services. The other approach to operations objectives is to develop a set of factors which are more generic in their nature and relate more to the internal workings of the operation. There is reasonable agreement among authors as to this generic set. It usually includes such factors as quality (both high absolute level of performance and consistency of performance), dependability of delivery (the ability to consistently meet delivery schedules or promises), speed of delivery (the ability to react quickly to customer orders), FLEXIBILITY (the ability to change the design, mix, volume, or delivery of products and services), and COST (producing and distributing products and services at low cost) (*see* QUALITY MANAGEMENT SYSTEMS, TIME-BASED PERFOR-MANCE, DELIVERY DEPENDABILITY, and PRODUCTIVITY).

In addition, some authors include the objective of "innovativeness" as part of the set of operations objectives. By this they mean the ability of the operation to introduce novel products or services, or introduce new process technologies or methodologies into their operations. An alternative way of treating innovativeness is to include it as either a sub-set or consequence of flexibility.

Other terms which are used to describe operations objectives include "competitive factors," "critical success factors," "order-winners," and "competitive priorities."

See also **performance measurement; manufacturing strategy; service strategy; design chain management; lifecycle effects; sandcone model of improvement; importance–performance matrix**

Bibliography

Hill, T. J. (1993). *Manufacturing strategy*. 2nd edn. London: Macmillan.

Leong, G. K., Snyder, D. L. & Ward, P. T. (1990). Research in the process and content of manufacturing strategy. *OMEGA, The International Journal of Management Science*, **18**, 2, 109–22.

NIGEL SLACK

operations role   The "role" of the operations function refers to the set of long-term strategic responsibilities which are seen as being its prime concern, and from that the part it has to play in achieving competitive success. Usually the term is used to mean the underlying rationale of the function.

The best known approach to defining operations role considers the organizational aims or aspirations of the operations function. Hayes and Wheelwright (1984) developed a four-stage model which can be used to evaluate the competitive role and contribution of the operations function of any type of company. The model traces the progression of the operations function from what is the largely negative role (called stage 1 operations) to it becoming a central element of competitive strategy (called stage 4 operations).

Stage 1, or "internal neutrality," is the very poorest level of contribution by the operations function. In a stage 1 organization the operation is considered a "necessary evil." The other functions regard the operations function as holding them back from competing effectively. Operations has little which is positive to contribute towards competitive strategy; it is unlikely even to have developed its resources so as to be appropriate for the company's competitive position. The best that the function can hope for is to be ignored inasmuch as when operations is being ignored it is not holding the company back. The rest of the organization would not look to operations as the source of any originality, or competitive drive. In effect the operations function is aspiring only to reach the minimum acceptable standards implied by the rest of the organization. It is trying to be "internally neutral," a position it attempts to achieve not by anything positive but by avoiding the more obvious mistakes.

Stage 2, or "external neutrality," envisages the operation breaking out of stage 1 by meeting the minimum internal performance required and comparing itself with similar companies or organizations in the outside market. This may not immediately result in the company taking a leading position in the market, but at least it is aspiring to reach that position and is measuring itself against the performance of competitors. Although not particularly creative in the way they manage, such operations are trying to "be appropriate," by adopting "best practice" from their competitors. In taking the best ideas and norms of performance from the rest of their industry they are trying to be "externally neutral."

Stage 3, or "internally supportive," operations have probably reached a leading position in their market. They may not be better than their competitors in every aspect of operations performance but they are broadly up with the best. Nevertheless, good as they may be, stage 3 operations aspire to be clearly and unambiguously the very best in the market. They try to achieve this by gaining a clear view of their competitive or strategic goals after which they organize and develop operations resources to excel in the things which the company needs to compete effectively. Not only are they developing "appropriate" resources, they are taking on the role of the "implementers" of strategy. The operation is trying to be "internally supportive" by providing a credible operations strategy.

Stage 4, or "externally supportive," operations go further in attempting to capture the emerging sense of the growing importance of operations management. In essence, a stage 4 company is one which sees the operations function as providing an important foundation for its future competitive success. Operations looks to the long term. It forecasts likely changes in markets and supply, and it develops operations-based strategies which provide the company with the performance which will be required to compete in future market conditions. In effect the operations function is becoming central to strategy making. Stage 4 operations are creative and proactive. They are likely to organize their resources in ways which are innovative and capable of adaptation as markets change. Essentially they are trying to be "one step ahead" of competitors in the way that they create products and services and organize their operations, which Hayes and Wheelwright describe as being "externally supportive." Operations are not only developing "appropriate" resources and "implementing" competitive strategy, they are also an important long-term "driver" of strategy.

The Hayes and Wheelwright four-stage model may be a simplification but two points are worth considering. First, it assesses the performance of operations by the function's aspirations. Second, as companies move from stage 1 to stage 4 there is a progressive shift in the contribution of operations from being negative and merely operational to being positive and strategic. For both reasons the model has become widely used by both academics and practitioners.

See also **manufacturing strategy; service strategy; operations activities; operations objectives**

Bibliography

Hayes, R. H. & Wheelwright, C. (1984). *Restoring our competitive edge: Competing through manufacturing.* New York: Wiley.

Slack, N., Chambers, S., Harland, C., Harrison, A. & Johnson, R. (1995). *Operations management.* London: Pitman Publishing.

NIGEL SLACK

operations strategy Operations strategy is a term which is often used to indicate one of two departures from the better known term MANU-FACTURING STRATEGY.

The first use of the term is to imply a broader approach to manufacturing strategy so that it includes the whole chain of functions which deliver products to customers and provide on-going support to customers. Functions represented in this approach include purchasing, manufacturing itself, PHYSICAL DISTRIBUTION MANAGEMENT, and CUSTOMER SUPPORT OPERATIONS. In this sense manufacturing strategy is expanded to include all the SUPPLY CHAIN MANAGEMENT issues.

The second use of the term is to indicate the strategic management of the resources which create goods or services in any type of organization. Here the term is being used to include both manufacturing strategy and SER-VICE STRATEGY. This latter approach is some-times criticized for failing to reflect the differences between manufacturing and service organizations. So, for example, it is argued that the far larger overlap between "operations" and "marketing" activities in service operations precludes a common approach to the strategic management of their operations functions.

See also **operations management; service operations; service processes**

NIGEL SLACK

optimized production technology Optimized production technology (OPT) is both a philosophy (the OPT concept) and a planning and scheduling software (OPT); the name OPT being a registered trademark of the Scheduling Technology Group Ltd. The OPT philosophy and software aim to achieve the stated goal of manufacturing which is to make money now and in the future. It does this by synchronizing manufacturing by concentrating on the capacity constraining resources of the business.

The philosophy of OPT has been widely expounded by Dr Eliyahu Goldratt, most notably in his book *The Goal.* Goldratt introduced three new measures that he claimed are needed to assist in decision making at the operational level in a manufacturing company. These are throughput, inventory, and operating expense. While these may sound familiar terms, the measures are unique to Goldratt because of his precise definitions of them.

Throughput is defined as the rate at which the company makes money through sales. Thus, for example, the sale of factored goods would be covered by the definition; as would the sale of spares. Inventory is defined as what the company has purchased with the intention of selling. In this definition, items which are normally classified as inventory, but which are not ultimately for sale are ignored. Thus engineering spares and consumable items are excluded. Also implicit in the definition is the concept of valuing all inventory at raw material value. Finally, operating expense is defined as all the money required to turn inventory into throughput. The argument for putting together both direct and indirect expenditure under one heading is that, in practice, direct labor is fixed.

The three measures are in a form that can be used as a guide to operational decision making. It is reasonable to ask a foreman to consider whether running overtime, which will certainly increase operating expenses, will also increase throughput or merely end up as inventory. These three measures can be shown to have direct impacts on the traditional measures of business performance, namely, profit, return on investment, and cash flow. The ideal situation would therefore be to schedule a factory in such a way that throughput is increased while, simultaneously, operating expenses, and inventory are reduced.

The OPT scheduling approach focuses attention on those resources that constrain capacity and hence the throughput of a plant. These are called capacity constraining resources or CCRs. This name was adopted because the term BOTTLENECKS was found to be too restrictive when applied using the definition given by Goldratt (a resource whose capacity is equal to or less than the demand placed upon it).

The CCR is seen as the heartbeat of the plant. It is, essentially, the resource (or resources) that controls the flow of materials. It is referred to as the "drum" by Goldratt, indicating it provides the drumbeat to which the total operation should work. The relationship between the CCR or the final stage after the CCR and those resources which feed them, is referred to as the "rope," this being the mechanism which triggers the release of material to the first manufacturing stage in synchronization with the CCR schedule. Finally, there is a requirement to buffer the most vulnerable parts of the operation against uncertainty. These are the CCR, because production lost through the CCR is lost sales, and before final assembly. Note that one obviously cannot prevent the CCR from breaking down. The "buffer" is to ensure that the CCR is never starved of work because of breakdowns elsewhere. The inherent slack associated with all other operations acts as its own buffer. The entire scheduling concept is referred to as the drum, buffer, and rope.

The ideas of synchronization are incorporated, to a degree, in the OPT software. However, there is an important distinction in the software between scheduling and modeling. The basic premise is that the OPT scheduling rules are the correct ones for scheduling a plant; what varies between plants is manufacturing strategies, operations and product structures, resources, working practices, and quality policies. In consequence, it is possible to build a model using the OPT software that is unique to each plant and then apply the scheduling rules to that model to validate it by producing feasible schedules.

Models in the OPT system have two major components, dynamic and static data. The dynamic data include orders, inventories, and open purchase orders. The static data include the BILL OF MATERIALS, routings, and resource listings. All these data are usually to be found on the database of a MANUFACTURING RESOURCES PLANNING (MRPII) system. The OPT modeling language is flexible enough to permit quite complicated operations to be represented.

In the scheduling part of the OPT software there are three major program elements corresponding to the drum, buffer and rope. The first uses a simulation technique to schedule the CCRs identified to it, forwards in time to finite capacity to derive delivery dates. It works on the basis that since these resources are CCRs, they should aim always to be fully loaded. The rope is provided by a backwards scheduler which ignores capacity and uses the forward schedule of the CCR as its MASTER PRODUCTION schedule. As such it is a pull system. The buffers are inserted using predetermined rules, in the key areas identified in the theory.

The OPT scheduling software also takes account of the fact that increased throughput can only come about by better utilization of the CCR facilities, and increased batch sizes are one way to increase utilization. OPT calculates different batch sizes throughout the plant, depending on whether a work center is a CCR or not. The key to lot sizing in OPT is distinguishing between a transfer batch (that quantity that moves from operation to operation) and a process batch (the total lot size released to the shop). The basic concept is to move material as quickly as possible through non-CCR work centers in small batches until it reaches the CCR. There, work is scheduled for maximum utilization of the CCR in large batches. Thereafter, work again moves at maximum speed in small batches to finished goods. What this means for lot sizing is very small transfer batches to and from the CCR, with a large process batch at the CCR (see LOT SIZING IN MRP).

The OPT philosophy has evolved. To more clearly separate OPT's philosophical concepts from the computer software, Goldratt and his associates have coined the term "theory of constraints" (TOC) to represent their ideology. Here the definition of a constraint has been extended beyond the factory shop floor and the goal is to break the constraints and thereafter identify the next constraint in a continuous improvement program.

See also **just-in-time; planning and control in operations**

Bibliography

Goldratt, E. M. & Cox, J. (1984). *The goal.* New York: North River Press.

Luscombe, M. (1993). *MRPII: Integrating the business.* Oxford: Butterworth Heinemann.

Vollmann, T. E., Berry, W. L. & Whybark, D. C. (1992). *Manufacturing planning and control systems.* New York: Irwin.

PETER BURCHER

order-winners and qualifiers The order-winners/qualifiers distinction ascribed to Hill (1984) is a widely adopted approach to distinguishing between the different competitive factors (*see* OPERATIONS OBJECTIVES) which operations may choose to emphasize. The basis of the classification is that different competitive factors can play different roles in determining the competitive contribution of the operations function.

An order-winning competitive factor (simply called order-winners by Hill) are those factors which directly and significantly contribute to an organization winning business. Implicitly they are regarded by customers as the key reasons for purchasing a product or service. Implicitly, therefore, they are the most significant factors in defining the operations contribution. Increasing performance in an order-winning factor will result in more business, or an increased chance of gaining more business. Conversely, reduced performance in order-winning factors will reduce the amount of business won by the organization, or reduce the chances of winning business.

A qualifying competitive factor (called qualifiers by Hill) may not be the most obvious determinant of competitive success, but can be equally important in a different way. Qualifiers are those aspects of competitiveness where the operations performance has to be above a particular level in order to be considered by the customer. This gives rise to their name, performance in these factors has to be above a certain (qualifying) level for the organization to "qualify" to be considered by customers at all. Above this qualifying level the organization will be considered as a potential supplier but will be judged mainly in terms of its performance on order-winning factors. Any further improvement, therefore, in qualifying factors is unlikely to gain significant competitive benefit.

The distinction between order-winners and qualifiers as a concept is widespread in the operations strategy literature. It has been taken up by many authors and is generally regarded as being both practical and conceptually useful.

Similar concepts are evident in other areas of management. Most notably the distinction between motivating and hygiene factors in describing behavior can be viewed as a strong influence on the order-winner/qualifier concept. The "success producer" and "failure preventer" concept used in competitive strategy also represent a similar distinction.

Although widespread the order-winner/qualifier distinction is not without its critics. The first criticism is that order-winners and qualifiers might change over time. However, Hill does emphasize that both order-winners and qualifiers should be regarded as context and time dependent. The second criticism concerns the generality of using such concepts as order-winners and qualifiers. Hill recommends specific competitive factors to be assigned as order-winners or qualifiers by considering the way individual purchasers make decisions as to whether to buy or not. Some authors argue that the purchasing behavior of whole market segments cannot be generalized from such data.

See also **manufacturing strategy; process of manufacturing strategy formulation; importance–performance matrix; performance measurement; zone of tolerance**

Bibliography

Hill, T. J. (1985). *Manufacturing strategy.* London: Macmillan.

NIGEL SLACK

organization of development Effective product and process development requires project management structures that promote the efficient use of available resources. There are a variety of organizational structures under which product development (or other projects) can be organized. The choice of structure will be subject to, among other things, the availability of resources, the competitive environment (such as the speed of product introduction), and the age and variety of the product base. For example, as the management of product and process development has recognized the need for cross-functional co-ordination, reductions in lead times and so forth, there has been a movement away from a traditionally organized functionally dominated structure, towards alternatives which promote tighter PROJECT MANAGEMENT. These alternative organizational structures may also enable development tasks to be undertaken simultaneously (*see* SIMULTANEOUS DEVELOPMENT).

A spectrum of alternative structures can be considered from a pure functional organization, to those with a much greater emphasis on tighter project management such as pure project-based teams. Lying between these extremes are structures based on the combination of these two pure forms, usually called matrix organizations.

Functional Organizations

This is the traditional hierarchical organization under which a project is subdivided and assigned to specialist groups operating within functional areas (such as engineering, production, marketing, and administration), and whereby authority for the development project cascades down through the organization from senior management, through the ranks of middle management and to the lower management levels. In this way, the project is passed sequentially (as a completed task), like a baton in a relay race from one team member to the next. The main responsibility for the project shifts from function to function as it progresses, and is co-ordinated by the respective functional heads. Any liaison will be conducted through the head of function.

Projects organized in this way have several advantages. First, the simple structure makes economical use of managerial tasks and control. Second, it enables the centralization (or pooling together) of available experts and resources, especially important in the innovation process where specialist technical expertise is critical, costly, and often scarce. Third, clearly defined career paths, and peer grouping, can assist the hiring and retaining of specialist staff. However, there are weaknesses with this form. When a multitude of projects are being undertaken simultaneously, competition for resources can lead to conflicts over the relative priorities of individual projects. Functional speciality can lead to an over-emphasis of the departmental goals, rather than to achieving the goal of the project. Finally, there may be a lack of motivation or enthusiasm when commitment of personnel is spread across projects.

Project Teams

This type of development organization is also called an autonomous team, venture team, tiger team, and task force. It consists of a project manager who is given responsibility for a development project team composed of a core group of personnel from several functional areas, assigned on a full-time basis for the duration of the project, while other staff may be seconded to the team as required. This team is separated from the functional structure of the rest of the company and controlled by a manager responsible for the completion of the project. The company's functional managers need have no formal involvement in the team. The project manager has responsibility for both internal co-ordination and external integration, and has direct control of all personnel throughout the life of the project. In this way, responsibility is centered on one individual, who co-ordinates the entire process, rather than the distributing of authority inherent in the functional structure.

The advantages of this structure are the singleness of purpose and unity of command, the clear focus of a single objective, the effectiveness of informal communication, and the central authority of all the necessary resources. In particular, the development of team work, together with a single leader, enables conflict to be managed efficiently. On the downside, this structure disrupts the regular organization, since the individual project is only a temporary event (even if "temporary" means several years). Facilities are inevitably duplicated and therefore may be used inefficiently, and personnel may have problems re-entering the organization after project completion, such as personnel losing their "home" in the functional structure while working away on the project.

Matrix Organizations

Firms are unlikely to adopt either of these pure forms. Instead they usually choose a balance between the two. They may consider adopting a structure combining the characteristics of both the functional and project organization. This is matrix management, a "mixed" organizational form in which the functional hierarchy is "overlaid" by some form of lateral authority, influence, or communication. In a matrix, there are usually two chains of command, one along functional lines and the other along project lines. Three forms of matrix are commonly defined: functional matrix, balanced matrix, and project matrix.

The Functional Matrix (or Lightweight Project Manager)

This lightweight (or weak) form of matrix maintains personnel in their functional groups, but designates a project manager with limited authority to co-ordinate the project across the different functional areas. The project is entirely under the control of the project manager, who co-ordinates, liaises, and monitors its progress. Each functional area is represented through a liaison representative who co-ordinates related issues to the project manager. However, the functional managers retain responsibility and authority for the design and completion of technical requirements within their discipline (specific to elements of the project), and hence to the allocation of resources.

The project manager is lightweight in three ways. First, there is no direct influence over engineers at the working level, and the product manager has little leverage over the activities outside of engineering (such as manufacturing and marketing), despite having liaison representatives. Second, the project manager has little status or power within the organization, since he has a middle-management or junior position to command such respect. Third, the project manager is a co-ordinator, utilizing concepts developed by others to co-ordinate and manage potential conflicts.

The Balanced Matrix

In this form, the project and functional managers share the responsibility and authority for completing the project. They jointly direct many work-flow elements and jointly approve many decisions. More specifically, project managers schedule, control, and monitor the timing and activities of the project, and integrate the contributions of the various disciplines, while functional managers assign personnel and execute their part of the project according to the plans of the project manager.

The Project Matrix (or Heavyweight Project Manager)

This form of matrix requires a stronger project manager than under the previous matrix structures. A project manager is assigned to oversee the project and has primary responsibility and authority for completing the project. Staff working on the project will be under the control of the project manager, although they are likely still to reside in their specific functions. Similarly, functional managers will assign personnel as needed, provide technical expertise, and oversee the long-term career development of their own personnel. It is essential that the project manager is able to command authority over the functional heads, hence it is likely that he or she will be relatively senior, or at least equal to them.

The heavyweight project manager can be characterized as follows. First, the project manager will have direct influence over the personnel working in the various functions – engineering, marketing, and manufacturing. Second, since the project manager will be of senior management level (head of function, or chief engineer of a division), he or she will wield considerable status and power within the organization. Third, the project manager plays an active role in directing and evolving the product, thus performing more than mere co-ordination of activities.

Formation of Project Teams

The results of several studies provide a strong preference towards strong project leadership in product development activities. Most argue that the heavyweight project manager and the project team are the most efficient forms of organization for product competitiveness, shorter lead time, and engineering efficiency. Furthermore, when project complexity is analyzed, only the project team structures showed considerable suitability for very complex projects. It is not surprising, therefore, that from the late 1980s onwards as TIME TO MARKET became a driving competitive weapon, the formation of multifunctional project teams, under heavyweight project management, has been widely advocated.

See also **design–manufacturing interface; design for manufacture**

Bibliography

Bower, J. L. & Hout, T. M. (1988). Fast-cycle capability for competitive power. *Harvard Business Review*, **66**, *6*, 110–18.

Clark, K. B. (1991). High performance product development in the world auto industry. *International Journal of Vehicle Design*, **12**, *2*, 105–31.

Larson, E. W. & Gobeli, D. H. (1988). Organizing for product development projects. *The Journal of Product Innovation Management*, **5**, *3*, 180–90.

Youker, R. (1977). Organization alternatives for project managers. *Management Review*, **66**, *11*, 46–53.

DAVID TWIGG

P

P:D ratios The P:D ratio of an operation is the ratio of its customer lead time to the total throughput time of its materials. An external customer of an operation judges the speed of any operation by the total waiting time between asking for a product and receiving it. This is the "demand" time, D. But to the operation it is the whole throughput cycle, P, which is important because that is how long the operation will have to manage the flow of materials and information. In a typical make-to-stock manufacturer such as those making consumer durables, customer's demand time, D, is the sum of the times for transmitting the order to the company's order processing system, processing the order to the warehouse or stock point, picking and packing the order, and its physical transport to the customer (the "deliver" cycle). Behind this visible order cycle lie other cycles. The "make" cycle involves scheduling work to the various stages in the manufacturing process. Physically this involves withdrawing materials and parts from input inventories and processing them through the various stages of the manufacturing route and the "purchase" cycle (the time for replenishment of the input stocks) involving transmitting the order to the supplier and awaiting their delivery. For this type of manufacturing the "demand" time which the customer sees is very short compared with the total throughput cycle, the sum of the deliver, make, and purchase cycles, P (*see* DEMAND RESPONSE).

Contrasting with the make-to-stock company is the company which both makes and develops its products to order. Here D is the same as P. Both include an "inquiry" cycle, a "develop" cycle for the design of the product, followed by "purchase," "make," and "delivery" cycles.

Most companies operate with more than one P and more than one D (*see* RUNNERS, REPEATERS, AND STRANGERS).

Reducing total throughput time P will have varying effects on the time the customer has to wait for demand to be filled. For many customized products, P and D are virtually the same thing. The customer waits from the material being ordered through all stages in the production process. Speeding up any part of P will reduce the customer's waiting time, D. On the other hand, customers who purchase standard "assemble to order" products will only see reduced D time if the "assemble" and "deliver" parts of P are reduced and savings in time are passed on.

Generalizing, D is smaller than P for most companies. How much smaller D is than P is important because it indicates the proportion of the operation's activities which are speculative, that is carried out on the expectation of eventually receiving a firm order for the work. The larger P is compared with D, the higher the proportion of speculative activity in the operation and the greater the risk the operation carries.

But the speculative element in the operation is not there only because P is greater than D; it is there because P is greater than D and demand cannot be forecast perfectly. With exact or close to exact forecasts, risk would be non-existent or very low no matter how much bigger P was than D. When P and D are equal, no matter how inaccurate the forecasts, speculation is eliminated because everything is made to a firm order. Reducing the P:D ratio becomes, in effect, a way of taking some of the risks out of manufacturing planning.

See also **supply chain management; dependent and independent demand; planning and control in operations**

Nigel Slack

Pareto analysis   Pareto analysis (also referred to as *A B C* analysis) is a method of classifying items, events, or activities according to their relative importance. It is frequently used in inventory management where it is used to classify stock items into groups based on the total annual expenditure for each item, although it is increasingly used in other areas of operations management such as Quality Management Systems. In most organizations the number of different items which must be stocked in order to run their business effectively is extremely large. It is unlikely to be economic or even practical to give the same high level of detailed attention to the control of every single stock item. What is needed is a method of identifying those items for which detailed control would produce the greatest pay-off. The most commonly used way of achieving this is through Pareto analysis.

The first step in the analysis is to identify the factors which make a high degree of control of a stock item important. Two possible factors might be the rate at which the item is used and its unit value. For fast moving items with a high unit value then very close control is justified. On the other hand, with slow-moving, low unit value items the cost of the stock control system may exceed the benefits to be gained so that only very simple methods of control can be justified.

One way of combining these two factors is to calculate for each stock item the total value of annual usage, called the annual requirement value (ARV):

$$\text{Annual requirement value (ARV)}$$
$$= \text{unit value} \times \text{annual usage}$$

If the stock items are then placed in descending order of ARV then the really important items will appear at the top of the list. If cumulative ARV is then plotted against number of items then a graph known as a Pareto curve is obtained. A typical Pareto curve is shown in Figure 1.

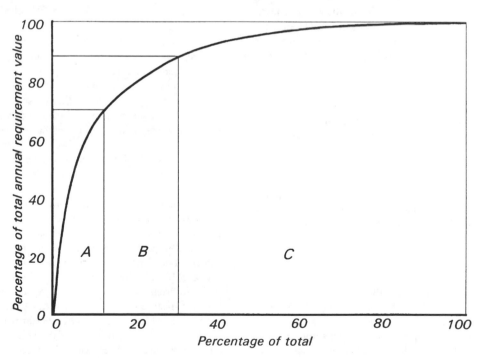

Figure 1 Pareto curve

The precise shape of the Pareto curve will differ for each organization but typically, the first 20 percent of items stocked will account for approximately 80 percent of cumulative ARV. For a company with a stock list of 10,000 different items this means that control of the top 2,000 items will give control of about 80 percent of total stock investment. These items are known as category A items and will require fairly sophisticated methods of control. The next 40 percent of items, called category B items will, typically, account for a further 15 percent of cumulative ARV. Obviously the B items will need some measure of control but much less precise methods than for category A can be used. The last 40 percent of items, called category C items, will account for a mere 5 percent of ARV. The C items are either very cheap or very slow moving and simple methods of stock control can be used. Even if this results in stocks of C items being rather greater than is strictly necessary this will not increase total costs significantly, and is likely to be much less than the cost of operating a more complicated system of stock control.

Other examples of the use of Pareto analysis in operations management include classifying quality problems in order of their frequency of occurrence, failure modes in order of their impact on a system's performance, and work tasks in order of the total amount of time they occupy.

See also **inventory management; tools of quality management**

Bibliography

Flores, B. E. & Whybark, D. C. (1987). Implementing multiple criteria ABC analysis. *Journal of Operations Management*, 7, 1–2, 79.

JOHN MAPES

PDCA cycle The PDCA cycle is frequently used in the context of CONTINUOUS IMPROVEMENT. The repeated and cyclical nature of continuous improvement is well summarized by the PDCA cycle (or Deming wheel – see DEMING). The PDCA cycle is the sequence of activities which are undertaken on a cyclical basis to improve activities.

The cycle starts with the P (for plan) stage, which involves an examination of the current method or the problem area being studied. This involves collecting and analyzing data so as to formulate a plan of action which is intended to improve performance. Once a plan for improvement has been agreed the next step is the D (for do) stage. This is the implementation stage during which the plan is tried out in the operation. This stage may itself involve a mini PDCA cycle as the problems of implementation are resolved. Next comes the C (for check) stage where the new implemented solution is evaluated to see whether it has resulted in the expected performance improvement. Finally (at least for this cycle), comes the A (for act) stage. During this stage the change is consolidated or standardized if it has been successful. Alternatively, if the change was not successful, the lessons learned from the "trial" are formalized before the cycle starts again.

See also **quality; total quality management**

NIGEL SLACK

performance measurement Performance measurement is the process of quantifying action, where measurement is the process of quantification and performance is the result of action. According to the marketing perspective, organizations achieve their goals by satisfying their customers with greater efficiency and effectiveness than their competitors. The terms efficiency and effectiveness have specific meanings in this context. Effectiveness refers to the extent to which customer requirements are met, while efficiency is a measure of how economically the firm's resources are utilized when providing a given level of customer satisfaction. This is an important point because it not only identifies two fundamental dimensions of performance, but also highlights the fact that there can be internal as well as external reasons for pursuing specific courses of action (*see* OPERATIONS OBJECTIVES). The level of performance a business attains is a function of the efficiency and effectiveness of the actions it undertakes, and thus:

- Performance measurement can be defined as the process of quantifying the efficiency and effectiveness of action.

- A performance measure can be defined as a metric used to quantify the efficiency and/or effectiveness of an action.

- A performance measurement system can be defined as the set of metrics used to quantify both the efficiency and effectiveness of actions.

These definitions highlight the fact that a performance measurement system can be analyzed both at the level of the system, and at the level of the individual performance measures which together constitute the system.

The Performance Measurement System

Traditionally, businesses have used financially orientated performance measurement systems, relying on derivatives of measures, such as return on investment (ROI). By the time Johnson and Kaplan's *Relevance lost* was published (1987) there was widespread dissatisfaction with these traditional, cost accounting based performance measurement systems, not least because they were seen to encourage short-termism and lacked strategic focus. Additionally they failed to provide data on quality, responsiveness or flexibility, encouraged local optimization, for example manufacturing inventory to keep people and machines busy, encouraged managers to minimize the variances from standard rather than continually seek to improve, and failed to provide information on what customers wanted and what the competition was doing.

Many organizations are now actively involved in the process of reviewing their performance measurement systems, not simply to get a better means of monitoring performance, but also to enable them to: (1) assess health; (2) stimulate learning; and (3) improve communication.

Assessing health. One of the primary roles of senior management in any organization is to keep track of whether the organization's resources are being used in a way that will help it survive and prosper. Traditionally, financial measures of performance have been the tools used to do this, but increasingly senior managers are looking for a more rounded picture of the health of their businesses. As a result they are turning to measurement systems which combine the financial and non-financial dimensions of performance. This trend is encapsulated by Kaplan and Norton's (1992, 1994) balanced scorecard which is based on the assumption that an organization's measurement system should enable its managers to answer each of the following questions:

- How do we look to our shareholders (financial perspective)?

- What must we excel at (internal business perspective)?

- How do our customers see us (customer perspective)?

- How can we continue to improve and create value (innovation and learning perspective)?

Although popular, the balanced scorecard is not the only performance measurement framework that is available. In the US and Europe the Malcolm Baldrige and the European Quality Awards, respectively, have proved to be popular ways of assessing the health of businesses (*see* QUALITY AWARDS).

Stimulate learning. Initially BENCHMARKING was primarily seen as a means of determining an organization's competitive standing. More recently, however, the emphasis has shifted to benchmarking practices rather than performance. In large, multinational corporations, this concept has important implications, because within such organizations, there is scope to transfer knowledge or learning from one part of the business to another. Having comparable measures of performance in different parts of the business simplifies the process of identifying which knowledge could valuably be transferred.

Improve communication. It has long been recognized that the effect of measurement is to stimulate action. The final way in which businesses are now seeking to use performance measures is as a means of communicating what they care about, thereby stimulating appropriate behaviors. (See section on "Formula".)

The Individual Performance Measures

Information is needed to specify a performance measure. This can be incorporated in a ten-step procedure.

(1) *Measure*: this step should fix the title of the measure. A good title is one that explains what the measure is and why it is important. It should be self-explanatory and not include functionally specific "jargon."

(2) *Purpose*: if a measure has no purpose then one can question whether it should be introduced. Hence in the second step the rationale underlying the measure should be specified. Typical purposes include: enabling us to monitor the rate of improvement thereby driving down the total cost; ensuring that all delayed orders are eliminated ultimately; stimulating improvement in the delivery performance of suppliers; insuring that the new product introduction lead time is continually reduced.

(3) *Relates to*: if the measure being considered does not relate to any of the business objectives then one can question whether the measure should be introduced. Hence, in the third step, the business objectives to which the measure relates should be identified.

(4) *Target*: the objectives of any business are a function of the requirements of its owners and customers. The levels of performance the business needs to achieve to satisfy these objectives are dependent upon how good its competitors are. Without knowledge of how good the competition is, and an explicit target, which specifies the level of performance to be achieved and a timescale for achieving it, it is impossible to assess whether performance is improving fast enough and hence whether the business is likely to be able to compete in the medium to long term. Typical targets include: X percent improvement year on year; Y percent reduction during the next twelve months; achieve Z percent delivery performance (on time, in full) by the end of next year.

(5) *Formula*: this step is one of the most difficult to complete because the way performance is measured affects what people do. Take, for example, a measure such as value of new products won. This appears to be an appropriate measure for a sales manager. But if the formula is value,

in terms of dollars, the measure may encourage sales managers to seek large contracts, rather than profitable ones. Hence perhaps the measure should be contribution; but the problem with this is it may stop sales managers pursuing new business opportunities, even if they are of strategic significance.

There clearly can be problems if the formula is inappropriately defined, but it should be noted that the converse is also true. That is, it is often possible to define the formula in such a way that it induces good business practice.

(6) *Frequency*: the frequency with which performance should be recorded and reported is a function of the importance of the measure and the volume of data available.

(7) *Who measures*: this step should identify the person who is to collect and report the data.

(8) *Source of data*: this step should specify where the data come from. The importance of this question lies in the fact that a consistent source of data is vital if performance is to be compared over time.

(9) *Who acts on the data*: this step should identify the person who is to act on the data.

(10) *What do they do*: this step is probably the most important, not because it contains the most important information, but because it makes explicit the fact that unless the management loop is closed (unless the measure stimulates appropriate action) there is no point having it. It is not always possible to detail the action that will be taken if performance proves either to be acceptable or unacceptable, as this is often context specific. It is, however, always possible to define in general the management process that will be followed should performance appear either to be acceptable or unacceptable. Typical information for this step includes: setting up a continuous improvement group to identify reasons for poor performance and to make recommendations as to how performance can be improved; publishing all performance data and an executive summary on the shop floor as a means of demonstrating commit-

ment to empowerment; identifying commonly occurring problems; setting up review teams, consisting of sales, development and manufacturing personnel, to establish whether alternative materials can be used.

These steps can be incorporated into a performance record sheet which provides a structured way of recording all the data necessary to specify a performance measure. In reality, of course, the act of specifying individual performance measures is but an element of the process of developing a performance measurement system.

See also **manufacturing strategy; operations objectives; operations activities**

Bibliography

Johnson, H. T. & Kaplan, R. S. (1987). *Relevance lost: The rise and fall of management accounting.* Boston, MA: Harvard Business School Press.
Kaplan, R. S. & Norton, D. P. (1992). The balanced scorecard: measures that drive performance. Harvard Business Review, January–February, *70, 1,* 71–9.
Kaplan, R. S. & Norton, D. P. (1993). Putting the balanced scorecard to work. *Harvard Business Review,* September–October, *75,* 134–47.
Neely, A. D. & Mills, J. F., Gregory, M. J., Richards, A. H. & Platts, K. W. (1995). *Performance measurement system design.* University of Cambridge, Manufacturing Engineering Group.

ANDY NEELY

physical distribution management   Physical distribution management usually refers to the storage of goods and their transport from one firm to another in the supply chain (*see* SUPPLY CHAIN MANAGEMENT). Most authors on physical distribution management now use the term LOGISTICS to include consideration of businesses processes and information flows as well as physical flows.

Many of the systems for physical distribution are "multi-echelon" systems with storage at different points in the supply chain. For example, a manufacturer stores products in its own warehouse. From there the products may be distributed to a regional warehouse for a retailer. Regional warehouses have several benefits. First, they act as an intermediate point which is located closer to the retailer than their manufacturing site, therefore facilitating quicker delivery. Second, they enable the manufacturer to deliver to a limited number of customer locations, rather than do store by store delivery. Third, the retailer has to request stocking up from only one source of supply. The introduction of a warehouse stage in the physical distribution network can therefore simplify communications and routes.

However, warehouse locations have costs – these costs include the opportunity cost of the capital tied up in the inventory contained in them, the cost of the facilities themselves (e.g. lease costs), the cost of running the facilities (e.g. labor, heating, security, lighting), the cost of inventory loss (e.g. obsolescence, deterioration, etc.). Therefore, warehouse decisions involve consideration of the costs and benefits as well as the location (*see* INVENTORY-RELATED COSTS).

As well as decisions on the structure of the physical distribution system, in terms of the number, size, and location of distribution centers, decisions have to be made on the mode of transport to use to move goods between the nodes in the network. The modes of transport available to the distribution manager are:

- road;
- rail;
- water;
- air;
- pipeline.

Each of these modes have certain characteristics which affect its suitability. For example, air transport is expensive, limited in the space available (in terms of the capacity of the aircraft and the number of flights scheduled on a particular route), and in access to suitable airports. Air transport is therefore typically used for high value, low volume items, such as jewelry or fresh lobsters. Conversely, bulk raw materials are often transported using slower, cheaper forms of transport such as water or rail. Some hazardous items, such as nuclear waste, have to be transported in special containers and are only allowed to use certain routes at certain times.

The choice of transport mode is not only determined by cost but also by physical product characteristics. It is not possible to transport discrete parts by pipeline because they do not flow, whereas a pipeline is an option for liquids such as oil and chemicals and for gases such as domestic supply gas.

The choice of transport mode is usually determined by the relative importance of delivery speed and reliability, quality and perishability (or contamination), costs, and flexibility (including ease of access, ease of movement, and capacities).

See also **capacity strategy; location; materials management; inventory control systems; supply chain dynamics**

CHRISTINE HARLAND

planning and control in operations Operations planning and control involves coordinating the internal activities of operations with the demands of customers. It is the process of reconciling supply and demand.

The resources of an operation have the capability to supply customers, but without a planning and control activity, they do not have the instructions on how to do so. Operations usually have a set of both general and specific demands from the actual and potential customers for the operation's products or services. Planning and control activities provide the systems procedures and decisions which bring these two entities together. They connect up the resources of the operation which are capable of supplying goods and services with the demand that it was designed to satisfy.

The constraints within which the planning and control activity takes place are as follows:

- *cost constraints*: products and services must be produced within an identified cost;

- *capacity constraints*: products and services must be produced within the designed capacity limits of the operation;

- *timing constraints*: products and services must be produced with the time when they still have value for the customer;

- *quality constraints*: products and services must conform to the designed tolerance limits of the product or service.

Although they can be viewed as separate activities most authorities treat planning and control together. This is because the division between planning and control is not always clear, either in theory or in practice. However, there are some general features that help to distinguish between the two.

A plan is a formalization of what is intended to happen at some time in the future. It does not guarantee that an event will actually happen, but is a statement of intention based on expectations concerning the future. When operations attempt to implement plans, things do not always happen as expected. For example, customers change their minds about what they want and when they want it, suppliers may not always deliver on time, machines may fail and staff may be absent through illness. For any of these reasons, and many others, the plan may not be carried out. Control is the process of coping with these changes, which may mean that plans need to be redrawn in the short term, and that an "intervention" will need to be made in the operation to bring it back "on plan." Control makes the adjustments which allows the operation to achieve the objectives which the plan set, even when the assumptions which the plan made do not hold true. We can define a plan as an intention and control as the driving through of the plan, monitoring what actually happens and making changes as necessary.

The nature of planning and control differs in the long, medium, and short term. In the very long term operations managers make plans concerning what they intend to do, what resources they need, and what objectives they hope to achieve. The emphasis is on planning rather than control because there is little to control as such. They will use forecasts of likely demand which are described in aggregated terms. Similarly, the resources will be planned in an aggregated form. In carrying out their planning activities the operations managers will place heavy emphasis on achieving financial costs and revenue targets.

Medium-term planning and control is concerned with both planning in more detail and replanning if necessary. It looks ahead to assess the overall demand which the operation must meet in a partially disaggregated manner. Similarly resources will be set at a more disaggregated level. Just as important, contingencies will have been put in place which allow for slight deviations from plans. These contingencies will act as "reserve" resources and make planning and control easier in the short term.

In short-term planning and control many of the resources will have been set and it will be difficult to make large-scale changes in resourcing. However, short-term interventions are possible if things are not going to plan. By this time demand will be assessed on a totally disaggregated basis. In making short-term intervention and changes to plan, operations managers might be attempting to balance the various aspects of performance on an *ad hoc* basis. It is possible that they will not have the time to carry out detailed calculations of the effects of their short-term planning and control decisions on all these objectives. However, a general understanding of priorities will form the background to their decision making.

See also **capacity management; push and pull planning and control; scheduling; finite and infinite loading; sequencing; dependent and independent demand; demand response**

Bibliography

Vollmann, T. E., Berry, W. L. & Whybark, D. C. (1992). *Manufacturing planning and control.* 3rd edn. Burr Ridge, IL: Irwin.

NIGEL SLACK

predetermined motion time systems Predetermined motion time systems (PMTS) are WORK MEASUREMENT systems based on the analysis of work into basic human movements, classified according to the nature of the movement and the conditions under which it is made. Tables of data provide a time, at a defined rate of working, for each classification of each movement. The first PMTS (since designated as "first-level" systems) were designed to provide times for detailed manual work and thus consisted of fundamental movements and associated times. Large amounts of research,

data collection, analysis, synthesis, and validation are required to produce PMTS data and the number of such systems is very low. "Higher level" systems have since been devised, most commonly by combining these fundamental movements into common, simple manual tasks. Such higher level systems are designed for faster standard setting of longer-cycle activity.

Criticisms of PMTS relate to their inability to provide data for movements made under "unnatural" conditions (such as working in cramped conditions or with an unnatural body posture) or for mental processes and their difficulty in coping with work which is subject to interruptions. However, various systems have been derived for "office work," which include tasks with a simple and predictable mental content.

Many PMTS are proprietary systems and users must either attend a designated and approved training course and/or pay a royalty for use of the data.

Bibliography

Whitmore, D. (1991). Systems of measured data: PMTS and estimating. In T. J. Bentley (Ed.), *The management services handbook.* 2nd edn. London: Pitman.

JOHN HEAP

preventive maintenance Preventive maintenance is an approach to facilities care which aims to prevent failures which are caused by time-dependent factors such as component wear. Most operations plan their MAINTENANCE to include a level of regular preventive maintenance which gives a reasonably low but finite chance of breakdown. Usually the more frequent the preventive maintenance episodes, the less the chances of a breakdown. The balance between preventive and breakdown maintenance (intervening only when failure occurs) is set to minimize the total costs associated with care and breakdown. Infrequent preventive maintenance will cost little to provide but result in a high likelihood (and therefore cost) of breakdown maintenance. Conversely, very frequent preventive maintenance will be expensive to provide but will reduce the cost of having to provide breakdown maintenance. The total cost of maintenance is held to minimize at an "optimum" level. This optimum level indicates the recommended frequency of preventive maintenance.

However, the conventional representation of maintenance-related costs, although conceptually elegant, may not reflect reality in some operations and is being challenged by some academics. For example, the cost of providing preventive maintenance may not increase with increasing frequency of intervention as steeply as assumed. The relationship between preventive maintenance frequency and cost assumes that it is carried out by a separate set of people (skilled maintenance staff) whose time is scheduled and accounted for separately from the "operators" of the facilities. Furthermore, every time preventive maintenance takes place, the facilities cannot be used productively, which is why the relationship is often taken to increase marginal costs, because the maintenance episodes start to interfere with the normal working of the operation. Yet in many operations, at least some of the preventive maintenance can be performed by the operators themselves (which reduces the cost of providing it) and at times which are convenient for the operation (minimizing disruption). In addition it can also be argued that the cost of breakdowns could be higher than is traditionally assumed. Here the argument is that unplanned breakdowns may do more than necessitate a repair and stop the operation; they can take away stability from the operation which prevents it being able to improve itself (see DELIVERY DEPENDABILITY). The combination of these two adjustments to conventional PM have the effect of moving the "optimum" level of maintenance intervention significantly towards the use of preventive maintenance rather than run to breakdown maintenance.

See also condition-based maintenance; total productive maintenance; reliability-centered maintenance

NIGEL SLACK

principles of motion economy The principles of motion economy are guidelines to be used when examining and designing work station and workplace layouts and during METHOD STUDY. They are simple and empirical hints on work design which are based on a combination of simple ergonomic principles and common sense. They relate to both the design of the workplace and the design of the work. Thus, for example, they advise that gravity should be used, where possible, to deliver materials to their point of use and to remove completed work. They include the characteristics of easy movement which suggest that working methods and work places should be designed such that the motion patterns required of workers can comprise movements which are minimum, symmetrical, simultaneous, natural, rhythmical, habitual, and continuous.

See also ergonomics; layout

Bibliography

BS 3365. (1993). Part 2: Management services. Part 2: Guide to method study. London: British Standards Institution.

JOHN HEAP

process charts Process charts are a simple short-hand means of recording the details of work for subsequent analysis. Because they are in common usage, process charts are seen as a common "language" which facilitates analysis. A variety of process charts are designed for each particular level or stage of analysis. Their variety and flexibility means that they can be used at the work station and workplace level and at the wider system, process, or procedure level. All use a common core set of symbols, though some have additional symbols for specific and specialized process steps. The common symbols (of which there are only five) were first promulgated by the American Society of Mechanical Engineers and have become known as the ASME symbols (see Figure 1).

The simplest process chart is known as an outline process chart and records an overview of a process by recording only those steps of a process that can be represented by the ASME symbols of operation (which is a main process step that normally results in some change to the material being processed, or significant effort on behalf of the operator) and inspection (which is a verification of quality or quantity). This is

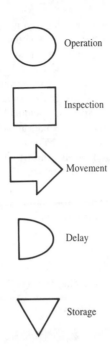

Figure 1 Process chart symbols

often a useful first step to identify key areas of concern before recording (part of) the process in more detail. In a "full" process chart, where all symbols are used, it is common to chart the process from the "viewpoint" of the material being processed, the worker carrying out the work or, less commonly, a piece of equipment. Thus, the same symbols can be used in different ways. As a simple example, a piece of equipment can be represented on an equipment-type flow process chart as a "delay" (because it is not in use) while a material-type flow process chart would show the material being transported to the next work station, and a man-type chart could show the operator involved in another operation on another machine. The chart to be used may be determined by the purpose of the investigation or by the relative costs involved in the process – a highly capital-intensive process may focus more attention on the equipment being used.

Process charts may also be used at a more micro level of analysis. An example is the two-handed process chart which records the motions performed by both hands during a task. The sequence of motion of each hand is charted

using the same symbols as before. There are slight changes to the meaning of the symbols, however. The delay symbol is used to indicate that the hand is waiting to carry out its next task. The storage symbol is used to indicate that the hand is holding on to a piece of material or a document. Two-handed process charts are usually drawn on a pre-formatted diagram.

See also **method study; service design; layout**

Bibliography

BS3375. (1993). Part 2: Management services. Part 2: Guide to method study. London: British Standards Institution.

Heap, J. P. (1991). *The analysis of work*. In T. J. Bentley (Ed.), BS3375. (1993) The management service handbook 2nd edn. London: Pitman.

JOHN HEAP

process layout A process (or functional) LAYOUT is one of the three basic options for laying out facilities to produce goods or deliver services, the other options being FIXED POSITION LAYOUT or PRODUCT LAYOUT. A fourth alternative, the CELL LAYOUT, is actually a hybrid facility arrangement which combines some of the principles of fixed position and product layouts.

The term "process layout" implies that all similar production processes are grouped together in the same department or area. This approach to laying out facilities can be applied to component production or assembly. In component production the "processes" might be different manufacturing processes such as milling, drilling, turning, grinding, plastic moulding, etc. In assembly the use of a process layout might involve having separate areas for producing different sub-assemblies, final assembly, testing, packing, etc. The use of process layouts is most common in batch operations where batches of parts (or perhaps customers in the case of services) are routed from one process area to another where a single production operation, or perhaps a limited number of operations, are carried out. Examples in service provision are less easy to identify, but in retailing the arrangement of shops in a high street could be considered to be a process layout since they each sell common products (bread, vegetables, hardware, etc.).

There is some debate concerning the relative advantages and disadvantages of process layouts. They are very popular, but this could simply be based on the historical situation where similar machines were grouped together because they were driven from a common power source. Advantages include the opportunity for specialized supervision, and there is a degree of flexibility involved because the priority of batches can be changed while they are being progressed through the production system. There are, on the other hand, a large number of disadvantages including high work in progress levels, frequent set-ups, extensive material movement, and long throughput times (*see* MANUFACTURING PROCESSES).

It is sometimes argued that process layouts enable greater economies of scale to be achieved. However, this is only true relative to using a fixed position layout; a product layout offers even greater scale benefits. The use of group technology and a cell layout can overcome the disadvantages associated with process layouts.

When process layouts are used they should be designed in such a way that they offer the best "efficiency." This can be achieved by ensuring that total material movement (or cost of material movement) is minimized. Alternatively, or additionally, other factors may be taken into account such as the movement of workers or the need for information to be exchanged between process areas. A number of computer software packages are available which are designed to calculate the "optimum" process layout; these include CRAFT (computerized relative allocation of facilities technique) and CORELAP (computerized relationship layout planning). The input to these packages would normally include such data as the number of material movements per unit of time between the various processes and the cost of movement per unit of distance. Secondary factors such as the desired "closeness" of processes for the purpose of information exchange, etc. can be represented on a "relationship chart."

One of the problems with using such techniques is that they only provide the solution to a "static" problem (i.e. for a particular mix of products and fixed operation sequences). In practice, however, the layout problem is a dynamic one because the situation is continuously changing and the "best" solution today may not be so tomorrow. For this reason "simulation" is growing in popularity as a tool for analyzing and designing process layouts (and indeed any type of layout). A computer simulation enables changes to a layout, or its operating information, to be modeled so that the effect can be seen almost instantaneously. Moreover a "visual interactive" simulation will allow the designer to see a graphic representation of the layout on a computer screen and to quickly determine the effect of any modifications made.

Bibliography

Francis, R. L. & White, J. A. (1987). *Facility layout and location: An analytical approach*. Englewood Cliffs, NJ: Prentice-Hall.

DAVID BENNETT

process of manufacturing strategy formulation   The process of manufacturing strategy (as opposed to the CONTENT OF MANUFACTURING STRATEGY) means the steps, procedures, and methods by which organizations can decide how they wish to develop their manufacturing or operations function. There are many alternative procedures available which have been suggested as providing suitable outline frameworks for developing manufacturing strategy. Although these frameworks and procedures are generally explained in terms of manufacturing (as opposed to service) strategy formulation they are, for the most part, reasonably well suited to developing an OPERATIONS STRATEGY in a wide range of operations. Three issues are emerging as being of interest to operations management academics (and to a lesser extent operations management practitioners). They are, first, how should the outcome from the manufacturing strategy process be judged? Second, what prescriptive stage models and frameworks are effective in helping operations managers to frame strategies for their functional area? Third, notwithstanding the prescriptive models of manufacturing strategy formulation, how do operations managers actually behave when formulating manufacturing strategies?

Judging the Effectiveness of Manufacturing Strategy

In general it seems to be agreed that effective manufacturing strategies should clarify the links between overall competitive strategy and the development of the company's operations resources. In that sense the key attribute of an effective manufacturing strategy is that it must be appropriate for the organization's competitive strategy. Although appropriateness is necessary, it is not sufficient to indicate an effective manufacturing strategy. A manufacturing strategy must also be comprehensive, not in the sense of defining every minor operational decision, but rather to indicate how all parts of the manufacturing function are expected to perform. It must also be coherent in that it avoids clashes between different elements of the resulting manufacturing strategy. Similarly, a manufacturing strategy needs to exhibit some degree of consistency over time. Finally, a manufacturing strategy needs to be credible in so much as it is regarded as achievable by the rest of the organization.

Manufacturing Strategy Formulation Procedures

One of the most widely known and influential formulation procedures is the so-called Hill methodology (Hill, 1985). Hill's model follows the relatively conventional approach of providing a connection between different levels of analysis in strategy making. It is a five-step procedure which moves from developing an understanding of overall corporate objectives through to specific structural and infrastructural (see OPERATIONS ACTIVITIES).

Step one involves understanding the corporate objectives of the organization. The justification for this is first to provide a clear basis for strategic direction and, second, to delineate the boundaries within which manufacturing strategy must operate. Issues such as the relative importance of profitability and growth, investment targets, employee policies, and environmental issues are suggested as being appropriate for consideration in this stage. Step two involves understanding the marketing strategy of the organization as it derives from corporate objectives. The objective of this is to understand product markets and segments and the range, mix and volumes of products intended for each

segment. Other issues suggested for consideration at this stage include the degree of standardization or customization of products, the appropriate level of innovation and product development, together with the timing of any changes in marketing strategy.

Step three of the process is regarded by many as being the pivotal stage of Hill's methodology. It involves asking the question with which this methodology has become identified, namely "How do products win orders in the marketplace?" (See ORDER-WINNERS AND QUALIFIERS.) This step is essentially a process of translating the corporate and marketing objectives of the organization into terms which have more specific meaning for the operations or manufacturing function. However, Hill does stress that at this stage competitive factors other than those under the sole responsibility of manufacturing need to be considered. It is suggested that as well as identifying order-winners and qualifiers it will be necessary to distinguish between the relative importance of each competitive factor in each category. Hill also suggests distinguishing between qualifiers which are critical in terms of the customers or markets requirements with those which are less so. The former might be labeled as "order-losing sensitive qualifiers." Step four involves identifying the appropriate process choice for the manufacturing operation. Step five involves determining the relevant infrastructural issues suggested by the identified set of order-winners and qualifiers.

The methodology is not intended to be a simple, sequential movement from step one through to step five. Although primarily a "top-down" model, the process is an iterative one whereby operations managers cycle between an understanding of the long-term strategic requirements of the organization and the specific resource developments which support the strategy. The process as a whole is intended to provide two outputs. The first is a comprehensive statement of the implications for manufacturing of future market projections. The second is an understanding of the way in which the capabilities and resources of manufacturing can themselves influence the strategic direction of the organization as a whole.

Another influential formulation methodology is the so-called Platts–Gregory procedure. This process uses an audit-based procedure intended to guide operations managers through a logical process of identifying manufacturing objectives, measuring current manufacturing performance, determining the effects of current manufacturing practices and identifying where changes are required. The procedure uses a series of pro forma work sheets for groups of managers to complete thereby analyzing and auditing their manufacturing processes. Overall the procedure has three stages. Stage one involves developing an understanding of the market position of the organization by assessing opportunities and threats within the competitive environment. More specifically, it also involves identifying the factors which are required by the market in order to compete effectively. In this it is similar to the Hill methodology. However, where it differs from the Hill methodology is in comparing the requirements of the market with the achieved level of performance in terms of the operation's ability to satisfy the market. Whereas the Hill methodology places its main emphasis on the manufacturing strategy being developed from a customer's view of competitive factors, the Platts–Gregory procedure is explicit in making a comparison between the requirements of the market and the performance of the operation. In this sense it is similar to the IMPORTANCE–PERFORMANCE MATRIX. However, rather than use a matrix procedure to identify performance gaps, the Platts–Gregory procedure uses a profiling process to superimpose a profile of market requirements on a profile of achieved performance. Stage two of the procedure involves auditing the capabilities of the manufacturing operation in order to identify current operations practice and assess the extent to which this practice helps to achieve the type of performance indicated as being required in stage one. Stage three develops a new set of manufacturing strategies by reviewing the various options available to the organization and selecting those which best satisfy the criteria which have emerged from the previous two stages.

Manufacturing Strategy in Practice

Several researchers have examined the way in which organizations formulate their manufac-turing strategies in practice. Among the findings of these studies are the following.

Most organizations are comfortable with working in an approximate top-down manner starting with a "manufacturing mission" and working through operations objectives towards their implications for resource development. In this sense, formulation practice mirrors the prescriptive models. Implicit in this finding is that most firms have an intuitive understanding of the order-winning concept.

Many firms incorporate some procedure which provides an analysis of both strengths and weaknesses. The purpose of this analysis is usually to assess the ability of the manufacturing function to respond to current industry condi-tions. The overall objective, however, is usually to align future developments in the manufactur-ing function to some concept of competitive support.

Often there is a single stimulus which prompted the organization to reassess its manufacturing strategy. This may have been an external stimulus such as a deterioration in trading conditions, or an internal stimulus such as the appointment of a new chief executive officer.

Implementing manufacturing strategy is usually seen as a process of building consensus among employees for the strategy. Often this involves a team approach in managing imple-mentation, even if the same team was not involved in formulating the strategy initially.

Other findings of the formulation and implementation of manufacturing strategies closely shadow the more general implementa-tion literature inasmuch as they emphasize the importance of organizational culture, consistency of implementation, top manage-ment support, and the importance of project management.

See also **operations role; performance mea-surement; trade-offs**

Bibliography

Anderson, J. C., Schroeder, R. G. & Cleveland, G. (1991). The process of manufacturing strategy: some empirical observations and conclusions. *International Journal of Operations and Production Management*, 11, 3, 86–110.

Hill, T. J. (1985). *Manufacturing strategy*. London: Macmillan.

Leong, G. K., Snyder, D. L. & Ward, P. T. (1990). Research in the process and content of manufacturing strategy. *OMEGA, The International Journal of Management Science*, 18, 2, 109–22.

Marucheck, A., Pannesi, R. & Anderson, C. (1990). An exploratory study in the manufacturing strategy process in practice. *Journal of Operations Management*, 9, *1*, 101–11.

Platts, K. W. & Gregory, M. J. (1990). Manufacturing audit in the process of strategy formulation. *International Journal of Production and Operations Management*, 10, *9*, 5–27.

Voss, C. A. (1992). *Manufacturing strategy process and content*. London: Chapman and Hall.

NIGEL SLACK

process technology   Process technologies are the machines, equipment and devices which contribute to an operation transforming materials and information and customers in order to add value (*see* TRANSFORMATION MODEL). Almost all operations use process technologies, even the most labor-intensive.

It is necessary to distinguish between product or service technology on the one hand and process technology on the other. In manufacturing operations it is a relatively simple matter to separate product from process technology. However, in some service operations it is far more difficult to distinguish process from "product" technology. For example, an aircraft is process technology or an airline. It "transforms" customers by transporting them. But the technology is also part of the product. In fact customers may choose an airline partly to experience its superior aircraft. In cases like this, product or service technology and process technology are, in effect, the same thing.

The management of process technology, as far as operations managers are concerned, involves being able to articulate how technology could improve effectiveness, being involved in the choice of the technology itself, integrating the technology into the rest of the operation, and upgrading or replacing the technology when necessary. To do this operations managers need to understand the technology with which they are dealing.

Although this does not mean that all operations managers must also be experts in the core science on which their technology is based, they do need to know enough about the principles behind the technology to understand the managerial implications of technology choice. Significant questions include the following:

- What does the technology do which is different to other similar technologies?

- How does it do it? That is, what particular characteristics of the technology are used to perform its function?

- What benefits does using the technology give to the operation?

- What constraints does using the technology place on the operation?

See also **advanced manufacturing technology; flexible manufacturing systems; computer-integrated manufacturing; process technology; robotics; automated guided vehicles; service innovations**

NIGEL SLACK

product families   The idea of grouping products or component parts into families arose in response to the problems associated with batch operations using a PRODUCT LAYOUT. One of the major limitations of this traditional approach to production relates to the frequent and time consuming resetting that needs to take place when facilities are changed over between the production of different batches of products or parts. This results in a significant loss of capacity and also causes management to produce larger batches than may be required to satisfy immediate demand.

A major cause of long resetting times is the dissimilarity of design features, and hence processing operations, across the whole range of products and parts being made in any particular production plant. In conventional batch operations production planning does not take design features into account when a facility is changed from one product to another. As a result the sequence in which batches are processed is, from a design point of view, random and the change-over time is consequently maximized.

The identification of families of products and parts addresses this problem by taking design into account in the production planning process. A family is simply a group of products which exhibits the same or similar design characteristics. Hence there is some commonality of processing operations which results in shorter overall setting times when they are produced on the same machine or group of facilities.

Families are normally created using coding and classification (see CELL LAYOUT) where products or parts are identified by a numerical or alphanumeric coding system. Using this approach the identification numbers of products are actually coded descriptions of their design which can be used to sort them into groups, or "families," for the purpose of processing on a common set of facilities.

DAVID BENNETT

product layout A product (or operation sequence) LAYOUT is one of the three basic options for laying out facilities to produce goods or deliver services, the other options being a FIXED POSITION LAYOUT or PROCESS LAYOUT. A fourth alternative, the CELL LAYOUT, is actually a hybrid facility arrangement which combines some of the principles of fixed position and product layouts.

As its name implies a product, or operation sequence, layout is determined by the design of the product. In other words, it is where machines, equipment and workplaces are arranged according to the sequence of operations required for a defined product. In this context the product could be the complete end product, a sub-assembly or a component part.

Product layouts usually take the form of lines with unidirectional flow. Although cell layouts are also based on the design of products they differ in that the operation sequence and flow direction can usually be varied.

There are two basic types of product layout. First, there is the assembly type, where at each work station materials are added and resources applied to produce discrete end products.

Second, there is the analytical (or "disassembly" type) where a single raw material input is separated into parts and subsequently processed. Examples of this second type are oil refining and abattoirs; in fact Henry Ford revealed that his idea of building the Model T car using an assembly line came from seeing lines used in the Chicago meat packing industry.

There is a third type of product layout, the transfer line, where there is only one material input at the beginning of the line and its form is modified, usually by machining processes, as it stops at each work station. However, this is conceptually similar to the assembly type and can be designed in the same way.

Some of the advantages of product layouts are that they require relatively infrequent set-ups, involve low work in progress levels, have minimum material movement, need lower labor skills, and can be easily automated. They gained great popularity in the early part of the twentieth century after their possibilities for improving efficiency were demonstrated by Henry Ford. More recently, however, a number of problems have come to light. Among these are the "human" problems of recruitment difficulties, absenteeism, high turnover, etc. and the "physical" problems of high capital cost, risk of stoppage (if one machine fails the whole line stops) and inflexibility (in terms of product variety and operation sequence).

The design of product layouts is very important because they are normally used in high product volume situations where there is price competition in the marketplace. Efficiency is therefore a prime consideration and there is a need to minimize the amount of idle time at each work station. The approach used in their design is usually termed LINE BALANCING, which as well as minimizing idle time seeks to spread it evenly across work stations. A further consideration is to minimize the SYSTEM LOSS which results from differences between the operators' work times and the fixed cycle time of the line (*see* WORK TIME DISTRIBUTIONS).

A popular belief with product layouts is that they can only be used in connection with highly standardized products. This may have been true at one time, but now a wide variety of different products can be made using variations on the basic product layout known as multimodel and mixed-model lines. One of the difficulties with

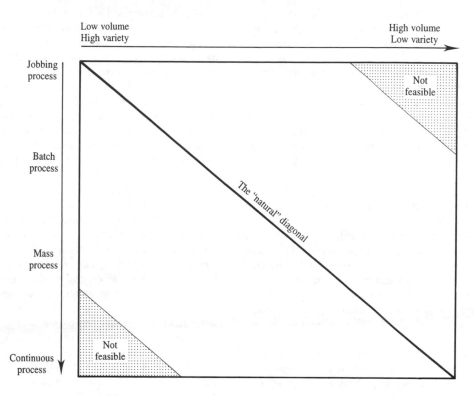

Figure 1 The product—process matrix

building a wide variety of products on a line was the need to schedule the correct item of material to the correct work station at the correct time. However, this can now be achieved relatively easily under computer control.

See also **job design; division of labor; "scientific" management**

Bibliography

Wild, R. (1972). *Mass production management.* London: Wiley.

DAVID BENNETT

product–process matrix   The product–process matrix is a model which is used to demonstrate the combination of a product's (or product group's) volume and variety characteristics, and the nature of the processes which make it. It was originally devised by Hayes and Wheelwright (1979) who saw it as "one way in which the interaction of the product lifecycle and process lifecycle can be represented." In its original form the two dimensions of the matrix were seen in lifecycle terms, one of the authors' intentions being to show that processes progress through a predictable lifecycle which corresponds to the better known concept of the product lifecycle. Since then the model has been used primarily to show the different operations needs of products (or product groups) which have different competitive characteristics and to indicate the consequences of failing to match product and process characteristics.

The product–process matrix is an array whose horizontal dimension represents points on the volume–variety continuum (*see* VOLUME and VARIETY) from low volume one-off products, through to high volume, high standardization products. Its vertical dimension represents MANUFACTURING PROCESSES from jobbing, through batch and mass, to continuous (see Figure 1).

Product–process combinations can occupy most parts of the matrix, although the two extreme areas of the bottom left and upper right portions of the matrix can be taken as representing combinations which are, for all practical purposes, infeasible. It would be difficult to imagine the circumstances under which any operation would wish to manufacture one-offs on a continuous basis or high volume standardized products on a jobbing basis. However, the other parts of the matrix represent the choices open to operations managers.

Hayes and Wheelwright use the matrix to make three important points. The first is that for all points on the volume–variety continuum there is a corresponding position on the process continuum. This is represented by the "natural" diagonal of the matrix. So companies which supply customized products in low volume will find the flexibility of jobbing process particularly appropriate for their type of business. Companies who supply high volumes of standardized products will regard the low-cost production possible with mass or continuous processes as enabling them to compete effectively. Likewise all points on the volume–variety continuum will correspond to an appropriate process type.

The second important point made by Hayes and Wheelwright is that companies might move away from the "natural" diagonal, perhaps deliberately in order to achieve some kind of competitive advantage, or because they "drift" into using inappropriate processes. Either way, there are predictable consequences of moving off the diagonal. Moving from the diagonal in the upper right direction means that the process used to manufacture a product group is more flexible (in terms of being able to cope with ahigher variety of product types) than is strictly necessary. The "excess" FLEXIBILITY might mean that the COST of manufacture is higher than if the manufacturing process was positioned "on the diagonal." Moving from the diagonal towards the bottom left of the matrix results in less flexibility than would seem to be necessary for the product group's variety. Such an inappropriately rigid process could incur extra costs, either of lost market opportunities or through the effort and lost capacity needed to change over the process between products.

The third point to be drawn from the matrix is that companies can define their product groups using the model in order to FOCUS their manufacturing resources more effectively. The matrix encourages companies to analyze their products in such a way as to distinguish between the different product groups which require different processes. In this way it encourages companies to explore alternative product classification boundaries and the consequences of segmenting their manufacturing operations to concentrate on their individual competitive priorities.

Developments of the product–process matrix include substituting other dimensions for the vertical process dimension. For example, the similar argument can be made for a matrix which incorporates scales representing the various dimensions of process technology such as the scale (capacity increment) of technology, the degree of automation, or the extent of its integration. The matrix can also be adapted for use with service operations, either by using the same manufacturing process types (which Hayes and Wheelwright (1984) do) or by substituting SERVICE PROCESSES for the original MANUFACTURING PROCESSES.

See also **manufacturing strategy**

Bibliography

Hayes, R. H. & Wheelwright, S. C. (1979). Link manufacturing process and product life cycles. *Harvard Business Review*, **57**, *1*, 133–40.

Hayes, R. H. & Wheelwright, S. C. (1984). *Restoring our competitive edge: Competing through manufacturing*. New York: Wiley.

NIGEL SLACK

productivity   Productivity is usually taken to mean the ratio of what is produced by an operation to what is required to produce it. Put in terms of the TRANSFORMATION MODEL, it is the ratio of outputs from the transformation to the transforming and transformed resources which form its inputs. High productivity is generally assumed to be a "good thing" inasmuch as a productive operation is more likely, other things being equal, to have lower COST – products or services. It is this close connection with the cost performance of opera-

$$\text{TFP} = \frac{\text{total output of all products and services}}{\text{total resource inputs}}$$

which can be disaggregated to refer to only particular outputs:

$$\text{TFP (for product } X) = \frac{\text{output of product } X}{\text{total resources to make product } X}$$

or particular inputs, when the ratio is called single factor productivity (SFP):

$$\text{SFP (input } Y) = \frac{\text{total output of all products and services}}{\text{input of resource } Y}$$

or both:

$$\text{SFP (output } X, \text{ input } Y) = \frac{\text{output of product } X}{\text{input of resource } Y}$$

Figure 1

tions which accounts for the interest in understanding and measuring productivity.

Productivity combines the concepts of effectiveness and efficiency, where effectiveness is the degree to which end results are achieved and efficiency is associated with the amount of input resources used.

Productivity as a Ratio

Although the ratio-based definition of productivity is conceptually straightforward, the idea becomes complex either when extended beyond the basic concept, or when it is used to measure the actual productivity of operations.

In terms of the measurement units, outputs can be measured in physical terms such as tonnes, cars or kilowatts, or financial terms such as revenue, profit or added value. Likewise, inputs can be measured in physical terms such as tonnes of material inputs, staff hours worked, or financial terms such as cost of material, cost of labor or value of assets.

The total factor productivity (TFP) of an operation can be described by the equation shown in Figure 1.

It is also important to decide whether inputs and outputs should be considered at their actual or optimal levels (see Figure 2). In cell 1 we consider the actual output relating to an actual input. Such a ratio on its own tells the analyst little about performance, since he is unable to

state whether the ratio is good or bad. He therefore needs to compare it with a standard in order to make such a judgment. This standard may be provided by:

- a ratio relating to a previous time period;
- a ratio relating to a similar activity carried out at the same time elsewhere (in the enterprise or outside),
- or to the industry as a whole (this is the essence of inter-firm comparisons);
- a ratio of the maximum output that can be obtained for a given level of input (cell 2 in the matrix);
- a ratio of the minimum input needed to produce the actual level of output (cell 3 in the matrix).

Thus, an evaluation of performance may be based on a comparison of ratio 1 with itself (for other time periods or other operations) or with ratio 2 or with ratio 3. (Eilon, 1982)

Measuring Productivity

In practice, operations predominantly take one of three approaches to measuring productivity. Partial productivity measurements are used where total output is divided by an incomplete (often a one factor) measure of input.

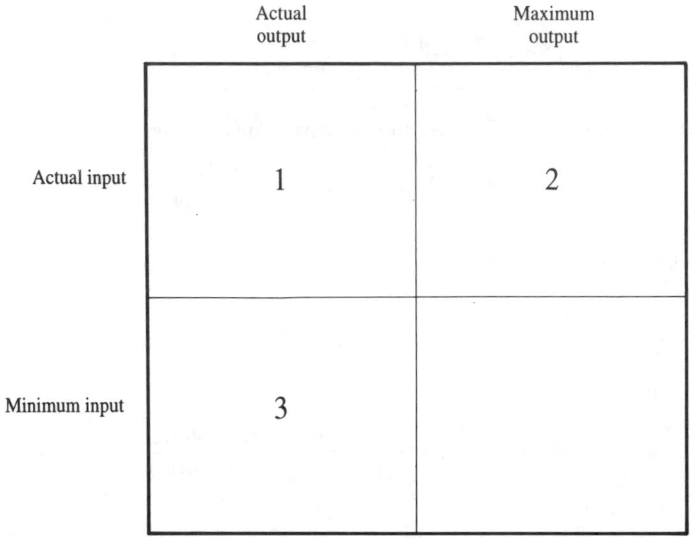

	Actual output	Maximum output
Actual input	1	2
Minimum input	3	

Figure 2 Choice of input and output in productivity measurement

- Total factor productivity where all outputs are divided by all inputs.
- Added value indices which compare the value of outputs and inputs minus the value of bought-in goods and services.

Although partial measures of productivity are by far the most straightforward way of measuring productivity, taken alone they can be misleading by their inability to take in all factors in the operations process which may be relevant. For example, output per labor hour might be improving, but this could be at the expense of inefficiently used capital resources. A natural tendency might be to pick a measure which, although convenient, is not as important as other partial measures. The partial measure may even, over time, become regarded as a comprehensive measure of productivity.

Total factor productivity provides a much more comprehensive picture of the way an operation is converting its input resources into outputs. However, this more representative picture is gained only at the expense of considerable complexity. Although relatively successful attempts to use total factor productivity have been reported, nearly all report difficulties in obtaining satisfactory data and incorporating realistic assumptions. Reported difficulties include managerial confusion between total factor productivity and traditional accounting concepts, choosing a suitable base period against which to compare changes in productivity, measuring the value of capital inputs, satisfactorily accommodating technological economies of scale, and coping with changes in product or service mix over time.

Using the value added approach to productivity measurement can considerably simplify some of the problems conventionally encountered in other productivity measurement approaches. Most notably, changes in bought-in material and service prices are excluded from the calculations. Two particular problems with value added approaches have been identified. First, it can make it difficult to determine how much productivity change is caused by changes in the use of purchased goods and services. Second, it may even take changes in productivity which are due to bought-in goods and services and attribute them instead to changes in energy or labor productivity.

See also **service productivity; flexibility; capacity strategy; inventory management**

Bibliography

Eilon, S. (1982). The use and misuse of productivity ratios. *OMEGA, The International Journal of Management Science*, **10**, 6, 575–80.

Eilon, S., Gold, B. & Soesan, J. (1976). *Applied productivity analysis for industry*. Oxford: Pergamon.

Hayes, R. H., Wheelwright, S. C. & Clark, K. B. (1988). *Dynamic manufacturing*. New York: Free Press.

NIGEL SLACK

has meant that diffusion has been extensive; reports suggest that by the early 1990s over 50 percent of all control was being carried out using PLCs in some form.

See also **advanced manufacturing technology; flexible manufacturing systems; computer-integrated manufacturing; process technology; robotics**

JOHN BESSANT

programmable logic controllers Programmable logic controllers (PLCs) are computer-based devices which are used to control production processes. The first PLC was developed in the 1960s by General Motors Hydromatic Division as a solid-state control panel which could have its control functions changed without wiring alterations. By the mid-1970s PLCs began to find application in many different sectors and applications, and by the 1980s the original concept of a simple digital controller acting in isolation had all but disappeared, to be replaced by an integrated, multifunction model. Current generations of PLCs support a wide range of applications, and include digital and analogue signal processing, high level languages for simpler programming, communication with other PLCs, and within computer hierarchies and beyond. Importantly, too, they are available in standardized modules which can be built up into tailor-made systems to suit particular applications. Thus the same basic family of general-purpose PLCs can find application in industries as diverse as steel making, aerospace engineering, and food processing.

A major advantage of PLC technology is that it can be used in a step-by-step pattern, moving up from simple material handling and packing or monitoring type applications where they operate in stand-alone mode, through sequential and interlocking control of processes right up to complex integrated machine control, energy management systems, etc. Thus they can be seen as building blocks of integrated and flexible automation in a wide range of industries. Their role as a low-cost, general-purpose controller

project control Project control is part of PROJECT MANAGEMENT and comprises a cycle of which control is the last stage. The cycle is: Plan; Monitor; Control. Control only happens when action is taken subsequent to monitoring to correct deviation from a valid and well-established plan. It is vital for effective control to establish baselines and measure progress against them. So attention to the planning process is the foundation of control. The control focus in most projects is on time and cost, however, the principles apply to any set of major project deliverables such as materials and specifications.

The control stage encompasses assessing where the project is and, more importantly, "where it is going." Figure 1 illustrates not only the cyclic nature of project control, but also the various actions that need to be taken depending on the extent of the variance between the planned and actual situation.

Monitoring

The objective of monitoring is to accumulate progress data, analyze differences from the plan and forecast what is likely to happen to the project.

Monitoring comprises gathering of data, consolidation of the data into reports and graphics, and then analyzing the information to draw conclusions and recommendations for action. Data gathering on a large project is not a trivial task; as much automation as possible should be employed. Employing the aid of techniques such as bar coding and linking constituent systems with an integrated database, can help to keep down the cost of monitoring.

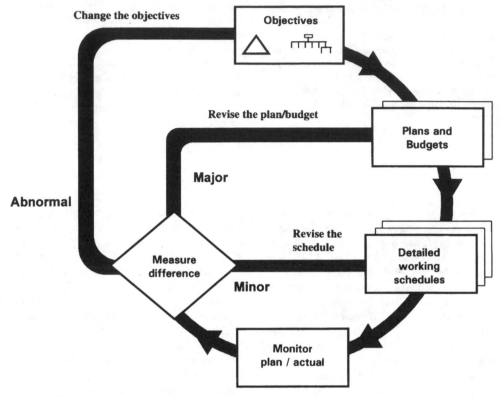

Figure 1 The project control cycle

In large projects the cost of management and control can be in the order of 5 percent of the project cost. The frequency of monitoring depends on the overall project duration and what stage the project has reached. At peak progress and often towards completion, monitoring is more crucial and its frequency should increase.

Change Control

If the difference between plan and actual values is greater than can be accommodated by just minor revisions to the schedule, then the plans and/or budgets have to be changed. At this point, organizations with suitable change control procedures use them to identify the extent of the change and formally incorporate it into the project. The effect of the change on both time and cost should be estimated before agreement, and funding for it should be obtained. This is especially important if the project is a formal contract.

Good control is exemplified by making rational decisions and taking corrective action as necessary.

Communication

The final stage of any control procedure will be to communicate any changes to plans or budgets. This may be part of the review meeting held regularly by the project team, but it is essential that agreed decisions and changes are reported back to the project participants and stakeholders. Amendments to the project plan should be published and distributed.

Methods and Procedures

Many organizations have developed standards for not only project control, but the wider issues of project management, including organization structures and the role of the sponsoring organization. These procedures and methods are as much a part of project management as corresponding quality standards are to the operations of the business. Over the past few years the project management community has seen the development of a number of standard methodologies. Many of these standard methodologies have been assembled by consultants who sell both the method and its implementation. They have their roots in the development of software systems.

Bibliography

Archibald, R. D. (1976). *Managing high technology programs and projects*. Chichester: John Wiley.

RALPH LEVENE

project cost management and control The management of costs in project management will always be judged by how close the final cost is to the budget. The final budget will not necessarily be the original budget as this may well have been amended by incorporating project changes, both plus and minus. The original budget will relate to the cost estimate approved for the project. The process of estimating starts when the project is conceived and continues at different levels throughout the project. The final part of managing the cost will be to produce a historical report which is essential for improved future estimates. Accurate recording of costs throughout the project is therefore of prime importance. In many projects a large proportion of the project cost is generated from the time that people spend: accurate and timely timesheet recording is therefore essential.

The basic phases of most projects are the same: concept, feasibility, planning, realization and (organization) implementation. At the end of each of these phases an estimate is produced that increasingly matches the final cost. The concept phase produces a ballpark figure that will only be used to gain agreement to move onto the feasibility phase when a more detailed preliminary estimate is produced. This should aim to be in the order of 25 percent of the final cost. The planning phase should refine this estimate to the range ±10 percent to provide the working budget for the major proportion of the project expenditure in its realization and final project delivery.

Data gathered throughout each phase contribute to the definition of the cost estimate and increase its accuracy. Mature and experienced organizations collate costs to an estimating database regularly. Some industries such as petrochemical engineering and construction have the benefit of commercial estimating/cost databases to which they can subscribe. For software development projects there are also parameterized standard models.

Data can also be collected at work package level and future projects can be estimated using a building block approach via the WORK BREAKDOWN STRUCTURES.

Once the project is in its realization phase the "estimate" becomes a budget and costs start to incur. The project cost should continue to be "estimated" and take into account actual costs and forecast information. Cost management should always be concerned with the final project cost during this phase, and it concentrates on trends, evaluating work still to do by looking at the elements that make up the actual costs, e.g. workhours (labor), materials, equipment, and overheads. Some of the actual costs come from the organization's financial accounting system. Links between the project cost system and the finance systems have to ensure data integrity and timeliness.

Sophisticated cost management systems not only track actuals in cost terms but also in terms of work achievement and its value. Such systems are termed project performance measurement systems and their techniques originate from standards developed by the US military for monitoring complex defense projects. The principle, as with all powerful tools, is simple: the practice is more difficult especially in relation to measuring the value of work achieved. The cost budget is not just considered as a single value but the planned spend through time is compared throughout the project both to actual expenditure and the value of work achieved. The key issue in performance measurement systems is the link between time and cost, i.e. the time phasing of costs.

If the cumulative costs of a project are plotted against time then the shape of the line will be an S curve. Many organizations report actual

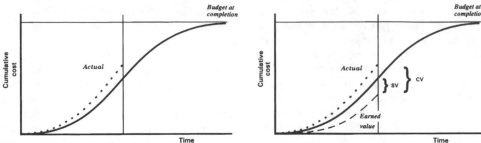

Figure 1 Examples of project cost management and control graphs

expenditure to date against this curve. If the expenditure to date is not the same as the budgeted sum to date the project has either spent more or less than planned although not necessarily "over" or "under" spent. The important issue is to compare how the value of the work done compares to the budget spend and the actual spend. The value of work achieved is commonly called the "earned value." Figure 1 illustrates a typical situation. From this it appears that the project has spent more than planned by half way through its duration. It also shows that it has it overspent and that its earned value is less than the budget. Had the earned value line been coincident with the actuals line, the project would have been ahead of schedule.

There is a specific terminology for performance management which relates to the time phasing of the costs. The costs to date are referenced by:

- Actuals = actual cost of work performed (ACWP)

- Budget = budget cost of work scheduled (BCWS)

- Value of work done = budget cost of work performed (BCWP) or the earned value

In addition, useful measures of how close the project is performing to budget are measured by the differences between earned value and actuals, that is the cost variance (CV), and earned value and budget, that is the schedule variance (SV).

A number of performance indicators are usefully recorded through the project:

- Cost performance index (CPI) = BCWP/ACWP, where less than 1 represents poor performance

- Schedule performance index (SPI) = BCWP/BCWS, where less than 1 represents poor performance

- To complete performance index (TCPI) = (BAC – BCWP)/(BAC – ACWP), where less than 1 represents good performance, and BAC is the budget at completion

The difficulty, in practice, is determining appropriate measures of earned value and putting monitoring systems in place. Objective measures of work accomplishment are easy to establish when physical accomplishment is visible but more difficult in design oriented projects. Measurement can range from subjective assessment to methods for counting physical accomplishment via units of work complete. Appropriate and objective measures of work should be established, taking into account the capability of the organization to regularly monitor progress. Project performance measurement systems are frequently oriented to the project work breakdown structure so that budget, actual and earned values can be aggregated or "rolled up" through the structure.

See also **project control; project risk management**

Bibliography

Clark, F. D. & Lorenzoni, A. B. (1988). Applied cost engineering. New York:. Marcel Dekker.

Fleming, Q. W. (1988). *Cost/schedule control systems criteria: The management guide to CSCSC.* Chicago:. Probus Publishing Co.

RALPH LEVENE

project leadership Within PROJECT MANAGEMENT the role of the project manager is developing in importance in many organizations as the need to work across the organization increases. The traditional skills of many project managers have had to be augmented by financial and strategic skills as organizations orient towards a project style of working and managing change.

An essential ingredient to the success of any project will be the project manager or leader. Although strong leadership may seem to be a vital skill in a task force environment where the authority of the project manager is high, by contrast, in a matrix environment, negotiation skills and diplomacy are more valuable to secure resources. Building the project team and blending them into a cohesive unit is the major challenge in most matrix structures (*see* ORGANIZATION OF DEVELOPMENT).

As well as completing the project within its time, cost, and quality all the stakeholders including the team have to be satisfied. This frequently requires addressing competing agendas. Therefore, a project manager must have skills over and above those of a "functional" manager to include those of leadership and motivation in a team environment that often includes temporary resources. The working life of a project manager will be a series of temporary assignments (projects) within which there are many changes in emphasis as each project moves through its lifecycle.

Typically a project manager would need the following knowledge and skills to manage both the project objectives and its team:

- the scope of the project and its objectives;

- the business need for the project;

- the stakeholder requirements and their criteria for success;

- the decision-making processes necessary to ensure a successful project;

- an appreciation of the systems and procedures required to provide effective project planning and control;

- an ability to present well and communicate;

- report-writing capability;

- motivational and interpersonal abilities;

- the leadership qualities necessary to create a team and provide the enthusiasm, dedication, and commitment to drive the team to achieve difficult targets;

- negotiation and diplomatic skills to be able to resolve conflicts that arise at organizational interfaces;

- the management of resources, time schedules, and cash flow;

- the use of output from computerized project control systems;

- an understanding of the supply chain process and how to deal with vendors and suppliers;

- a commitment to quality and safety programs;

- contracts and the contracting process and how to deal with subcontractors;

- a financial control ability to obtain value for money through sound management;

- style, in order to engender the trust and confidence of senior management and other stakeholders.

To some extent or other a project manager takes on the following, often competing, roles throughout a project career:

- director;

- delegator;

- disciplinarian;

- motivator;

- coach and developer (of people);

- team builder;

- sympathizer;

- decision maker;

- diplomat;

- negotiator;

- manipulator;

- company loyalist;

- rule breaker;

- co-ordinator;

- resource allocator;

- orator/presenter.

An ideal project manager would possess the following attributes to a high level of competence: charisma, charm, assertiveness, inspiration, empathy, a logical approach, and knowledge.

Bibliography

Briner, W., Geddes, M. & Hastings, C. (1990). *Project leadership*. Aldershot: Gower.

RALPH LEVENE

project management The traditional image of a project is one of physical endeavor such as a major construction project or perhaps a new product development. Yet project management is needed when introducing any new entity or making a change that involves moving from one state to another. Project management is the processes of managing that change by planning the work, executing it and co-ordinating the contribution of the people and organizations with an interest in the project.

The view that project management is purely a set of "practical" techniques is belied by its emphasis on team working, a perspective that crosses functional boundaries, an orientation to process and logical progression together with strong leadership. (*See* PROJECT LEADERSHIP).

The Origins of Project Management

Modern project management techniques date from the development of NETWORK TECHNIQUES which started in the 1950s with its origins in operational research, although prior work on activity planning was pioneered by Henry Gantt at the turn of the century. (*See* GANTT CHART). Since then project management has moved to encompass techniques other than those of the planning and scheduling of activities. There have been many developments over the past 40 years to extend project management into detailed methods for the management and control of cost, resources, quality, and performance.

Project management has developed into a blend of both mechanistic techniques that are designed to help plan and control of the project, and behavioral or "soft" techniques to help the people processes. In general the "hard" techniques are oriented around the planning, monitoring, and control of time, cost and deliverables; project management software is designed as an aid to these processes. Techniques for project definition, activity tracking and work measurement are typified by WORK BREAKDOWN STRUCTURES, network analysis and cost/performance measurement.

Team leadership and building a cohesive team are key elements to insure project success. Best practice for the use of any of the planning and control techniques involves a team rather than individual effort; for example a competent planner will involve the key members of the project team in construction of the plan, to insure their commitment to it. Team building techniques which involve role identification and team cohesion are frequently employed to increase the chances of success in major projects.

The Essential Characteristics of a Project

Organizations will carry out two distinct types of project: those that can be classified as development projects and those that relate to organizational improvements and changes.

The "development" projects are those which arise from the need to create new or improved products or facilities. The "change" projects will comprise projects that arise from business process improvements to create new ways of working or new organizational forms. These change projects are often classified as BUSINESS PROCESS REDESIGN (BPR) projects as their size and scope in many cases, parallels traditional engineering projects.

Whatever the source of the project it has the same basic characteristics of objectives, organization and resources to carry it out that distinguish it from a continuous operation.

Specific objectives and goal. A project involves people working together to complete a particular end product or specific deliverable (result):

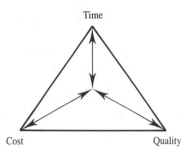

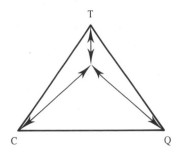

Figure 1 The "objectives triangle" in project management

- by a required or specified date;
- to a specified budget;
- to a specific quality or standard of performance.

These parameters are frequently represented by forces in a state of equilibrium or balance. A change to the state of any of them will affect the others. A triangular model of these elements illustrates the trade-off nature of the parameters for the defined scope of the project (see Figure 1). For example, if the project time needs to be decreased to meet a market need, then either the cost or quality or both will be affected. It is often useful to draw the triangle and agree a new balance with the key team members.

One-off and unique.   Projects are by their nature unique. A similar project may previously have been carried out, perhaps in a different timeframe or circumstance, or with a similar technology, but each project is "one-of-a-kind" in some way.

Defined duration.   Planned projects have a timeframe or finite duration, the end date of which is often related to a business need. This need may well dictate the project timespan, influencing when it should start. This in turn will determine when resources are needed to carry out the project.

Project lifecycle.   Projects can be divided into distinct phases. Projects start with a feasibility phase, then the project is realized and finally

implemented into the organization. The project realization phase is frequently expanded into more detailed phases such as design, material purchase, and fabrication. In some industries these phases are sequential, while in others they are overlapped to a large extent, frequently in an attempt to shorten the overall project duration. (*See* SIMULTANEOUS DEVELOPMENT.)

People issues.   Commitment and backup from senior management is essential to the success of the project. The project manager should have authority over the project team. Frequently the team is made up of people from several different disciplines from various parts of the organization and in international projects from different countries.

Priorities between projects have to be clear when the project manager has to negotiate the provision of resources with functional managers, especially when in competition with other project managers. Leadership as well as sound management becomes all important where the (project) organization structure is a form of matrix. (*See* ORGANIZATION OF DEVELOPMENT.)

The project organization chosen should strengthen the leadership of the project. A project manager needs to be adaptable to the project circumstance and manage the project in a style appropriate to both the business organization and the type of project.

Managing project change.   The scope of the project can change, often by a large amount due to changing needs and market conditions.

Although good project management should avoid unnecessary change, project teams must have the ability to assess and control these changes in an effective and timely manner. It is important to keep the client or sponsor advised at all times of potential changes and negotiate their incorporation into the project and with an agreed effect on schedule and cost.

Strategic and Tactical Project Management

The management of the project work within the organization is crucial to turning strategy into reality. Projects can combine into programs of work or project portfolios; managing these becomes an added dimension of project management, using financial appraisal, resource management and decision-making techniques across the organization. These projects in turn may lead to further projects, some of a radical nature, that change the organization to enable it to survive in its "new" environment.

Strategic project management.   The management of groups of projects is known as either program management or multiproject management, an area of current development in the discipline. Aspects of program management are concerned with: consolidation of the component projects for both directional and planning and control purposes, with a business aim or need as a driver.

There are some examples of organizations who claim to run their entire organizations in a project fashion, this being known as "management by projects."

Program management can be classified into three major areas:

(1) mega-projects such as the proposed space station or the channel tunnel project;
(2) all projects for a single client;   .
(3) projects grouped together for line of business reasons.

Some organizations would also group organizational change projects together.

Program management raises a number of key issues that require careful consideration:

● the decision-making processes that link the projects to and within the program for the selection of projects, their prioritization and the allocation of resources;

● who makes decisions about selection or prioritization within the organization;

● the supporting information systems to help make the decisions;

● an appropriate organizational structure for such a multiproject environment.

Tactical project management.   In most organizations projects are treated as a series of single entities and responsibility for their success is vested in the project manager. The project organizations are frequently chosen to fit with the prevailing culture of the company.

The appropriate management style will depend on: the skill and competence of the project manager, the type of project – development or change and its complexity – runner, repeater, or stranger. It will also depend on the ability of the organization to employ project management techniques.

See also **design; manufacturing processes; fixed position layout; project cost management and control; project control**

Bibliography

Cleland, D. I. & King, W. R. (1988). *Project management handbook.* New York: Van Nostrand Reinhold.

Gerais, R. (Ed.) (1990). *The handbook of management by projects: Proceedings of the 10th conference on project management.* Zurich: International Project Management Association.

Morris, P. G. M. (1994). *The management of projects.* London: Thomas Telford Publications.

RALPH LEVENE

project risk management   Risk analysis and management spans the whole project lifecycle in PROJECT MANAGEMENT. All projects will have areas of uncertainty; analyzing, reducing, and managing it is essential to a well-run project. Risks have to be identified, their impact and likelihood assessed, and their reduction or elimination planned and implemented.

Some risks are more obvious than others; for example technical problems and poor scope identification will almost certainly cause the project to be late and/or over budget. Other risks such as those due to an inexperienced team or bad planning can have a serious effect on the project but can remain hidden.

Causes of risk that can lead to poor performance include: poor understanding of scope, lack of estimating methods, novel technology, untrained teams, lack of understanding of client or user needs, bad choice of contractors and suppliers, a lack of project management experience, and uncontrollable events (e.g. weather).

Within each area of risk, specific items that contribute to the risk can be identified, e.g. the design areas are broken down into specific elements of technical risk, and a quantitative value can then be estimated for each. In an ideal situation a probability distribution is assigned to each risk element. Then overall project risk is determined by combining the elements into a simulation model (Monte Carlo). Commercially available software packages exist for generalized models which can be formulated and used to explore risks in the cost estimate. Specialist packages that model the network plan and allow distributions to be applied to activity durations are also available. It is essential that the data used are as good as possible (many organizations neglect to collect actual and comparison data at the end of the project). Probabilistic analysis relies on good data. The PERT method for network analysis (see NETWORK TECHNIQUES) was designed to take into account a form of time risk assessment. The method requires three time estimates; "pessimistic" (*P*), "most likely" (*ML*) and "optimistic" (*O*) values for each activity. The PERT duration (*PD*) for each activity is then

$$PD = \frac{(P + 4ML + O)}{6}$$

Reducing the risk is an essential part of the management process. Where parts of the project can be subcontracted, this can also be a strategic decision. The form of the contract, which can range from fully reimbursable to fixed price, relates to the extent of risk that the client is willing to take. In a fixed price contract the contractor assumes all the risk.

The most vulnerable part of a project is often the definition of the scope; a thorough feasibility study can decrease the risk in such cases. Residual risk should be covered by contingency of both time and cost.

See also **failure analysis; project control**

Bibliography

Cooper, D. F. & Chapman, C. B. (1986). *Risk analysis for large projects.* Chichester: Wiley.

RALPH LEVENE

purchasing and supply management   Purchasing has been defined as a proactive function which manages the inputs to an organization (Baily et al., 1994). However, inputs to an organization include spend on people and capital equipment as well as transformed materials. The classic TRANSFORMATION MODEL can be used to define the categories of inputs which have to be purchased and supplied.

Organizations buy a range of services and goods from different markets; all these purchases, including labor bought on the labor market, and buildings bought on the property market, make up the total spend. But rarely are all of these the responsibility of the purchasing function. Figure 1 shows how the split of who buys what in an organization may be illustrated by considering the frequency of purchase and the value of the purchase.

The total materials spend of an organization as a percentage of its revenues varies depending on the nature of the industry, the task performed, the country of operation, and the amount of value added by the business. In some highly automated industries, such as petrochemicals, up to 90 percent of sales revenues are spent on purchasing goods and services. Many manufacturing firms spend over 70 percent of their revenues, components, and materials. However, some jobbing or craft businesses may only spend about 35 percent of their revenues on goods and services. Therefore the purchasing function will have greater effect and visibility in some organizations than in others.

The Purchasing Task

The scope and definition of the purchasing task in organizations vary, as do definitions on

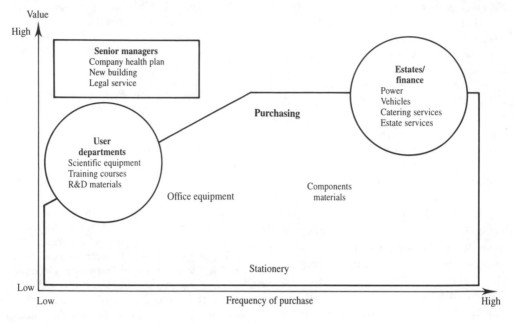

Figure 1 Example of who buys what

the scope of purchasing. Terms such as "procurement," "supply," "buying" and "purchasing" are used with similar meanings associated with them. Figure 2 offers some distinction between the terms.

Strategic purchasing has been defined as including four major contributions:

(1) monitoring supply market trends;
(2) interpreting the meaning of these trends for the firm;
(3) identifying the materials and services required to support company and strategic business unit strategies;
(4) developing supply options.

A purchasing strategy therefore provides the context and creates the supply base for the tactical and operational tasks of purchasing to be fulfilled within. Some authors prefer to use the term "procurement" for the strategic aspects of purchasing.

However, other authors take a more operational view of the role of the purchasing or sourcing function. Monczka and Morgan (1992) defined strategic sourcing management as "the integration of all decisions that affect the design and flow of purchased items and materials into and through a corporate entity to finished

products aimed at specific customers." This evokes the concept of internal SUPPLY CHAIN MANAGEMENT. Adopting this definition, sourcing would include planning and control of the internal operations between suppliers and customers.

Types of Purchases

There are many different classifications that can be used to categorize the types of purchase. One classification relates to the nature of the good or service being bought and its application.

● *Raw materials* usually refers to materials which have undergone little or no previous transformation operation.

● *Semi-manufactured materials* are materials which are received from a previous link in the supply chain that has processed them but not to the state that they would be visible in the finished product.

● *Components* are items which have already been transformed by a previous link in the supply chain into a semi-finished state.

● *Finished products* are complete items which some firms, such as distributors and retailers, purchase and sell on to the next link in the supply chain, which may be the consumer.

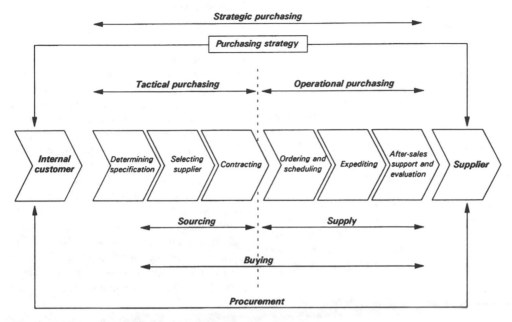

Figure 2 The scope of purchasing (adapted from Van Weele, 1994)

- *Packaging* is often separated out by firms when they categorize purchases. While not forming a part of the finished product that is used by the consumer, packaging is a necessary part to sell or move a finished product.

- *Maintenance, repair and operating (MRO) supplies* are consumables which are necessary for the transformation process but are not part of the package that is sold to the next link in the supply chain.

- *Capital items* are expensive items which are bought infrequently and include items such as buildings, plant and equipment, and vehicles.

- *Services* represent a very broad category of purchases which are usefully broken down into types of services. Subcontract services are typically those where an operation is performed on semi-finished items which are sent out to the subcontractor by the purchasing organization. The materials return to the purchasing organization with the service completed to them; the purchasing organization retains responsibility for the management of the material and the whole process. In other circumstances, the purchasing

organization passes all responsibility for routinized services out to the supplier – these can be termed "contract services."

Instead of categorizing purchases by the nature of the good or service, it may also be useful to categorize them by the familiarity of the organization with the purchase. These distinctions have been termed "straight rebuy," "modified rebuy," and "new buy" (Robinson et al., 1967). Not only does this affect the familiarity of the organization with the purchase, but it also often affects who is involved with the purchasing decision. Lower value straight rebuys, such as cleaning materials and stationery, are often dealt with by the purchasing function. However, larger value straight rebuys such as energy may not be; this may be purchased by the finance and administration team. Many new buys will involve a cross-functional team to consider a range of technical and financial aspects of the decision.

The Objectives of Purchasing

The underlying objectives of purchasing which are true for all services and materials procured are known as the "five rights of purchasing."

These are purchasing:
- at the right price;
- for delivery at the right time;
- of goods and services of the right quality;
- in the right quantity;
- from the right source.

Purchasing at the right price. Any reduction in purchase cost is added directly to the bottom line. Price reductions in purchasing can have a tremendous impact on profitability of a business because of the "leverage" effect of the high proportion of purchased items for most companies. Relatively small reductions in purchase costs are equivalent to far larger increases in sales revenue in their effect on profitability. The higher the percentage of bought-in materials and services, relative to turnover, the greater is this effect.

Purchasing for delivery at the right time and in the right quantity. These aspects of purchasing performance impact on a firm's ability to be able to supply its own products and services on time, quickly and flexibly to customers. The volume and timing requirements for supply are usually determined by a requirements planning process of some sort (*see* MATERIAL REQUIREMENTS PLANNING), then existing INVENTORY MANAGEMENT policies are taken into consideration. However, given requirements for certain volumes at certain times, purchasing may choose to, or be obliged to purchase different amounts and at different times.

Purchasing at the right quality. Increasingly suppliers are being made responsible for the quality of the goods and services they supply. Supplier quality assurance programs are a form of supplier development to ensure that suppliers are capable, through their technology, systems, processes, people, and purchases, to provide the right quality first time. One of the benefits of this is that the purchaser no longer has to perform the non-value added operation of inspection.

Purchasing from the right source. The key issue here is the choice between single or multi sourcing (purchasing an item from one or several suppliers). The relative merits of single sourcing and multi sourcing as shown in Table 1.

Network Sourcing and Lean Supply

"Lean supply" involves the total removal of waste from the supply system (Womack et al., 1990). A common view of how lean supply is implemented in Japan is through the Japanese subcontracting system. This has been viewed as a closed, highly integrated pyramidal and hierarchical structure. However, the Japanese supply structure is evolving to become an extensive network system involving complex, integrated relationships and collaborations with much more open, flexible, and mutually beneficial structures. This is facilitated by greater collaboration between suppliers through the supplier associations present in Japan. Potentially this should reduce some of the disadvantages of sourcing with few suppliers, in particular their ability to innovate and transfer technologies from other industries and supply systems.

See also **international location; materials management; logistics; supply chain dynamics; vertical integration**

Bibliography

Baily, P. & Farmer, D., Jessop, D. & Jones, D. (1994). *Purchasing principles and management.* London: Pitman Publishing.

Browning, J. M., Zabriskie, N. B. & Huellmantel, A. B. (1983). Strategic purchasing planning. *Journal of Purchasing and Materials Management,* Spring, 19–24.

Lamming, R. (1993). *Beyond partnership: Strategies for innovation and lean supply.* Prentice-Hall.

Monczka, R. M. & Morgan, J. P. (1992). Strategic sourcing management. *Purchasing,* **23,** 1, June, 52–5.

Robinson, P. J., Faris, C. W. & Wind, Y. (1967). *Industrial buying and creative marketing.* Boston, MA: Allyn and Bacon.

van Weele, A. J. (1994). *Purchasing management: Analysis planning and practice.* London: Chapman and Hall.

Womack, J., Jones, D. & Roos, D. (1990). *The machine that changed the world.* New York: Rawson Associates.

CHRISTINE HARLAND

Table 1 Relative merits of single and multisourcing

	Single sourcing	*Multisourcing*
Advantages	Potentially better quality because more SQA possibities	Purchasers can drive price down by competitive tendering
	Strong relationships which are more durable	Can switch sources in case of supply failure
	Greater dependency encourages more commitment and effort	Wide sources of knowledge and expertise to tap
	Easier to co-operate on new product/ service development	
	More scale economies	
	Higher confidentiality	
Disadvantages	More vulnerable to disruption if a failure to supply occurs	Difficult to encourage commitment by supply
	Individual supplier more affected by volume fluctuations	Less easy to develop effective SQA
	Supplier might exert upward pressure on prices if no alternative supplier is available	More effort needed to communicate
	More difficult to obtain scale	Suppliers less likely to invest in new processes

push and pull planning and control

"Push" and "pull" are terms used in PLANNING AND CONTROL IN OPERATIONS to indicate the direction of the stimulus in the system which-causes materials to be moved and activities to be undertaken.

In a push system of planning and control each work center has responsibility for sending work to the succeeding part of the operation. The work centers "push" out work without considering whether the succeeding work center can make use of it. Activities are scheduled by means of a central system, and completed in line with central instructions, such as a MATERIAL REQUIREMENTS PLANNING system. However, because actual conditions differ from those planned, idle time, inventory, and queues often characterize push systems because, in the short term, activities are not influenced by actual operational conditions.

In a pull system of planning and control the pace and specification of what is done is set by the "customer" work station, who "pulls" work from the preceding (supplier) work station. The customer acts as the "trigger" for movement. If a request is not passed back from the customer to the supplier, the supplier cannot produce anything or move any materials. A request from a customer not only triggers production at the supplying stage, it will also prompt the supplying stage to request a further delivery from its own suppliers. In this way demand is transmitted back through the stages from the original point of demand by the original customer.

Push and pull systems have different effects in terms of their propensities to accumulate inventory in the operation. Pull systems being less likely to result in inventory build up and are therefore favored by JIT operations.

*See also **kanban**; **just-in-time***

NIGEL SLACK

Q

quality Quality and its management is looked upon by many organizations as the means by which they can gain and maintain competitive advantage. However, there are a variety of interpretations placed on the use and meaning of the word "quality." In a linguistic sense, quality originates from the Latin word *qualis* which means "such as the thing really is." More formally, the international definition of quality goes further, quality is the "totality of characteristics of an entity that bear on its ability to satisfy stated and implied needs" (ISO 8402 (1994)).

Definitions of Quality

There are a number of ways or senses in which quality may be defined, some being broader than others. These different definitions are now examined.

Quantitative. A traditional quantitative term (still used in some businesses) is the acceptable quality level (AQL) (*see* STATISTICAL QUALITY TECHNIQUES). *Using such an approach quality is being defined in terms of non-conforming parts per hundred, that is, as some defined degree of imperfection.*

Uniformity of the product characteristics or delivery of a service around a nominal or target value. The idea of reducing the variation of part characteristics and process parameters so that they are centered around a target value can be attributed to Taguchi, who saw the quality of a product as the minimum loss imparted by the product to society from the time the product is shipped. This is defined by a quadratic loss curve. Among the losses he includes consumers dissatisfaction, warranty costs, loss of reputation and, ultimately, loss of market share (*see* TAGUCHI METHODS).

Conformance to agreed and fully understood requirements. This definition is attributed to CROSBY. He believes that quality is not comparative and there is no such thing as high quality or low quality, or quality in terms of goodness, feel, excellence, and luxury. A product or service either conforms to requirements or it does not. In other words, quality is an attribute not a variable.

Fitness for purpose/use. JURAN classifies "fitness for purpose (or use)" into the categories of: quality of design, quality of conformance, abilities, and field service. Focusing on fitness for use helps to prevent the overspecification of products. The fitness of a product or service for use has to be judged by the purchaser, customer or user.

Satisfying customer expectations and understanding their needs and future requirements. A typical definition which reflects this sentiment is: "The attributes of a product or service which, as perceived by the customer, makes the product or service attractive to them and gives them satisfaction." In most situations customers have a choice; they need not place future orders with a supplier who does not perform as they expect. The aim of the superior performing companies is to become the supplier of choice of their customers.

Many company missions are based largely on satisfying customer perceptions. Some go beyond satisfying customers and emphasize the need to delight customers by giving them more than what is required.

The Importance of Quality

Several reasons have been suggested as to why quality is regarded as a particularly important OPERATIONS OBJECTIVE.

Quality is not negotiable. An order, contract or customer which is lost on the grounds of non-conforming product or service quality is much harder to regain than one lost on price or delivery. In a number of cases the customer could be lost forever; in simple terms the organization has been outsold by the competition. In today's business world the penalties for unsatisfactory product quality and poor service are likely to be punitive.

Quality is all pervasive. Recent views on quality (*see* TOTAL QUALITY MANAGEMENT) are much broader concepts than previous initiatives, encompassing not only product, service, and process improvements but those relating to costs and productivity, and people involvement and development.

Quality increases productivity, Cost, productivity, and quality improvements are complementary and not alternative objectives. Managers sometimes say that they do not have the time and resources to insure that product or service quality is done right the first time. They go on to argue that if their people concentrate on planning for quality then they will be losing valuable production and operating time, and as a consequence output will be lost and costs will rise. Despite this argument, management and their staff will make the time to rework the product and service a second or even a third time, spend considerable time and organizational resources on corrective action, and placating customers.

Quality leads to better performance in the marketplace. The profit impact of market strategy (PIMS), conducted under the Strategic Planning Institute in Cambridge (Massachusetts), have a database which contains over 3,000 records of detailed business performance. The database allows a detailed analysis of the parameters which influence business performance. A key PIMS concept is that of relative perceived quality (RPQ); this is the product and service offering as perceived by the customer. It has been established that the factors having most leverage on return on investment are RPQ and relative market share and that companies with large market shares are those whose quality is relatively high, whereas companies with small market shares are those whose quality is relatively low (see Buzzell and Galt, 1987).

The cost of non-quality is high. Based on a variety of companies, industries and situations, the cost of quality ranges from 5 to 25 percent of an organization's annual sales revenue. An organization should compare its profit to sales revenue ratio to that of its quality costs to sales turnover ratio, in order to gain an indication of the importance of product and service quality to corporate profitability.

Evolution of Quality Management

Recently simple inspection activities have been replaced or supplemented by quality control, quality assurance has been developed and refined, and now most companies are working towards total quality management. In this progression, four fairly discrete stages can be identified, inspection, quality control, quality assurance, and total quality management.

Inspection. At one time inspection was thought to be the only way of ensuring quality. Under a simple inspection-based system, one or more characteristics of a product, service or activity are examined and compared with specified requirements to assess conformity. The system is an after-the-event screening process with little prevention content. Simple inspection-based systems are usually wholly in-house and do not directly involve suppliers or customers in the activity.

Quality control. Under a system of quality control one might expect to find in place a paperwork and procedures control system, raw material and intermediate stage product testing, logging of elementary process performance data, and feedback of process information to appropriate personnel. With quality control there will have been some development from the basic inspection activity in terms of sophistication of methods and systems and the quality management tools and techniques which are employed. While the main mechanism for preventing off-specification products and services from being delivered to a customer is again screening inspection, quality control measures lead to greater process control and fewer incidence of non-conformances.

Quality assurance. Finding and solving a problem after a non-conformance has been created is not an effective route towards eliminating the root cause of a problem. A lasting and continuous improvement in quality can only be achieved by directing organizational efforts towards planning and preventing problems occurring at source. This concept leads to the third stage of quality management development, which is quality assurance.

Examples of additional features acquired when progressing from quality control to quality assurance are, for example, a comprehensive quality management system to increase uniformity and conformity, use of the seven basic quality control tools (e.g. histogram, check sheet, Pareto analysis, cause and effect diagram, graphs, scatter diagram and control chart), statistical process control (SPC), FMEA, and the gathering and use of quality costs. Above all one would expect to see a shift in emphasis from mere detection towards prevention of non-conformances.

Total quality management. The fourth and highest level that of TQM involves the application of quality management principles to all aspects of the business, including customers and suppliers.

Total quality management requires that the principles of quality management should be applied in every branch and at every level in the organization. It is a company-wide approach to quality, with improvements undertaken on a continuous basis by everyone in the organization. Individual systems, procedures, and requirements may be no higher than for a quality assurance level of quality management, but they will pervade every person, activity and function of the organization. It will, however, require a broadening of outlook and skills and an increase in creative activities over that required at the quality assurance level. The spread of the TQM philosophy would also be expected to be accompanied by greater sophistication in the application of quality management tools and techniques and increased emphasis on people. The process will also extend beyond the organization to include partnerships with suppliers and customers. Activities will be reorientated to focus on the customer, internal and external. (*See* TOTAL QUALITY MANAGEMENT).

Prevention Versus Detection

In tracing the development of quality management from inspection to TQM it was said that inspection and quality control are basically detection type activities while quality assurance and TQM are prevention based.

In a detection environment, the emphasis is on the product, procedures or service deliverables and the downstream producing and delivery processes. Considerable effort is expended on after-the-event inspecting, checking, screening and testing of the product or service to ensure that only conforming product and services are delivered to the customer. Detection will not improve service quality but only highlight when it is not present.

While a detection type system may prevent non-conforming product, services, and paperwork being delivered to the customer it does not stop them being made. Physical and mental fatigue decreases the efficiency of inspection and it is commonly claimed that, at best, 100 percent inspection is only 80 percent effective. It is often found that with a detection approach the customer also inspects the incoming product or service, thus the customer becomes a part of the organization's quality control system. In this type of approach a non-conforming product must be made and a service delivered before the process can be adjusted, and this is inherently inefficient in that it creates waste in all its various forms.

A prevention-based approach places the emphasis on product, service, and process design. By concentrating on source activities it stops non-conforming products being produced or non-conforming services being delivered. There is a clear change of emphasis from downstream to the upstream processes and from product to process. This change of emphasis can also be considered in terms of the PDCA CYCLE (plan, do, check, action). In the detection approach the action part of the cycle is limited, resulting in an incomplete cycle. Whereas with prevention it is an essential part of individuals and teams striving for continuous improvement as part of their everyday work activities.

See also **service quality; quality characteristics; quality management systems**

Bibliography

BS 4778. (1991). *Part 2: Quality vocabulary: quality concepts and related definitions*. London: British Standards Institution.

Buzzell, R. D. & Galt, B. T. (1987). *The profit impact of marketing strategy: Linking strategy to performance*. New York: Free Press.

Dale, B. G. (Ed.) (1994). *Managing quality*. 2nd edn. Herts.: Prentice-Hall.

Gallup Organization, Inc. (1991). *An international survey of consumers' perceptions of product and service quality*. Milwaukee: American Society for Quality Control.

Gallup Organization, Inc. (1992). *An ASQC/Gallup survey on quality leadership roles of corporate executive and directors*. Milwaukee: American Society for Quality Control.

Hutchens, S. (1989). What customers want: results of ASQC/Gallup survey. *Quality Progress*, **22**, *1, February*, 33–6.

ISO 8402-1. (1994). Quality management and quality assurance: vocabulary. Geneva: International Organization for Standardization.

Kano, N., Tanaka, H. & Yamaga, Y. (1983). *The TQC activity of Deming Prize recipients and its economic impact*. Tokyo: Union of Japanese Scientists and Engineers.

Larry, L. (1993). Betting to win on the Baldrige winners. *Business Week*, 18 October, 16–17.

McKenzie, R. M. (1989). *The production–inspection relationship*. Edinburgh and London: Scottish Academic Press.

McKinsey and Co. (1989). Management of quality: the single most important challenge for Europe. *Proceedings of the European Quality Management Forum*. 19 October, Montreux, Switzerland.

United States General Accounting Office (1991). *Management practices: US companies improve performance through quality efforts*. Washington DC: General Accounting Office.

Wisner, J. D. & Eakins, S. G. (1994). Competitive assessment of the Baldrige winners. *International Journal of Quality and Reliability Management*, **11**, *2*, 8–25.

Zairi, M., Letza, S. R. & Oakland, J. S. (1994). Does TQM impact bottom-line results? *The TQM Magazine*, **6**, *1*, 38–43.

BARRIE DALE

quality awards Quality awards are the formal recognition of quality achievement, given to organizations by quality bodies. Increasingly the frameworks behind such awards are being used by organizations for self-assessment purposes.

Many definitions of self-assessment are provided by writers, but an all embracing definition is provided by the European Foundation for Quality Management (EFQM). "Self assessment is a comprehensive, systematic, and regular review of an organization's activities and results referenced against a model of business excellence" (e.g. the Malcolm Baldrige National Quality Award (MBNQA) and the European Quality Award (EQA).

Self-assessment implies the use of a model on which to base the evaluation. There are a number of internationally recognized models, the main ones being the Deming Application Prize in Japan, the Malcolm Baldrige National Quality Award in America, and the European Quality Award in Europe. In addition there are many national and regional quality awards, most of which are close to the international models, with some modifications to suit issues of national or local interest.

The award models and the application guidelines are helpful in defining TQM in a digestible form. They also help organizations to develop and manage their quality improvement activities in a number of ways. For example, they provide a definition and description of TQM which gives a better understanding of the concept, improves awareness, and generates ownership of TQM among senior managers. They also enable measurement of the progress with TQM to be made, along with its benefits and outcomes, while the scoring criteria provide an objective measurement, gains consensus on strengths and weaknesses of the current approach, and helps to pinpoint improvement opportunities. Also benchmarking and organizational learning is facilitated and training in TQM is encouraged.

Deming Application Prize

The Deming Application Prize was set up in the honor of Dr W. E. Deming, back in 1951. It was in recognition of his friendship and achievements in the cause of industrial quality. The original intention of the prize was to assess a company's use and application of statistical method; later it was broadened out to assess how TQM activities were being practiced. The award is managed by the Deming Prize Committee and administered by the Japanese Union of Scientists and Engineers (JUSE). It recognizes outstanding achievements in quality

Table 1 Quality awards

Deming Application Prize	Maximum points
Company policy and planning	100
Organization and its management	100
Quality control education and dissemination	100
Collection, transmission and utilization of information on quality	100
Analysis	100
Standardization	100
Control	100
Quality assurance	100
Effects	100
Future plans	100
Total	1000

Malcolm Baldrige National Quality Award	
Leadership	90
Information and analysis	75
Strategic quality planning	55
Human resource development and management	140
Management of process quality	140
Quality and operational results	250
Customer focus and satisfaction	250
Total	1000

European Quality Award	
Leadership	100
People management	90
Policy and strategy	80
Resources	90
Processes	140
People satisfaction	90
Customer satisfaction	200
Impact on society	60
Business results	150
Total	1000

strategy, management, and execution. There are two separate divisions for the award, the Deming Application Prize and the Deming Prize for individuals. The Deming Application Prize is open to individual sites, a division of a company, small companies, and overseas companies. It is awarded each year and there is no limit on the number of winners. It is made to those businesses who have, in the designated year, achieved the most distinct improvement of performance through the application of company-wide control.

The Deming Application Prize has a checklist of ten primary factors (see Table 1) which in turn are divided into a number of secondary factors. This checklist is prescriptive in that it identifies factors, procedures, techniques, and approaches that underpin TQM. The examiners for the Deming Application Prize are selected by JUSE from quality management experts from not-for-profit organizations. The applicants are required to submit a detailed document on each of the prize's criteria and this is followed by an on-site visit. Considerable emphasis is placed on the on-site examination of the applicant organization's practices (*see* DEMING).

The Malcolm Baldrige National Quality Award

The Malcolm Baldrige National Quality Improvement Act of 1987, signed by President Reagan on August 20, 1987, established this annual US quality award, some 37 years after the introduction of the Deming Prize. The award is named after a former American Secretary of Commerce in the Reagan Administration, Malcolm Baldrige. Its purpose is to promote quality awareness, recognize the quality achievements of American companies, and publicize successful quality management and improvement strategies. The US Department of Commerce and the National Institute of Standards and Technology are responsible for administering the Award scheme.

Up to two awards can be given each year, in each of three categories: manufacturing companies or subsidiaries, service companies or subsidiaries, and small businesses (defined as independently owned, and with not more than 500 employees). The award is made by the President of the United States. The recipients receive a specially designed gold plated medal set in crystal. They may publicize and advertize their awards provided they agree to share information about their successful quality management and improvement strategies with other American organizations.

Every Baldrige Award application is evaluated in seven major categories with a maximum total score of 1,000. These are: leadership, information and analysis, strategic quality analysis, human resource development and management, management of process quality, quality and operational results, and customer focus and satisfaction (see Figure 1). Each of the seven categories is further divided into a number of items. The framework has four basic elements: driver, system, measure of progress, and goals. The evaluation by the Baldrige examiners is based on a written application and looks for three major indications of success:

- approach: the strategy, processes, practices and methodology used by the organization use in attempting to achieve world class quality;

- deployment: the resources being applied, and how widespread (i.e. broad or narrow) is the quality effort throughout the organization;

- results: evidence of sustained improvement.

Following a first-stage review of the application by quality management experts, a decision is made as to which organizations should receive a site visit. A panel of judges review all the data both from the written applications and site visits and recommend the award recipients. Quantitative results weight heavily in the judging process, so applicants must be able to prove that their quality efforts have resulted in sustained improvements. The thoroughness of the judging process means that even applicants not selected as finalists get valuable feedback on their strengths and areas for improvement.

The European Quality Award

The European Quality Award was first awarded in 1992. While only one European Quality Award is made each year, several European Quality prizes are awarded to those companies who demonstrate excellence in the management of quality through a process of continuous improvement. The EQA is awarded to the best of the prize winners. The winner of the award retains the EQA Trophy for a year; all prize winners receive a framed holographic image of the trophy. The winners are expected to share their experiences of TQM at conferences and

seminars organized by the EFQM. Only for profit European-based businesses are eligible to apply, thus, all forms of non-profit organizations such as government agencies, trade, and professional associations are excluded. There are currently two separate categories for the EQA – companies and public services organizations.

The EQA model is intended to help the management of European organizations to improve their understanding of best practices and to support them in their leadership role. The EQA is administered by the EFQM with the support of the European Organization for Quality and the European Commission. The EFQM in developing the EQA drew upon the experience in use and application of the MBNQA.

Applications for the EQA are assessed on nine criteria: customer satisfaction, people (employee) satisfaction, business results, processes, leadership, resources, policy and strategy, and impact on society (EFQM, 1996). The criteria which are shown in Figure 1 are split into two groups: "enablers" and "results." The nine elements of the model are further divided into a number of secondary elements. The model is based on the principle that processes are the means by which the organization harnesses and releases the talents of its people to produce results. In other words, the processes and the people are the enablers which provide the results. The results aspects of the award are concerned with what the organization has achieved and is achieving, and the enablers with how the results are being achieved. The rationale for this is that customer satisfaction, people satisfaction, and impact on society are achieved through leadership, driving policy and strategy, people management, and the management of resources and processes, leading to excellence in business results. Each of these nine criteria can be used to assess an organization's progress to business excellence.

The enablers are scored in terms of approach and deployment. The approach is concerned with how the requirements of a particular item are approached and met. The deployment is the extent to which the approach has been deployed and implemented vertically and horizontally within the organization. The results criteria are evaluated in terms of degree of excellence and the scope of the results presented. The scoring framework of 1,000 points with 500 points each being allocated to enablers and results.

The EQA model does not stipulate any particular techniques, methods, or procedures which should be in place. The organizations that put themselves forward for the award are expected to have undertaken at least one self-assessment cycle. Once an application has been submitted to the EFQM headquarters, a team of fully trained independent assessors examine the applications and decide whether or not to conduct a site visit. A jury reviews the findings of the assessors to decide who will win the award.

See also **quality management systems**

Bibliography

Brown, G. (1991). How to determine your quality quotient: measuring your company against the Baldrige criteria. *Journal for Quality and Participation*, June, 82–8.

Cole, R. E. (1991). Comparing the Baldrige and Deming Awards. *Journal for Quality and Participation*, July-August, 94–104.

European Foundation for Quality Management (1996). *Self-assessment: 1996 guidelines for companies*. Brussels: EFQM.

Nakhai, B. & Neves, J. (1994). The Deming, Baldrige and European Quality Awards. *Quality Progress*, April, 33–7.

BARRIE DALE

quality characteristics   Some approaches to QUALITY view it as a precise and measurable set of variables that are required to satisfy the customer. These variables, or quality characteristics, are those properties of a product or service that are to be evaluated against specifications. Quality characteristics are important for operations as they help identify the critical characteristics of the product or service that require a design specification. Their identification also means that appropriate control and measurement systems can be put in place to ensure that the specifications are met.

Product Quality Characteristics

There are two types of product quality characteristics, variables, and attributes. Vari-
ables are those quality characteristics that can be measured on a continuous scale, for example length or weight. Attributes are those characteristics that are either present or absent, for example acceptable or not acceptable, within tolerance or out of tolerance. Most operations texts explain in some detail how variables and attributes can be measured using statistical process control (SPC) and statistical quality control (SQC) (*see* STATISTICAL QUALITY TECHNIQUES). Few, however, provide comprehensive lists of product quality characteristics in the same way as service quality characteristics.

The most comprehensive list of product quality characteristics is provided by Garvin (1984); who defines the scope of "quality" as comprising performance, features, reliability, conformance, durability, serviceability, esthetics, and perceived quality. "Performance" comprises the set of "primary operating characteristics" – handling, cruising speed, and comfort of a car for example. "Features" are the secondary characteristics, supporting or enhancing features that supplement the primary characteristics, such as the color of the car's trim and types of accessories. "Reliability" is the chance of a failure occurring (*see* FAILURE ANALYSIS). "Conformance" is the degree to which the product meets its specification. "Durability" is a measure of product life. Garvin defined "serviceability" as the speed, courtesy and competence of repair – the servicing of the product. "Esthetics" refers to the customer's judgment of the look, sound or taste of a product. "Perceived quality" recognizes the fact that customers do not possess complete information about a product's attributes and that quality may be, in part, a function of the organization's image and brand names.

Some additional product characteristics have been identified by other authors, for example, the ease of installation and use function, a product doing what it is supposed to, availability, reliability, delivery, and maintainability.

Some authors have argued that reliability is not a quality characteristic. Wild (1980), for example, argued that it is a result or consequence of quality not a characteristic of quality itself. Others treated reliability separately and argued that it ranks equally with quality in importance in terms of competitive criteria.

Service Quality Characteristics

Research by Parasuraman et al. (1985) provided a list of ten determinants, or characteristics, of service quality; access, communication, competence, courtesy, credibility, reliability, responsiveness, security, understanding, and tangibles. In the next phase of their research, they found a high degree of correlation between communication, competence, courtesy, credibility, and security, and between access and understanding. Therefore, they created the two broad dimensions of assurance and empathy, i.e. five consolidated dimensions. They then used the five dimensions of tangibles, reliability, responsiveness, assurance, and empathy as the basis for their service quality measurement instrument, SERVQUAL (*see* SERVICE QUALITY).

They further reported that, regardless of the service being studied, reliability was the most critical dimension, followed by responsiveness, assurance and empathy. The tangibles were of least concern to service customers. These dimensions have been much criticized, though they have formed the basis for a considerable amount of research and application in the field of service management. Further research involved some testing of the comprehensiveness of Parasuraman et al.'s service quality determinants. This analysis, although generally supportive of the ten determinants, suggested a refined list of 12. This list was then increased to 18 quality characteristics to provide the most comprehensive set of service quality characteristics to date (Johnston, 1995). They are; access, esthetics, attentive/helpfulness, availability, care, cleanliness/tidiness, comfort, commitment, communication, competence, courtesy, flexibility, friendliness, functionality, integrity, reliability, responsiveness, and security.

Satisfiers Versus Dissatisfiers

Research has shown that the effect of some of the characteristics may be different to others (*see* SERVICE QUALITY; ZONE OF TOLERANCE). Johnston (1995) demonstrated that the causes of dissatisfaction are not necessarily the obverse of the causes of satisfaction. It was suggested that the predominantly satisfying service quality characteristics are attentiveness, responsiveness, care and friendliness, and that the dissatisfiers are integrity, reliability, responsiveness, avail-

ability and functionality. Responsiveness is identified as a critical determinant of quality as it is a key component in providing satisfaction and the lack of it is a major source of dissatisfaction.

See also **total quality management**

Bibliography

Garvin, D. A. (1984). What does "product quality" really mean? *Sloan Management Review*, **25**, 25–43.

Johnston, R. (1995). The determinants of service quality: satisfyers and dissatisfyers. *International Journal of Service Industry Management*, **6**, *5*, 53–71.

Johnston, R., Silvestro, R., Fitzgerald, L. & Voss, C. (1990). Developing the determinants of service quality. *Proceedings of the 1st International Research Seminar in Service Management*, La Londes les Maures.

Parasuraman, A., Zeithaml, V. A. & Berry, L. L. (1985). A conceptual model of service quality and implications for future research. *Journal of Market*, **49**, 41–50.

Parasuraman, A., Zeithaml, V. A. & Berry, L. L. (1988). SERVQUAL: a multiple-item scale for measuring consumer perceptions of service quality. *Journal of Retailing*, **64**, *1*, 12–40.

Wild, R. (1980). *Production and operations management*. London: Holt, Rhinehart and Winston.

ROBERT JOHNSTON

quality costing   Quality costing expresses an organization's quality performance in financial terms.

The benefits of quality costs are related to their uses which include the following:

- promotes quality as a business parameter;

- helps to keep quality aspects of the business under the spotlight;

- enables business decisions about quality to be made in an objective manner;

- helps to identify and justify investment in prevention-based activities, equipment and tooling;

- educates staff in the concept of total quality management (TQM) as a key business parameter and thereby gaining their commitment and reducing scepticism;

- facilitates performance measurement in terms of comparison with other parts of the business, decision making, and motivation;

- identifies products, processes and departments for investigation;

- focuses attention on the problems for which compensation has already been built into the system;

- assists in setting cost-reduction targets and to measure progress towards targets;

- provides bases for budgeting and eventual cost control.

Definition of Quality Costs

The importance of definitions to the collection, analysis, and use of quality costs is crucial. Without clear definitions there can be no common understanding or meaningful communication on the topic. Reaching an exact definition of what constitutes quality costs is not straightforward, and there are many gray areas where good production/operations procedures and practice overlap with quality related activities. Unfortunately there is no general agreement on a single broad definition of quality costs.

Some organizations may stretch their definitions to include those costs which have only the most tenuous relationship with quality. This may be to try and create a financial impact. Yet once costs have been accepted as quality related, there may be some difficulty in exerting an influence over the reduction of costs which are independent of quality considerations. If there is a serious doubt, the cost should not be considered as quality related where it is unlikely to be amenable to change by quality management influences. Other suggested criteria to assess whether or not an item is quality related include consideration of whether, if less is spent on it, failure costs will increase, and if more is spent, failure costs will decrease.

Collection of Quality Costs

The purpose of quality costing should be clarified at the start as this may influence the strategy of the exercise and will help to avoid difficulties later. If, for example, the main objective is to identify high-cost problem areas, approximate costs will suffice. If, on the other hand, the purpose is to set a percentage cost-reduction target on the organization's total quality-related costs, it will be necessary to identify and measure all the contributing cost elements in order to be sure that costs are reduced and not simply transferred elsewhere.

It is necessary to decide how to deal with overheads, since many quality-related costs are normally included as part of the overhead, while others are treated as direct costs and attract a proportion of overheads. Failure to clarify this can lead to a distortion of the picture derived from the quality-related costs analysis. It is also easy to fall into the trap of double counting. For these and other reasons quality-related costs should be made the subject of a memorandum account. Another issue to be decided is how costs are to be allocated to those components, materials, etc. which are scrapped.

There are a number of possible quality costing strategies, ranging from measuring and monitoring all quality costs to measuring only failure costs and costing only specific quality improvement projects and activities, and from "one-shot" exercises to regular monitoring and reporting. Another aspect which needs to be considered is whether to collect and allocate costs on a departmental or business unit basis or across the whole company.

It should not be forgotten that quality costs are already being incurred and the exercise is to identify these "hidden costs" from various budgets and overheads. The objective is to allocate them to a specific cost activity but some costs, even those directly associated with failure, are not easy to measure.

There are several approaches to classifying the costs of quality. Perhaps the best known is that which distinguishes between prevention costs which are incurred in trying to prevent errors occurring, appraisal costs which are incurred in controlling quality by checking for errors, internal failure costs which are the cost of coping with errors inside the organization, and external failure costs, which are the cost of the errors which are detected by customers.

Quality costing should be a joint exercise. If accountants try to do it alone, they are likely to miss some important details, or even be misled by people with hidden agendas. On the other hand, if quality assurance and/or technical people go it alone, they may fail to discover costs which accountants have tucked away out of sight.

Quality cost information needs to be produced from a company's existing system. It is often recommended that the system used to collect quality costs should be made as automatic as possible with minimum intervention of the cost owners and without significantly increasing paperwork or the burden on the accounts department.

Reporting of Quality Costs

It is important to collect and display all quality costs and to indicate those relevant costs which cannot yet be quantified. Some authorities recommend that for maximum impact, quality costs should be included in a company's overall cost reporting system or separate management report.

See also **performance measurement; quality management systems; total quality management**

Bibliography

BS 6143. (1990). Part 2: Guide to the economics of quality: prevention, appraisal and failure model. London: British Standards Institution.

BS 6143. (1992). Part 1: Guide to the economics of quality: process cost model. London: British Standards Institution.

Campanella, J. (1990). *Principles of quality costs: Principles, implementation and use.* Milwaukee: ASQC Quality Press.

Dale, B. G. & Plunkett, J. J. (1995). *Quality costing.* 2nd edn. London: Chapman and Hall.

Grimm, A. F. (1987). *Quality costs: Ideas and applications*, 1. Milwaukee: ASQC Quality Press.

BARRIE DALE

quality function deployment Quality function deployment (QFD) is a technique that was developed in Japan at Mitsubishi's Kobe shipyard, used extensively by Toyota, and now by many other companies in other parts of the world. It is also known as the "house of quality" (because of its shape) and the "voice of the customer" (because of its purpose). The technique tries to capture what the customer needs and how it might be achieved.

It is a structured procedure which is used to translate the expressed or perceived needs of customers into specific product or service design characteristics and features, and then on to process and operational characteristics. In doing so it attempts to prioritize the requirements of the design process (the whats) and reconcile them with the attributes embodied in the design "solution" (the hows). The central mechanism for doing this is the "what–how" matrix.

The procedure for using the matrix is as follows. In the first matrix (the house of quality) customers' requirements, which form the vertical axis of the matrix, are matched with the design attributes which form the horizontal axis of the matrix. The individual elements of the matrix are used to indicate the degree and direction of influence of the main design attributes on customer needs. To do this some kind of coding scheme is used, often using circles and triangles. It is important at this stage to clearly record all assumptions used in judging the nature of these relationships. In effect the process makes explicit what, without QFD, might have remained unexplained in the design process. At the same time other information is connected concerning both customer requirements and design attributes. First the correlation between different design attributes is recorded so that the consequence for other attributes of changing one attribute on other attributes is well understood. In addition, specific target values of each design attribute can be defined and, if the product or service is already in use, a competitive assessment comparing the product or service in question with competitors' offerings may be mapped. Similarly, perceived customer rating of each requirement comparing current product or service performance against competitors can also be recorded.

Once the important design attributes have been identified together with an understanding of their current state these can be transposed to a second matrix to form the "whats," which must be reconciled with the specific design features of the product or service. After a similar analysis these in turn form the whats of the process matrix which links the design features of the product or service with the attributes of the design of the process which will create the

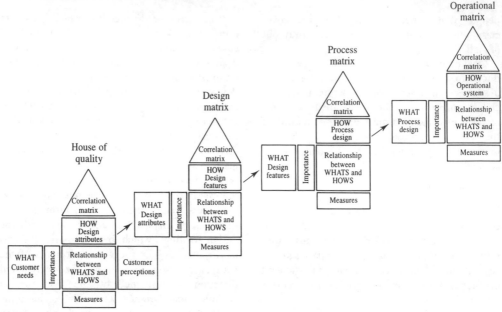

Figure 1 Translating customer needs through stages in the design process using Quality Function Deployment (QFD)

product or service. This in turn may be extended by the final operational matrix to help design the operational control system used in the process (see Figure 1).

The main advantages of using a QFD approach are first that it requires designers to be both analytical and explicit in terms of their design objectives (whats) as well their design solutions (hows) and the relationship between them. Second, it helps to integrate the various functions and departments commonly associated with design activities in large organizations. The main disadvantage cited by practitioners is the extreme complexity involved in using QFD in large design projects. The dilemma appears to be that unless the number of factors used in both axes of the matrix is kept under control then the whole process becomes unmanageable. However, a too strict a filtering of design factors and important relationships may be overlooked.

See also **design; design for manufacture; design–manufacturing interface; organization of development**

Bibliography

Griffin, A. (1992). Evaluating QFD's use in US firms as a process for developing products. *Journal of Product Innovation Management*, **9**, 171–87.

Hauser, J. R. & Clausing, D. (1988). The house of quality. *Harvard Business Review*, **66**, *3*, 63–73.

NIGEL SLACK

quality management systems A quality management system defines and covers all quality-related facets of an organization's operation. It deals with organization, responsibilities, procedures, and processes. The quality system must be developed against a reference base on which its adequacy can be judged and improvements made. This reference base is called a "quality system standard."

In some countries many organizations have developed their quality management system to meet the requirements of the ISO 9000 quality system series of standards. The objective of the ISO 9000 series of quality management system standards is to give purchasers an assurance that the quality of the products or services meets their requirements. Over 80 countries have adopted these standards as their national quality system standards.

The ISO 9000 series define and set out a list of features and characteristics which should be present in an organization's documented policies, manual, and procedures. The aim is systematic quality assurance and control. It is the broad principles of control, in general terms, which are defined in the standards, and not the specific methods by which control can be achieved. This allows the standards to be interpreted and applied in a wide range of situations and environments.

The ISO 9000 series consists of five individual standards (ISO 9000, ISO 9001, ISO 9002, ISO 9003, and ISO 9004) divided into four parts (guidelines, model for quality assurance in design, development, production, installation and servicing, model for quality assurance in production, installation and servicing, and model for quality assurance in final inspection and test).

The standards have two main functions. The first function is an introduction to the series and this identifies the aspects to be covered by an organization's quality system. The guidelines contained in ISO 9000 and ISO 9004 gives guidance in quality management and their application. The second function defines in detail the features and characteristics of a quality management system that are considered essential for the purpose of quality assurance in contractual situations, for three main different types of organization, depending upon the services they offer.

The Guidelines: ISO 9000, 1–4 and ISO 9004, 1–4

ISO 9000 *Guidelines for Selection and Use* and ISO 9004 *Guidelines for Specific Applications* consist of a number of parts and are intended only as guidelines. They cannot be used as reference standards with which to assess the adequacy of a quality management system. Organizations embarking on the development of a quality system to meet the requirements of ISO 9001, ISO 9002 or ISO 9003, should find ISO 9001, 1–4 and ISO 9004, 1–4 of considerable help in the initial stages where an overview is needed.

- ISO 9000-1 is a guide to the use of other standards in the series, and a thorough understanding of its content is essential if the series of standards are to be interpreted and used correctly.

- ISO 9000-2 is a guide for the application of ISO 9001, ISO 9002, and ISO 9003. This is a guidance document and is useful to organizations in understanding the requirements of these three standards. It is structured in line with ISO 9001 and should be read in conjunction with that part of the ISO 9000 series with which compliance is sought.

- ISO 9000-3 sets out guidelines to facilitate the application of ISO 9001 to organizations developing, supplying, and maintaining software.

- ISO 9000-4 is a guide to dependability (i.e. reliability, maintainability, and availability) program management and covers the essential features of such a program.

- ISO 9004-1 is a guide to good quality management practice and in this it provides more detail than ISO 9001, ISO 9002, and ISO 9003. It also contains reference to a number of quality aspects (e.g. quality risks, costs, product liability, and marketing) which are not covered in the same level of detail in ISO 9001, ISO 9002, and ISO 9003. Considerable emphasis is placed throughout on the satisfaction of customer needs and requirements.

- ISO 9004-2 gives guidance and a comprehensive overview for establishing and implementing a quality system specifically for services.

- ISO 9004-3 provides guidance on quality system elements for processed materials.

- ISO 9004-4 gives guidelines for quality improvement, covering concepts, principles, methodology, and tools and techniques.

Detailed Definition of Features, ISO 9001, ISO 9002, ISO 9003

ISO 9001 *Model for Quality Assurance in Design, Development, Production, Installation, and Servicing* covers circumstances in which an organization is responsible for conceptual design and development work, and/or where it may be required to cover post delivery activities such as commissioning and servicing. It contains 20 elements.

ISO 9002 *Model for Quality Assurance in Production, Installation, and Servicing* covers circumstances where an organization is responsible for assuring the product and/or service quality during the course of production or installation only. This part consists of 19 elements, excluding design control.

ISO 9003 *Model for Quality Assurance in Final Inspection and Test* is used when conformance to specified requirements can be assured solely at final inspection and test. This contains 16 of the elements of ISO 9001, excluding the clauses of design control, purchasing, process control, and servicing.

Principal Clauses in ISO 9001

The 20 principal clauses in ISO 9001 together with key factors of the quality system are given below.

1. Management responsibility:

- corporate quality policy development, statement, organizational goals, aims and objectives, deployment, implementation, communication, understanding, and review;

- organization, structure, resources, trained personnel, responsibility, and authority;

- management representative;

- management review and reporting of the system to ensure its effectiveness, including policy and objectives.

2. Quality system:

- documentation and implementation of procedures and instructions;

- quality manual – the first part of the manual should describe how the company operates, and the second part should list the requirements of various standards against which registration of approval may be sought and references the procedures to satisfy these requirements;

- quality planning, quality plans, work instructions, inspection instructions, etc.

3. Contract review:

- definition and documentation of customer (internal and external) needs and requirements, including records;

- contract and tender compatibility;

- quality planning;

- capability of compliance with requirements;

- amendment to contract.

4. Design control:

- design and development planning, including statutory and regulatory requirements;

- identify and allocate resources;

- organizational and technical interfaces;

- definition and control of design inputs, outputs, and interfaces;

- design verification to confirm outputs meet input requirements;

- design validation;

- review, approve, record, and control design changes.

5. Document and data control:

- "document" (in the form of any type of media) needs to be defined;

- formal review and approval of documents by authorized personnel;

- correct issues of necessary documents available at appropriate locations;

- obsolete documents removed or assured against intended use provided suitable documentation is maintained;

- changes to documents are authorized and recorded.

6. Purchasing:

- suppliers/subcontractors evaluation, monitoring of performance and capability;

- records of acceptable suppliers;

- formal written definition of requirements and specification;

- verification of subcontracted product by the customer, if required in the contract.

7. Control of customer-supplied product:

- verification, storage, and maintenance of "free issue" or customer-supplied material for use on their order.

8. Product identification and traceability:

- unique and positive identification of material, parts and work in progress from receipt and through all stages of production, delivery, and installation;

- demonstrated traceability and its recording as and to the extent specified.

9. Process control:

- identify and plan the processes;

- process control procedures, where the absence would adversely affect quality;

- monitoring of key characteristics and features during production;

- process definition and qualification;

- processes carried out under controlled conditions;

- criteria for workmanship;

- provision and control of equipment;

- maintenance of equipment to ensure process capability.

10. Inspection and testing:

- established procedures;

- goods receiving inspection and testing, or other means of verification;

- in-process inspection and testing;

- final inspection and testing;

- inspection and test records, including responsibilities.

11. Control of inspection, measuring, and test equipment:

- control, calibration, and maintenance of equipment needed to demonstrate compliance with requirements;

- consideration of other measurements needed;

- calibration procedures and processes defining equipment, location, methods of checking, acceptance criteria, etc.;

- documentation and calibration records;

- traceability to reference standards, where applicable;

- handling and storage.

12. Inspection and test status:

- identification of inspection and test status (i.e. untested, tested, checked, reject, meets the requirements) throughout all processes;

- confirmation that tests and inspections have been carried out;

- authority for release of conforming product.

13. Control of non-conforming product:

- identification and control to prevent unauthorized use;

- segregation of non-conforming materials, parts and products, where practicable;

- review and decide on appropriate remedial action (e.g. destroyed, repaired, reworked or regarded);

- reinspection.

14. Corrective and preventive action:

- procedures, routines and reporting of customer complaints, and product non-conformities;

- detection, investigation, and analysis of causes;

- elimination of causes and abnormalities;

- assignment of responsibilities;

- preventive action to analyze and eliminate potential problems;

- corrective action control;

- changes to procedures, working instructions.

15. Handling, storage, packaging, preservation, and delivery:

- methods and equipment which prevent product damage, preservation, segregation, and deterioration;

- maintenance of product integrity;

- use of designated storage areas to prevent damage and/or deterioration;

- receipt and delivery of items into and out of storage;

- procedures to ensure that the product is packed to prevent damage throughout the entire production to delivery cycle.

16. Control of quality records:

- adequate records relating to inspections, tests, process control, etc. to demonstrate achievement of product quality and effective operation of the quality system;

- traceability and full history;

- retention time for records;

- storage, retrievable, legibility, and identification;

- method of disposition when no longer required.

17. Internal quality audits:

- audit plan, verification, responsibility, and auditor independence;

- procedures to ensure that the audit method is clear;

- compliance with the documented system;

- assessment of the effectiveness of the actions taken;

- review and implementation of corrective action by management to bring activities and the quality system into agreement with the planned arrangements.

18. Training:

- assessment and identification of needs;

- provision of the required training;

- written job responsibilities and specification;

- determine degree and method of competency;

- planned and structured training program;

- training records.

19. Servicing:

- contractual specification;

- procedures for performing and verifying that needs and requirements are met.

20. Statistical techniques:

- the use of samples to determine product and service quality;

- identify the need for statistical technique;

- process capability determination, acceptability, and certification;

- product characteristic verification.

See also **total quality management; quality management systems**

Bibliography

ISO 9000-1. (1994). Quality management and quality assurance standards. Part 1: Guidelines for selection and use. Geneva: International Organization for Standardization.

ISO 9000-2. (1993). Quality management and quality assurance standards. Part 2: Generic guidelines for the application of ISO 9001, ISO 9002, ISO 9003. Geneva: International Organization for Standardization.

ISO 9000-3. (1991). Quality management and quality assurance standards. Part 3: Guidelines for the application of ISO 9001 to the development, supply, and maintenance of software. Geneva: International Organization for Standardization.

ISO 9000-4. (1993). Quality management and quality assurance standards. Part 4: Guide to dependability programme management. Geneva: International Organization for Standardization.

ISO 9001. (1994). Quality systems: models for quality assurance in design, development, production, installation, and servicing. Geneva: International Organization for Standardization.

ISO 9002. (1994). Quality systems: model for quality assurance in production, installation, and servicing. Geneva: International Organization for Standardization.

ISO 9003. (1995). Quality systems: model for quality assurance in final inspection and test. Geneva: International Organization for Standardization.

ISO 9004-1. (1991). Quality management and quality system elements. Part 1: Guidelines. Geneva: International Organization for Standardization.

ISO 9004-2. (1991). Quality management and quality system elements. Part 2: Guidelines for services. Geneva: International Organization for Standardization.

ISO 9004-3. (1993). Quality management and quality system elements. Part 3: Guidelines for process materials. Geneva: International Organization for Standardization.

ISO 9004-4. (1993). Quality management and quality system elements: Part 4: Guidelines for quality Improvement. Geneva: International Organization for Standardization.

BARRIE DALE

quality teams   The development of people and their involvement in improvement activities, both individually and through a formal process of team work, is a key feature in a company's approach to TOTAL QUALITY MANAGEMENT (TQM). There are a number of different types of teams with different operating characteristics, all of which can act as the means for getting people involved in improvement activities. Different types of teams can be used at different stages of an organization's development of TQM. Some teams have a narrow focus, with perhaps limited problem-solving potential, with members coming from one functional area, whereas others are wider and cross-functional, dealing with the organization's more deep-rooted problems.

Types of Teams

There are a variety of types of teams with differing characteristics in terms of membership, mode of participation, problem selection, scope of activity, problem-solving potential, and permanency which can be used in the quality improvement process. The following types are among the most popular.

Project teams.   If senior management identify the main problems facing the organization, key improvement issues can be developed, which are then allocated among the membership for consideration as one-off projects. The project owner then selects employees to constitute a team which will consider the improvement issue. The owner can either lead the team him or herself, or act as sponsor to the team. Through participation in project teams, managers better understand the problem-solving process and become more sensitive to the problems faced by other types of teams.

The typical characteristics of such teams are:

- The objective has usually been defined by senior management.

- The team is led by management.

- It is temporary.

- The project is specific and significant, perhaps addressing issues of strategic change, external customer issues, and new product introduction and will have clear deliverables within a set timescale.

- The team is organized in such a way to insure it employs the appropriate talents, skills, and functions which are suitable in resolution of the project.

- The scope of its activity tends to be cross-functional.

- Participation is not usually voluntary – people are requested by senior management to join the team.

- Team meetings tend to be long rather than short, although they occur on a regular basis.

Quality circles.   Quality circles (QCs), when operated in the classical manner, have characteristics which are different from other methods of team work. A quality circle is a voluntary group of between six and eight employees from the same work area. They meet, usually in company time, for one hour every week or fortnight, under the leadership of their work supervisor, to solve problems relating to improving their work activities and environment.

The typical characteristics of QCs are:

- Membership is voluntary and people can opt out as and when they wish.

- Members are usually drawn from a single department and are doing similar work. All members are of equal status.

- They operate within the existing organizational structure.

- Members are free to select, from their own work area, the problems and projects which they wish to tackle. These tend to be ones they have to live with every day.

- The QC members are trained in the use of the seven basic quality control tools, meeting skills, facilitation, team-building, project management, and presentation techniques.

- Appropriate data collection, problem-solving methodology and skills, and decision-making methods are employed by QC members to the project under consideration.

- Meetings are generally short, but a large number are held.

- There is minimum pressure to solve the problem within a set timeframe.

- A facilitator is available to assist the QC with the project.

- The solutions are evaluated in terms of their cost-effectiveness.

- The findings, solutions, and recommendations of the QC are shown to management for comment and approval, usually in a formal presentation.

- The QC implements its recommendations, where practicable.

- Once implemented, the QC monitors the effects of the solution and considers future improvements.

- The QC carries out a critical review of all its activities related to the completed project.

There have been a number of derivatives of QCs resulting in teams operating under a variety of names but with very similar characteristics to QCs.

Quality improvement teams.   Teams of this type can compromise members of a single department, be cross-functional, and include representatives of either or both customers and suppliers. The characteristics of quality improvement teams are more varied than any other type of team activity, but typically include the following:

- Membership can be voluntary or mandatory and can comprise of line workers, staff or a mixture of both. Some teams involve a complete range of personnel from different levels in the organizational hierarchy.

- Projects can arise as a result of management initiative, a need to undertake some form of corrective action, a high incidence of defects, supplier–customer problems and an opportunity for improvement. It is usual to agree the project brief with management and/or the team "sponsor."

- The team is usually formed to meet a specific objective.

- In the first place, the team leader will have been appointed by management and briefed regarding objectives and timescales.

- The team is more permanent than project teams but less so than QCs. In some cases teams disband after a project, in others they continue.

- Members are usually experienced personnel and well versed in problem-solving skills and methods.

- The team is self-contained and can take whatever action is required to resolve the problem and improve the process.

- The assistance of a facilitator is sometimes required to provide advice on problem-solving, use of specific quality management tools and techniques, and keeping the team activity on course.

See also **quality management systems; total quality management; group working; job design**

Bibliography

Aubrey, C. A. & Felkins, P. K. (1988). *Teamwork: Involving people in quality and productivity improvement*. New York: ASQC Quality Press.

Boaden, R. J. & Dale, B. G. (1993). Teamwork in services: quality circles by another name. *International Journal of Service Industry Management*, 4, 1, 5–24.

Fisher, K. (1992). *Leading self directed work teams*. New York: McGraw-Hill.

Hutchins, D. (1985). *Quality circles handbook*. London: Pitman.

Ryan, J. M. (1992). *The quality team concept in total quality control*. New York: ASQC Quality Press.

BARRIE DALE

R

reliability-centered maintenance Reliability-centered maintenance (RCM) is a systematic process of preserving a system's function by selecting and applying effective PREVENTIVE MAINTENANCE (PM) tasks. However, it differs from most approaches to PM by focusing on function rather than equipment. RCM governs the maintenance policy at the level of plant or equipment type. In general the concept of RCM is applicable in large and complex systems such as large passenger aircraft, military aircraft, oil refineries, and power stations.

The RCM approach arose in the late 1960s and early 1970s when the increasing complexity of systems (and consequent increasing size of the preventive maintenance task) resulted in a rethink of maintenance policy by manufacturers and operators of large passenger aircraft. Pioneering work on the subject was done by United Airlines in the 1970s to support the development and licensing of the Boeing 747.

The principles which define and characterize RCM are, first a focus on the preservation of system function, second the identification of specific failure modes to define loss of function or functional failure, third the prioritization of the importance of the failure modes, because not all functions or functional failures are equal, and finally the identification of effective and applicable PM tasks for the appropriate failure modes. (Applicable means that the task will prevent, mitigate, detect the onset of, or discover, the failure mode. Effective means that among competing candidates the selected PM task is the most cost-effective option.)

These principles, in turn, are implemented in a seven-step systems analysis process:

(1) system selection and information collection;
(2) system boundary definition;
(3) system description;
(4) functions and functional failures;
(5) FAILURE MODE AND EFFECT ANALYSIS;
(6) logic (decision) tree analysis (including a criticality classification of component failure);
(7) maintenance task selection.

Although one of the prime objectives of RCM is to reduce the total costs associated with system failure and downtime, evaluating the returns from an RCM program solely by measuring its impact on costs hides many other less tangible benefits. Typically these additional benefits fall into the following areas:

(1) improved system availability;
(2) optimizing spare parts inventory;
(3) identification of component failure significance;
(4) identification of hidden failure modes;
(5) discovery of significant, and previously unknown failure scenarios;
(6) providing a training opportunity for system engineers and operations personnel;
(7) identification of components where an increase in maintenance task periodicity or life can reduce costs;
(8) identification of candidate areas for design enhancements;
(9) providing a detailed review, and improvement where necessary, of plant documentation.

CONDITION-BASED MAINTENANCE (CBM) is often confused with RCM. However, after "the identification of effective and applicable PM tasks for the appropriate failure modes," on-condition maintenance might be one of a number of resulting policy/action at the component level, i.e. as a result of implementing the RCM approach a picture of the deterioration characteristics of components will emerge. These characteristics can then be used to make decisions on the desirability of monitoring the component, the techniques to be used and their periodicity. In practice RCM will usually result in a combination of policies at the system component level. These include simple inspection procedures (low-cost procedures designed to detect minor problems), condition-based monitoring of system components, trend monitoring (where little is known about system components deterioration characteristics, experience is accumulated in the monitoring process), operate to failure policies and opportunity maintenance policies.

See also **total productive maintenance; failure analysis**

Bibliography

Smith, A. (1993). *Reliability-centered maintenance*. New York: McGraw-Hill.

MICHAEL SHULVER

robotics A robot is an automatic position-controlled reprogrammable manipulator which is capable of handling materials, parts, tools, or specialized devices through variable programmed motions. It often has the appearance of one or several arms ending in a wrist. Its control unit uses a memorizing device and sometimes it can use sensing and adaptation appliances that take account of the environment and circumstances. These multipurpose machines are generally designed to carry out repetitive functions and can be adapted to other functions without permanent alternation of the equipment.

The term "robot" was first coined by a Czech playwright, Carel Capek, in his play *Rosum's Universal Robots* where it was used to refer to automatons capable of carrying out a range of human activities. Experiments aimed at developing such devices for industrial applications date back at least to the Second World War, but it was not until the emergence of IT that suitable control systems began to appear to facilitate practical robotics.

Early robots were mainly used for repetitive tasks like diecasting and found most applications in the large car manufacturing plants. The Norwegian firm, Tralfa, developed the first tool-handling robot for paint spraying in 1966 and welding applications emerged in the late 1960s; in each case the main applications were in high volume series. In the much bigger application area of high flexibility tasks where reprogrammability would be important it was not until ASEA in Sweden developed a robot using electric rather than hydraulic drives in 1973 that this field began to open up. This design offered greater precision of control over movements, and the emergence of microprocessor control during the following years opened up possibilities in smaller batch work, especially in assembly areas. Unimation's PUMA (programmable universal machine for assembly) was originally developed for General Motors in 1978 but found widespread application in a variety of tasks.

In the late 1970s the SCARA robot emerged as the product of a major research program in Japan. This pre-competitive project involved 13 manufacturers collaborating to develop a low-cost, general-purpose robot which aimed to be suitable for 80 percent of all industrial assembly work. Although successful in opening up the assembly automation market, there are still problems with the concept of general-purpose robots, particularly in the area of sensor technology where the lack of suitably powerful but low-cost systems for vision, touch, etc., limit their application.

Robotics has begun to diffuse widely, especially in its simpler form where re-programmable manipulators and "pick and place" devices are now commonplace. Sophisticated applications are less evident, partly because of the technological problems mentioned above and partly because the costs of robots are still high relative to manual labor for manipulative tasks. Thus most applications are in locations where labor costs are high or where tasks are too dangerous for human intervention.

It is widely accepted that assembly automation will represent a major growth area for robotics in the medium-term future, and it has already experienced the most rapid growth in most industrialized countries.

Among key technological developments currently being explored are:

- direct-drive robots, in which motors are directly connected to arm joins rather than via gears and transmissions;

- advanced sensors, especially in image processing for vision systems;

- improved, more sensitive grippers;

- artificial intelligence-based programming so that robots can "learn" from their own mistakes.

See also **advanced manufacturing technology; flexible manufacturing systems; computer-integrated manufacturing; process technology**

Bibliography

Bessant, J. (1991). *Managing advanced manufacturing technology: The challenge of the fifth wave.* Oxford: NCC-Blackwell.

JOHN BESSANT

runners, repeaters, and strangers Runners, repeaters, and strangers is a classification of product groups which is based on the frequency with which a manufacturing operation is called upon to make a product. It is related to the central concepts of VOLUME and VARIETY, and the assumptions about how different levels of each imply different methods of treating product groups.

- Runners are products or parts which are produced frequently, such as every week.

- Repeaters are products or parts which, although being produced regularly, are manufactured at longer time intervals.

- Strangers are products or parts which are products at long, irregular and possibly unpredictable intervals.

While the exact timescale of production intervals and boundaries between the three categories is almost certain to vary between different industries, the principle of distinguishing between different product groups in this manner has precedent. It is well accepted that the volume and variety characteristics of products will influence the design planning and control of the processes which are required to manufacture them.

See also **manufacturing processes; service processes; planning and control in operations; demand response**

Bibliography

Parnaby, J. (1988). A systems approach to the implementation of JIT methodologies at Lucas Industries. *International Journal of Production Research*, **26**, 3.

NIGEL SLACK

S

safety stocks in MRP Safety stocks in MRP systems are held, as in any manufacturing system, to cater for uncertainty. In a MATERIAL REQUIREMENTS PLANNING system the major cause of uncertainty, that of the future usage of the item, has been mainly eliminated since items should be produced to meet a plan; the MASTER PRODUCTION SCHEDULE. Therefore, overall, safety stocks in an MRP system should be significantly lower than in a system using classical inventory control policies (*see* INVENTORY MANAGEMENT).

However, safety stocks may still be needed because of uncertainties in supply both in terms of the variation of actual lead times and the variation of quantities supplied caused by process failures, inspection rejects, and material shortages. There may also be changes of demand caused by short-term (emergency) changes to the master schedule and unexpected demands for items for spares.

The statistical techniques of establishing safety stocks used in classical inventory control systems are not directly transferable to the material requirements planning environment. Alternative methods have therefore been developed for application to MRP which fall into three main categories: fixed quantity safety stocks, safety times, and percentage increases in requirements.

Fixed quantity safety stocks are introduced by triggering a net requirement whenever the projected stock on hand reaches a safety stock level rather than zero. The calculation of the size of the fixed quantity safety stock should be related to the cause of the unexpected usage or failure of supply during the lead time. For example, if an unplanned demand is primarily as a result of unforecast spares demand for the item, then a historical analysis of this variation may lead towards the setting of a safety stock level which gives a satisfactory service level.

The safety time, or safety lead time, approach for setting safety margins is essentially planning to make items available earlier than they are required. The introduction of safety time is straightforward in that the net requirements are offset by the lead time and the safety time to produce planned orders. It is important to realize that the introduction of safety time does not have the same effect as increasing the lead time, since the due dates on planned orders will be a lead time after the planned order release date; that is there will be a safety time before the actual net requirement due date. The choice of the length of the safety time could be related to the variability of the manufacturing or procurement lead time of the item being considered. However, since other factors may influence the use of the safety stock generated by the use of safety time, a safety time set taking account of the item value and the penalty of running out, and then subsequent adjustment based on the monitoring of the usage of the safety stock, may be satisfactory.

The setting of safety margins by the percentage increase in requirements method is particularly suitable for dealing with the variations in supply caused by scrap or process yield losses and are often implemented as "scrap factors," or "shrinkage factors." This type of safety margin is introduced by increasing the net requirements by a factor to produce planned orders. The size of the percentage increase in requirement should be directly related to the actual scrap or process yield loss for which it is supposed to be compensating. If this margin is to be used as a buffer against other variations, then an arbitrary setting may be made and subsequently modified, based on the feedback of the actual use of the safety stock generated.

Safety stocks of finished products to provide a predetermined customer service level should be set by analyzing the operation of the sales forecast and translating the resulting requirements into a master production schedule for the finished products.

See also **netting process in MRP; inventory control systems**

Bibliography

Vollmann, T. W., Berry, W. L. & Whybark, D. C. (1992). *Manufacturing planning and control systems.* New York: Irwin.

PETER BURCHER

sandcone model of improvement The sandcone model of improvement is an analogy which seeks to explain how assigning priorities to OPERATIONS OBJECTIVES may result in lasting improvements in performance.

Based on an interpretation of data from the Global Manufacturing Futures Survey to which they contribute, Ferdows and De Meyer (1990) suggest that lasting improvements in performance depend on effort being applied in creating a particular sequence of capabilities and that these capabilities should be considered as cumulative developments, building on each other. The model is called the sandcone model because the sand is analogous to the management effort and resources. To build a stable sandcone the base must be continually widened to support its increasing height.

The first "layer" of improvement, and a precondition to all lasting improvement, is effort applied to quality performance. Only when the operation has reached a minimally acceptable level in quality should it then tackle issues of internal dependability. But moving on to include dependability in the improvement process should not stop the operation making further improvements in quality. Indeed, improvement in dependability will actually require further improvement in quality. Once a critical level of dependability is reached, enough to provide some stability in the opera-

tion, the next stage is to turn attention to the speed at which materials flow through the operation. But again only while continuing to improve quality and dependability further. Now, according to the sandcone model, is the best time for COST to be tackled head on. Thus cost reductions are seen as a consequence of other improvements.

See also **trade-offs; manufacturing strategy; continuous improvement; quality management systems; time-based performance; delivery dependability**

Bibliography

Ferdows, K. & De Meyer, A. (1990). Lasting improvements in manufacturing management. *Journal of Operations Management*, **9**, *2*, 168–84.

NIGEL SLACK

scheduling A schedule is a plan which defines the sequence and time allocated to the activities of an operation. It is a detailed timetable showing at what time or date jobs should start and when they should end. Scheduling is the process of formulating the schedules for an operation which together will indicate which jobs will be completed within a given timescale. It is one of the central tasks of PLANNING AND CONTROL IN OPERATIONS.

The scheduling activity is one of the most complex tasks in operations management. Schedulers must deal with several different types of resource, most with different constraints, simultaneously. Also the number of possible schedules increases rapidly as the number of activities and processes increases. For example, if one machine has n jobs to process there are $n!$ different ways of scheduling the jobs through a single process. With m machines and n jobs there are $(n!)^m$ possible schedules. So with realistic values of many tens or hundreds of jobs and machines the scheduling task rapidly becomes very complicated. Within the very large number of schedules there are many acceptable options as to which are appropriate routes and sequences for any set of jobs. Even where a product is manufactured repeatedly there may be a number of different routes which that product could take. However, most of the schedules which are possible in theory will not be workable in practice and these can be rapidly eliminated.

The scheduling task may also have to be repeated on a frequent basis to allow for market variations and product mix changes. Even minor product mix changes may cause the capacity constraints within the facility to change over a comparatively short period of time, with BOTTLENECKS moving between machines.

The scheduling activity has three conflicting objectives. First, scheduling attempts to meet due dates (the time when the job is due to be completed). Second, it attempts to minimize the time the job spends in the operation, that is minimize the throughput time (*see* TIME-BASED PERFORMANCE). Third, it attempts to maximize work center utilization. The weight given to each of these objectives will depend on the competitive circumstances of the company and its prevailing manufacturing philosophy. For example JUST-IN-TIME philosophies stress throughput time and due date performance above utilization.

Forward and Backward Scheduling

Forward scheduling involves starting work as soon as it arrives. Backward scheduling involves starting jobs at the last possible moment to prevent them being late.

The choice of backward or forward scheduling depends largely upon specific circumstances and gives different advantages and disadvantages. The main advantages of forward scheduling are first that utilization of work centers is high (if work is available it is scheduled to be performed by the work center), and second that the schedule remains flexible so that unexpected work can be loaded. Backward scheduling, on the other hand, should progress material through the operation only when it is needed and therefore should keep work-in-progress inventory down. It is also less vulnerable to customers extending their required due date, but does tend to focus the operation on customer due dates. *See also* FINITE AND INFINITE LOADING.

In theory, both MATERIAL REQUIREMENTS PLANNING and JUST-IN-TIME use backwards scheduling; only starting work when it is required. In practice, however, users of material requirements planning may allow extra time for tasks to be completed, therefore each task is not started at the last possible time.

See also **Gantt chart; sequencing**

Bibliography

Conway, R. W., Maxwell, W. L. & Miller, L. W. (1967). *Theory of scheduling.* Reading, MA: Addison Wesley.

NIGEL SLACK

"scientific" management   In the last years of the nineteenth century and the first of the twentieth century, a number of management thinkers developed ideas and principles of JOB DESIGN and WORK ORGANIZATION which collectively became known as "scientific" management. The term "scientific" management became established in 1911 with the publication of the book of the same name by Fredrick Winslow Taylor. This whole approach is sometimes referred to, pejoratively, as "Taylorism." In this work he identified what he saw as the basic tenets of scientific management.

- All aspects of work should be investigated on a scientific basis to establish the laws, rules, and formulae governing the best methods of working.

- Such an investigative approach to the study of work is necessary to establish what constitutes a "fair day's work."

- Workers should be selected, trained, and developed methodically to perform their tasks.

- Managers should act as the planners of the work (analyzing jobs and standardizing the best method of doing the job), while workers should be responsible for carrying out the jobs to the standards laid down.

- Achieve co-operation between management and workers based on the "maximum prosperity" of both.

Other contributors to the "scientific" management movement included Gilbreth, Gantt, and Bedaux, all working in the United States. Between them all two separate, but related, fields of study emerged. One, METHOD STUDY, concentrates on methods and activities; the other, WORK MEASUREMENT, is concerned with measuring the time which should be taken for performing jobs. Together these two fields are often referred to as WORK STUDY.

From its earliest days, "scientific" management attracted criticism. Two themes evident in this early criticism are important. The first is it inevitably results in standardization of highly divided jobs and thus reinforces the negative affects of excessive DIVISION OF LABOR. Second, that it formalizes the separation of the judgmental, planning, and skilled tasks, done by "management," from the routine, standardized, and low-skill tasks, which are left for "operators." Such a separation deprives the majority of staff of the opportunity to contribute in a meaningful way to their jobs. Therefore jobs designed under strict "scientific" management principles lead to low motivation among staff, frustration at the lack of control over their work, and alienation from the job. However, more recent applications of some of the principles of "scientific" management claim to have partly overcome the objections to it by moving responsibility for the use of its methods and procedures from "management" to the staff who are being studied. Furthermore, some of the methods and techniques of "scientific" management (as opposed to its philosophy), can, in practice, prove useful in critically re-examining job designs. It is the practicality of these techniques which may explain their survival.

Bibliography

Adler, P. S. (1993). Time and motion regained. *Harvard Business Review*, 71, *1*, 97–108.
Bailey, J. (1983). *Job design and work organisation*. London: Prentice-Hall.

NIGEL SLACK

sequencing   Sequencing is the decision which is taken on the order of the jobs which will be tackled by a work station. Typically in batch processes (*see* MANUFACTURING PROCESSES) and some SERVICE PROCESSES, each work station has a queue of jobs waiting to be processed from which it must select one to

work on. This is the sequencing decision. There are several sequencing rules which can be used to make this decision. Some of these are as follows.

Customer Priority

Operations may allow an important customer, or item, to be "processed" prior to others, irrespective of their order of arrival. This approach is typically used by operations whose customer base is skewed, containing a mass of small customers and a few large, very important customers. However, sequencing work by customer priority may mean that "large volume" customers receive a very high level of service, while service to other customers is eroded. This may lower the average performance of the operation.

Due Date

Prioritizing by due date means that work is sequenced according to when it is due for delivery, irrespective of the size of each job or the importance of each customer.

LIFO

Last in first out (LIFO) is a method of sequencing usually selected for practical reasons. For example, unloading an elevator is more convenient on a LIFO basis as there is only one entrance and exit. However, it is not an equitable approach.

FIFO

Some operations process jobs in exactly the sequence they arrive in on a first in first out (FIFO) basis. In high-contact operations, arrival time may be viewed by customers in the system as a fair way of sequencing, thereby minimizing customer complaints, enhancing service performance. However, because there is no consideration of urgency or due date, some customers' needs may not be served as well as others. It is also difficult to be flexible in a system where this prioritization is visible to customers.

Longest Operation/Longest Total Job Time First

Under certain circumstances operations may feel obliged to sequence their longest jobs first. This has the advantage of occupying the work centers within the operation for long periods. Relatively small jobs progressing through an operation will take up time at each work center which will need to change over from one job to the next. Especially where staff are under some incentive to keep utilization high, such a sequencing rule might seem attractive.

Shortest Operation/Shortest Total Job Time First

This rule involves choosing jobs to process on the basis of their processing time, either for their next operation or the sum of their process times. Because this rule launches shorter (faster) jobs through the system first, they are less likely to dwell in the system and slow down subsequent (slower) jobs. In fact this rule is generally agreed to provide fast throughput and reasonably good due date performance on average. Its main disadvantage is that it can ignore larger jobs which may be continually superseded by later but shorter jobs. This means that a high "percentage on time" performance may be gained at the expense of a poor "average lateness" performance.

See also **planning and control in operations; time-based performance; delivery dependability**

Bibliography

Conway, R. N., Maxwell, W. L. & Miller, L. W. (1967). *Theory of scheduling*. Reading, MA: Addison Wesley.

NIGEL SLACK

service design It is claimed that, until relatively recently, many large and small organizations, both product and service oriented, have given little thought to the design and development of their services. "The development of a new service is usually characterized by trial and error ... No one systematically quantifies the process or devises tests to ensure that the service is complete, rational, and fulfils the original need objectively. No R&D departments, laboratories or service engineers define and oversee the design" (Shostack, 1984).

The service design activity:

- is concerned with specifying the characteristics of service (*see* QUALITY CHARACTERISTICS);

- is concerned with designing out fail-points (*see* SERVICE RECOVERY and FAILURE ANALYSIS);

- requires a clear understanding of customer needs and expectations, and a clear and shared service concept (*see* SERVICE STRATEGY);

- involves decisions concerning the selection and training of staff, and the design of jobs (*see* JOB DESIGN);

- includes the design of service technology;

- involves the detailed design of the service delivery system, service package, service process, and the service environment (*see* SERVICE OPERATIONS).

The Service Delivery System

The service delivery system, or the service operation, is the part of the organization that designs, creates, and delivers the service package to the customer. In many personal and social services it involves dealing directly with the customer, as in leisure and health services. In other organizations, the delivery system may be concerned with the provision of facilities for the customer, as in telecommunications and travel, or the provision of goods for the customer as in retail and distribution activities. Within most service delivery systems there are two distinct types of operations, back office and front office. The back office is the part of the service operation which the customer does not usually see, or have access to. This is often referred to as the "manufacturing" part of the service operation, for example the kitchen in a restaurant. The front office is the part of the operation that provides the service to the customer, usually involving some contact with the customer, that is the place where the customer is processed.

The Service Package

The service package comprises the bundle of goods used in the delivery of service or removed from the system by the customer, the environment in which the goods and services are provided, and the way the customers or their belongings are treated. Each service operation usually provides several services and several types of goods. These can be classified as the core, supporting and facilitating goods and services (*see* TRANSFORMATION MODEL).

The core service is the fundamental service of the organization, without it the remaining supporting and facilitating services would be of little use. For example, the core service in an hotel is the provision of an acceptable bedroom. If this service was not provided, however excellent the hotel restaurant or however polite the staff, the "service" would have little point. Supporting services are the services that enhance the core service. Such services might include, in the case of an hotel, the restaurant, pool, recreation facilities, and tour services. Facilitating services facilitate the organization's provision of the core and supporting services. These activities may not directly involve the customer, for example guest billing or cleaning in hotels.

The Service Process

Service is often described as a process rather than a product, and while most services do process material objects and information, customer processing is usually a core and critical function.

The customer process is the part of the front office that delivers the service package to the customer. This involves contact with the customer which may be personal and direct, for example face to face with a bank clerk, or personal but indirect, for example discussing an overdraft with the bank manager over a telephone, or non-personal and involve customers interacting with equipment, a cash machine for example. The provision of service involving contact and interaction with customers is usually a "real time" activity (*see* SERVICE PROCESSES).

The Service Environment

Bitner (1992) coined the phrase "servicescapes" to describe the physical surroundings of the service delivery system. She uses the word servicescape to convey more than just an environment but also the "landscape" or backdrop that should give context to, and support for, the service concept (*see* SERVICE STRATEGY). The physical setting and atmosphere of a service operation will influence the behavior and attitude of not only the service employees but also the customers. LAYOUT can enhance or discourage social interaction for example. Decor can influence the perceived image of an organization. Other environmental cues, such as dress and furniture, can influence customers' beliefs about the nature of the service they are to receive.

Service Design Tools

There are a number of tools and techniques that can be used to aid the design of services. These include blueprinting, QUALITY FUNCTION DEPLOYMENT, walk-through audits, CRITICAL INCIDENT TECHNIQUE, failsafing (*see* FAILURE ANALYSIS). However, the best known and most widely used design technique is blueprinting.

Service Blueprinting

Blueprinting is a means of evaluating, developing, and designing service processes. The term "blueprinting" refers to the documentation of a service process. Blueprinting is not just confined to documenting customer processes but is intended to help design the interrelationships between material, information, and customer flows.

There are several ways of documenting service processes, for example, decision charts, PROCESS CHARTS, customer processing framework, and blueprints (as described by Shostack, 1984). All of these methods essentially involve the identification of the different stages in a service process. They can be made more sophisticated by the addition of lines of visibility, lines of interaction, time frames, the identification of control points and mechanisms, and the location of responsibility for each stage of the process. The benefits of blueprinting in the design of service processes is that the process can be checked for completeness and over-complexity, to see whether it meets the strategic intentions of an organization and to help identify and remove potential fail-points, and help identify potential improvements.

The Customer Processing Framework

One blueprinting tool designed specifically for documenting and analyzing customer flows through a service operation is the customer processing framework (Johnston, 1987). This framework identifies the series of generic stages through which customers usually pass, including selection, point of entry, response time, point of impact, delivery, point of departure, and follow up. By identifying and analyzing the activities at each of these stages, managers may better understand how they can ensure that the process is both efficient and effective. This involves not only assessing the productivity or efficiency of the process but also how it creates customers' perceptions of service, reshapes their expectations for further stages in the process and affects their future purchase intentions (*see* SERVICE QUALITY).

Bibliography

Bitner, M. J. (1992). Servicescapes: the impact of physical surroundings on customers and employees. *Journal of Marketing*, **56**, 57–71.

Fitzsimmons, J. A. & Fitzsimmons, M. J. (1994). *Service management for competitive advantage*. New York: McGraw-Hill.

Johnston, R. (1987). A framework for developing a quality strategy in a customer processing operation. *International Journal of Quality and Reliability Management*, **4**, *4*, 35–44.

Shostack, G. L. (1984). Designing services that deliver. *Harvard Business Review*, **62**, *1*, 133–9.

ROBERT JOHNSTON

service innovations Technology in a service business can take forms very different from industrial-based definitions. Examples such as the wheel, automobile, refrigeration, aeroplane, telephone, satellite, automatic teller machine, space shuttle, personal computer, plastic automobile bodies and rapid manufacturing prototyping represent advances in hard technology. These hard technology examples are physical apparatus that help create and deliver goods and services. They are easy to recognize because people can see and touch them as physical items.

At the other end of the technology spectrum, soft technologies also increase productivity and improve our standard of living. Soft technologies are more than computer software. Soft technologies include human intellect, information processing, and ways of thinking and acting. The written word, self-service, customer service script dialogues, US Bill of Rights, insurance, service guarantees, corporations, service-provider empowerment training, and object-oriented computer software are examples of soft technologies. They are not so easy to recognize. They are usually associated with a novel procedure such as self-service, managing information or an intangible characteristic such as a person's psychological well-being.

Service innovations are usually combinations of hard and soft technologies, they include electronic mail, buyer and computer clubs, health maintenance organizations, and newspaper wire service associations.

The study of service technologies is relatively new. In a 1983 article titled "The service sector revolution: the automation of services," Collier identified examples of service technology in many service industries. A subsequent case book was titled *Service Management: The Automation of Services* (1985). Examples of service technology in the financial services industry include encoded check processing machines, electronic funds transfer, automated trust portfolio analysis, electronic checkbooks and home banking, and automatic teller machines. For the utility and government services industries, service technology examples include automated one-person garbage trucks, optical mail scanning and sorting machines, airborne warning and control systems, and highly automated power generating plants. In the hotel/motel industry, service technologies include electronic reservation systems, elevators/escalators, electronic key and lock systems, and automatic sprinkler systems.

Yet these 1983 examples of service technology understate a service management view of service innovation. Innovation in all forms encapsulates human knowledge. Proven technical, process or social innovations, a customer and market that is receptive and ready to pay; and excellent management decisions must all converge at the right time to create a successful innovation.

One dictionary definition of automation is "the technique of making an apparatus, a process, or a system operate automatically." The ability to do physical and intellectual tasks often unassisted by human beings is automation. Technology may be defined as a technical method of achieving practical purposes. Innovation is "something that deviates from established doctrine or practice, something that differs from existing forms." Quinn (1979) defines innovation as "creating and introducing original solutions for new or already identified needs." More specifically, service innovation is "any new or modified doctrine, practice, or way of creating and delivering service encounters." Here innovation includes discovery and the practical application or commercialization of a device, method, or idea. Service innovations include both backroom and frontroom initiatives (*see* SERVICE DESIGN) that affect service encounter design and execution. Service innovation reflects the broadest view of technology. It is most appropriate for services to view service technology as a subset of service innovations.

For example, Wendy's Salad Bar (a restaurant chain) in the US fast food industry is a service innovation. The salad bar service innovation is not automated (at least not yet). But it did combine at its time of introduction many new ideas of facility and process design, and self-service. Service innovations do not have to include new physical layouts or the use of new technology (equipment). A process-based service innovation coupled with existing technology can sometimes differentiate offered products and services, and service encounters, from those of competitors.

For example, shop at home by phone capabilities have been in existence for a long time. The US-based Kroger supermarkets offer The Shoppers Express where a customer places an order verbally over the telephone or by fax machine. The customer can call 24 hours a day, 7 days a week. Temperature-controlled vehicles deliver the groceries right to the customer's door with same day or next day service. Prices vary according to delivery requirements, faxed orders get a discount, and so do senior citizens. Senior citizens and time-starved professional workers are two target markets for this time- and convenience-based consumer benefit package. This service innovation is process-based using existing telephone technology.

Many service innovations are information-based, making the location of work places increasingly irrelevant. Therefore service firm managers and service-providers do not necessarily need a permanent workplace. For information-intensive jobs, electronic networks allow work to be done almost anywhere in the world. In effect the time and place of service encounter execution becomes portable. Technology such as a portable personal computer, a fax machine, and a car telephone defines a mobile office for many professional and routine service-providers. Consultants, engineers, lawyers, and so on are mobile and now have the capability to leverage every minute of their time. The capability to create and execute service encounters can now follow the customer. The terms convenience-, time- and place-utility, may assume an enhanced meaning as both customers and staff are connected to a global electronic network.

In summary, service innovations take many forms, most of which are not recognized as such based on the traditional ideas of product innovations. Service innovations help define the capabilities of the consumer benefit package, and its service process and service encounters. However, because service innovations have less copyright and patent protection than product innovations, service firm managers must be very alert to new ideas and innovations within and outside their industry. Constant innovation, both product and service, is taken by many to be a predictor of marketplace success.

See also **advanced manufacturing technology; computer-integrated manufacturing; process technology; service operations; service processes**

Bibliography

Collier, D. A. (1983). The service sector revolution: the automation of services. *Long Range Planning*, **16**, 6, 10–20.

Collier, D. A. (1985). *Service management: The automation of services*. Englewood Cliffs, NJ: Prentice-Hall.

Quinn, J. B. (1979). Technological innovation, entrepreneurship, and strategy. *Sloan Management Review*, **20**, 19–29.

DAVID COLLIER

service operations Whereas goods-producing industries include agriculture, manufacturing, mining, construction, fishing, and forestry, service industries include all other economic and social activity such as government, education, telecommunication, finance, health care, and retail/wholesale services. However, although the body of knowledge on operations management for goods-producing organizations is extensive, the stature of service operations management historically is less well developed. For example, in 1955 about one-half of the United States workforce worked in the service sector. Yet, it was not until 1978 when Sasser, Olsen and Wyckoff wrote a text and case book titled *Management of Service Operations*, that service operations management was recognized. Johnston (1994) documents the evolution of production management to operations management to service management. He concludes that

> From an operations perspective the subject seems to be dominated and driven by marketers whose work sometimes ignores the constraints imposed, and the opportunities afforded, by the operation in the delivery of service promises. Some of these people appear to disregard, or not understand, the role and importance of operations management and do not use or refer to the large body of knowledge that has been developed on service operations.

Service industries typically account for 50 to 80 percent of the jobs in developed economies. Considering that at least 50 percent of employment in goods-producing industries are in service processes, then 75 to 90 percent of the jobs in modern economies are in service processes. Clearly, a key to national and organizational competitiveness lies in improving service process performance.

It is generally held by both academics and practitioners that providing services is intrinsically different than producing physical products. Four distinct characteristics that make the management of service-providing organizations different from goods-producing organizations were first defined by Sasser et al. (1989).

Services are intangible. Thus, they are difficult to describe, as well as demonstrate to the buying public, and illustrate in promotional material. Services are perishable: they cannot be inventoried. For example, three very perishable commodities are an airline seat, a hotel room, and an hour of a lawyer's day. In essence, the service manager is without the important "shock absorber" called inventory that is available to managers in goods-producing firms to absorb fluctuations in demand. Services are characterized as providing heterogeneous output. The

heterogeneity characteristic means that it is difficult to establish standards for the output of a service firm and even harder to insure that standards are met each time the service is delivered. Services require simultaneous production and consumption, which compounds the problems caused by intangibility, perishability, and heterogeneity. Unlike a manufacturing system, the consumer interacts with, and participates in, the service delivery process with production and consumption occurring simultaneously.

Collier (1994) extends these four ideas and adds a few more by defining nine characteristics that distinguish goods-producing and service-providing organizations. He defines a consumer benefit package (CBP) as a clearly defined set of tangible (goods content) and intangible (service content) attributes (features) that the customer recognizes, pays for, uses, or experiences. It is some combination of goods and services configured in a certain way. A CBP includes the purchase of a primary (core) good with peripheral goods and/or services or of a primary (core) service with peripheral goods and/or services. The final set of CBP features or attributes fulfills certain customer needs and wants.

Customer participation in the service encounter recognizes that the customer is frequently engaged in the service process, activity or transaction. That is, the customer is "in your factory." When a customer, for example, checks into your hotel or calls the credit card processing center to resolve a dispute, the customer "enters your factory." Some service firms try to take advantage of the customer being in their service delivery system by encouraging self-service (supermarkets, cafeterias, libraries) and self-clean-up (fast-food restaurants, campgrounds, vacation home rentals).

The characteristic of time-dependent demand recognizes that the demand for services is more difficult to predict than the demand for products over equal planning horizons. Inventory cannot be used to store the service encounter. Therefore, the nature of demand for services, especially over the short term (say by hour or day), places great pressures on service firm managers and service-providers. Customer arrival rates and demand patterns for service delivery systems such as those of banks, airlines, supermarkets, telephone service centers, and courts are highly variable and very difficult to forecast.

The simultaneous production and consumption of most services preclude the use of inventory. For service delivery systems, capacity is the surrogate for inventory. For example, safety capacity for a hospital can take the form of safety beds (equipment) for the purpose of meeting unanticipated patient demand. A float pool of nurse (labor) capacity can alleviate shortfalls in hospital nurse capacity.

Service-provider skills, the fifth distinguishing service characteristic, are paramount to a successful service encounter. The customer and service-provider (sometimes called buyer–seller) interface is where the service-provider is simultaneously providing (performing) marketing, human resource management, and operations (technical) tasks. The service-provider has a significant effect on the perceived value of the service as viewed by the customer.

Service organizations typically consist of small units of capacity in close proximity to the customer. For example, post offices, hotels, and branch banks fit these size and proximity requirements. This spatial relationship of service facilities scattered over a wide geographical area is called multisite management. Multisite management complicates the task of managing a service business.

The intangible nature of a service makes it difficult to keep a competitor from copying service encounters. Thus, in terms of patent protection, service packages are not as well protected as physical products. The seventh distinguishing service characteristic is that there is no patents on services. However, services are protected to some extent by copyrights, trademarks, and by establishing a standard consumer benefit package, facility and process design, and so on.

For most services, an inventory build up of service encounters cannot occur during a reduction in demand. For goods-producing firms, on the other hand, inventories can rapidly build up during a business downturn. Future demand for goods can be filled from these inventories, whereas service output is time-dependent and perishable. These characteristics have led some to argue that the services are more recession proof than the goods-producing

sector. Some experts suggest that the recession-proof argument for service firms is most realistic for financial, public utility, health care, government, and some professional services. Discretionary services such as leisure, insurance, hotel/motel, restaurant/food, telecommunications, retail trade, and adult education are thought to be affected by the vitality of the nation's economy. A Toyota can be transported to the USA and sold, but legal services, individual financial services, or medical services, to name just a few, are different. How transportable is a service firm's consumer benefit package in the world economy? Some services simply cannot be transported between countries because of physical, cultural, or regulatory barriers. For example, the VISA credit card is a world class financial service, whereas Blue Cross and Blue Shield find it difficult to export their insurance services across national borders. In summary, many services today are not as transportable as physical products in the global economy. These nine distinguishing service characteristics are another way to conceptualize differences between goods versus services.

See also **operations management; transformation model; service processes; service innovations**

Bibliography

Collier, D. (1987). *Service management: Operating decisions*. Englewood Cliffs, NJ: Prentice-Hall.

Collier, D. A. (1994). *The service/quality solution: Using service management to gain competitive advantage*, Milwaukee, WI: ASQC Quality Press, and Burr Ridge, IL, Irwin Professional Publishing.

Johnston, R. (1994). From factory to service management. *International Journal of Service Industries Management*, **5**, *1*, 49–63.

Sasser, W. E., Olsen, R. P. & Wyckoff, D. D. (1978). *The management of service operations*. Boston, MA: Allyn and Bacon.

DAVID COLLIER

service processes The MANUFACTURING PROCESSES model has occupied a central position in the operations management literature for several decades. By contrast there has been a distinct lack of agreement within the service operations literature as to how to classify services so as to develop a corresponding understanding of the similarities and differences in the management of service operations. "Service industries remain dominated by an operations orientation that insists each industry is different" (Lovelock, 1983).

The manufacturing process model is so prominent in the operations management field that attempts have been made to fit service examples into it. Such attempts have met with considerable criticism because they are insufficient for diagnosing service systems and fail to capture the inherent variability of service operations created by the existence of the customer in the process. A number of authors in the service management field have therefore proposed service typologies which more appropriately differentiate between different types of service. The distinctions described below by no means represent a complete list but include the main classification schemes in use:

(1) Equipment or people focus: examples of equipment-based services include airlines, automatic car washes, and vending machines; examples of people-based services are appliance repair and management consultants. This distinction attempts to move managers' strategic thinking away from a "product-orientated language" to a service management approach which differentiates between businesses on the basis of the way in which service is provided. While the traditional assumption has been that services are invariably and undeviatingly personal, as something performed by individuals for other individuals, the strategic requirements for equipment-based businesses are obviously quite different from those in which individuals perform services for other individuals. A similar distinction is that between different types of services on the basis of the degree of labor intensity of the service process.

(2) Level of customer contact: some authorities suggest classifying services along a continuum from high to low contact, where contact refers to the length of time the customer is in contact with the service. This concept may also be operationalized slightly differently. Instead of considering the duration of customer contact it may be preferable to focus on where value is added, whether in the front or back office. It is then argued that services where value is added primarily in the back office are more akin to production operations and the lessons of modern production-line management methods can be brought to bear.

(3) Extent of customization: here services are differentiated according to the extent to which they are tailored to meet individual requirements, an idea closely related to VARIETY. Customized activities involve compiling a service package for each customer. At the other extreme, standardized activities are non-varying processes; although there may be several routes or choices, their availability is always predetermined. For example, rail transport systems provide passengers with a wide variety of routes between many locations, but the service offered cannot be tailored (at least in the short term) to meet individual passenger needs.

(4) Degree of discretion given to personnel in meeting customer needs: this dimension can be defined as the extent to which customer contact staff exercise judgment in meeting individual customer needs. Clearly the more highly customized the service process, the more discretion staff need to respond to customer requirements.

(5) Product/process focus: some authors distinguish between product and process focused services. In a product focused organization the emphasis is on what the customer buys, while in a process focused business the emphasis is on how the customer buys, that is, the way the service is delivered. It is often argued that many service organizations tend to focus their control and measurement systems on product and outcome, rather than on the process.

A multidimensional service classification scheme can be constructed drawing upon and integrating the typologies described above. Just as production volume is the unifying characteristic in the manufacturing processes model, the volume of service activity, measured in terms of numbers of customers processed per business unit per period, similarly correlates with the service dimensions mentioned above. As the number of customers processed by a typical unit per day increases, the following service characteristics obtain:

- focus moves from a people to an equipment orientation;

- length of contact time moves from high to low;

- degree of customization moves from high to low;

- level of employee discretion moves from high to low;

- value added moves from front office to back office;

- focus moves from a process to a product orientation.

The framework, analogous to the manufacturing process model, is illustrated in Figure 1, which identifies three service archetypes: professional services, service shops and mass service. Just as there are hybrid manufacturing processes, not all services share all the characteristics of one service type, although most services will predominantly be characterized as either professional, service shop or mass services. The three types of services are defined as follows.

Professional services are organizations which process relatively few transactions, provide highly customized service, with relatively long contact time. These services tend to be people-based, with most value being added in the front office, where considerable judgment is applied in meeting customer needs.

Mass services are organizations where there are many customer transactions involving limited contact time and little customization. Often equipment based, the service offering is predominantly product oriented with most value being added in the back office and little judgment applied by the front office staff.

The service shop is a categorization which falls between professional and mass services with each of the service characteristics falling between the other two extremes.

Professional Services

In customized service processes, the customer often actively participates in the process of defining the service specification, detailing his/ her individual requirements. Customers (or clients) of professional services typically build long-term relationships with individual members of staff who will have personal responsibility for their individual customer accounts. The low volume of customers and the high relative value of their accounts mean that, for managers of professional services, customer retention, and managing service recovery so as to obviate customer defections, are likely to be central concerns. Being people based, the opportunities for substituting labor by equipment or technology are limited, while there is likely to be a high ratio of front office staff to customers. Human resource issues therefore tend to dominate the resource management agenda. Key issues of labor-intensive businesses are the hiring and training of staff; management, scheduling and control of the workforce, and employee welfare.

The customized nature of professional services, requiring high discretion by front line staff in meeting customer requirements, often means that front line staff are highly qualified, with valuable skills which are difficult to acquire. Controlling jobs in customized services is often highly complex due to the low specificity of tasks, limited repetitive learning opportunities, and the "craft-skill specialization," making individual work difficult to pace and standardize. Assignments are often long term and job completion times tend to be uncertain, variable, and difficult to estimate. Managing the career advancement of employees delivering the service, generating employee loyalty and staff retention rates are likely to be key concerns, also organization structures are likely to be flat, with loose rather than rigid control relationships between superiors and subordinates.

With labor being the key resource, control of labor costs is likely to be critical and labor productivity will be the key measure of resource utilization. Costs are usually readily traceable in professional services with the price charged to the customer often being based on the number of labor hours spent on a job, making the use

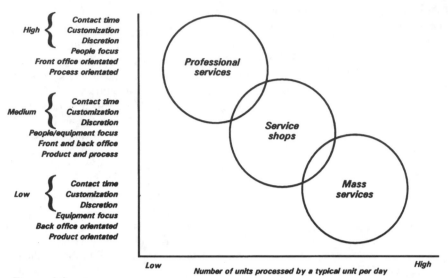

Figure 1 Service processes

of diary systems to quantify, document, and control resources appropriate. Capacity is defined primarily in terms of available labor in professional services. Such services tend to be more flexible in the short term than mass services, being better able to accommodate changes to the service process and adjust capacity to meet demand fluctuations. Service flexibility tends to be provided through job scheduling, negotiation of delivery dates with the customer, multiskilling, cross-training, job rotation, and the transfer of staff between business units.

It may be argued that the nature of the customer relationship in professional services has implications for the control and measurement of service quality, which is essentially about the performance of staff. Investment in staff training, supervision, and chargeable ratios are typical quality measures in professional services; for if there is inadequate investment in training, insufficient number of supervisory staff and too much time spent on chargeable work, quality is likely to suffer. Formal quality audits and staff appraisals are also central to the control and measurement of service quality. Methods for the measurement of customer satisfaction tend to be informal, being based on individual customer interviews and unstructured reports rather than standardized ques-

tionnaires or surveys. Unlike mass services, it is often feasible to measure the satisfaction of every customer rather than basing the measurement on samples; and the identification of customer dissatisfaction may well result in action being taken to recover the service for the individual customer.

Mass Services

Mass services are often equipment based, and offer opportunities for the substitution of service by equipment or technology. In non-labor-intensive mass services the choice of plant and equipment, and monitoring and implementing technological advantages, are likely to be key issues. Capacity tends to be defined in terms of availability of plant, equipment, and facilities and can be difficult to change in the short term. Mass services therefore tend to be less flexible than professional services, not only in terms of their ability to change the service process, but also in terms of being able to adjust capacity to meet demand. Average response and throughput times are often built into the service design so that flexibility is designed into the system in the long term, with limited scope for short-term flexibility. Level AGGREGATE CAPACITY MANAGEMENT and management of demand in order to smooth peaks and promote off-peak demand therefore tend to be typical of the approach to capacity management.

Customer/staff relationships are best characterized as being between the customer and the organization rather than with an individual, so given the limited scope for tailoring the service to meet individual needs, highly standardized services need to carefully manage customer expectations and invest in customer training. This may imply the pre-selection of customers, providing signals so that only customers whose expectations can be matched by the service delivery system actually select the service and participate in the process.

When levels of customer interaction are low there are fewer opportunities to interface and therefore cross-sell products and services to customers than is typical in high contact, customized services. Similarly, efforts need to be focused on making the service environment "warm," even though there is limited scope for the provision of individual, personal attention. The nature of tasks for employees in high volume, standardized services may be highly specified, well defined, teachable and of known duration. Workers therefore tend to become proficient in one type of operation and tasks may require staff who are tolerant of repetition. When demand is stable, units tend to be highly productive due to the division of labor, specialization and learning that occurs with scale. Control through the application of standard operating procedures will be typical, with relatively rigid, hierarchical organization structures.

Part-time and casual staff may well be used in mass services to increase flexibility in meeting different levels of demand, whereas in professional services the high skill levels of service providers and the length of time taken to train staff and bring them up to speed can prohibit short-term recruitment possibilities. However, the opportunities for providing service flexibility through multiskilling and job rotation tend to be more limited than in professional services, since the trade-off with productivity is costly. Service variety and choice is often provided to the customer by giving many options and routes through the service process, making the tracing of costs of providing services to individual customers very difficult. Therefore, typically a high proportion of costs are allocated, so the profitability of individual services may be difficult to ascertain. Resource utilization is likely to be measured using a number of different ratios. Although labor productivity may well be an important indicator, ratios measuring the utilization of other resources are also likely to be used. The measurement of quality tends to be relatively routinized and systematic. Mystery shoppers and management inspections are typical mechanisms for monitoring quality, using standardized checklists to evaluate service provision on a routine basis. Similarly the measurement of customer satisfaction is usually formal and structured in mass services. Satisfaction will normally be measured on a sample basis and the identification of customer dissatisfaction is unlikely to result in action being taken for the individual, but, rather, feeds into service design decision making.

Bibliography

Chase, R. B. (1978). Where does the customer fit in a service operation? *Harvard Business Review*, **56**, *4*, 137–42.

Lovelock, C. H. (1983). Classifying services to gain strategic marketing insights. *Journal of Marketing*, **47**, 9–20.

Maister, D. & Lovelock, C. H. (1982). Managing facilitator services. *Sloan Management Review*, **24**, *1*, 19–31.

Schmenner, R. (1986). How can service businesses survive and prosper? *Sloan Management Review*, **27**, *Spring*, 21–32.

Thomas, D. R. E. (1975). Strategy is different in service businesses. *Harvard Business Review*, **53**, *4*, 158–65.

RHIAN SILVESTRO

service productivity   While PRODUCTIVITY in manufacturing operations is well understood the same cannot be said of services. The development of improvements in service productivity lags behind manufacturing. Why this should be so is not altogether clear. However, there are problems with definition, with measurement, and with issues of how productivity impacts on SERVICE QUALITY in the service encounter (*see* SERVICE OPERATIONS) and SERVICE PROCESSES).

Measurement of service productivity is difficult for a number of reasons associated with the nature of the inputs and outputs from service processes. These can be easily recognized by considering the problems associated with measuring and comparing the service productivity for a network of service branches which have a complex mix of inputs and outputs. Measuring inputs pose similar problems to manufacturing processes; however, measuring outputs pose specific problems for services.

The intangible nature of service makes precise definition of outputs difficult. So the higher the intangible content of a service the more difficult it is to define the output and hence to devise appropriate measures. Professional services present the greatest challenge. How, for example, might the output from a session with a psychoanalyst be defined? The situation is easier for mass services where the tangible aspect of the service rises, for instance when providing information about travel times for trains or plane and travel prices.

The mix of services being offered though the same set of service resources present difficulties. The greater the VARIETY of service offered in a given time period the more difficult it becomes the measure at an aggregate level. Professional services are more difficult in this respect than mass services.

There is uncertainty as to whether the service output is constrained by lack of customer demand or other resources. The question is whether the service process is working at the rate set for the level of resources present to achieve the target levels of service quality and productivity. If demand is erratic, and unless resource levels change, then the time at which measurements are made will influence the recorded service productivity. It is possible to establish the state of an operation by asking, is it busy or slack for the resource level present at the time of measurement?

It is necessary to balance service quality and service productivity. It is easy to increase productivity by serving more customers, but this should not be at the expense of service quality. Service productivity measurements should only be taken with a counter-check on service quality and customer satisfaction.

Customers may act as a resource for the provision of service by completing some or all of the task themselves. An issue is where to count this component or to ignore the contribution and count only the resources provided by the service providers.

The choice of measurement of service productivity depends on the level of analysis. It is convenient to think in terms of the service network, the service branch, the service team or section, and an individual resource.

The higher the level of aggregation the greater the move away from simple measures relating work achieved to measured standards to the use of financial ratios. Problems still arise in making comparisons between service units within the same network. Individual characteristics of the units associated with factors including location, customer base, level of staff training, staff turnover, all often act to confound sensible discussion about relative performance. The technique of data envelopment analysis offers service organizations a means of measuring relative performance across a service network.

COLIN ARMISTEAD

service quality   Service quality has been one of the most widely covered subjects in the service management literature over the last ten years. Despite this, it is only quite recently that there has been a degree of consensus emerging about the definition, nature and determinants of service quality.

Service quality is traditionally defined from a customer's point of view as "perceived service quality," i.e. quality is what the customer thinks it is. The emerging view of perceived service quality is that it is the customer's overall impression of the relative inferiority or superiority of the organization and its services. Service quality is usually expressed as a function of the customer's expectations of the service to be provided (which may be based on, for instance, previous experience, word of mouth information and the organization's image), compared with the customer's perceptions of the actual service experience. This assessment of the organization's service will also be tempered by knowledge of competitors' offerings and perceptions of price and value (*see* QUALITY).

Expectations Versus Perceptions

The underlying concept of service quality as perceptions versus expectations, which is similar to customer satisfaction (see later), has been developed from the disconfirmation theory.

The disconfirmation theory holds that service quality and customer satisfaction with a service is related to the size of the disconfirmation experience, where disconfirmation is related to the person's initial expectations. More specifically, an individual's expectations are:

(1) confirmed when a service or product performs as expected;
(2) negatively disconfirmed when the service or product performs more poorly than expected;
(3) positively disconfirmed when the service or product performs better than expected.

Simply put, if the customer's perceptions are matched by their expectations then they are satisfied with the service (*see also* ZONE OF TOLERANCE). If the experience was better than expected then perceived service quality is high and the customer is "delighted." If the experience did not meet expectations then service quality is perceived to be poor and the customer is dissatisfied. It is generally agreed that these three outcomes of satisfaction, delight, and dissatisfaction, are three states along a continuum of degrees of satisfaction.

Some organizations are content to define service quality as matching perceptions with expectations. They might then design their service operation to try to reduce or remove any dissatisfying situations while at the same time not necessarily trying to exceed expectations as this could raise a customer's expectations for future occasions, resulting in lower perceived service quality on the next occasion. Some leading edge organizations, however, are defining service quality as exceeding customer expectations and they continually seek ways in which they might delight their customers.

Just as there is a range of outcome states, the customer's expectations (i.e. that which the customer believes to be likely) are also usually regarded as being on a continuum whose scale goes from minimum tolerable to ideal, with desired, deserved, and adequate being somewhere in between.

There is some controversy about the relative importance of expectations of overall service quality compared with the service performance itself. In some cases expectations may be a greater determinant of the perceived service quality; in other cases the service performance itself may be a greater determinant of the outcome, especially where the customer has little prior knowledge of the service.

Customer Satisfaction

A service experience is often comprised of many individual service transactions or encounters, each of which will play a contributory part in the development of the customer's overall view of the quality of the service. The outcome of each of these experiences has been defined as "service encounter satisfaction" which is the consumer's satisfaction or dissatisfaction with a discrete service encounter. The customer's assessment of each encounter is based on the same expectation/performance/perception model as overall service quality, but at a micro level. A customer's overall satisfaction or dissatisfaction with the total service experience, based on all the service transactions experienced, is usually referred to as "overall service satisfaction."

It is this overall perception of satisfaction and dissatisfaction with the service that is tempered by other information, such as previous highly satisfying or dissatisfying experiences with the organization, or views about the overall value of the service relative to other alternative offerings of organizations. Together these factors create an impression of overall service quality in the customer's mind. Thus satisfaction with the service may serve to reinforce feelings of service quality about a service.

Service Quality Models

Several models have been developed and tested that have helped operationalize the service quality construct. The best known is that proposed by Parasuraman et al. (1985) which identified four quality gaps which contribute to the fifth gap, a mismatch between expectations and perceptions. The four gaps are the gap between customers' expectations and managers' perceptions of those expectations; the gap between managers' perceptions of service quality and the service quality specification; the gap between the service quality specification and that which is delivered; and the gap between that which is delivered and the external communications to the customers. By removing each of the four gaps, managers can minimize the fifth gap, that between expectations and perceptions.

Several instruments have been designed to try to measure service quality. The best known is SERVQUAL developed by Parasuraman et al. (1988). SERVQUAL is a concise multiple-item skeleton questionnaire that asks questions of customers about their expectations and perceptions of the services of a particular company. It encompasses five consolidated quality dimensions (*see* QUALITY CHARACTER-ISTICS) of assurance, empathy, reliability, responsiveness, and tangibles, with 22 items for perceptions and 22 for expectations using a seven-point Likert scale. A perception gap score is then calculated for each pair of statements (expectations versus perceptions), the difference being the SERVQUAL score.

See also **critical incident technique; quality management systems**

Bibliography

Berry, L. L., Zeithaml, V. A. & Parasuraman, A. (1985). Quality counts in services, too. *Business Horizons*, May–June, 44–52.

Bitner, M. J. & Hubbert, A. R. (1994). Encounter satisfaction versus overall satisfaction versus service quality: the consumer's voice. In R. T. Rust & R. L. Oliver (Eds), *Service quality: New directions in theory and practice*. Thousand Oaks: Sage Publications.

Cronin, J. & Taylor, S. A. (1994). SERVPERF versus SERVQUAL: reconciling performance-based and perceptions-minus-expectations of service quality. *Journal of Marketing*, 58, *1*, 125–31.

Grnroos, C. (1984). A service quality model and its marketing implications. *European Journal of Marketing*, 18, *4*, 36–44.

Parasuraman, A., Zeithaml, V. A. & Berry, L. L. (1985). A conceptual model of service quality and implications for future research. *Journal of Marketing*, 49, 41–50.

Parasuraman, A., Zeithaml, V. A. & Berry, L. L. (1988). SERVQUAL: a multiple-item scale for measuring consumer perceptions of service quality. *Journal of Retailing*, Spring, 12–40.

Parasuraman, A., Zeithaml, V. A. & Berry, L. L. (1994). Reassessment of expectations as a comparison standard on measuring service quality: implications for further research. *Journal of Marketing*, 58, *1*, 111–24.

Rust, R. T. & Oliver, R. L. (1994). Service quality: insights and management implications from the frontier. In R. T. Rust & R. L. Oliver (Eds), *Service quality: New directions in theory and practice*. Thousand Oaks: Sage Publications.

ROBERT JOHNSTON

service recovery   Service recovery can be described as "doing the service very right the second time" (Berry and Parasuraman, 1991). It is the action of seeking out and dealing with failures in the delivery of service. Service recovery can also be used to support the drive for CONTINUOUS IMPROVEMENT by focusing managerial attention on specific problem areas.

The term "service recovery" is believed to have originated from British Airways "Putting the Customer First" campaign.

> It had never occurred to us in any concrete way. "Recovery" was the term we coined to describe a very frequently repeated concern. If something goes wrong, as it often does, will anybody make special efforts to get it right? Will somebody go out of his or her way to make amends to the customer? Does anyone make effort to offset the negative impact of a screw-up? (Zemke and Schaff, 1990)

Research has shown that effective service recovery can significantly influence customer perceptions of service quality, increase loyalty and repurchase intentions and lead to positive word-of-mouth recommendations. Wherever the responsibility for the failure might lie, customers have expectations of recovery, just as they do for the service itself (*see* SERVICE QUALITY) and thus organizations have the opportunity to satisfy or delight their customers when things go wrong. "While companies may not be able to prevent all problems, they can learn to recover from them. A good recovery can turn angry, frustrated customers into loyal ones" (Hart et al., 1990). It is often suggested that organizations should see failure as an opportunity to create satisfied customers, reinforce customer relationship, and build customer loyalty. "Breakthrough" service organizations, according to Heskett et al. (1990), are those which have recovery systems in place. They believed that an effective response to failure may have a high pay-off in terms of customer loyalty.

Conversely, it has also been shown that the lack of service recovery when a breakdown or failure has occurred has a dramatic negative effect on customer perceptions of service quality, loyalty, and repurchase intentions. Research also found that the effect on word-of-mouth recommendations was significant. "Customers, we found, are searching for opportunities to get even. They don't tell the retailers, manufacturers and service providers that they have served them poorly – they tell their friends and colleagues. As the bad word passes along, it creates a time bomb" (Davidow and Uttal, 1989).

The critical issue about service recovery is that it is not necessarily the failure itself that leads to customer dissatisfaction, as most customers do accept that things can go wrong. It is more likely to be the organization's response (or lack of response) to a failure that causes dissatisfaction. The crucial point is that while mistakes may be inevitable, dissatisfied customers are not.

A failure is any situation where something has gone wrong, irrespective of responsibility (Johnston, 1995). Failures may be of the service itself or the goods or facilities provided or of the customer's physical self. The failure may have been a result of faulty systems or procedures, incorrect actions by staff, poor design or even as a result of the customer's own actions (see FAILURE IN OPERATIONS). Failures may be classified into two types: those that create annoyance and those which leave the customer feeling victimized. Annoyance, they defined, is the minor feeling of frustration when experience falls slightly short of what was hoped for. On the other hand, victimization is a major feeling of ire and frustration.

If mistakes and failures are an inevitable part of service then there are many opportunities for organizations to create very satisfied customers.

Indeed, research has shown that most highly satisfying experiences encountered by customers are as a result of effective recoveries of service failures.

The first way of managing service recovery is to try to ensure that failures do not occur in the first place by designing them out of the service system. Some authors contended that many service failures are not "failures" but are faults that have been designed into the service system, and recommended the use of blueprinting the service in order to identify and remove failpoints (see SERVICE DESIGN and FAILURE ANALYSIS).

Second, recovery needs to be planned. Organizations need to design appropriate responses to failure, linked to the cost and the inconvenience caused by the failure to the customer, that will meet the needs and expectations of the customer. Such recovery processes need to be carried out either by empowered front-line staff or trained personnel who are available to deal with recovery in a way which does not interfere with day-to-day service activities.

Bell and Zemke (1987) identified five ingredients for service recovery: apology, urgent reinstatement (either actual reinstatement or a demonstration of "gallant intent"), empathy, symbolic atonement, and follow up. They further suggested that the first two of these are necessary to recover annoyed customers and all five are required for customers who feel victimized.

Research has also found that the recovery process requires staff who appear pleasant, helpful, and attentive, who show concern for the customer and can act quickly and be flexible. The key activities to bring about recovery are, first, to provide information about the problem and what is being done; second, to take action, either in response to the customer or preferably without needing to be asked; third, that staff should appear to put themselves out to try to solve the problem; and fourth, ideally, that the customer should be involved in the decision making.

Bibliography

Bell, C. R. & Zemke, R. E. (1989). *Service wisdom: Creating and maintaining the customer*. Minneapolis: Lakewood Books.

Berry, L. L. & Parasuraman, A. (1991). *Marketing services: Competing through quality*. New York: Free Press.

Davidow, W. H. & Uttal, B. (1989). *Total customer service*. New York: Harper Perennial.

Hart, C. W. L., Heskett, J. L. & Sasser, W. E. (1990). The profitable art of service recovery. *Harvard Business Review*, **68**, *4*, 148–56.

Heskett, J. L., Sasser, W. E. & Hart, C. W. L. (1990). *Service breakthroughs: Changing the rules of the game*. New York: Free Press.

Johnston, R. (1995). Service failure and recovery: impact, attributes and process. *Advances in Services Marketing and Management: Research and Practice*, **4**, 211–28.

Zemke, R. & Schaff, R. (1990). *The service edge: 101 companies that profit from customer care*. Plume Books.

ROBERT JOHNSTON

service strategy Service organizations, like all businesses, need to have overarching strategies in place to try to prevent non-aligned and disjointed activities and decisions. A strategy is usually seen in market terms as an organization's plan to achieve an advantage over its competitors. Some organizations, however, may not wish to achieve advantage but see their role as maintaining their position in the marketplace. Others operate in non-competitive situations and wish to ensure that they are able to adapt to their own changing environments. Service strategy can therefore be defined as the set of plans and policies by which a service organization aims to meet its objectives. In this sense service strategy is a means of directing and managing change. It is not a one-off activity as organizations need to respond to the two main forces of change that operate upon them, the external and internal environments. These changing internal and external conditions are the drivers of strategic change.

Strategy Drivers

Modifications to service strategy may be driven by changes in the organization's external environment, either actual or anticipated. Such changes might include new competitors entering the marketplace or the strategic developments of competitors through different positioning or service developments, or the changing needs of customers as a result of the activities of the competition, or the loss of customers because their needs are not being met.

Changing internal conditions might include the requirements of the board or the shareholders for a greater return on assets or for expansion, for example. Opportunities for change may arise from new developments from within the organization such as new services, skills, technologies, or processes. Change may be required because of declining staff loyalty or morale which may in, turn, affect the level of service provided by the organization.

Without constant appraisal of the changes to the internal and external environments and consequent adjustments to strategy, organizations may decay. Lovelock (1994) refers to this process as "institutional rusting." Strategy therefore involves the process of continually checking the organization's plans for direction, progress, and cohesion in terms of the continually changing environment.

Creating a Strategic Plan

A strategic plan should harness the various elements of an organization and insure that they support each other and are consistent with the direction indicated by the drivers of change. Five critical areas for service organizations include; the creation of corporate objectives; an understanding of the environment; the development of an appropriate service concept and degree of focus; the identification of appropriate operations performance objectives; and the development of an appropriate delivery system.

Corporate objectives. The development of clear corporate objectives is based on the strategy drivers; the internal or external pressures or opportunities for change. The objectives may well be expressed in financial or competitive terms over a set period of time, for example, return on investment, profit, number of new customers or market share. These objectives need to be clearly stated and will provide the means of measuring and monitoring the success or otherwise of the strategy.

The environment. In order to insure that those objectives can be achieved, there is a need to develop a clear understanding of the market and the environment in which the organization currently operates, or plans to be operating. This will include an understanding of the size and nature of the competition, the nature and size of the market or potential market, existing competing and complementary products and services, the ways the market is currently segmented, and the likely reaction of the competition. One key outcome of this activity is the identification of a potential target market and an assessment of the perceived needs and expectations of the target customers.

Service concept and focus. "A service concept describes the way in which an organization would like to have its services perceived by its customers, employees, shareholders and lenders" (Heskett, 1986). The development of a service concept may be based upon existing services, the activities in the external environment or from internal drivers such as the activities of design departments or ideas of staff and managers. The concept is a description of the form, function, purpose, and benefits of the service to be provided. The concept may require to be screened for viability, feasibility, appropriateness, and checked to insure that it will meet the needs and expectations of the target market.

The notion of focus is an important one in assessing how an organization's service concept compares to, or is differentiated from, the offerings of alternative organizations (*see also* FOCUS). Two dimensions can be considered, the range of services provided and the scope of the target market. Service concepts may thus range from doing "everything for everybody" (unfocused) to those tightly focused on providing a narrow range of products to a small and well-defined target market.

Operations objectives. Having identified a target market and developed a service concept, the operation needs guidance as to how it should manage its resources and activities. This will ensure that the service it provides will meet the corporate objectives, the needs of the target market and establish how it will differentiate itself from the competition. Clear statements about the relative importance of price, quality, availability, reliability, and flexibility, for example, are required to create an operations strategy

to guide the design and operation of an appropriate delivery system (*see* OPERATIONS OBJECTIVES).

Delivery system. The design of an appropriate delivery system is a complex affair requiring decisions about the number and location of sites, the activities of each of the sites, the characteristics of service, the selection and training of staff, the design of jobs, the design of service technology and the detailed design of the service delivery system, service package, service process and the service environment (*see* SERVICE DESIGN). The concept of focus at different levels in an organization can also be used to help identify the alternative ways of designing a service operation.

The critical questions that the design must answer include:

- Does the proposed design provide the desired service concept?
- Is the design consistent with operations strategy and the operations performance objectives?
- Will it meet the perceived needs of the target market?
- How will it create value in the minds of customers?
- What will be the products and services?
- What is the relationship between core, supporting and facilitating products/services?
- How will the processes be designed?
- How will the services and products be monitored and controlled?
- How will the operation cope with variation in demand without compromising the service levels required?
- How can the operation harness energy within the organization to effect the changes required?

This detailed plan has then to be checked against the corporate objectives to ensure that the total strategy is consistent and will achieve the objectives that have been set. Thus the process may have to go through several iterations before a consistent and cohesive strategy is created.

See also **manufacturing strategy; operations strategy; service processes**

Bibliography

Heskett, J. L. (1986). *Managing in the service economy.* Boston, MA: Harvard Business School Press.

Heskett, J. L., Sasser, W. E. & Hart, C. W. L. (1990). *Service breakthroughs: Changing the rules of the game.* New York: Free Press.

Johnston, R. (1996). Achieving focus in service organisations. *Service Industries Journal*, **16**, *1*, 10–20.

Lovelock, C. H. (1994). *Product plus.* New York: McGraw-Hill.

ROBERT JOHNSTON

set-up reduction   Set-up reduction (SUR) is often seen as one of the most directly useful techniques associated with JUST-IN-TIME philosophies of operations management. The purpose of SUR is to reduce the time, effort, and cost associated with changing a process from one activity to another. Traditional thinking in this area has been constrained by the economic batch quantity formula (*see* ECONOMIC ORDER QUANTITY) which models a perceived trade-off between the carrying cost of inventory and a fixed set-up cost. The set-up cost is determined by the time and resources necessary to change over equipment from good product of one type to good product of another. However, if set-up times can be reduced, the benefits can be translated into reduced batch sizes.

The advantages of small batch sizes are that smaller batches are used quickly, so defectives are found earlier and corrective action taken earlier. More significantly, smaller batches mean that less inventory is needed and throughput times are reduced. In general, material control becomes an easier task, and many of the routine transactions can be removed from central systems and delegated to the shop floor. Similar principles apply to other operations which do not involve setting up machines. Assembly lines which can be changed over more quickly from one product to another mean that shorter production runs can be planned.

Shingo's (1985) target for set-ups was encapsulated in his "SMED system." SMED stands for "single minute exchange of dies," and reflects Shingo's view that set-ups can always be reduced to less than ten minutes. Set-up reduction has become fairly routinized in many companies. A typical eight-step approach (Harrison, 1992), is summarized here:

(1) Select the set-up to be tackled. Criteria could include that it is the longest, or a bottleneck operation.

(2) Record the method as it currently stands. A popular way to record set-ups is by time-lapse video.

(3) Analyze the activities according to a classification scheme. This could include clamp/unclamp, load/unload, transport, adjustment, and cleaning activities.

(4) Eliminate wasteful activities. Search time for tools can, for example, be eliminated by provision of a dedicated tool trolley.

(5) Simplify remaining activities by, for example, pre-setting tools and improved material-handling devices.

(6) Classify the remaining activities as internal work (which must be carried out after the machine has stopped), and external work (which must be carried out before the machine has stopped). The emphasis is on transferring internal to external work, and on reducing internal work to a minimum. This way, the machine is kept running for as long as possible, and the disruption of set-ups is kept as short as possible.

(7) Develop methods and equipment to support the new internal and external activities.

(8) Implement the new procedures as standard practice, and record the new method for training and as a challenge for further improvement.

Much of the literature on set-up reduction emphasizes the low-cost nature of the improvements, such as elimination of search time referred to above. It is also significant that set-up reduction along the above lines is carried out by the work teams themselves. While industrial engineers could carry out this work, there are held to be many advantages to this approach. Team members "own" the solutions, and are therefore more likely to make them work effectively.

See also flexibility; inventory management; trade-offs; JIT tools and techniques; leveled scheduling

Bibliography

Harrison, A. S. (1992). *Just-in-time manufacturing in perspective.* Hemel Hempstead: Prentice-Hall.
Shingo, S. (1985). *A revolution in manufacturing: The SMED system.* Cambridge, MA: Productivity Press.

ALAN HARRISON

simultaneous development Product and service development consists of the movement of a product or service idea from concept through to market availability. This process involves a number of distinct phases which have been traditionally viewed as individual, predetermined steps, each of which required completion before subsequent stages could begin.

This step-by-step process has been likened to a relay race in which the baton is passed from one runner to the next: the work of an upstream stage (such as product engineering) is only passed downstream (such as to process engineering) when the stage is complete. Only when senior management is ready to accept responsibility for the completed work of its area is the project signed off for work by the next group.

The sequential approach is held to have several advantages. First, the distinct stages make the process easy to manage and control since each stage is predetermined and can be reviewed. Second, uncertainty is reduced before the next phase begins, since the information received downstream is assumed to be complete. In this way, risk can be better managed if the appropriate control (review) mechanisms are in place. Third, the sequential approach assists in optimizing functional expertise, since each manager can focus on a limited number of tasks. Finally, engineers can be kept busy by participating on a variety of projects (*see* ORGANIZATION OF DEVELOPMENT).

However, this approach may create products that are difficult to make, inappropriate for customers, and slow to reach the market. One explanation for this delay to market is the need for product redesign, resulting from a failure to involve manufacturing early enough in the design phase. If the principles of DESIGN FOR MANUFACTURE, QUALITY FUNCTION DEPLOYMENT and TAGUCHI METHODS were incorporated, much time, effort and money could be minimized by the early interaction of product, process, and customer needs in the design stage (*see* TIME TO MARKET).

Simultaneous engineering, concurrent engineering, forward engineering, integrated problem solving, parallel engineering, team approach, and lifecycle engineering are some of the terms that have been applied to overlapping the phases of design. "Simultaneous engineering attempts to optimize the design of the product and manufacturing process to achieve shortened lead times and improved quality and cost by the integration of design and manufacturing activities and by maximizing parallelism in working practices" (Broughton, 1990).

In studies of development projects, overlapping the phases of product development is identified as a factor that assists firms to reduce total development cycle time. Overlapping development is where downstream activities receive resources prior to the completion, but after the start, of the upstream task. Two further types of overlapping development model can be identified. First, those where successive tasks are undertaken in parallel, as information (and sometimes as technology) is transferred at each interface. Second, those where a greater overlap extends across several phases and, thus, several tasks may be undertaken simultaneously. In addition to the benefits of faster speed of development and increased flexibility, overlapping development aids the sharing of information and a variety of human resource management issues.

Experience of successful users of overlapping phases has shown that effective simultaneous engineering requires a combination of the early release of information, intensive two-way flows of information, effective computer and organizational integration, analytical methods and tools, and multifunctional teams.

Bibliography

Broughton, T. (1990). Simultaneous engineering in aero gas turbine design and manufacture. *Proceedings of the 1st International Conference on Simultaneous Engineering.* London: Status Meetings Ltd. 25–36.

Imai, K., Nonaka, I. & Takeuchi, H. (1985). Managing the new product development process: how Japanese companies learn and unlearn. In K. B. Clark, R. H. Hayes & C. Lorenz (Eds), *The uneasy alliance: Managing the productivity-technology dilemma*. Boston, MA: Harvard Business School Press. 337–75.

Wheelwright, S. C. & Clark, K. B. (1992). *Revolutionizing product development*. New York: Free Press.

DAVID TWIGG

statistical quality techniques Statistical quality techniques are generally taken to be those techniques which are used in managing QUALITY MANAGEMENT SYSTEMS and are based on the theories of applied probability (as opposed to the simpler TOOLS OF QUALITY MANAGEMENT). Although the theory behind these techniques has often been known for many decades, their widespread use is more recent and connected with the increasing interest in quality-related issues.

Acceptance Sampling

Acceptance sampling is an inspection method in which decisions, based on a sample of the batch or product, are made to accept or reject a product. It is based on the mathematical theory of probability and employed in situations where there is a continuous flow of batches between supplier and customer. The general assumption is that a manufacturer presents batches to an inspector who accepts or rejects them on behalf of a customer in the light of clearly defined laid down requirements. The manufacturer may be a department internal to an organization or an outside supplier. In the case of the latter, acceptance sampling is generally carried out at the customer's goods inwards department. It is sometimes a requirement of a major customer that a supplier takes regular samples of their production output using acceptance sampling to determine whether or not the product is of the acceptable quality. The customer's quality systems standard will outline the circumstances where this is applied along with the sampling plan to be used.

Sampling does involve risks which, although they cannot be eliminated, can be assessed by statistical techniques. The objective of a statis-tically designed sampling plan is to ensure that batches of the acceptable quality level (AQL), or better, have a high probability of acceptance and that batches with higher non-conformity levels will almost certainly be rejected.

It is important that all decisions regarding acceptance or rejection of a batch of product are based on a random sample. Most sampling schemes relate sample size to batch size because of the need to ensure a representative sample, which becomes increasingly difficult as the batch size increases. Accordingly, the penalty for rejecting a good batch or accepting a bad batch, based perhaps on insufficient sample data, also increases.

To be of value, sampling inspection has to be carried out in a systematic manner. The acceptance procedure can be based on attributes or variables data, the latter having been little used in industry to date. The purpose of systematic sampling is to induce a supplier, through the economic and psychological pressure of lot non-acceptance, to maintain a process average at least as good as the specified AQL, while at the same time minimizing the risk to the consumer of accepting the occasional poor lot. Sampling plans are intended primarily to be used for a continuing series of lots sufficient to allow the switching rules to be applied, which provide for:

• An automatic protection to the consumer, should a deterioration in quality be detected (by a switch to tightened inspection or discontinuance of inspection);

• An incentive to reduce inspection costs (at the discretion of the responsible authority) should consistently good quality be achieved (by a switch to reduced inspection). The responsible authority may be: the quality department within a supplier's organization (first party); the purchaser or procurement organization (second party); or an independent verification of certification authority (third party).

Acceptance sampling is a screening technique based on after-the-event detection. The use of acceptance sampling by a customer at goods inward might be seen as diverting some of the responsibility for quality from supplier to customer. Thus the customer's inspection becomes a vital ingredient in the supplier's quality control system. Furthermore, the idea of employing a certain proportion of defectives as a measure of the quality required in the product is contrary to the aim of trying to get suppliers to deliver batches of product which are free from non-conformities and also to pursue continuous improvement.

Statistical Process Control

Statistical process control (SPC) is generally accepted to mean management of the process through the use of statistical methods. It has four main uses:

- to achieve process stability;

- to provide guidance on how the process may be improved by the reduction of variation;

- to assess the performance of a process;

- to provide information to assist with management decision making.

The first step in the use of SPC is to collect data to a plan and plot the gathered data on a graph called a control chart. The control chart is a picture of what is happening in the process at a particular point in time; it is a line graph. The data to be plotted can be in variable or attribute format.

Variable data are the result of using some form of measuring system. It is essential to insure the capability of the measuring system to minimize the potential source of errors which may arise in the data. The measurements may refer to product characteristics (e.g. length) or to process parameters (e.g. temperature). Attribute data are the result of an assessment using go/no-go gauges or pass/fail criteria. It is important to minimize subjectivity when using this pass/fail type of assessment. Reference standards, photographs, or illustrations may help and, where possible, the accept/reject characteristics should be agreed with the customer.

The objective of data collection is to get a good overall "picture" of how a process performs. A data-gathering plan needs to be developed for collection, recording, and the plotting of data on the control chart. The data collected should accurately reflect the performance of the process.

Different data-gathering plans may give different pictures of a process, and there are many economic models of control charts. However, consideration of statistical criteria and practical experience has led to organizations formulating general guidelines for sample size and intervals between samples. For example, in the automotive-related industry it has led to the widespread acceptance (for variables) of a sample size of five, a one-hourly sampling frequency, the taking of at least 20 subgroups as a test for stability of a process, and the use of three standard error control limits. To obtain a meaningful picture of process performance from attributes data, and to ensure that the statistical theory supporting the design of the control chart is valid, larger samples (no more than 25) and more subgroups are often required.

Construction of control charts using variables data. Control charts using mean and range are the most popular variables charts in use and they are now used to discuss the methods of control chart construction. There are four steps to producing the chart.

(1) Calculate each subgroup average ($\overline{X}$) and range value ($\overline{R}$); these data are plotted on the chart.

(2) Calculate the process average ($\overline{\overline{X}}$) and process mean range ($\overline{R}$). These statistics are plotted on the chart as heavy broken lines.

(3) Calculate and plot on the chart the control limits. These control limits are drawn on the chart as solid lines and are set at three standard errors or A_2 ($\overline{R}$) for the mean control chart, and D4 ($\overline{R}$) and D_7 ($\overline{R}$) for the range control chart from the reference value.

(4) Analyze and interpret the control charts for special and common causes of variation.

The process average ($\overline{\overline{X}}$) is the mean of all the sample means, and the mean range ($\overline{R}$) is the average of all the sample ranges. These are used to calculate control limits and are drawn on the chart as a guide for analysis. They reflect the natural variability of the process and are calculated using constants, appropriate to the sample size, and taken from statistical tables.

Interpreting a variables control chart. The range and mean charts are analyzed separately, but the patterns of variation occurring in the two charts are compared with each other to assist in identifying special causes which may be affecting the process. The range chart monitors uniformity and the mean chart monitors where the process is centered.

These causes of variation influence some or all the measurements in different ways. They occur intermittently and reveal themselves as unusual patterns of variation on a control chart. Special causes should be identified and rectified, and with improved process or product design, their occurrence should in the long term be minimized. It is important in the management and control of processes to record not only the occurrence of such causes, but any remedial action that has been taken, together with any changes that may occur or have been made in the process. This provides a valuable source of information in the form of a "process log," to prevent the repetition of previous mistakes and in the development of improved processes.

Indications of special causes include the following:

- a data point falling outside the control limits;

- a run of points in a particular direction, consistently increasing or decreasing; in general, seven consecutive points is used as the guide;

- a run of points all on one side of the reference value $(\overline{\overline{X}})$ or $(\overline{R})$; in general, seven consecutive points is used as the guide;

- if substantially more or less than two-thirds of the points plotted lie within the mid-third section of the chart; this might indicate that the control limits or plot points have been miscalculated or misplotted, or that data have been edited, or that process or the sampling method are stratified;

- any other obvious non-random patterns.

Common causes influence all measurements in the same way. They produce the natural pattern of variation observed in data when they are free of special causes. Common causes arise from many sources and do not reveal themselves as unique patterns of deviation, consequently they are often difficult to identify. If only common cause variation is present the process is considered to be stable, hence predictable.

If properly maintained, the chart will indicate to operational personnel when they need to do something to the process and, on the other hand, when to do nothing. It discourages operators from interfering needlessly with the process.

Construction of control charts using attribute data. An argument in favor of inspection by attributes is that it is not such a time consuming task as that for variables, so the sample size can be much larger and it is also less costly to undertake. Experience shows that attribute data often exists in a variety of forms in an organization, although they may not necessarily be analyzed statistically.

A variety of charts can be used to organize attribute data in order to assist with process control. The choice of chart is dependent on whether the sample size is kept constant and whether the inspection criterion is a non-conforming item or a non-conformity within an item. The main types of attributes chart for non-conforming items are proportion/percentage (p) and number defective (np) charts; while for non-conformities they are proportion (u) and number (c) charts.

The collection and organizing of data is almost identical to that described for variables, except that for each sample, the number (or proportion or percentage) of non-conforming items or non-conformities are recorded and plotted. The reference value on attribute charts is the process average. The control limits are again three standard errors from the process average. The interpretation of attributes data on control charts is similar to that for variables data.

The capability of the process is a measure of the acceptability of variation of a process. The simplest measure of capability (C_p) is given by the ratio of the specification range to the "natural" variation of the process (i.e. ± 3 standard deviations).

$$C_p = \frac{UTL - LTL}{6s}$$

where UTL is the upper tolerance limit, LTL is the lower tolerance limit and s is the standard deviation of the process variability.

Generally, if the C_p of a process is greater than one it is taken to indicate that the process is just "capable," and a C_p of less than one to indicate that the process is not "capable," assuming that the distribution is normal.

The simple C_p measure assumes that the average of the process variation is at the midpoint of the specification range. Often the process average is offset from the specification range, however. In such cases one-sided capability indices are required to understand the capability of the process.

$$\text{Upper one-sided index } C_{pu} = \frac{UTL - X}{3s}$$

$$\text{Lower one-sided index } C_{pl} = \frac{X - LTL}{3s}$$

where X is the process average.

Sometimes only the lower of the two one-sided indices for a process is used to indicate its capability (C_{pk}):

$$C_{pl} = \min(C_{pu}, C_{pl})$$

See also **quality; JIT tools and techniques; quality management systems**

Bibliography

Dale, B. G. & Oakland, J. S. (1994). *Quality improvement through standards.* 2nd edn. Cheltenham: Stanley Thornes.

Montgomery, D. C. (1991). *Introduction to statistical quality control.* 2nd edn. New York: John Wiley.

Oakland, J. S. & Followell, R. F. (1990). *Statistical process control: A practical guide.* 2nd edn. London: Heinemann.

BARRIE DALE

supply chain dynamics   Industrial dynamics authors have applied elements of systems control theory which treat amplification to considering supply chains. Much of the theory on which their work is based is attributed to Forrester (1961) and Burbidge (1961).

Forrester's (1961) work considered a production and distribution system whose component echelons were a factory, a warehouse, a distributor, and retailers. Between these he simulated flows of goods, information, and delays in the system. The effect he described,

also known as the Forrester effect, is one where real demand information from the end of the chain is distorted as it is interpreted, processed, and passed up the supply chain. The distortion is amplified the further in the chain a company is from the consumer.

Some of the reasons why the Forrester effect occurs in supply chains relate to what has been called a just-in-case approach to managing materials. In contrast to a JUST-IN-TIME approach, just-in-case ordering has the following characteristics:

- Members of the supply chain keep safety stocks, just in case there should be a supply failure. Sometimes the orders they place are to replenish their safety stocks, rather than because of a real end customer demand. The nature of the demand is not visible to their suppliers who endeavor to supply with the same vigor as if a real end customer were waiting.

- Orders are placed regularly and periodically, rather than as and when they are needed. The order period tends to become greater the further upstream you go.

- Requirements are batched up to round numbers or to economic order quantities, price break quantities, lot sizes or minimum order quantities.

The principle was developed further by Burbidge (1961) who described the relationship between process flow rate, fluctuations in demand, and inventory variation within a manufacturing operation. In 1984, Burbidge used the term "the law of industrial dynamics" and concluded that: "If demand for products is transmitted along a series of inventories using stock control ordering, then the demand variation will increase with each transfer."

The principles of industrial dynamics have been applied in the 1990s to considering the management of supply chains. Central to this is the recognition of perceived demand rather than real demand as being one of the causes of the Forrester effect. More recently, work has demonstrated the Forrester effect on perceptions in supply chains. Upstream relationships in supply chains suffered more from misperceptions between the purchaser/supplier than downstream relationships. This misperception was correlated to dissatisfaction in the relationships; that is, upstream customers were more dissatisfied than downstream customers. So, in addition to the conventional hard Forrester effect, this showed that supply chain dynamics also affected softer, behavioral aspects of the chain (Harland, 1995).

See also **supply chain management; time-based performance; inventory management; inventory control systems**

Bibliography

Burbidge, J. L. (1961). The new approach to production. *Production Engineer*, **40**, *12*, 769–84.

Burbidge, J. L. (1984). Automated production control with a simulation capability. *Proceedings of IFIP Conference WG 5-7*. 1–14.

Forrester, J. W. (1961). *Industrial dynamics*. Cambridge, MA: MIT Press.

Harland, C. M. (1995). Dynamics of customer dissatisfaction in supply chains. *Production Planning and Control*, **6**, *3*, 209–17.

Towill, D. (1991). Supply chain dynamics. *Computer-Integrated Manufacturing*, **4**, *4*, 19–208.

Towill, D. (1992). Supply chain dynamics: the change engineering challenge of the mid-1990s. *Proceedings of the Institute of Mechanical Engineers*, **206**, 23.

CHRISTINE HARLAND

supply chain management Supply chain management is a term used to mean many different things. Three different but related definitions in common use are provided and described here.

Definition 1: Supply Chain Management is the Management of the Internal Supply Chain

All operations transform inputs to produce goods or services (*see* TRANSFORMATION MODEL). When some organizations use the term "supply chain management" they may be referring to the flow of materials and information from their immediate suppliers, through their operation and out through distribution to their immediate customers.

Various authors have examined the internal supply chain from different perspectives, depending on their backgrounds and fields of interest. One perspective considers the management of materials and information flows within

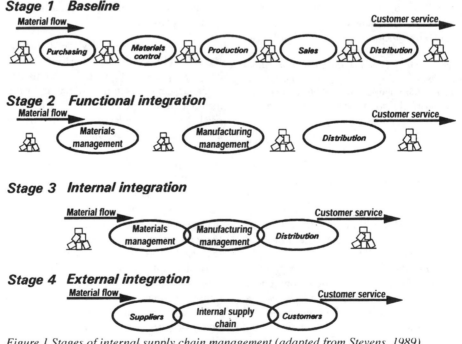

Figure 1 Stages of internal supply chain management (adapted from Stevens, 1989)

Table 1   Exchange in different types of relationship

Relationship type	Exchange elements	Examples
Integrated hierarcy	People, materials, goods and services, technologies, information, money, equity	Single product firm, e.g. paper, aluminum
Semi-hierarchy	People, materials, goods and services, technologies, information, money, equity, centralized control, divisional reporting	Multidivisional firm, holding company, e.g. chemicals, food
Co-contracting	Medium-/long-term contract, technologies, people, specification, materials, goods, services, knowledge	Co-makership, joint venture, e.g. automotive
Co-ordinated contracting	Specification, payment, planning and control information, materials	Projects e.g. construction
Co-ordinated revenue links	Contract, performance measures, specification of processes and products/services, brand package, facilities, training	Licensing, franchising, e.g. fast food chains
Long-term trading commitment	Reservation of future capacity, goods and services, payment, demand information	Single and dual source, blanket order, e.g. electronics
Medium-term trading commitment	Partial commitment to future work, reservation of capacity, goods and services, specifications	Preferred supplier, e.g. defense
Short-term trading commitment	Goods and services, payment, order documentation	Spot orders e.g. stationery purchases

Adapted from Slack et al. 1995.

an organization. Supply chain management can be viewed as the integration of previously separate operations functions within the organization (see Figure 1).

The business issues which arise when companies take this view are, the reduction of inventory, the integration of separate business functions, the quicker flow through the operation, possibly reducing lead time to customers, and reduced cost.

Definition 2: Supply Chain Management is the Formation of Long-Term Partnerships or Relationships with Suppliers

"Partnership" sourcing involves forming stronger bonds between a purchasing and a supplying organization whereby they work together to get business that benefits both parties. Rather than a distant and confrontational relationship, partnership sourcing involves jointly improving design, reducing costs, improving quality, and developing products to market faster.

There are many different types of relationships that can be formed between a purchasing and a supplying organization. Depending on which type of relationship is being applied, different elements are "exchanged" between the two parties, as shown in Table 1.

Recent research in this area has identified the reduced popularity of hierarchical relationships and short-term trading relationships. Instead, companies are tending to form relationships that are between these two polar extremes.

Although "relationships" are an important aspect of business management, longer-term relationships are not a radical business development. Rather they are a trend that favors some types of relationships more than others. Therefore, like the first, this second definition does not represent a major new strategic challenge for businesses.

Definition 3: Supply Chain Management is Managing the Entire Network of Supply from Original Source through to Meeting the Needs of the End Customer

The first definition concentrated on the firm and what went on, largely, inside it. The second definition concentrated on the relationship between elements of the chain. This third

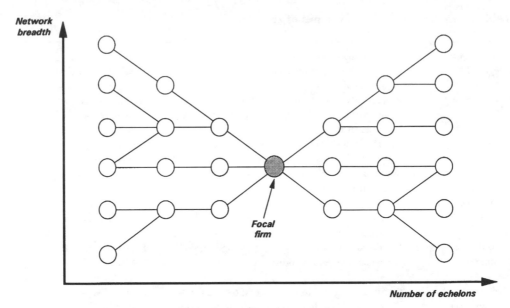

Figure 2 Firms have a network of relationships

definition is broader still and relates to the network. This implies managing beyond boundaries to develop strategies, influence, invest in and connect with suppliers, suppliers' suppliers and so on upstream, also customers, customers' customers and so on downstream, ultimately to the end customer.

Any site that is chosen to focus on has its own unique network of relationships, as shown in Figure 2.

Some firms manage their whole network. For example, Toyota has a network strategy which it has implemented in a systematic way to achieve its performance targets. Toyota redesigned its network structure, in terms of who it bought from, who its suppliers bought from and so on, who it sold to and who its distributors sold to, right down to the ultimate car buyers. Having redesigned its network structure, it was able to improve the network infrastructure, i.e. the information flows, the materials flows, the design of work, payment and reward, etc.

The Strategic Importance of Supply Chain Management

Supply chain management has become strategically important to most businesses for several reasons.

- *Increasing competition worldwide*: markets have become increasingly competitive and many markets have excess capacity, thereby increasing the intensity of competition of players fighting for a share. Therefore, increasingly innovative solutions are required often beyond the capability of any one firm operating in isolation.

- *Transferability of technology*: where technology transfer has become easier it is more difficult for firms to stay competitive exclusively through technology. Yet this is also an opportunity insomuch as it may be easier to network with other firms.

- *Globalization*: global players source globally, manufacture off-shore, distribute and service globally. Because it is not easy for firms to be excellent worldwide at manufacturing, sourcing, distributing, and servicing, most global players are likely to network strategically. Some authorities believe that effective network management is how global firms will succeed (*see* INTERNATIONAL LOCATION).

- *Time compression*: time is seen as critical in many manufacturing and service industries. It is difficult to achieve radical time improvements where customer–supplier relationships are confrontational. Network approaches with increased communication, shared destiny and commitment provide enhanced potential for time to be taken out of supply chains (*see* TIME-BASED PERFORMANCE).

- *Increased customer expectation*: in most markets customers' expectations for VARIETY, DELIVERY DEPENDABILITY, service, quality, and reliability are increasing, possibly without any concomitant expectation of higher prices. As single companies alone may not be able to satisfy this entire spectrum of customer expectations, forming close bonds with other players in co-operative networks may allow improvement on all performance dimensions, rather than trading off between dimensions (*see* TRADE-OFFS).

Supply Chain Management

Several advantages have been put forward as deriving from a strategic perspective of supply networks.

Networks Enable Strategic Intent rather than Strategic Fit

The traditional view of strategy is one of strategic fit between existing resources and current opportunities, identifying core strengths to tackle a focused set of those opportunities. However, strategic intent is where a business' ambitions stretch well beyond its current resources, thereby causing an extreme misfit. Yet some global players have a strategic intent stretching far beyond their in-house capabilities. Their success has been attributed to their inventive use of other businesses' resources to close the resource-opportunity gap through relationships such as licensing (*see* MANUFACTURING STRATEGY).

Networks may Provide Economies of Scale

Economies of scale apply to activities rather than companies or products. Activities which may attract scale economies include those with high R&D (e.g. pharmaceuticals), highly capital-intensive processes (e.g. flat panel display manufacture), bulk purchasing possibilities (e.g. food), high investment in advertizing (e.g. personal consumer products), and distribution economies (e.g. international freight forwarding). These different types of scale

economies may be traded off against each other. For example, locating worldwide manufacturing in one location may provide manufacturing scale economies but the products then have to be shipped worldwide. High value, low bulk or weight items are more likely to be produced further away from the customer markets as the cost penalties of distribution are less than the scale economies of manufacturing (*see* CAPACITY MANAGEMENT, INTERNATIONAL LOCATION).

Networks may Provide Economies of Scope

While scale refers to the size of a plant, scope refers to the range of significantly different products, processes, markets, and geographical regions that a plant serves. Some economies can be gained through spreading fixed costs over a greater number of smaller batches of products or service. In entering global markets, capturing economies of scope demands inter-business co-ordination. Inter-business networks are becoming increasingly important; increasingly these networks are also inter-country networks.

Networks can Enable Management of the Value System

As each firm contains a value chain, a network of firms contains a value system, which is the connection of all their value chains, i.e. the sum of the value chains of suppliers, manufacturers, distributors, and end customers.

It is often possible to benefit the firm and its suppliers by influencing the configuration of suppliers' value chains to optimize joint performance, and improving co-ordination between a firm and its suppliers' value chains or its channel value chains to lower cost or enhance differentiation. This latter point particularly is an opportunity for improved information systems and transfer.

Networks may Provide Comparative Advantage

Comparative advantage is advantage gained through planned location of the links of a supply chain internationally. As different countries and cultures offer different benefits, they may suit different firms' strategies to a varying extent, *see* PURCHASING AND SUPPLY MANAGEMENT. Networks can combine competitive advantage and comparative advantage globally. Configuration relates to organizational design and physical/geographical location of facilities; it is a phrase used to cover aspects of competitive advantage through management of the value system and also comparative advantage through location decisions(*see* INTERNATIONAL LOCATION).

See also **design chain management; logistics; physical distribution management; supply chain dynamics**

Bibliography

Coyle, R. G. (1982). Assessing the controllability of a production and raw material system. *IEEE Transactions on Systems, Management and Cybernetics*, **SMC-12**, 867–76.

Forrester, J. W. (1961). *Industrial dynamics.* Cambridge, MA: MIT Press.

Harland, C. M. (1995). Dynamics of customer dissatisfaction in supply chains. *Production Planning and Control, Special issue on Supply Chain*, **6**, *3*, 209–17.

Jarillo, J. C. (1983). *Strategic networks: Creating the borderless organisation.* Oxford: Butterworth Heinemann.

Jones, T. C., Riley, D. W. (1985). Using inventory for competitive advantage through supply chain management. *International Journal of Physical Distribution and Materials Management*, **15**, *5*, 16–26.

Slack, N., Chambers, S., Harland, C., Harrison, A. & Johnston, R. (1995). *Operations management.* London: Pitman Publishing.

Stalk, G. H. & Hout, T. (1990). *Competing against time: How time based competition is reshaping global markets.* New York: Free Press.

Stevens, G. C. (1989). Integrating the supply chain. *International Journal of Physical Distribution and Materials Management*, **19**, *8*, 3–8.

Towill, D. R. (1982). Dynamic analysis of an inventory based production control system. *International Journal of Production Research*, **20**, 671–87.

CHRISTINE HARLAND

system loss   System loss is a phenomenon which occurs with PRODUCT LAYOUT, or lines, when tasks are being carried out by human operators rather than being automated. Where operators are involved they are often subject to "pacing," which is the need to keep working at the speed of the line. Since the work times of any operator will inevitably be subject to natural variability, lines are designed such that the cycle time allows the operator at the busiest work station to complete the task (*see* WORK TIME DISTRIBUTIONS).

System loss in such paced lines is the loss that occurs when operators either cannot complete all their work within the cycle time or have idle time on a cycle. It is particularly prevalent on mixed-model lines where the variability of work times is greatest. The effect of system loss is that either the line needs to be stopped for work to be completed, or products remain unfinished at the end of the line and need to be completed later or workers further down the line are forced to have idle time. Normally, system loss can be minimized by increasing the time for which items are available to operators. This can be achieved in two ways. First by slowing down the line while reducing the distance between products (thereby retaining the same cycle time), and second by introducing a buffer stock of parts between each work station to "absorb" any losses that occur due to excessive work times. However, despite these measures, losses cannot be totally avoided where lines are being used because there will always be unexpectedly long work times due to unforeseen circumstances. The only way to completely solve the problem of system loss is to use a wholly different approach, such as a CELL LAYOUT, which is not subject to pacing.

System loss can also occur in unpaced lines which consist of a series of work stations with inter-stage buffer inventories. If, over a period of operation, a preceding station processes several items at times shorter than its succeeding station, the available buffer inventory space will eventually become full, forcing the preceding station to cease work. This is called "blocking." Conversely, if the succeeding station processes several items faster than its supplying station it will exhaust the buffer inventory and have no items to work on. Again this will cause the station to stop work, this time through "starving." Together, blocking and starving result in system loss.

In such unpaced lines the degree of system loss will depend on the extent of variation in the station's individual work time distribution, the number of stations arranged in series, and the amount of buffer inventory space provided between each stage. System loss will increase with increasing work time variation and the number of stages, but reduce with increasing buffer inventory space. However, larger inventory space will mean higher work-in-progress levels.

See also job design; division of labor; "scientific" management

Bibliography

Buxey, G. M., Slack, N. & Wild, R. (1973). Production flow line design: a review. *AIIE Transitions*, 5, *1*, 37–48.

DAVID BENNETT

T

Taguchi methods Taguchi methods are usually taken to refer to two related ideas. The first is that, by the use of statistical methods concerned with analysis of variance, experiments may be constructed which enable the important design factors responsible for degrading product performance to be identified. The second related idea is that in judging the effectiveness of designs, the degree of degradation or loss is a function of the deviation of any design parameter from its target value.

The first of these ideas was reportedly developed by Dr Genichi Taguchi when he worked at the Japanese telecommunications company NTT in the 1950s and 1960s. His concept of off-line quality control involved attempting to attain both high quality and low-cost design solutions through the effective use of experimental techniques. He proposed that the design process should be seen in three stages, systems design, parameter design, and tolerance design. Systems design is intended to identify the basic elements of the design which will produce the desired output, such as the best combination of processes and materials. Parameter design takes the system design elements of the design and sets the most appropriate parameter values for them. This stage identifies the "settings" of each parameter which will minimize variation from the target performance of the product. Tolerance design identifies the components of the design which are sensitive in terms of affecting the quality of the product and establishes tolerance limits which will give the required level of variation in the design.

Taguchi methodology emphasized the importance of the middle (parameter design) stage in the total design process. A stage which is held to be neglected in industrial design practice. The Taguchi methodology proposes identifying the parameters which are under the control of the designer, and conducting a series of experiments which establish the parameters which have the greatest influence on the performance and variation of the design. Through this approach designers are able to identify the aspects of a design which most influence the desired outcome of the design process.

The second related aspect of Taguchi methodology is the "quality loss function." This holds that there is an increasing loss, both for producers and for society at large, which is a function of the deviation or variability from a target value of any design parameter which represents the "ideal state" of that parameter. The greater the deviation from target or variability, the greater is the loss (*see also* ZONE OF TOLERANCE).

The concept of loss being dependent on variation has always been well established in design theory, and at a systems level is related to the benefits and costs associated with dependability (*see* DELIVERY DEPENDABILITY). Variability inevitably means waste of some sort, however operations managers also realize that it is impossible to have zero variability. Their response to this has been to set not only a target level for performance but also a range of tolerance about that target which represents acceptable performance. This is usually interpreted in practice as implying that if performance falls anywhere within the range it is regarded as acceptable, while if it falls outside that range it is not acceptable. The Taguchi methodology suggests that instead of this implied step function of acceptability, a more realistic function is used based on the square of the deviation from the ideal target.

This function, the quality loss function, is given by the expression

$$L = k(x - a)^2$$

where

L = the loss to society of a unit of output at value x

a = the ideal state target value, where at a, $L = 0$

k = a constant

While the form of the loss function may be regarded as being in most cases more realistic than a step function, the practicalities of determining the constant of k with any degree of accuracy can be formidable. Although even the shape of the function can be questioned where the consequences of variation are not symmetrical. Quoted successful applications of the Taguchi methodology are frequently associated with relatively limited aspects of design (for example single parts), rather than very complex products or services. Some designers and academics also argue that the results of Taguchi methodology may not always provide better design solutions than obtained by conventional means.

See also **quality management systems; design; design for manufacture**

Bibliography

Taguchi, G., El Sayed, M. & Hsaing, C. (1989). *Quality engineering and production systems.* New York: McGraw-Hill.

Tribus, M. & Szonyl, G. (1989). An alternative view of the Taguchi approach. *Quality Progress*, **22**, 46–52.

NIGEL SLACK

time study Time study is a structured process of directly observing and measuring (using a timing device) human work in order to establish the time required for completion of the work by a qualified worker when working at a defined level of performance. It follows the basic procedure of WORK MEASUREMENT of analysis, measurement and synthesis. The observer undertakes preliminary observation of the work (a pilot study) to identify suitable elements which can be clearly recognized on subsequent occasions and are convenient, in terms of their length, for measurement. Subsequent studies are taken during which the observer times each occurrence of each element (using a stopwatch or other timing device) while at the same time making an assessment of the worker's rate of working on an agreed rating scale. (One of the prime reasons for measuring elements of work, rather than the work as a whole is to facilitate the process of rating. The rate at which a worker works will vary over time; if elements are carefully selected, the rate of working should be consistent for the relatively short duration of the element.) This assessment of rating is used to convert the observed time for the element into a basic time – a process referred to as "extension." It is essential that a time study observer has been properly trained in the technique and especially in rating. The technique, when properly undertaken, involves the use of specific control mechanisms to ensure that timing errors are within acceptable limits. Increasingly, timing is by electronic devices rather than by mechanical stopwatch; some of these devices also assist in subsequent stages of the study by carrying out the process of "extending" or converting observed times into basic times.

The number of cycles that should be observed depends on the variability in the work and the level of accuracy required. Since time study is essentially a sampling technique in which the value of the time required for the job is based on the observed times for a sample of observations, it is possible using statistical techniques to estimate the number of observations required under specific conditions. This total number of observations should be taken over a range of conditions (where these are variable) and, where possible, on a range of workers. Once a basic time for each element has been determined, allowances are added to derive a standard time.

Time study is a very flexible technique, suitable for a wide range of work performed under a wide range of conditions, although it is difficult to time jobs with very short cycle times (of a few seconds). Because it is a direct observation technique, it takes account of specific and special conditions but it does rely on the use of the subjective process of rating. However, if properly carried out it produces consistent results and it is widely used. Additionally, the use of electronic data capture devices and personal computers for analysis makes it much more cost effective than previously.

Bibliography

BS 3365. (1993). Part 3: Management services. Part 3: Guide to work measurement. London: British Standards Institution.

Whitmore, D. A. (1987). *Work measurement.* 2nd edn. London: Heinemann.

Whitmore, D. (1991). Work measurement techniques: timing. In T. J. Bentley (Ed.), *The management services handbook*. London: Pitman.

JOHN HEAP

time to market Time to market is the elapsed time between product or service definition (concept) and its availability (market introduction). Many companies attempt to reduce the time to market of their products and services because this can increase competitive advantage. Being faster to market enables a greater market share and price realization. For example, it has been estimated that in the electronics industry, introducing a product nine to 12 months late can cost it 50 percent of its potential revenues. A long development process exposes the project to the risk of changes in the market and environment. Especially when product lifecycles are short, product modifications, and replacements need to be managed more effectively if market share and profits are not to be lost (*see* TIME-BASED PERFORMANCE).

Time to market is an important measure of the performance of development projects, together with productivity and quality. Typical measures include: frequency of new product introduction; time from initial concept to market introduction; number of products started and completed (actual versus planned); and the percentage of sales resulting from new products.

As Wheelwright and Clark (1992) indicate "a six-month jump on competitors in a market accustomed to eighteen to twenty-four-month design lives can translate into as much as three times the profit over the market life of the design. Conversely, being late to market with a new product can lead to break-even results and

zero profit." Thus, over the long term, a significant performance gap can appear between a fast cycle and slow cycle competitor.

Many benefits can be realized from reducing time to market (see Stalk and Hout, 1990). Companies may become technological leaders – actual and perceived by the customer – supported through being able to incorporate the latest technology into the product closer to the time of market introduction; additionally, being fast to market can establish the product or service as the market standard. This can lead to a higher price realization, as the product or service becomes sought after by customers. Similarly, customer relations can improve as companies gain flexibility to respond quickly to a changing marketplace.

Reduced time can lead to reduced costs. Total development costs can be lowered since the early exchange of information and resolution of conflicts results in the need for fewer engineering changes and review procedures. Less inventory can result from shorter cycle times, followed by lower overhead costs – such as reduced breakdown costs, delays, and number of working hours.

Bibliography

Stalk G, Jr & Hout, T. M. (1990). *Competing against time.* New York: Free Press.

Wheelwright, S. C. & Clark, K. B. (1992). *Revolutionizing product development.* New York: Free Press.

DAVID TWIGG

time-based performance The time taken to deliver products or services (sometimes referred to as just "speed") is widely assumed to be one of the more important OPERATIONS OBJECTIVES for most companies. As a generic attribute of an operation, speed manifests itself in three related aspects of operations performance. The first is the time taken by an organization to develop new products or services from concept through to the point where they become available to customers (often referred to as TIME TO MARKET). The second is the time taken to manufacture an already designed product or create an already specified service within the operation. The third is the time to deliver or transport the product or service to the customer. The last two aspects are often treated together for operations which produce standardized products or services and all three aspects may be treated together in operations which routinely produce customized products or services (*see* DEMAND RESPONSE). The elapsed time from customer request to customer receipt of the product or service is taken to be the prime element of time or speed performance.

Customer Benefits of Speed

The most obvious benefit of speedy operations is that customers receive their good or services faster. In some competitive circumstances reduced delivery lead times can be vital, in others it is less important, though rarely totally unimportant.

Speed is seen as giving direct competitive benefits, including the potential to command a premium price, developing long-term relationships based on responsiveness to delivery changes, or extending product or service range. In addition, fast response can minimize some of the effects of the supply chain amplification of demand fluctuations (*see* SUP-PLY CHAIN DYNAMICS).

The Internal Benefits of Speed

From an operations management perspective the main interest in speed is that it can result in benefits within the operation. In this sense "speed" is used to refer to the time taken for the transformed resources of the operation (*see* TRANSFORMATION MODEL) to move through the sequence of processes which effect their transformation; this is usually known as the throughput time for the operation. The increase of interest in reducing internal throughput times is partly due to the realization of the benefits it can bring, partly due to the closely related interest in JUST-IN-TIME philosophies.

The specific internal benefits of speed are widely held to be as follows. First, speed reduces speculative activity. Reducing through-put time prior to finished goods stocks (if used) reduces the proportion (and often the absolute amount) of speculative activity in the operation. The production of goods prior to a specific customer order being placed for them is always to some extent speculative and carries the risk of the effort put into their production being wasted. An operation with long throughput times would need to start production (and hence speculation) considerably in advance of the products being required.

Second, speed allows better forecasts, not only by providing some protection against poor forecasts but in making better forecasts more likely. Events well in the future are more difficult to forecast than imminent events and forecast error is directly proportional to how far ahead is the event being forecast.

Third, speed reduces overheads, or at least provides the potential to do so. The longer an order or a batch spends in the operation the more overheads it attracts. An order which moves quickly through the operation takes less "looking after" than one which lingers. It needs less heating, lighting, and space, it does not need as much controlling, checking, and monitoring.

Fourth, speed lowers work in progress. When material passes quickly through the operation it cannot spend as much time in the form of work in progress, waiting to be processed. The time which material or information takes to move through the operation is either taken in being processed, traveling between processing stages, or waiting to be processed. Waiting time is by far the largest element in the throughput cycle and is seen as the obvious part to be reduced.

Fifth, speed exposes problems and helps to reduce intrinsic inefficiencies in an operation. This is largely because stocks, either of materials or information, have the effect of obscuring problems in the operation. With work stored about the operation it becomes difficult to "see" the processes themselves. Problems are hidden and improvements smothered (*see* JUST-IN-TIME).

It is generally agreed that in most industries the potential for reducing throughput time is very great. The usual measure of internal speed is throughput efficiency (TE), the ratio of the total processing time for a batch of products to the total throughput time for the batch. Because in most traditionally organized manufacturing operations materials spend much of their time waiting to be processed, throughput efficiency is usually very low, typically between 5 and 0.05 percent.

The attention of both academics and practitioners has increasingly focused on how throughput time may be shortened. Several prescriptions have been proposed which either identify the sources of potential improvement or change the way processing is organized so as to minimize delays.

There are several "mapping". techniques which follow the route of materials, customers or information. They usually try to distinguish between the "real time" where some value is being added by a process, and those times which are "non-value-added." In essence most mapping techniques are similar to PROCESS CHARTS but used at a more macro level of analysis. The types of activity which may be considered non-value adding will depend on the type of operation being mapped. Yet whatever activities are classed as non-value-added, it is they which can be simplified, merged, or eliminated in order to shorten throughput times without detracting from the value adding activities. There is also common agreement that operations can gain benefit from BENCHMARKING their time-based measurements of performance against other similar operations.

A related approach concentrates on methods of avoiding delays. Decision-making delays, especially, seem to be cited as worthy of attention. This involves identifying the number of formal decisions needed during the throughput cycle. Some decisions may be eliminated, while others may be made by exception and, where decisions are necessary, they may be made by the lowest competent authority.

See also **demand response; delivery dependability; flexibility; lifecycle effects**

Bibliography

Blackburn, J. D. (1990). *Time based competition.* Homewood, IL: Irwin.

Blackburn, J. D., Elrod, T., Lindsley, W.B. & Zahorik, A. J. (1992). The strategic value of response time and product variety. In C. A. Voss (Ed.), *Manufacturing strategy.* London: Chapman and Hall.

Bower, J. L. & Hout, T. M. (1988). Fast cycle capability for competitive power. *Harvard Business Review,* **66**, 6, 110–18.

Stalk, G. & Hout, T. M. (1990). *Competing against time.* New York: Free Press.

NIGEL SLACK

tools of quality management   To support and develop a process of CONTINUOUS IMPROVEMENT in QUALITY it is necessary for an organization to use a selection of quality management tools and techniques. Most of these tools and techniques are simple, although not all. There are a considerable number of quality management tools and techniques, all with slightly different roles to play in the process of quality improvement.

When selecting quality management techniques there are two factors which organizations should consider. First, the application of any tool and technique in isolation without a quality strategy and long-range management vision will only provide short-term benefits. Second, no one tool or technique is more important than another, they all have a role to play at some point in the quality improvement process.

A common mistake is to use quality management techniques without thinking through their implications. Research indicates that many companies using specific tools and techniques as the springboard to launch quality improvement single out a specific technique, sometimes at random, and apply it with undue haste without giving sufficient thought to issues such as:

- How will the technique facilitate quality improvement?

- What is the fundamental purpose of the technique?

- What will it achieve? Will it produce benefits if applied on its own?

- Is the technique right for the company's product, processes, people, and culture?

- What organizational changes are necessary to make the most effective use of the technique?

- What is the best method of introducing and then using the technique?

- What are the resources, skills, information, training, etc. required to introduce the technique successfully?

- How will it fit in with, complement, or support other techniques, methods, and quality systems already in place, and any that might be introduced in the future?

- What are the potential difficulties in using the technique?

- What are the limitations, if any, of the technique?

Some of the basic tools of quality control are as follows.

Checklists

Checklists are used as prompts and aids to personnel. They highlight the key features of a process, equipment, system, product, or service to which attention needs to be given, and to ensure that the procedures for an operation, housekeeping, inspection, maintenance, etc. have been followed. Checklists are also used in audits of both product and systems. They can be a useful aid for quality assurance although their variety, style, and content is extensive (*see* QUALITY AWARDS).

Flowcharts

Process mapping, in either a structured or unstructured format, is necessary to obtain an in-depth understanding of a process. A flowchart is employed to provide a diagrammatic picture, by means of a set of symbols, showing all the steps or stages in a process, project, or sequence of events, and is of considerable assistance in documenting and describing a process as an aid to examination and improvement.

Analyzing the data collected on a flowchart can help to uncover irregularities and potential problem points. It is also a useful method for dealing with customer complaints, by establishing the cause of problems in the INTERNAL CUSTOMER–SUPPLIER RELATIONSHIPS chain. In some organizations people are only aware of their own particular aspect of a process, and process mapping helps to facilitate a greater understanding of the whole process. It is essential to the development of the internal customer–supplier relationship (*see* SERVICE DESIGN).

Checksheets

A checksheet is a sheet or form used to record data. It is a simple recording method for determining the occurrence of events such as non-conformities, non-conforming items, breakdown of machinery and/or associated equipment and non–value–adding activity. They are prepared, in advance of the recording of data, by the operatives and staff being affected by a problem. The data collected on a checksheet provides the factual basis for subsequent analysis and corrective action, using for example a PARETO ANALYSIS.

Tally Charts and Histograms

Tally charts are a descriptive presentation of data and help to identify patterns in the data. They are used with measured data to establish the pattern of variation displayed, prior to the assessment of process capability. Tally charts are regarded as simple or crude frequency distribution curves.

A histogram is a graphical representation of individual measured values in a data set according to the frequency of occurrence. They take measured data from the tally sheet and display its distribution using the class intervals or value as a base. The histogram helps to visualize the distribution of data and there are several forms which should be recognized (i.e. normal, skewed, bimodal, isolated island), and in this way they reveal the amount of variation within a process. There are a number of theoretical models which provide patterns and working tools for various shapes of distribution (*see* STATISTICAL QUALITY TECHNIQUES).

Graphs

Graphs, whether presentational or mathematical, are used to facilitate understanding and analysis of the collected data, investigate relationships between factors, attract attention, indicate trends, and make the data memorable. There is a wide choice of graphical methods available for different types of application.

Pareto Analysis

This is a technique employed for prioritizing problems of any time. The analysis highlights the fact that most problems come from a few of the causes and it indicates what problems to solve and in what order. In this way improvement efforts are directed at areas and projects that will have the greatest impact (*see* PARETO ANALYSIS).

Cause and Effect Diagrams

These are used to determine and break down the main causes of a given problem. Cause and effect diagrams are often called "fishbone" diagrams because of their skeletal appearance. They are usually employed where there is only one problem and the possible causes are hierarchical in nature.

The effect (a specific problem or a quality characteristic/condition) is considered to be the head of the fish and the potential causes and sub-causes of the problem, or quality characteristic/condition to be its bone structure. The diagram illustrates in a clear manner the possible relationships between some identified effect and the causes influencing it. They also assist in helping to uncover the root causes of a problem and in generating improvement ideas.

Brainstorming

Brainstorming, is a method of free expression and is employed when the solutions to problems cannot be deduced logically and/or when creative new ideas are required. It is used with a variety of quality management tools and techniques. Brainstorming works best in groups. It unlocks the creative power of the group through the synergistic effect and in this way stimulate the production of ideas. It can be employed in a structured manner in which the group follow a set of rules, or in an unstructured format which allows anyone in the group to present ideas randomly as they occur.

Scatter Diagram

Scatter diagrams are used when examining the possible relationship or association between two variables, characteristics or factors. They indicate the relationship as a pattern. For example, one variable may be a process parameter and the other may be some measurable characteristic of the product. As the process parameter is changed (independent variable) it is noted together with any measured change in the product variable (dependent variable), and this is repeated until sufficient data have been collected. The results when plotted on a graph will give a scatter diagram. Variables that are associated will show a linear pattern and those that are unrelated will portray a random pattern (*see also* STATISTICAL QUALITY TECHNIQUES).

See also **total quality management; quality management systems**

Bibliography

Dale, B. G. (1994). *Managing quality.* 2nd edn. Herts.: Prentice-Hall.
Ishikawa, K. (1976). *A guide to quality control.* Tokyo: Asian Productivity Organization.
Ozeki, K. & Asaka, T. (1990). *Handbook of quality tools.* Cambridge, MA: Productivity Press.

BARRIE DALE

total productive maintenance Total productive maintenance (TPM) is productive MAINTENANCE carried out by all employees through small group activities.

The dual goal of TPM is zero breakdowns and zero defects. When breakdowns and defects are eliminated, equipment operation rates improve, costs are reduced, spare parts inventory can be minimized, and as a consequence, overall productivity increases.

It has been reported that typically, within three years from the introduction of TPM, companies show 15–25 percent increases in equipment operation rates while others show a 90 percent reduction in process defects. Labor productivity is generally increased by 40–50 percent.

In the years following the Second World War the Japanese industrial sectors imported PREVENTIVE MAINTENANCE (PM) from the United States. Preventive maintenance was introduced in the 1950s and remained well established until the 1970s. Japan's PM consisted mainly of time-based maintenance featuring periodic servicing and overhaul. During the 1980s PM was rapidly being replaced by predictive maintenance, or condition-based maintenance (*see* RELIABILITY-CENTERED MAINTENANCE).

TPM is often defined as productive maintenance involving total participation. Frequently, management misconstrues this to imply that only shop floor staff need be involved. However, TPM should be implemented on a company-wide basis.

TPM aims to establish good maintenance practice in operations through the pursuit of "the five goals of TPM" as follows:

(1) *Improve equipment effectiveness*: examine how the facilities are contributing to the effectiveness of the operation by examining all the losses which occur. Loss of effectiveness can be the result of downtime losses, speed losses or defect losses.

(2) *Achieve autonomous maintenance*: allow the people who operate or use the operation's equipment to take responsibility for, at least some, of the maintenance tasks. Also encourage maintenance staff to take responsibility for the improvement of maintenance performance. There are three stages in which staff take responsibility for maintenance, the repair level; where staff carry out instructions, but do not predict the future, they simply react to problems, the prevention level; where staff can predict the future by foreseeing problems, and taking corrective action, and the improvement level; where staff can predict the future foreseeing problems, they not only take corrective action but also propose improvements to prevent recurrence.

(3) *Plan maintenance*: have a fully worked out approach to all maintenance activities. This should include the level of preventive maintenance which is required for each piece of equipment, the standards for condition-based maintenance, and the respective responsibilities of operating staff and maintenance staff. The respective roles of "operating" and "maintenance" staff are seen as being distinct. Maintenance staff are seen as developing preventive actions and general breakdown services, whereas operating staff take on the "ownership" of the facilities and their general care. Similarly, the respective responsibilities of the two types of staff are seen as distinct. Maintenance staff are held to be responsible for the training of operators, problem diagnosis, and devising and assessing maintenance practice.

(4) *Train all staff in relevant maintenance skills*: the responsibilities of operating and maintenance staff require that both have all the skills to carry out their roles. TPM places a heavy emphasis on appropriate and continuous training.

(5) *Achieve early equipment management*: this goal is directed at going some way to avoiding maintenance altogether by "maintenance prevention" (MP). MP involves considering failure causes and the maintainability of equipment during its design stage, its manufacture, its installation, and its commissioning. In this way TPM attempts to trace all potential maintenance problems back to their root cause and then tries to eliminate them at that point.

The first principal feature of TPM, total effectiveness or profitable PM is also emphasized in predictive and productive maintenance. The second feature, a total maintenance system is another concept first introduced during the productive maintenance era. It establishes a maintenance plan for the equipment's entire life-span and includes maintenance prevention (MP: maintenance-free design), which is pursued during the equipment design stages. Once equipment is assembled, a total maintenance system requires preventive maintenance and maintainability improvement (MI: repairing or modifying equipment to prevent breakdowns and facilitate ease of maintenance). The last feature, autonomous maintenance by operators (small group activities), is unique to TPM.

TPM works to eliminate what are termed the "six big losses" that are regarded as formidable obstacles to equipment effectiveness. They are:

Downtime:
(1) equipment failure from breakdowns;
(2) set-up and adjustment from exchange of dies in injection moulding machines, etc.

Speed losses:
(3) idling and minor stoppages due to the abnormal operation of sensors, blockage of work on chutes, etc.;
(4) reduced speed due to discrepancies between designed and actual speed of equipment.

Defects:
(5) process defects due to scraps and quality defects to be repaired;
(6) reduced yield from machine start-up to stable production.

See also **condition-based maintenance; failure analysis**

Bibliography

Nakajima, S. (1988). *Introduction to total productive maintenance*. Cambridge, MA: Productivity Press.

MICHAEL SHULVER

total quality management Total quality management (TQM) is a management philosophy embracing all activities through which the needs and expectations of the customer and the community, and the objectives of the organization are satisfied in the most efficient and cost effective way by maximizing the potential of all employees in a continuing drive for improvement. It is the latest in what have been several stages in the development of QUALITY management. While the many authors who write on the subject may choose to stress slightly different aspects of the TQM philosophy, there is reasonable consensus concerning some central elements.

Many authorities agree that without the total commitment of the CEO and his or her senior managers any improvement stands little chance of being permanent. They have to take charge personally, provide direction, set goals, and exercise forceful leadership. However, while some specific actions are required to give it a focus, eventually it must be seen as the natural way of operating a business.

An emphasis on planning and organization features in a number of facets of the quality improvement process. This will take the form of developing a clear long-term approach for TQM which is integrated with other strategies such as information technology, operations and human resources and the business plans of the organization, and of building product and service quality into designs and processes, developing prevention-based activities, and putting quality assurance procedures into place which facilitate closed loop corrective action. Similarly, planning the approach to be taken to the effective use of quality systems, procedures, and quality management tools and techniques, in the context of the overall strategy is important, as is developing the organization and infrastructure to support the improvement activities and pursuing standardization, systematization, and simplification of work instructions, procedures and systems.

The use of quality management tools and techniques is stressed in order to support and develop a process of continuous quality improvement. Without the effective employment and mix of tools and techniques it will be difficult to solve problems. The tools and techniques should be used to facilitate improvement and integrated into the routine operation of the business. The organization should develop a route map for the tools and techniques which it intends to apply. The use of tools and techniques helps to get the process of improvement started, employees using them are involved and feel that they are making a contribution, quality awareness is enhanced, behavior and attitude change starts to happen, and projects are brought to a successful conclusion (*see* TOOLS OF QUALITY MANAGEMENT).

Education and training are seen as a central TQM issue. Employees should be provided with the right level of education and training to insure that their general awareness of quality management concepts, skills, and attitudes are appropriate and suited to the continuous improvement philosophy; it also provides a common language throughout the business. A formal program of education and training needs to be planned and provided on a timely and regular basis to enable people to cope with increasing complex problems. It should suit the operational conditions of the business. Without training it is difficult to solve problems and without education, behavior and attitude change will not take place. It also has to be recognized that not all employees will have received and acquired adequate levels of education. The structure of the training program may incorporate some updating of basic educational skills in numeracy and literacy, but it must, promote continuing education and self development.

Involvement of employees and a commitment to their development is a reoccurring theme. All available means from suggestion schemes to various forms of team work must be considered for achieving broad employee interest, participation and contribution in the process of quality improvement. This also involves seeking and listening carefully to the views of employees and acting upon their suggestions. Part of the approach to TQM is to ensure that everyone has a clear understanding of what is required of them and how their processes relate to the business as a whole. The more people who understand the business and what is going on around them, the greater the role they can play in quality improvement. People have got to be encouraged to control, manage, and improve the processes which are within their sphere of responsibility (*see* INTERNAL CUSTOMER–SUPPLIER RELATIONSHIPS).

Similarly team work needs to be practiced in a number of forms. Consideration needs to be given to the operating characteristics of the teams employed, how they fit into the organizational structure and the roles of member, team leader, sponsor, and facilitator. TQM also may stress a need to recognize positive performance and achievement, and celebrate and reward success. This needs to be constantly encouraged through active communication (*see* QUALITY TEAMS).

Measurement and feedback needs to be made continually against a series of key results indicators, both internal and external. The latter are the most important as they relate to customer perceptions of product and service improvement. The indicators should be developed from existing business measures, external (competitive and functional), and internal BENCHMARKING, as well as customer surveys and other means of external input. This enables progress and feedback to be assessed against a roadmap or checkpoints. From these measurements, action plans must be developed to meet objectives, and to identify and bridge gaps.

TQM stresses the need to create an organizational environment which is conducive to continuous quality improvement, and in which everyone can participate and work together. Quality assurance also needs to be integrated into all an organization's processes and functions (*see* CONTINUOUS IMPROVEMENT). This is often framed in terms of changing peoples' behavior, attitudes, and working practices. The following are typical:

- Everyone in the organization must be involved in "improving" the processes under their control on a continuous basis and take personal responsibility for their own quality assurance.

- Employees must be inspecting their own work.

- Defects must not be passed, in whatever form, to the next process.

- Each person must be committed to satisfying their customers, both internal and external.

- External suppliers and customers must be integrated into the improvement process.

- Mistakes must be viewed as an improvement opportunity.

- Honesty, sincerity, and care must be an integral part of daily business life.

The Benefits of TQM

Various benefits of TQM are mentioned by most of those writing on the subject. Monetary benefits include:

- reduction in internal rejection rates;
- reduction in warranty claims;
- reduction in field failures;
- reduction in the cost of quality;
- savings resulting from quality improvement projects and suggestions;
- increased customer satisfaction.
Qualitative benefits include:
- greater involvement and participation;
- common language leading to improved communication;
- increased pride, encouragement, and support;
- enhanced job ownership and support;
- increased employee awareness;
- willingness to identify and eliminate waste;
- improved systems and procedures;
- development of problem solving and leadership skills.

How do Companies get Started on TQM?

Many writers on TQM develop approaches to the subject which reflect their own background and experience. These approaches often include: (1) a listing of TQM principles which are presented in the form of a TQM implementation plan and a set of guidelines; (2) prescriptive step-by-step approaches; (3) methods outlining the wisdom, philosophies and recommendations of the internationally respected experts on the subject; (4) non-prescriptive methods in the form of a framework or model. In total they represent a body of advice, from which organizations have to identify the approach which best suits their needs and business operation.

Applying the wisdom of the quality management "gurus". The writings and teachings of the internationally respected quality experts may be a sensible starting point for any organization introducing TQM. The usual approach is for an organization to adopt the teachings of one of the quality management experts and attempt to follow the program. The argument for this approach is that each expert has a package which works, and by adopting one of the packages it helps to reduce confusion; some organizations have purposely opted for the simplest package. Organizations adopting this approach eventually start to use the ideas of other quality management experts. Crosby followed by Juran and then Deming are the most frequently cited experts (*see* CROSBY, JURAN, and DEMING).

Applying a consultancy package. Some companies decide to adopt the program of one of the major management consultancies on the grounds that it is a self-contained package which can be suitably customized for application throughout their organization. Most of the "gurus" have their own consultancy activities to help organizations implement the ideas and principles of the expert in question.

Frameworks and models. A framework or model is usually introduced to present a picture of what is required in introducing TQM. They are the means of presenting ideas, concepts, pointers, and plans in a relatively non-prescriptive manner, as are guides to action. They are often more concerned with the destination than the route to get there.

Developing a tailor-made organizational route map. A variation on these approaches is to absorb the "received wisdom" and the experiences of other companies and extract the ideas, methods, systems, and tactics which are appropriate to the particular circumstances, business situation and environmental culture of the organization. This implies that management have to think through the issues and develop for themselves a vision, quality objectives, policy, strategy, an approach, a route map for quality improvement and the means of deploying the philosophy to all levels of the organization. A feature of organizations following this approach is that senior management will have visited other companies with a reputation for being "centers of excellence" to see at first hand the lessons learned from TQM and have become involved in meetings relating to TQM with executives of like minds from different companies.

The process of change involved in integrating the philosophy of TQM into an organization is complex and wide ranging. If the process is to be effective, it requires the creation of an environment where employees are motivated to want to improve on a continuous basis. If the managers cannot create this environment then any systems, tools, techniques, or training employed will be ineffective.

See also **quality teams; quality awards; quality costing**

Bibliography

Chu, C. H. (1988). The pervasive elements of total quality control. *Industrial Management*, **30**, 5, 30–2.

Crosby, P. B. (1979). *Quality is free.* New York: McGraw-Hill.

Dale, B. G. (1994). *Managing quality.* 2nd edn. Herts.: Prentice-Hall.

Dale, B. G. & Boaden, R. J. (1993). Improvement framework. *The TQM Magazine*, 5, *1*, 23–6.

Dale, B. G. & Cooper, C. L. (1992). *Total quality and human resources: An executive guide.* Oxford: Blackwell.

Deming, W. E. (1982). *Quality, productivity and competitive position*. Cambridge, MA: Massachusetts Institute of Technology, Center of Advanced Engineering Study.

Feigenbaum, A. V. (1991). *Total quality control*. 3rd edn. New York: McGraw-Hill.

Juran, J. M. (1988). *Quality control handbook*. New York: McGraw-Hill.

BARRIE DALE

trade-offs Trade-off theory is concerned with the manner in which OPERATIONS OBJECTIVES relate to each other. The assumptions made about these relationships are important because they influence the strategic expectations that the organization should have regarding the performance of its operations function, as well as the expectations that the operations function should have regarding its own potential to improve operations performance.

The basis of the trade-off paradigm is that the improvement in one aspect of operations performance, to some degree, necessarily implies a reduction in some other aspect of performance. Put another way, it must consider trading off one aspect of performance with another. Taken to its extreme, the trade-off paradigm implies that improvement in one aspect of an operation's performance can only be gained at the expense of performance in another. "There is no such thing as a free lunch" is often quoted as a summary of the trade-off theory.

Probably the best known summary of the trade-off idea comes from Skinner (1969), the most influential of the originators of the strategic approach to operations.

> Most managers will readily admit that there are compromises or trade-offs to be made in designing an airplane or truck. In the case of an airplane, trade-offs would involve matters such as cruising speed, take-off and landing distances, initial cost, maintenance, fuel consumption, passenger comfort and cargo or passenger capacity. For instance no one today can design a 500 passenger plane that can land on an aircraft carrier and also break the sound barrier. Much the same thing is true in manufacturing.

Skinner's view was that all operations are, in effect, technically constrained systems. They have the potential to excel in a limited (one or two) number of operations objectives but cannot be equally good at everything. Therefore to realize their potential as a positive force, operations must focus on those objectives which best support the organization s competitive strategy (*see* FOCUS and OPERATIONS ROLE). This implies that a major task of any operations manager is to determine the most appropriate operations objectives contingent upon competitive strategy.

The relevance of the trade-off paradigm has been challenged by more evangelical approaches, most notably the "world class manufacturing" (WCM) movement (Schonberger, 1986) which takes a clear anti-trade-off stance. It holds that operations can indeed excel at many different objectives simultaneously.

The underlying philosophy of WCM is improvement oriented and radical when compared with the more conservative trade-off paradigm. One way of characterizing the difference between the two approaches is by visualizing a lever, pivoted in the middle and free to move one end up at the expense of the other end going down, but also with the pivot able to move up and down. The height of each end is then analogous to the level of performance achieved by the operations objectives which they represent. In terms of this "lever" model there are two ways to improve the position of one end of the lever. One is to depress the other end thereby improving one aspect of performance at the expense of another. The other way is to raise the pivot of the lever. This would raise one end of the lever without depressing the other end, or alternatively it could raise both ends. The "pivot" in a real operation represents the set of constraints which prevent both aspects of performance being improved simultaneously. These may be technical, or attitudinal, but the "pivot" is stopping one aspect of performance improving without it reducing the performance of another. Overcoming these constraints are seen as the main improvement task by proponents of the WCM approach.

Two compromises have been suggested which attempt to bridge the gap between trade-off and WCM approaches. One (New,

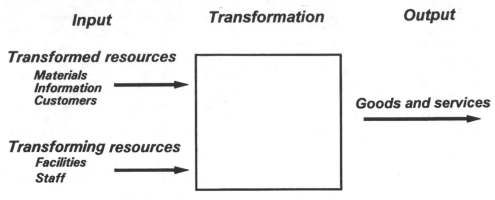

Input   **Transformation**   **Output**

Transformed resources
  Materials
  Information
  Customers

                                              Goods and services

Transforming resources
  Facilities
  Staff

Figure 1 The general transformation model

1992) distinguishes between different trade-offs. Some trade-offs, it is argued, do indeed appear to have been overcome by a combination of technological advances and alternative methods of organizing operations (*see* JUST-IN-TIME and TOTAL QUALITY MANAGEMENT). Most notably, the relationship between delivery speed and delivery dependability, product or service specification and specification consistency, or specification consistency and cost, do not necessarily trade off against each other. However, others, such as specification and cost, product or service range and delivery speed, product or service range and cost (and to some extent) delivery speed and volume flexibility, do exhibit a trade-off relationship.

The other compromise (Slack, 1991) sees the trade-off paradigm as being appropriate under some, but not all, circumstances. The timescale of any change in the relative performance levels of objectives is held to be especially important. In the short term the trade-off paradigm corresponds closely with observed system behavior. So an operation which was required to increase the range of its products or services, would, in the very short term, have little choice but to suffer increased costs for doing so. However, if the same operation is allowed a longer period to reshape its resources with the specific goal of achieving an extended range of offerings, the probability of its doing so without the same increase in costs is greatly increased. Thus long-term changes have, at least, the potential to overcome trade-off relationships.

Bibliography

New, C. (1992). World class manufacturing versus trade-offs. *International Journal of Operations and Production Management*, **12**, 6, 19–31.

Schonberger, R. J. (1986). *World class manufacturing*. New York: Free Press.

Skinner, W. (1969). Manufacturing: missing link in corporate strategy. *Harvard Business Review*, **52**, *3*, 136–45.

Slack, N. (1992). *The manufacturing advantage*. Didcot, UK: Business Books 2000.

NIGEL SLACK

transformation model   All operations produce goods and services by a process of transformation by using their resources to change the state or condition of something to produce outputs. This concept is central to the general transformation model (see Figure 1) which is frequently used to describe the nature of all operations, as taking in a set of input resources, and using them either to transform something, or to be transformed themselves, into outputs of goods and services. For this reason it is also known as the input–transformation–output model of operations. It is based on the open systems model of systems theory.

The difference between operations has led to further development of the simple transformation model. Manufacturing operations produce largely physical goods, SERVICE OPERATIONS produce sometimes intangible changes in the output. The nature of the processes within operations are also different. However, the most important difference between operations is the nature of their inputs. Whereas some operations transform materials or information (inanimate inputs), others transform the customers themselves.

Inputs to the Transformation Process

The inputs to operation can be classified as either transformed resources, which are the resources that are treated, transformed, or converted in some way, and transforming resources, which are resources that act upon the transformed resources. The transformed resources which operations take in are usually some mixture of materials, information, and customers, although often only one of these is dominant in an operation.

There is less variation between different operations' transforming resources. Two types of transforming resource are usually identified as forming the basic structure of all operations. Namely, facilities, which are the buildings, equipment, plant, and process technology of the operation, and staff, who operate, maintain, plan, and manage the operation. Also, sometimes included as transforming resources are consumable items which, although strictly material resources, are not the main subject of transformation, only incidental to it.

The Transformation Process

The purpose of the transformation process in operations is closely connected with the nature of its transformed input resources. Operations which process materials could do so to transform their physical properties such as physical shape, or composition or characteristics, as do most manufacturing operations. Other operations which process materials do so to change their location, such as transport companies. Some, like retail operations, do so to change the possession or ownership of the materials, and finally some such as warehouses, do so primarily to store or accommodate them.

Operations which process information, do so either to transform their informational properties (the form of the information); accountants are an example. Some change the possession of the information, as do market research companies. Others, such as libraries, store or accommodate the information, while others change the location of the information, such as telecommunication companies.

Operations which process customers might change their physical properties in a similar way to material processors, as do hairdressers and cosmetic surgeons. Some store or accommodate them (hotels for example). Airlines, mass rapid transport systems and bus companies transform the location of their customers, while some transform the physiological state of their customers, such as hospitals. Others transform the psychological state of their customers, for example most entertainment services.

Outputs from the Transformation Process

The outputs from (and purpose of) the transformation process are goods and services, which are generally seen as being different (*see* SERVICE OPERATIONS).

Most operations produce a mixture of goods and services, and can be positioned on a continuum from "pure" goods producers to "pure" service producers. Some extraction companies are concerned almost exclusively with their product. Other "commodity-like" goods producers, such as steel makers, are again largely concerned with the production of products, although they might also produce some services such as technical advice. Capital goods manufacturers are similar insomuch as they too primarily produce goods, but to an even greater extent they also produce facilitating services such as technical advice, applications engineering services, installation, maintenance, and training. However, the services produced by restaurants are an important part of the operation's output. Computer services company will also produce products, for example software products, but is primarily providing a service to its customers. Further along the continuum a management consultancy, although producing reports and documents, is a service provider which uses facilitating goods. Finally, some pure services do not produce products at all, for example, a psychotherapy clinic which provides therapeutic treatment for its customers without any facilitating goods.

See also **operations management; hierarchy of operations; operations activities**

Bibliography

Chase, R. B. (1977). Where does the customer fit in a service operation? *Harvard Business Review*, **56**, 137–42.

Wild, R. (1977). *Concepts for operations management.* Chichester: Wiley.

NIGEL SLACK

V

value engineering The purpose of value engineering is to try to develop products of low COST or high value. Value engineering is usually taken to apply to products prior to their manufacture, while "value analysis" treats products which are currently manufactured. However, both attempt to eliminate any costs that do not contribute to the value and performance of the product (or service, but the approach is more common in manufacturing).

The origins of the approach is credited to the General Electric company in the USA who engaged in a systematic study during the Second World War to investigate alternative materials, designs, and production processes in order to maintain production levels. The company found that in most cases the alternative materials and processes performed at least as well and often better in terms of both specification and cost. This led them to formalize their procedures for analyzing the value of each part and product. Value is seen as the primary concept rather than cost. Previous "design to cost" approaches had assumed a trade-off between product features which could be manipulated to achieve a required cost (*see* TRADE-OFFS). Value engineering, however, starts by critically assessing the value or worth of each feature of a design and then goes on to provide the same value but at lower cost.

Different types of value are recognized by the approach. "Use value" is the cost to the user of the attributes of a product which enable it to perform its function. "Cost value" is the total cost of producing the product. "Esteem value" is the additional cost which a product can attract because of its intrinsic attractiveness to purchasers. "Exchange value" is the sum of the attributes which enable the product to be exchanged or sold. Although the relative magnitude of these different types of value will vary between products, and also probably over the life of a product, the value approach attempts to identify the contribution of each feature to each type of value through systematic analysis and structured creativity enhancing techniques.

Value engineering programs are usually conducted by project teams consisting of designers, purchasing specialists, operations managers, and financial analysts. PARETO ANALYSIS is often used to identify the parts of the total design package that are worthy of most attention. The chosen elements are then subject to rigorous scrutiny. The team analyzes the function and cost of those elements and tries to find any similar components that could do the same job at lower cost. For example, the team might attempt to reduce the number of components, use cheaper materials, or simplify the processes.

See also **design; design for manufacture**

Bibliography

Mudge, A. E. (1971). *Value engineering: A systematic approach*. New York: McGraw-Hill.

NIGEL SLACK

variety The term "variety" can be used in at least two different ways. One is the variety of activities which result in the range of different products or services an operation produces. The other is the variation of an operation's outputs over time, not only in terms of how the range of products or services varies (e.g. product introductions or changes, and breadth of the product range) but also in terms of how the volume, both aggregate and per product, the mix and timing of the demanded output, vary along the time. The former aspect of variety is the more usual usage.

COST is generally sensitive to variety. The actual cost of variety is held by operations managers to be greater than accounting systems report it to be. An organization which manufactures only one product for only one customer at constant quantities would be very simple to manage. Production time lost in set-ups would be negligible, each step of the process would have matched capacities and be operated in synchronization, quality costs would be low, as would inventories. Management costs would be low because everything would be almost perfectly stable.

All this changes with the introduction of additional products or services. It is difficult to maintain production of one product or service at a constant rate when demand for the others must also be satisfied. Production schedules must be created and managed. Change-overs will require both scheduling and management as products and services compete for the same facilities. Quality could become more expensive, since with each change-over, the process has to be brought into tolerance. Additional process steps are likely to be required. Because it is much more difficult to match the capacities of each step of the process, it is unlikely that processes can be operated in unison. A greater variety of purchased items will be needed (in what is now an irregular pattern) to meet the production schedules. Work in process inventories are expected to increase as inventories are built up to enable the many parts of the process to continue operating. Finished goods inventories will possibly increase because while one product is being manufactured, stocks of other products have to be maintained to satisfy demand. Customer priorities must be weighed against the priorities for smooth operation of the factory, as a consequence, the process is rarely in balance.

The disadvantage of excessive variability is also behind Skinner's (1974) concept of FOCUS.

See also **volume; flexibility; manufacturing processes; service processes; planning and control in operations**

Bibliography

Johnson, H. T. & Kaplan, K. S. (1987). *Relevance costs: The rise and fall of management accounts.* Boston: Harvard Business School Press.

Skinner, W. (1974). The focused factory. *Harvard Business Review,* May-June, 113–21.

NIGEL SLACK

vertical integration Vertical integration is the extent to which an organization owns the network of processes which together give products or services their value. It involves an organization assessing the benefits of acquiring suppliers or customers. At a more micro level, it is the decision of whether to make a particular individual component or to perform a particular service itself, or alternatively buy it in from a supplier (*see* DO OR BUY). At the strategic level, vertical integration is a topic more of interest to economists. However, operations managers are required to assess its practical effects. It is also included as an element of the CONTENT OF MANUFACTURING STRATEGY by some authorities.

An organization's vertical integration strategy can be defined in terms of the following (Hayes and Wheelwright, 1984):

● the direction of vertical integration;

● the extent of the process span required;

● the balance among the resulting vertically integrated stages.

The strategy of expanding on the supply side of an organization's supply network (*see* SUPPLY CHAIN MANAGEMENT) is sometimes called backward or "upstream" vertical integration, and expanding on the demand side is sometimes called forward or "downstream" vertical integration. Backward vertical integration through an organization taking control of its suppliers is sometimes used either to gain cost advantages or to prevent competitors gaining control of important suppliers. For this reason it is sometimes considered a strategically defensive move. Forward vertical integration, on the other hand, takes an organization closer to its markets and allows more freedom for an organization to make contact directly with its customers. For this reason forward vertical integration is sometimes considered an offensive strategic move.

Having established its direction of expansion, an organization must then decide how far it wishes to take the extent of its vertical integration. Some organizations deliberately choose not to integrate far, if at all, from their original part of the supply chain. Alternatively, some organizations choose to become very vertically integrated.

The third dimension of vertical integration does not strictly concern the ownership of the supply chain; it concerns the capacity and, to some extent, the operating behavior of each stage in the chain which is owned by the organization. The balance of the part of the chain owned by an organization is the amount of the capacity at each stage in the chain which is devoted to supplying the next stage. So a totally balanced relationship is one where one stage produces only for the next stage and totally satisfies their requirements. Less than full balance in the stages allows each stage to sell their output to other companies or to buy in some of their supplies from other companies. Fully balanced networks have the virtue of simplicity and also allow each stage to focus on the requirements of the next stage along in the network. Having to supply other organizations, perhaps with slightly different requirements, might serve to distract from what is needed by their primary customer. However, a totally self-sufficient network is sometimes not feasible.

See also **capacity strategy; purchasing and supply management**

Bibliography

Hayes, R. H. & Wheelwright, S. C. (1984). *Restoring our competitive edge: Competing through manufacturing.* New York: Wiley.
Harrigan, K. R. (1983). *Strategies for vertical integration.* Lexington, MA: Lexington Books.

NIGEL SLACK

volume   The volume of activity in an operation is usually taken to mean the number of broadly similar products or customers it is required to process, or similar tasks it is required to perform, per unit of time. Volume (together with VARIETY) is often taken to be one of the main determinants of the nature of operations management in an organization (*see* MANUFACTURING PROCESSES and SERVICE PROCESSES).

In a high-volume operation there is inevitably a high level of repeatability of the tasks staff are performing. Because tasks are repeated frequently it makes sense to specialize the tasks, with one person assigned to each part of the total production task. When tasks are divided in this way it also allows the systemization of the work. Many high volume operations have standard procedures, set down formally, with instructions on how each part of the job should be carried out. Systemization can also lead to higher capital intensity of the operation, through the development of specialized technology. The most important implication of high volume, however, is that it gives relatively low COST because the fixed costs of the operation are spread over a large number of products or services.

Low-volume operations are subject to the opposite pressures. Here the degree of repetition will be far lower because of the lower volume. Furthermore the number of staff will be lower and, therefore, the amount of the whole job of producing the product or service which each staff member performs will be greater. This may be more rewarding for the staff, but less open to systemization. Lower volume also makes it less feasible to invest in specialized equipment. For all of these reasons it follows that the cost per product or customer served is likely to be higher than that in higher volume operations.

However, it is advisable to take care when applying the conventional generalization regarding high- and low-volume operations. For example, aircraft manufacture is relatively low volume compared with television manufacture. Yet much of the comments on high-volume operations still apply to aircraft production. It is highly systematized, with specialized jobs, performed by staff who only undertake a small part of the total job. Aircraft are even made on an assembly line basis (albeit a very slow one) like televisions. This seeming anomaly is partly due to the care taken in the construction of aircraft because of safety considerations. Mainly, though, it is due to the amount of work which goes into each aircraft. The number of products made may be relatively low, but the number of staff hours which are devoted to a day's production is very high, as is the number of repetitions (the number of times a rivet is inserted and a cable is joined) each day.

See also **job design; capacity management**

NIGEL SLACK

W

work breakdown structures Creating a work breakdown structure (WBS) is a systematic way of defining the scope of a project (*see* PROJECT MANAGEMENT). The process can be defined formally as breaking down (or decomposing) the project into natural elements for management and control purposes. Effectively this means creating "more manageable chunks of work." Carrying out the process of determining the WBS has immense value in helping to identify missing scope items and areas for further definition. Graphically, presentation is a pyramidal representation showing a hierarchical subdivision of the project, normally drawn similar to a family tree.

The structure and content of the WBS should be agreed by, at least, the key team members. Drawing the WBS is often a consensus group process, involving the relevant parties who will carry out the project. The WBS diagram and its structural detail provides the basis for: responsibilities to be identified, relating elements of work to each other and to the end product (deliverable). It also provides the basis for the organization of work for subsequent integration and the planning and control system. Above all it is an excellent visual way to communicate the scope of the project.

In breaking the project down to its component parts or products, any associated management services should be included to encompass all the project. The elements of the lowest level of breakdown are generally called work packages. These must be unique and clearly distinguishable from each other. Constructing the WBS can be approached in a number of ways, the most common are: project lifecycle, functional use, component or product, and geographical area. A view of these approaches shows the advantage of a diagrammatic representation (see Figure 1).

The breakdown shows the work to be done, and associated with each work package will be products or deliverables. The work packages then form the basis for control and are defined further by a description of the work to be performed as part of the package, who is responsible for its delivery, and a budget and timeframe for completing the work. Although the product or component form is most commonly used, a WBS is often of a mixed approach, e.g. the top levels may be phase oriented and the lower levels product or function oriented.

A number of factors influence how the WBS is created, i.e. the type of project (lifecycle for software projects), the use of organizational standards, and the preferences of the project manager and team.

Work Packages

Work packages represent units of work at levels where the work is performed and they are assignable to a single responsible organizational element, their definition, therefore, is very important. Each work package is unique and will have its own start and an end point that represent physical accomplishment. It will also have a budget, together with the resources required and associated products or deliverables that will include "management products" such as reports and specifications. Frequently work packages are used to represent a high-level program that details how the project will be carried out, i.e. the execution plan of the project (*see* NETWORK TECHNIQUES).

Having defined the work packages they provide the benefits of baseline definition for subsequent change control, risk identification and assessment, assignment of responsibility, and identification of resources. The approach ensures completeness by the discipline of a standard approach. Future projects also benefit, as work packages can form building blocks as an aid to estimating future projects.

A Framework for Control

The WBS can be the heart of an integrated project management information system by relating the work to be performed, the organization structure plus the individual responsibilities for the work. It forms the foundation for planning and budgeting and subsequent detailed activity or task planning (*see* PROJECT COST MANAGEMENT AND CONTROL and NETWORK TECHNIQUES). A valuable side benefit is to formulate packages of work for subcontracting to other organizations to reduce the risk to the project due to lack of expertise or resources (*see* PROJECT RISK MANAGEMENT). Most modern project management information systems provide analysis, reporting, and control based on WBS structures to enable decisions to be made with the overview information given by a WBS.

Bibliography

Harrison, F. L. (1985). *Advanced project management.* Aldershot: Gower.

RALPH LEVENE

work measurement   Work measurement is the process of establishing the time that a given task would take when performed by a qualified worker working at a defined level of performance. There are various ways in which work may be measured and a variety of techniques have been established. The basic procedure, irrespective of the particular measurement technique being used, consists of three stages. First, an analysis phase in which the job is divided into convenient, discrete components, commonly known as elements. Second, a measurement phase in which the specific measurement technique is used to establish the time required (by a qualified worker working at a

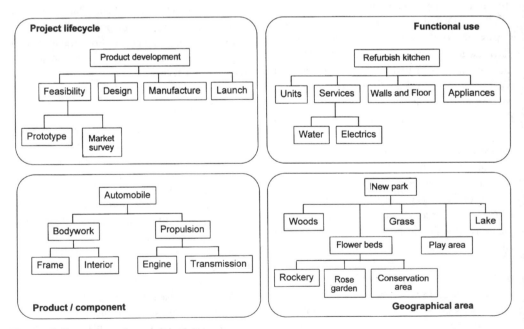

Figure 1 Examples of work breakdown structures

defined level of performance) to complete each element of work. Third, a synthesis phase in which the various elemental times are added, together with appropriate allowances (see below), to construct the standard time for the complete job.

The techniques used to measure work can be classified into those that rely on direct observation of the work, and those that do not. For example, some techniques, such as PREDETERMINED MOTION TIME SYSTEMS and the use of synthetic or standard data can provide times from simulation or even visualization of the work. However, the data on which such techniques are based were almost certainly based on earlier observation of actual work.

Direct observation techniques (such as TIME STUDY and ANALYTICAL ESTIMATING) include a process for converting observed times to times for the "qualified worker working at a defined level of performance." The commonest of these processes is known as rating. This involves the observer (after appropriate training) making an assessment of the worker's rate of working relative to the observer's concept of the rate corresponding to standard rating. This assessment is based on the factors involved in the work – such as effort, dexterity, speed of movement, and consistency. The assessment is made on a rating scale, of which there are three or four in common usage. Thus on the 0–100 scale, the observer makes a judgment of the worker's rate of working as a percentage of the standard rate of working (100). The rating is then used (in a process known as "extension" in time study) to convert the observed time to the basic time using the simple formula:

Basic time = observed time × observed rating/ standard rating

Rating is regarded by many as a controversial area of measurement since it is a subjective assessment. Where different observers rate differently, the resulting basic times are not comparable. It is seen as important by work measurement practitioners to ensure that those undertaking the rating are properly trained, and that this training is regularly updated (to maintain a common perception of standard rating) through rating clinics.

When carrying out work over a complete shift or working day, workers obviously suffer from the fatigue imposed both by the work undertaken and the conditions under which they are working. The normal practice is to make an addition to the basic time (commonly referred to as an "allowance") to allow the worker to recover from this fatigue and to attend to personal needs. The amount of the allowance depends on the nature of the work and the working environment, and is often assessed using an agreed set of guidelines and scales. It is usual to allow some of the recovery period inherent in these allowances to be taken away from the workplace (and it is essential in adverse working conditions). Thus, work design should include the design of an effective work–rest regime. The addition of allowances should never be used to compensate for an unsafe or unhealthy working environment.

One minority school of thought suggests that relaxation allowances are unnecessary. When work which involves, say, the carrying of heavy weights, this school suggests that the observer automatically adjusts the concept of standard rating to allow for the weight. Thus, if the standard rate of performance for walking on level ground carrying no weight is equivalent to four miles per hour, then an observer rating a worker walking while carrying a weight will not expect the equivalent rate. Thus, it is argued, that the weight has been allowed for in the adjustment of standard rating and any relaxation allowance is simply a duplication of this adjustment.

In many jobs there are small amounts of work that may occur irregularly and inconsistently. It is often not economic to measure such infrequent work and an additional allowance is added to cover such work and similar irregular delays. This allowance is known as a contingency allowance and is assessed either by observation, by analysis of historical records (for such items as tool sharpening or replacement), or by experience.

The end result is a standard time which includes the time the work "should" take (when carried out by a qualified worker) plus additional allocations in the form of allowances, where appropriate, to cover relaxation time, contingency time and, perhaps, unoccupied time which increases the overall work cycle (such as waiting for a machine to finish a processing cycle).

The choice of a suitable measurement technique depends on a number of factors including: the purpose of the measurement, the level of detail required, the time available for the measurement, the existence of available predetermined data, and the cost of measurement.

To some extent there is a trade-off between some of these factors. For example, techniques which derive times quickly may provide less detail and be less suitable for some purposes, such as the establishment of individual performance levels on short-cycle work.

The advantage of structured and systematic work measurement is that it gives a common currency for the evaluation and comparison of all types of work. The results obtained from work measurement are commonly used as the basis of the planning and scheduling of work, manpower planning, work balancing in team working, costing, labor performance measurement, and financial incentives. They are less commonly used as the basis of product design, methods comparison, work sequencing, and workplace design.

See also **work time distributions; learning curves**

Bibliography

Whitmore, D. A. (1987). *Work measurement.* 2nd edn. London: Heinemann.
Whitmore, D. A. (1991). Part 5: work measurement. In R. J. Bentley (Ed.), *The management services handbook.* 2nd edn. London: Pitman.

JOHN HEAP

work organization   Work organization is a general term which is used to describe the way in which the people in the production or operation system can be organized and directed towards meeting its output objectives. In some respects work organization is closely related to JOB DESIGN and the two terms are sometimes used interchangeably. However, work organization is a wider concept which can embrace the organization of the entire production function of an enterprise, whereas job design focuses on the structure of individual jobs at the work place, or groups of jobs around a discrete production system such as a line or cell.

A particular feature influencing work organization has been the increasing effect of mechanization and automation of operations, which in turn has led to greater differentiation and predetermination of work. Set against this trend has been the demand for greater self-actualization and the need to create "higher levels" of work to satisfy an increasingly better educated workforce. Because of this, the organization of work is no longer a straightforward matter of applying the simple principles of "SCIENTIFIC" MANAGEMENT which were developed in the early part of this century. Rather it needs to take account of human behavior, group dynamics, and the socio-technical systems concepts which recognize the interaction between workers and technology.

Although work organization is a complex subject, it is helpful to understand that in practice there are only a limited number of basic ways the human resources in a production or operation system can actually be orientated. These are by product, by process, or by task.

Product-orientated work organization is based on the idea of a worker, or group of workers, completing an identifiable "product" (which could be a discrete part of the final product, the final product itself, or a service). The required tasks are grouped (though not necessarily carried out together nor in a particular order) and there is usually some discretion as to how they are carried out.

Process-orientated work organization exploits the principle of DIVISION OF LABOR by enabling similar operations to be performed repeatedly on a whole range of components and products (or service elements). Here the products, rather than the tasks, are grouped and there is less discretion as to how the work is carried out.

Task-orientated work organization takes the idea of division of labor and specialization to its logical conclusion by adopting the approach of repeated performance of short cycle time tasks on part-completed components and products (or services) which, by virtue of their demand, are produced continuously. Here there is neither grouping of tasks, nor of products, and there is virtually no discretion as to how the work is to be carried out.

Much of the recent research on work organization has tended to focus on the problems associated with task and process orientation. These problems largely result from the alienation of people who are employed in these repetitive types of work. As a result, many of the alternative forms, such as GROUP WORKING based on a CELL LAYOUT have a product orientation which can allow a greater degree of association with the product and the wider enterprise.

See also **job enrichment; job enlargement; job rotation; layout**

Bibliography

Bennett, D. J. & Forrester, P. L. (1993). *Market-focused production systems: Design and implementation.* London: Prentice-Hall.

DAVID BENNETT

work study Work study is a general term for the study of human work, based originally on the principles of "SCIENTIFIC" MANAGEMENT. It includes a number of techniques which are generally divided into those which contribute to METHOD STUDY and those which contribute to WORK MEASUREMENT. These two topics are generally seen as the two sub-categories of work study activity. The aim of work study is a systematic investigation of work which will lead to improvements, especially in the efficiency with which the work is carried out.

See also **"scientific" management; job design**

NIGEL SLACK

work time distributions A characteristic of human work is that, when engaged on repetitive work, a person will not always take the same amount of time in performing a task. Most studies hold that when working under motivated and unpaced conditions (that is where machines are not directly limiting or accelerating individual work times) a qualified person will work in such a way that the distribution of task times is positively skewed. Exceptions to this general rule are where the person performing the task is not either experienced or trained in the task, in which case the distribution of work times is more likely to be symmetrical, or where some element of artificial pacing is present in the task, which again has the effect of producing a symmetrical work time distribution.

Although unanimous in describing the shape of unpaced work time distributions as being positively skewed with a lower limit below which the task cannot be completed, there is less agreement over the extent of variability and skewness to be expected. Partly this is explained by the fact that no one value of either variability or skewness will uniquely represent all unpaced work time distributions since the nature of the task itself will largely determine such values. However, an understanding of typical values is important insomuch as it directly affects the performance of production systems connected in series (*see* SYSTEM LOSS). Most studies seem to indicate a surprisingly close range of results for the variance of work time distributions, usually quoting a figure between 0.25 and 0.3 for the coefficient of variation of such distributions. There is less consensus over the degree of skewness to be found. However, skewness levels (measured by Pearson's first coefficient of skewness) of around 0.5 have been found to be typical.

See also **work measurement; time study**

Bibliography

Buxey, G. M., Slack, N. & Wild, R. (1973). Production flow line design: a review. *AIIE Transactions,* **5**, *1*, 37–48.

NIGEL SLACK

Z

zone of tolerance "The zone of tolerance is a range of service performance that a customer considers satisfactory. A performance below the tolerance zone will engender customer frustration and decrease customer loyalty. A performance level above the tolerance zone will pleasantly surprise customers and strengthen their loyalty" (Berry and Parasuraman, 1991). The zone of tolerance is a useful construct to understand the zero or satisfied state (*see* SERVICE QUALITY).

The importance of the zone of tolerance is that customers may accept variation within a range of performance, and any increase in performance within this area will only have a marginal effect on perceptions. It is only when performance moves outside of this range will it have any real effect on perceived service quality.

If a customer's zone of tolerance is narrow then he or she may be highly sensitive to the service experience with a greater likelihood of dissatisfying or delighting outcomes. Conversely, if a customer has a wide zone of tolerance then he/she may be much less sensitive to the service experience, thus increasing the likelihood of a satisfactory or acceptable outcome.

The width of the zone of tolerance may vary from customer to customer and from situation to situation. There are three things that might affect the width of a customer's zone of tolerance: the customer's involvement with the service, the importance of individual quality factors, and the outcomes of encounters during the service process itself.

First, the width of the zone of tolerance is affected by the customer's degree of involvement in the service. Involvement concerns a customer's perceived importance of the service. This may be influenced by, for example, the customer's emotional involvement with the service, past experiences, knowledge of alternative service offerings. The greater the involvement the more sensitive is the customer to the service, and the narrower is the width of their zone of tolerance.

Second, the width of the zone may vary for each individual quality factor (*see* QUALITY CHARACTERISTICS). Berry and Parasuraman (1991) suggested that the more important a characteristic the narrower its zone of tolerance. Reliability, they suggested, tends to be the most important and therefore the one where customers' perceptions are the most sensitive to service performance.

Third, the width of the zone of tolerance may be affected during the service itself by particularly dissatisfying or delighting service encounters or transactions (*see* SERVICE QUALITY). A failure in a single transaction or encounter may sensitize customers to negative aspects of the service. Customers may become more aware of, and indeed actively seek out, other negative experiences. A dissatisfying transaction will therefore have the effect of raising the lower threshold making a dissatisfying outcome more likely. Conversely, a delighting transaction during the service process may sensitize the customer to notice other successes thus lowering their upper threshold and making a highly satisfactory outcome more likely. Transactions that might previously have been seen as satisfying may now be seen as delighting as the customer has become more positively disposed toward the service.

See also **order-winners and qualifiers**

Bibliography

Berry, L. L. & Parasuraman, A. (1991). *Marketing services: Competing through quality*. New York: Free Press.

Johnston, R. (1995). Managing the zone of tolerance: some propositions. *International Journal of Service Industry Management*, **6**, *2*, A6–61.

Strandvik, T. (1994). *Tolerance zones in perceived service quality*. Helsingfors: Swedish School of Economics and Business Administration.

ROBERT JOHNSTON

— INDEX —

Index compiled by Meg Davies